P9-BIW-422

Crime and Culture

Refining the Traditions

Livy A. Visano

Canadian Scholars' Press Inc.   Toronto   1998

Crime and Culture: Refining the Traditions

Livy A. Visano

First published in 1998 by
Canadian Scholars' Press Inc.
180 Bloor Street West, Ste. 1202
Toronto, Ontario
M5S 2V6

We acknowledge the financial support of the Government of Canada through the Book Publishing Industry Development Programme for our publishing activities.

Canadian Cataloguing in Publication Data

Visano, L.A.
    Crime and culture: refining the traditions

Includes bibliographical references.
ISBN 1-55130-127-X

1. Criminology. I. Title.

HV6018.V57 1998   364   C98-931213-5

Page layout and cover design by Brad Horning

To beautiful Franco, always my "big" brother,
who like countless others, died alone in the workplace
while exploited for corporate greed.

To the many women and men who continue
to be condemned for just doing their jobs.

Perhaps, one day soon we too will learn to carry their "baggage".

And to the missing smiles and quiet tears of abused children
and youth—rejected, deprived, punished—forever in pain
in their innocent solitudes.

To all those criminalized unjustly:
"once we embark on different journeys,
feeling the joys and pains of growing,
of learning,
being together and remaining apart,
we will forge a fresh frontier into our estranged souls
enriched in a caring communion with the inner self that transcends
time and space"

Acknowledgments

Clearly, this book is the product of numerous emotional, spiritual and intellectual connections. Marked by pain and pleasure, this journey required considerable growth, and for this I thank those many who live in my soul and wish to remain anonymous. Their suffering will never be in vain.

A special note of thanks is extended equally to those who have been instrumental in shaping my early interests in the politics of deviance, crime, inequality and law, especially Sharon Stone, Dennis Magill, John Lee, Larry Ross, Gord West, Richard Ericson, the late Robert Harney, and Austin Turk. Intellectually, this book has been guided by the critical contributions of Antonio Gramsci, Paul Robeson, bell hooks, Sacco and Vanzetti, Angela Davis and my dear mentor—the late Mat Petranovich. I remain indebted to the many colleagues and friends from whom I have gained scholarly confidence, pedagogical directions, critical insights and continued personal encouragement, especially at times when my life, let alone this project, was interrupted by a series of misfortunes. They include Denis Bracken, Tom Fleming, the late Wilson Head, Nancy Mandell, Bob Doyle, Jan Newson, Gottfried Paasche, Richard Weisman and Steve Schklar.

As always, my work reflects much of what I have learned ideologically in different communities, from my former association with the SDS, Canadian Party of Labour, Correctional Services of Canada to the community activists on the Social Planning Council of Metropolitan Toronto. Likewise, over the long life of this enterprise a large number of graduate and undergraduate students have made this project conceivable by injecting a sense of bold imagination and uncompromising integrity into the politics of learning and teaching. Over the years the task of effectively balancing my teaching, service and scholarly responsibilities has been made possible by the always extremely heartening accommodation of members of the administrative and support staff in the departments of sociology, faculty of arts and Atkinson

College. Members of the dean's office at Atkinson College were always accommodating in balancing my administrative duties and academic interests.

The enthusiasm of the late Sandra Magico, acquisitions editor at Butterworth's, will always be appreciated. Lastly, I am grateful to Jack Wayne and Brad Lambertus of Canadian Scholars' Press for their ceaseless commitment to critical thought and social justice concerns. Canadian Scholars' Press has always encouraged innovative and progressive projects. Jack Wayne's support has been inimitable in the publishing industry.

Editing requires considerable industry, patience and discipline both intellectually and spiritually throughout all stages of this work. A loyalty to this commitment invites continued sacrifices and compromises. Lisa Jakubowski relentlessly steered the course of this project; her generosity remained endless and her command of critical pedagogies unmatched.

The preparation of this manuscript is indebted to Robynne Neugebauer, whose careful editing stimulated much valued discussions of the significance of this exercise. Her faith sustained much of the frustrations attendant with my impatience. She helped piece together some of the more thorny issues by carefully scrutinising more recent conceptual formulations of normative and conflict approaches. I thank her for fully appreciating and accepting the existential, intellectual and emotional life of what often was a very distressing journey. I shall always remain indebted to her.

A special note of thanks to Emily Tjimos without whom I could never hope to meet my current decanal duties while completing this project.

Stephanie McMahon's intellectual and personal insights were always challenging. Her demanding Gramscian and humanist analysis, formidable questions and intuitive grasp were always boldly courageous, painfully honest and endlessly encouraging. Were it not for her ongoing supportive push to "light the fire" under the project, this exercise would never have been published. Thank you for restoring the much appreciated confidence in completing this enterprise and for introducing me to an intellectual culture of compassion.

My family has always been patient in excusing the eccentricities attendant with prolonged excursion into critical enquiries. My brothers and sisters have always been helpful during this and other studies. I am grateful to my mother, Maria, for always being there as a dear friend, as an anchor. Her winning smile continues to guide my career. My father, Gino, has been extremely supportive as a loving parent and as a covert criminologist. And of course, there is Anthony! Words cannot capture my gratitude for his appreciation of my work and for just being a real treasure. His input on this topic and more important life issues is cemented deeply. I thank him for sacrificing many of our evenings and weekends to ensure the completion of this long-overdue project. I thank you for being the consummate expression of love. Likewise, I thank Marina for reaching out, holding on and moving along with us.

L.A.V.
Toronto, June, 1998

FOREWORD

Cultural Traditions: Towards a Critical Criminological Pedagogy

Lisa Marie Jakubowski

In traditional criminological discourses, crime is often simply described as rule violative behaviour. However, if one probes more deeply into the nature of criminality, it becomes clear that such simplicity can be quite misleading. My own experiences researching and teaching in the areas of the sociology of law, race and racism, and social inequality have often incited challenges to hegemonic criminological narratives. For example, in the classroom I have frequently used Makeda Silvera's (1989) *Silenced* to explore issues related to social inequality, crime and deviance. *Silenced* is a book within which Caribbean domestic workers discuss their experiences working and living in the homes of well-to-do Canadians. The moving and courageous accounts provided by these women, all of whom arrived in Canada between 1971 and 1980, overwhelm the reader with evidence that elements of slavery are "alive and well" in twentieth-century Canada. In their initial reading of this text, many of my students find it to be simultaneously enlightening and disturbing, but they cannot understand why I would link the text to a discussion of crime. Clearly, the book does not fit their stereotypical, simplified images of the exotic and fascinating world of crime.

The above scenario is not uncommon. Students habitually take courses in criminology anticipating a focus on enticing topics like prostitution, sexual assault and murder. Symbolic of actions that depart from, or are in violation of, some pre-established standard, norm, value or rule, these issues undoubtedly represent legitimate sites of inquiry. Customarily, when interpreting these matters, criminological discourses bifurcate identities, social relations and activities, i.e., as either criminal or conformist in the interests of protecting a particular social order. However, can one simplify definitions of the criminal to such a degree? Or does this bifurcation misrepresent and further mystify the already complex and elusive concept of crime?

In his book *Crime and Culture*, Livy Visano addresses these important questions. Providing a long overdue alternative to the more traditional analyses of crime, *Crime and Culture* challenges hegemonic narratives. With a compelling presentation of how social, cultural and political processes influence definitions of crime and criminal behaviour, Visano invites students to suspend their commonsensical perceptions and radically reappraise conventional definitions of crime.

Under the general headings of "normative", "interpretive," and "conflict" paradigms, the text begins by providing students with a necessary overview and critique of various classical perspectives on crime. Subsequently, the author addresses the possibility of a critical cultural alternative. In a way that is admittedly challenging for a student being introduced to the domain of criminology, Visano probes the interrelationship among concepts fundamental to this reconceptualization of crime—ideology, hegemony, political economy and the state. When this perspective is employed to analyze culture, the centrality of power is clarified. The criminal practices of institutions (e. g., the media, the law) are highlighted, with a particular emphasis on how these institutions interact to effectively discipline, dominate and devalue certain elements of the population.

This theoretical and substantive reformulation has significant implications for the teaching and learning of criminology. In order for the student to suspend and move beyond commonsensical perceptions, beliefs and ideas, instructors must empower the student with the analytical skills necessary to question and/or evaluate the usefulness of conventional ideas and practices. Such a transition necessitates that the instructor move away from conventional schooling practices towards a more critical pedagogy.

Traditional teaching—the implications of schooling

Educational institutions have typically promoted an ideology of equality of educational opportunity. That is, we are socialized or led to believe that we all start out with the same access to education; that we all have the same chances for success. Social differences then, stem not from lack of opportunity, but rather from the lack of individual motivation or ability. The implication, of course, is that social inequality is a problem stemming from the individual and not the system.

Instead of addressing systemic problems, it is much easier to blame social inequality on the deficiencies of particular individuals. Traditionally, however, educational institutions have been guilty of both reproducing social inequality and reinforcing its naturalness. The success of this process of reproduction and reinforcement is attributable to a number of factors, including the utilization of a banking method of instruction (Freire, 1970). According to Freire (ibid., 58), this kind of learning process is analogous to "an act of depositing in which students are the depositories and the teacher is the depositor. Instead of communicating, the teacher issues communiques and makes deposits which the students receive and memorize." This method of instruction, along with educational practices like I.Q. testing, streaming/tracking and "cooling out" (Goffman, 1952), serve to psychologically reinforce, within the minds of the less advantaged, the naturalness and inevitability of their positions of subordination. Essentially, students are socialized to develop commonsensical perceptions about their differential qualifications and location in social life based on, among other things, race, class and gender.

This kind of schooling fosters disrespect towards those individuals who are engaged in the learning process. Specifically, participants are not respected as knowing subjects. Instead, already marginalized individuals are further subordinated and objectified by the educator. Both the subjectivity and experiential wisdom of the students are downplayed. Knowledge, stemming from both their past and present real-life experiences, is, in general, disregarded and relegated to the periphery.

Schooling and its attendant implications preclude the possibility of students engaging in a critical pedagogical process. However, if one was educated rather than schooled, independent and critical thought would be encouraged. Education, through a constant unveiling of reality, invites students to develop a critical awareness of their social worlds. It promotes both consciousness-raising and societal intervention. Students receive challenges in the form of problems relating to themselves "in the world and with the world," and are urged to respond to those challenges. Education, thus, becomes a practice of freedom rather than domination (Freire, 1970: 68-69). Instructors committed to critical pedagogy recognize the importance of ongoing consultation with all those engaged in the learning process throughout all of its phases. Traditional approaches, on the other hand, fail to invite more marginal elements of this population to participate in discrete decision-making processes. Focusing on a university or college level setting, and in reference to the more substantive areas of the selection of course material, the creation of a course outline, and the structuring of tutorials, this marginalization is increasingly apparent.

Constructing a teaching framework involves the sorting of course-related theories, methods and applications into topics. In order for the educating process to be effective, the outline must be constructed in a way that will be meaningful to all participants. Accordingly, while creating a syllabus, the instructor is encouraged, through role-taking, to take into account the differing perspectives of the students. Implicit in this idea is the hegemonic perception of instructor as authority figure. If one acknowledges that the cultural diversity of the classroom might constitute a relatively foreign or alien context for the educator, it is also possible that the instructor's conception of reality will not correspond with the social realities of the students. Thus, it is both ethnocentric and paternalistic to assume that she or he will have the capability to determine what will be most meaningful to the students in the context of the classroom. The outline, nonetheless, is organized around the instructor's opinion of what constitutes sensible topics or categories, thereby tainting or influencing the course before it has begun. Similar problems of power can emerge in seminars.

One purpose of the seminar is to allow the student to critically reflect upon and discuss his or her perceptions of the reading and lecture materials. In this sense, tutorials become guided conversations between instructors and students. That is, students are invited to provide commentary on a set of concerns that have, in some sense, been imposed on the interaction by the course director. The whole notion of guided conversations carries with it the image of instructor as authority, whose mandate is to aid or direct those who are less capable. This type of direction becomes even more apparent if educators utilize probing questions to sensitize students to those issues which they, as authority figures, feel might be important—i.e., was such and such a consideration? Probes then, might be characterized as a subtle way of eliciting an instructor's preferred response from a student.

This brief discussion of the tutorial alerts the reader to the kind of unilateral power relationship that traditionally exists between instructors and students. Educators come to regard themselves as "social engineers" (Bodemann, 1978: 410) destined to save those who are less capable. Thus, rather than promoting a cooperative relationship between teacher and student, the instructor tends to invade and take control of the classroom.

Under such conditions, the probability of generating a liberating pedagogical environment decreases. Instructors may genuinely believe that by utilizing their academic expertise individuals can be liberated from an oppressive educational environment. While such expertise has an important role to play in the pedagogical process, it is not enough. Educators must recognize that the subjectivity of the student, articulated through experience, is an equally essential component of a successful emancipatory pedagogy.

Given the above, the traditional role of the instructor must be altered. From the earliest stages of the learning process, the notion of invade and control must be abandoned. The educator's role needs to become one of facilitator, wherein the individual strives towards empowering his or her students with the ability to think critically and, if necessary, effectively intervene in their social realities. Within such a context, the instructor and students must collectively take responsibility for, and work towards, creating a liberating, pedagogical environment.

Collective responsibility and dialogue—a critical alternative

> Whether [teaching] is a science, a craft, or a philosophy, it is nothing if it fails to discuss the experienced problems of ordinary people; and it is nothing if it fails to do this in a way that people can understand. (Corrigan, 1979: 16)

This quotation is an appropriate starting point for the discussion of critical alternatives. Specifically, it reinforces the idea that teaching is both alienating and meaningless if it does not address, in a comprehensible way, the concerns that emerge from the social realities of the ordinary student. Having internalized this message, the facilitator sets out to create teaching techniques that are commensurate with this critical philosophy. First and foremost, the stratified, unequal relationship that traditionally exists between instructor and student must be destroyed.

The destruction of this hierarchy begins with a reconceptualization of the identities of teacher and student. The stereotypical images of the educator as a social engineer and the student as a less capable individual are abandoned. Instead both actors come to be re-constituted, in a Gramscian (1971) sense, as intellectuals. That is,

> regardless of one's social and economic function, all human beings perform as intellectuals by constantly interpreting and giving meaning to the world, and by participating in a particular conception of that world. (Giroux in Freire, 1985: xxiii)

By treating all those who participate in the education process as intellectuals, there is an implicit understanding that they are social equals. Consequently, they will have equally significant, albeit different roles to play as teaching and learning unfold.

This newly established, unstratified relationship among the participants must be accompanied by philosophically compatible techniques. For instance, guided conversations can be eliminated in favour of dialogue. The notion of dialogue does not signify power and inequality. Instead, it facilitates intersubjectivity—an authentic and open interchange of ideas between all educational participants, wherein each participant is respected as "an equally knowing subject" (Kirby and McKenna, 1989: 129).

Given the subjective nature of education, pedagogical methods cannot be relegated to a strict inventory of rules, roles and recipes. Thus, other than acknowledging that effective critical skills will evolve within environments where social equals engage in dialogue, it is dangerous, if not counter-productive, to detail specific techniques to be used throughout the process. There is, however, a theoretical concept, known as the dialectic, that can be used by instructors to enhance the learning process within a critical context.

Emerging from the works of Hegel and Marx, the dialectic represents a "logic, a way of seeing the world" (Norman and Sayers, 1980: 2). When the idea of the dialectic is applied to a consideration of social life, it highlights how life circumstances continue to change and evolve through the struggles of real people. Because people are continually engaged in a process of "movement and becoming, of development and change" (ibid., 4), the nature of the social world within which they exist continues to change. What happens when this way of thinking is applied to a classroom setting?

Thinking dialectically enables the instructor to more fully appreciate the importance of the student in all phases of the learning process. Specifically, the educator must be particularly cognizant of the dialectical relationship between the individual and the social world (Corrigan and Leonard, 1978). The real-life experiences of students play a crucial role in all dimensions of social transformation. Consequently, when examining any societal issue, it is imperative that the instructor consults and gives equal credence to the views of all educational participants.

Using this conceptual framework as a guide, the educator first applies a method that creates a context wherein both student and teacher are treated as social equals. The application of the learning process incorporates four interrelated phases: articulation of social experience, codification, decodification and empowerment.

During the first phase, the articulation of social experience, the instructor invites students to share their insights on a particular theme or issue, thereby initiating the process of dialogue. As this exchange unfolds, individuals rely on personal experience to guide their reflections. When these personalized reflections are concretized in the form of textual or visual impressions, a codification is created. Codifications are objectifications or representations of students' real-life situations (Freire, 1985: 51).

This process of articulation and codification alerts students to their creative and vital presence in a critical learning process. The students' experiences become the starting point for dialogue. Specifically, situations representative of their orientations to the world are proposed to the students, in the form of codifications, as objects of critique (ibid.). Individuals are then able to reflect upon their experiences as they appear in these codified forms. This collective reflection develops, within both students and facilitators, a more critical awareness of the issue at hand. This reflection also marks the beginning of the decodification process.

Decodification invites the group as a whole to engage in an interchange of ideas in order to highlight the meaningfulness of the real-life experiences of students, as depicted in the codification. To some extent, the burden of responsibility shifts to the instructor during the decodification phase as efforts are made to draw linkages between experience and theoretically relevant course concepts. In continued consultation with students, the instructor draws from the discussion of the codification one or more generic concepts to facilitate the process of critical social analysis. Here, a generic concept is a panoptic tool that imposes order on diverse observations. In essence, generic concepts represent themes or issues of the subject matter that the collective has determined to be of fundamental significance.

With this collective accomplishment, the educator raises the dialogue from an individual to a structural level, where the potential for diversified discussion increases. Consider, as a more concrete example, the following elaboration.

Thematically, the course is "Criminology". In particular, we want to look at media representations of crime in North American society. How then, do we begin to effectively address, analyze and challenge the images by which we are constantly bombarded? Assume we are taking as codifications the students' written reflections on a series of newspaper articles and TV newsclips. From these codifications, the following generic concepts emerge: race, gender, class, stereotyping, prejudice, discrimination and alienation. The theme of inequality clearly emerges from the generic concepts. With respect to unequal portrayal or treatment, one might discuss discrimination, prejudice, or stereotyping in institutions like the media. Specifically, how do these expressions of inequality shape societal definitions of crime? Furthermore, how can these expressions influence the current life situations of racial minorities, women and the economically disadvantaged?

If throughout this extensive period of dialogue an exchange of ideas among social equals does indeed occur, students will become empowered. They will have developed a critical awareness of their own social realities inside the classroom, and they will better appreciate the dialectical relationship that exists between themselves and society. This consciousness-raising process has the potential to establish a politically literate population in two ways. First, it sensitizes students to their significant and creative presence in, and beyond, the classroom. Second, the process encourages instructors to recognize their own pedagogical limitations.

The failure to be responsive to critical alternatives increases the probability of marginalizing parts of the student body. Accordingly, restricting one's teaching practices to traditional methods has a number of serious implications. Aside from inhibiting the success of critical education, traditional teaching tends to adhere to and reinforce the hegemonic culture, replete with Eurocentrism, ethnocentrism and paternalism. These distortions, which systematically relegate to the periphery the views of some and not others, impede the creation of learning environments sensitive to the needs of traditionally marginalized elements of the population.

This brief overview serves to highlight the problematic nature of traditional teaching practices. The exploration of more appropriate alternatives sets the stage for a commitment to the creation of learning environments that will empower rather than silence. Fittingly, successful empowerment is the first step in generating a program of action to effectively confront those individuals and social institutions that unjustly discipline, dominate and devalue human beings.

Crime and Culture succeeds remarkably well in accepting and respecting the significance of empowerment as a strategic life experience that enhances effective teaching and learning. Theoretically and substantively, this book will be recognized as advancing the consciousness of social justice and the need to transform traditional thoughts about crime.

Lisa Marie Jakubowski
Department of Sociology
Brescia College
London, Ontario, Canada

Works Cited

Bodemann, M. "A Problem of Sociological Praxis: The Case for Interventive Observation in Fieldwork" in *Theory and Society* 5, 1978: 387-420.

Corrigan, P. *Schooling the Smash Street Kids* London: The MacMillan Press, 1979.

Corrigan, P., and P. Leonard. *Social Work Practice Under Capitalism: A Marxist Approach* London: MacMillan Publishers Ltd., 1978.

Freire, P. *Pedagogy of the Oppressed* NY: Herder & Herder, 1970.

—————————*The Politics of Education-Culture, Power and Liberation* Massachusetts: Bergin and Garvey Publishers, Inc., 1985.

Goffman, E. "On Cooling the Mark Out—Some Aspects of Adaptation to Failure" in *Psychiatry—Journal for the Study of Interpersonal Processes*, 15(4) Nov., 1952: 451-463.

Gramsci, A. *Selections from the Prison Notebooks* New York: International Publishers, 1971.

Kirby, S. and K. McKenna. *Experience, Research, Social Change—Methods from the Margins* Toronto: Garamond Press, 1989.

Norman, R., and S. Sayers. *Hegel, Marx and the Dialectic—A Debate* New Jersey: Humanities Press, 1980.

Silvera, M. *Silenced* Toronto: Sister Vision, 1989.

Audre Lorde (1934-1992)

"But I had no sense, no understanding at the time, of the connections, just that I was that woman. And that to put myself on the line to do what had to be done at any place and time was so difficult, yet absolutely crucial, and not to do so was the most awful death. And putting yourself on the line is like killing a piece of yourself, in the sense that you have to kill, end, destroy something familiar and dependable, so that something new can come, in ourselves, in our world. And that sense of writing at the edge, out of urgency, not because you choose it but because you have to.... Once you live any piece of your vision it opens you to a constant onslaught. Of necessities, of horrors, but of wonders too, of possibilities."

An Interview: Audre Lorde and Adrienne Rich, in Audre Lorde *Sister Outsider* Freedom, Calif: The Crossing Press/The Crossing Press Feminist Series, 1984: 107.

Angela Davis

"Jails and prisons are designed to break human beings, to convert the population into specimens in a zoo—obedient to our keepers, but dangerous to each other. In response, imprisoned men and women will invent and continually invoke various and defenses.... In an elemental way, this *culture is one of resistance*, but a resistance of desperation."

(emphasis added)
Angela Davis *On Becoming a Fugitive* 1974 cited on p 106 Deidre Mullane *Words to Make My Dream Children Live* NY: Anchor 1995.

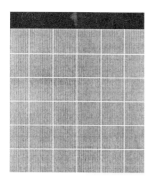

Contents

Introduction: Connecting Crime and Culture

" ... the meaning of a text is always the site of a struggle"
(Grossberg, 1986: 86)

Conceptualizing crime: criminal knowledge as criminology

The study of crime is an analysis of being, becoming and experiencing "otherness". Crime is a challenge to a particular socially constructed and historically rooted social order. The study of crime, therefore, is an inquiry into expressions of power, cultural controls and contexts of contests. Accordingly, the designated criminal is set apart and relegated to the margins according to a disciplining discourse about differences.

Criminality, as rule violative conduct, ranges from relatively minor legal infractions against property to extremely violent acts of omission and commission against communities. Similarly, criminal actors equally vary from single, simple, so-called locally situated and clearly pathologized individual offenders to more elusive, complex, global, sovereign and corporate organizations. Just as criminal acts differ according to penalties, so too do criminal actors differ considerably in terms of privilege (resources). And reactions to crime may range from subtle accommodation to coercive containment. Indeed, powerful reactors (individuals, collectivities or organizations) secure compliance to rules by adopting a variety of strategies that persuade (bend the mind) and penalize (break the body).

In general, the study of crime is about discipline, domination and devaluation. The origin, construction and subsequent definitions of crime are linked to the social organization of conformity—control. Control, constituting the social dimension of crime, represents the institutional or patterned responses to differences designated as threatening. All societies take crime seriously, especially when relations of power are challenged. Punishment is manipulated as a disciplinary device to compel conformity.

For punishment to be effective, however, it too must be flexible, ranging from the more arbitrary use of deadly force to seemingly innocuous community-oriented remedies. This criminalization creates and promotes legal regulation that, in turn, enhances the surveillance of real, imagined and symbolic troubles. Regulation consists of a set of ubiquitous and panoptic responses to resistance; these measures are the all-scanning and forever vigilant controls that strip suspects of individuality and create docile bodies. Interestingly, criminals become "subjected, used, transformed and improved" (Foucault, 1979: 136) in order to secure obedience to roles and rules. To be effective, discipline defies definition precisely because control extends beyond the juridic to include the moral, political and intellectual regulations. As Foucault explains (ibid., 216):

> Discipline may be identified neither with an institution nor with an apparatus; it is a type of power ... comprising a whole set of instruments, techniques, procedures, levels of application, targets ... it may be taken over either by "specialized" institutions (penitentiaries), or by institutions that use it as an essential instrument for a particular end (schools, hospitals), or by pre-existing authorities that find in it a means of reinforcing or reorganizing their internal mechanisms of power....

Despite its obvious connections to criminal codes, the concept of crime remains a mystification. This elusive idea continues to be paraded in traditional criminological canons simply as a departure from or a violation of legalized social norms. More appropriately, however, crime is the articulation of trouble in the maintenance of moral rules and ordered worlds. Within the everyday world of crime talk there is a belief held by some that something is wrong in the behaviour, views or even the appearances of others. Clearly, crime becomes translated as a social intrusion, a real or symbolic injury, that warrants an official response.

Interestingly, sanctions are legalized and legitimated to protect a particular peace. But the application of sanctions, the conduct of "criminalizers" varies significantly especially on the basis of non legal criteria. Given that this designation of crime is essentially a judgment grounded in the prevailing politics of rule making and rule enforcement, we must be encouraged to ask: Whose order is protected and what kinds of phenomena are singled out for control? Upon closer scrutiny we soon discover that definitions of crime which rely on elements of rule violative behaviours or departures from standards, conventions or norms are exceedingly limited primarily because they fail to critically address the problematic relationship between crime and rules. What roles do rules play?

Basically, rules are created to protect and promote particular perspectives, and their meanings are always negotiated among more powerful participants. Crime always implicates others by affirming a certain privilege to this proscription. Typically, crime originates with certain classifications of activities, actors and contexts—categoric guidelines that govern the appropriateness of behaviour, attributes, appearances, identities, or relations. Appropriateness, crime and the attendant responses are all culturally grounded. Culture frames interpretations by supplying experiences from which inferences are quickly drawn. Specifically, culture legitimates the decisions of authorities by deferring to a history of social obligations and a generic loyalty to rules. This negative imputation attendant with rule violative behaviour stresses the significance of the social nature of roles. Within this crime calculus the other is produced, that is, a marginalized other is transformed into a prospective alien, a suspect, accused or convict. This construction of the other is determined by a variety of dominant discourses—political, legal as well as cultural.

Lamentably, traditional criminological canons reflect the primacy of a binary code. Identities, relations and activities are presented as either criminal or conformist. This bifurcation, however, misrepresents multi-layered identities and phenomena. For example, social order involves more than a false either-or dichotomy of right or wrong, black or white, guilty or innocent, moral or immoral, good or bad, sinner or saint, ugly or beautiful, sane or mad, sacred or secular, cerebral or visceral. Rather, in this book, criminal actors and reactors are equally appreciated as acting subjects and subjected actors, both constituting and constituted within contexts of differential defiance or deference that characterize the politics of protest. Equally, the criminal actor and reactor are presented as active agents situated within wider, more complex and often overlooked contests. Actors and reactors, as cultural subjects within discourses of power, are engaged in micro-political (local) struggles shaped by more macro-cultural influences (global). Also, as will be explained in this book, the so-called criminals are multiple subjects, enjoying a plurality of meanings displaced and re-constructed in concert with wider reproductions of regulation. Crime, therefore, as a juridic judgment negotiates between the more micro politicized processes and the more macro structures of politics.

How then do we begin to approach the subject of crime? Essentially, crime cannot be understood without a meaningful discussion of the nature of ideas, that is, a basic concern for knowledge that informs prevailing perspectives. The contours of criminological canons and current commonsensical accounts of crime are shaped by the articulation of certain knowledge claims. Our first task, therefore, requires a scrutiny of ideas circulated as truths by confronting both the authoring subject and the authored text.

Crime as figurative: facts, fiction and function

Knowledge of crime is framed routinely within symbolic processes of over-categorization, coding and selective simplification (Simmons, 1965: 225). Programmatic stereotypes are convenient and simplistic mechanisms for understanding countless crime figures and facts. As Mohr (1973: 42) details:

> We forget the gross reduction and oversimplification that are involved in those terms.... We draw on the pool of typifications in our mind ... which are composites of thrillers, newspaper reports, soap operas and movies, liberally sprinkled with our own fantasies and take this to be social reality around us.

Knowledge of crime is statistically mediated. The currency of crime statistics claims to restore rationality within the mindless marketplace of distorted images. Statistics seek to homogenize, neutralize and formalize perceptions of crime according to apparently non-partisan and scientific evidence. The drama of crime is paraded within an organizationally constructed and subjectively interpreted framework that mathematizes crime trends. For example, the general categories into which statistics fall include: all crimes (reported and unreported); crimes of violence; crimes causing death; murder rates; crimes with firearms; juvenile crimes, etc. Interestingly, crimes of the powerful (government and corporate) escape mention let alone counting. Statistics have become, especially for the media, a catechism of self-evident truths, an essential part of an infallible dogma that demands reverence. As embodied moral statements, these caricatured fragments portray crime by acceding to convoluted logic, obfuscating symbols and mystifying rituals. Unqualified deference is extremely evident in the media coverage of "official statistics".

Official statistics are formal constructions originating from the office of authorized agencies of the criminal justice system. These statistics are standardized definitions of crime that satisfy organizational interests and reflect corporate priorities. The collection and subsequent public distribution of statistics serve to justify a particular position or argument. To illustrate, it is common for police forces to release detailed statistics documenting increased crime rates whenever local politicians threaten to limit or, at best, monitor police operational budgets. Since statistics are often used to justify police practices, they constitute an integral component of the growing arsenal of propaganda conveniently available to policing systems.

In general, official crime statistics result from a series of decisions made in institutions like the police force. In turn, politicians manipulate these rates by either trivializing or alarmingly amplifying the incidence of crime to express their respective ideological commitments to crime control and their obvious moral indignation with disorder. This championing of tough talk framed within law and order, especially during election campaigns, serves to support the power of state agents.

Statistics are presented by experts who employ alienating vocabularies and sophisticated techniques that flaunt alleged objectivity while often distorting and impeding effective communication with a more general public. The general public is rendered helpless and held hostage to the power of organizations that edit statistics according to their respective operational needs. But, many questions still warrant attention. What is crime? Whose definition of crime triumphs? How are statistics made official? To what extent do the police, for example, "torture their numbers until they too confess"? What official interpretations have been made and at what levels in the hierarchy? How transparent are these processes of governance? Why are only those acts defined according to legal criteria the only crimes that come to the attention of authorities? What crimes are deliberately excluded because of hidden negotiations, multiple charges, bias in reporting and recording procedures, flagrant negligence, etc.?

Crimes known to the police become officially incorporated into formal criminological computations. But crime counts cannot account for crime. To illustrate, even victims of violence often refuse to register a complaint with the police. Victims refuse to respond according to their situational roles as victims or complainants for many legitimate reasons, including fears of reprisals, insensitivity of the criminal justice system, inadequate or limited options, to name only a few. Clearly, crime rates depend on the willingness of people to complain and report as well as the willingness of the criminal justice system to take these complaints seriously.

Crime statistics also disclose much about the nature of organizations that collect data. More importantly, crime statistics are measures of police activity not the crime itself. Obviously, less police attention or enforcement leads to less crime recording or reporting. Police practices influence official crime rates. Moreover, these statistics are filtered through police organizationally defined activities. In addition, many interrelated contingencies influence official statistics. They include, for example, the following: the methods and resources of police crime reporting and recording; police access to information; plea bargaining; selective law enforcement; general policing strategies (reactive or proactive practices); the deployment of personnel in different departmental units; political pressures from the community and politicians; levels of confidence citizens feel towards the criminal justice system; the public's feelings of impotence if not incompetence in doing anything about their respective victimization; preference for informal resolution of conflict; the ambiguities in law; confusing organizational criteria and inconsistent data collecting procedures; increases in population, urbanization, poverty; police efficiency, response rates, advances in technology. Understandably, official statistics are riddled with many conceptual problems.

Equally, current methods for generating official statistics are generally limited. Police tallies are based on the number of offences as opposed to counting criminal incidents. The police note that a single incident may result in several charges such as break and enter, theft and possession of stolen goods. This methodology will obviously record a higher crime rate than the crime counting federal agencies in North America. Typically, politicians and police officials scream that rates are alarmingly high. In this instance, police forces argue that crime statistics are down because of less enforcement; less enforcement results from reduced personnel, inadequate police budgets, etc. Likewise, the police argue that the rates are high because their poor resources (budget, personnel, hardware) ill equip them to prevent crime.

Similarly, the rates of incarceration do not represent the actual number of people sentenced, convicted, prosecuted, caught or even reported to the police. Obviously, official rates are considerably less than the incidence of actual crime. Crime reporting continues to be inaccurate, unreliable and of limited value. The reportability of crimes also depends on activities known to the victim. Injuries may be suffered and yet remain unknown even to the victim as in the cases of victim-less crimes. Hidden crimes continue to be grossly under-reported, such as the traffic and possession of stolen merchandise, drugs or sex, gambling, loan sharking, internal pilferage, embezzlements, stock market manipulations, smuggling of contraband goods. Corporate, white-collar, professional or elite crimes, and also crimes against the environment and injuries in the workplace, are largely disregarded. And, interestingly, only the so-called conventional criminal code violations are ever reported and recorded. What finally gets registered as a conviction is but a residual, as the following overview suggests:

SERIES OF DECISION POINTS

ACTUAL CRIMES: total known and unknown
DETECTED CRIMES: by all victims and their agents
CRIMES REPORTED: to public police and private security
CRIMES RECORDED: officially documented
ARRESTS: single, multiple, included, negotiated charges, etc.
PROSECUTIONS: strength of the evidence, plea bargain, political climate, community interests, seriousness of crime, organizational factors such as resources, skills, etc.
CONVICTIONS: strength of the prosecution's arguments
NON CUSTODIAL PENALTIES: fines, probation, community service, etc.
CUSTODIAL: organizational and personal factors, levels of risks (perceived), levels of violence, penal orientations, etc.

Note the following statistics for the early 1990s. According to the US Justice Department's Annual National Crime Survey of 48,000 households, in 1991, only 37% of all crimes and only 49% of all violent crimes were reported to the police; these figures have remained constant for years (Bureau of Justice Statistics Update, 1991: 4; *Globe and Mail*, 20, 04, 1992: A10). Also, the Canadian General Social Survey estimated that in 1987, only 31% of violent crimes were reported to the police (Statistics Canada, 1992: 3). In Great Britain, only 7% of all crimes lead to police charges and only 2% lead to a conviction (*Globe and Mail*, 25, 11, 1993: A17)! Moreover, close to 1.2 million violent crimes against youths were not reported to the police in the USA (Bureau of Justice Statistics Update, 1991: 3).

For official statistics to be meaningful, they must move beyond the banal conclusions about crime causes derived from isolated local events. Rather than parochial pathologies, basic trends in social institutions and structures need to be incorporated. In constructing official meanings of crime, historical and cultural features of the political economy are woefully ignored by the media and other socializing influences. Regrettably, current public thought and public talk about crime remain reduced to numbers that entertain for the emotional moment; the quick fix that dazzles, pacifies or terrifies into inaction. Within the dominant culture, numbers carry considerable currency in popular discourse. Witness, for example, the incredible dependency on official statistics in routine talk of crime in social settings. Parenthetically, this "crime as a commodity" fetish is significant in signalling the cultural capital of crime, thereby avoiding any serious analysis of inherent social justice issues.

The collection of official data from different sectors of the criminal justice system using a diversity of approaches would contribute immensely to more depth and breadth, that is, a more thorough appreciation of crime rates. Although all measurements of crime suffer from imperfections, a wider variety of techniques would enhance validity. There are many sources that presumably may supplement extant official surveys. Data reported and interpreted should be based upon a flexible use of convergent methods ranging from official and non-official observations and interviews to more formal open-ended interviews and case histories (Plummer, 1983), documents (textual and content analyses), surveys of all respective actors in different situational roles-victims, offenders, complainants, witnesses, investigators, (self-report, first person accounts and victimization surveys), case studies, impact studies, effectiveness studies and critical ethnographies. A set of procedures, with more depth and breadth, is required to capture the exigencies of counting crime. Triangulation (Denzin, 1978)—the examination of single empirical events from the vantage of different methods and viewpoints—is highly congruent with this task. The accuracy of individual responses is checked by comparing accounts of all subjects, especially those that differ widely in the levels of participation in a specific activity.

The application of a wide repertoire of methods reduces flaws inherent in appropriating a single approach. With interviews of victims, for example, there may be cases of memory loss, uncomfortable and limited reconstructions of past encounters. Interviews with offenders require considerable effort in ensuring trust, confidentiality and anonymity. Surveys may have ambiguous, culturally biased items in the instrument. On the other hand, observational approaches demand considerable time in contacting key informants and in inducing cooperation.

In summary, the measurement of crime is a social enterprise that tells us just as much about the individual or organization counting as about the phenomenon being counted—crime. Because triangulation is not routinely applied in the measurement of crime, the information that readers obtain about crime statistics is very narrow. There is no one true picture of crime; rather, statistics are series of snapshots and captured moments that reflect the preferences of the photographer and the subject under focus. Some images will remain over- or underexposed, while others are frequently blurred, discarded or never even developed because of the associated costs.

Despite the dubious validity of official statistics, crime figures function to encourage citizens to express extraordinarily high levels of support for and confidence in the crime pictures police forces draw. For example, a 1992 International Crime Survey reported that 82% of Canadians think that the police are doing a good job in controlling crime (Department of Justice, 1993: 9).

The ideology of fear and the culture of violence

Because of the widespread circulation of official statistics, a general perception about the nature of society has emerged. The numbing numbers that are officially released on a daily basis dramatically reinforce the notion that crime is dangerously rampant. Individual and aggregate tallies have assumed an exaggerated significance; they have also become well-publicized benchmarks or criteria for policy changes. Crime statistics, as persuasive indicators of a crisis, are manipulated for political interests. These numbers discipline us as readers, viewers and general spectators to position ourselves as particular kinds of consumers. The categorizations of these numbers produce a knowledge of crime mediated by powerful organizations. As products of power, crime statistics are sites of objectified accounts. These textual forms perpetuate hegemonic narratives necessary for crystallizing justifications. Once contextualized within the sociology of emotions, notably fear, the social organization of crime statistics acquires considerable conviction. What then binds public interest or cements a collective conscience?

Within this numerical text, personal safety, protection of property and a sense of a healthy community are used to guide one's interpretation of crime. What about fear? Fear has become a contagion that erodes the sense of confidence in the local community. Admittedly, fear is not totally unproductive; this emotion prompts caution and reduces opportunities. On the other hand, an exaggerated sense of fear, a constant worry about crime, has in itself become a social problem as it tends to generate counterproductive responses such as alarmingly high levels of anxiety leading to a fortress mentality, "a cocooning" orientation—staying at home, arming oneself and avoiding the strange others out there.

Within the traditions of criminology, theoretical models have been developed to explain fear of crime; they include indirect victimization, incivilities or social disorder perspective, community concern, subcultural diversity and, cultural setting (Covington and Taylor, 1991; Bennett and Flavin, 1994: 359). First, victimization perspectives maintain that the fear of crime is determined by perceptions of vulnerability to crime based on individual demographic factors such as age, gender, race, ethnicity and experiences with victimization. The greater the perceived vulnerability, the greater one's fear of crime (ibid.). Vulnerability includes both physical and social elements. In our communities, the defensive reactions attendant with fears of victimization are expressed more deeply by more vulnerable individuals or groups; notably, women, the young, elderly, newcomers / immigrants, the poor, gays and lesbians, and non-whites. For instance, blacks expressed more fear of crime than whites, the poor more than the wealthy, and inner-city dwellers more than suburbanites (Moore and Trojanowicz, 1988: 2). The elderly experience greater rates of victimization by assaults, robberies, muggings and extortions. The elderly, who are most likely to live alone, feel more socially vulnerable and fear to be out alone at night.

The second perspective, incivilities or social disorder, examines the perceived breakdown or attenuation of social control that makes the residents feel more vulnerable and therefore more afraid (ibid., 361). Third, fear of crime is generalized as a result of the perceived community disintegration. Fourth, the subcultural diversity perspectives note that this fear of crime is attributable to living close to others whose cultural backgrounds are different from one's own (ibid.). The fifth perspective entails an analysis of the effects of cultural settings on fear (ibid.; Thompson et al., 1990).

Public concern about crime, however, is influenced more by abstract formulations than concrete experiences. Another factor, besides the fear of crime, which may affect one's appreciation of crime statistics, is the "suspiciousness" of strangers (Garofalo and Laub, 1978). An individual's perception of the level of risk is related to the fear of being tyrannized especially by strangers; that is, to be controlled as an object and subject to another's wants in a predator-prey relationship. Xenophobia, the fear of strangers, has been transformed into a fear of foreigners, the unknown or the unaccustomed. These perceptions imprison or self-incarcerate as these processes overestimate the coercive consequences of crime: violence at the hands of a stranger. Crime control has become grounded in this overstated fear of strangers. Official evidence indicates that there were 633 Canadian homicides in 1996, forty-five more than in 1995 (*Toronto Star*, July 31, 1997: A1). Four out of ten murdered women had an intimate relationship with the attacker, while 90% of the women killed knew their attacker (ibid.). Most murderers are familiar with their victims—relatives, family, lovers, friends and work colleagues. Similarly, of the 56,772 reported cases of missing children in 1992, only seventy cases were attributable to the foul play by strangers. Another 42,518 were runaways and another 635 were abducted by one of their parents (ibid., 15, 08, 1993: B5). Most murders in the USA do not occur as the result of an attack by a stranger but stem from arguments between people who know each other and are often related. In fact, only 14% of all reported cases of murder were caused by strangers (Sugarman and Rand, 1994: 32).

A great disparity exists between the incidence of crime and public perception. Statistics suggest that as a society we still overestimate the dangers inherent in the crimes of the powerless while refusing to acknowledge the crimes of the powerful. There is a public belief that phenomena like mass murder and serial killings are increasing. Admittedly, Canadians and Americans are no more likely to be victims of crime than they were five years ago, and yet a distorted perception prevails resulting in exaggerated fears. Panic may be attributable to a blood-thirsty media, an issue to be pursued in subsequent chapters.

Public perceptions about crime are problematic. There is also a general public opinion that Canada's criminal justice system is all too lenient; that tougher judges, stiffer penalties and a return to the death penalty are all warranted. Many people still maintain that capital punishment is a deterrent to crime despite the proliferation of exhaustive research that questions this widely held assumption. Canada may enjoy one of the highest rates of imprisonment in the world, but public opinion may easily overstate and also understate the rate of actual offences—suite or street crimes. In Canada, more than one-third of inmates are doing time for a failure to pay fines (*Toronto Star*, 14, 01, 1994: A10). Opinions about parole are equally ill-informed. For decades the general public mood as expressed or interpreted by the media has been hostile to parole. The whole parole process is repeatedly singled out as a costly failure. But, the rate of recidivism There are 113,000 people on probation or parole from the federal and provincial systems (*Toronto Star*, Jan 25, 1996: A14). Jim MacLatchie of the John Howard Society of Canada notes: "We anticipated this, due to the effect of public pressure on parole boards to release fewer people, on judges to impose higher sentences and on the police to charge more youths" (ibid.).

According to Statistics Canada, one-quarter of more than the 10,000 people surveyed in 1993 said that they were victims of at least one crime, the same number as 1988. (*Toronto Sun*, 15, 06, 1994: 17). Although these data indicate that today Canadians are no more likely to be victims of crime than they were five years ago, the perception that crime is dangerously rampant persists. A 1997 Angus Reid Poll of 1516 Canadians showed that 59% said they believed the crime has gone up in their community (*Toronto Star*, July 31, 1997: A22). Why are Canadians and Americans overly panicked around crime? Why does mainstream knowledge about crime perpetuate or exacerbate this culture of fear?

To what then is the attention of the general public directed? What currency is exchanged in crime talk? The following review of the more salient official statistics is offered in order to delve into both the incidence of crime and more importantly the social implications of official crime trends. What then do official statistics reveal and conceal? It is instructive to note that statistics fall under several general categories: all crimes (reported and unreported), crimes of violence, crimes causing death, murder rates, crimes with firearms, juvenile crimes, etc. Interestingly, crimes of the powerful (government and corporate) escape mention let alone counting. Throughout the 1990s US crime rates have been falling (Thomas, 1996: 3). The reduction in violent crime was fuelled by a dramatic drop in the rate of murders, along with a smaller decline in rapes, robberies and aggravated assaults. Criminologists explain that we are getting older and are less likely to commit violent crimes. Despite declining crime rates, Irvin Waller of the University of Ottawa notes in his studies of international comparisons that Canada's violent crime rate is two or three times greater than most European countries and nine times that of Japan. He adds that Canadians are too complacent (*Toronto Star*, 31, 07, 1992: A11) about their crimes. According to Waller's international report on crime comparisons of industrialized nations, Canada has the second-highest crime rate in the Western world, second only to the US although the homicide rate there is four times higher than that of Canada.

The murder rate for the US hovers around 10 per 100,000 compared to Canada's 1996 rate of 2.11 per 100,000 (Yakabuski, 1994: C4; *Toronto Star*, July 31, 1997: A1; A22). While Canada's murder rate is one-quarter of the US rate, it is still higher than many European countries and 30% higher than England and Wales (*Toronto Star*, July 31, 1996: A20). In addition, in 1995 sixty-five youths were charged with murder or manslaughter—the highest number in twenty years. And violent crime for youth rose 2.4%, more than twice the rate in 1986 (*Toronto Star*, August 1, 1996 A20).

In response to a public panic and the concomitant pressures to crackdown on violent youth crime, authorities in North America have moved to lower the age limit from eighteen to sixteen for young offenders. Youth court sentences have increased for those convicted of first degree and second degree murder. The American juvenile justice system was designed 100 years ago to reform youths found guilty of minor crimes. Increasingly, the system is overwhelmed by teenage drug runners and murderers. In September 1994, California governor Wilson signed a bill reducing the age of transfer to adult facilities to fourteen, as did Arkansas and Georgia. Youths aged fourteen to seventeen charged with certain crimes will be tried as adults automatically. Note the tenor of New York's democratic representative Charles Schumer. "Disturbing figures about violence in America are released so often we treat them as if they were a box score from yesterday's baseball game. Our country has to take radical action to counter this trend of violence." (*USA Today*, 18, 07, 1994: 3A). Changes to parole eligibility ensure that youths sentenced in the adult system will serve longer periods in custody. Despite their obvious quick-fix appeal, the above changes will falter in resolving youth violence. Why replicate and model the juvenile justice system after the adult criminal justice system, which has remained ineffective in deterring violent crimes? Youths will inevitably develop worse problems than when they entered adult facilities. Moreover, juvenile laws were historically designed to intervene and redirect youths in trouble within a child-saving protectionism. Since their inception, youth laws in practice were always punitive, contradicting the principles of "doing good". Juvenile laws have had difficulties balancing "doing justice" with "doing good", getting serious rather than getting tough. Getting tough has been costly with limited results. This money could be better spent on prevention and rehabilitation such as the development of a wider range of community alternatives and programs that include specialized foster care, intensive tracking, day centres, etc. For instance, the pressure to reduce violence in schools, especially as a result of the possession and use of weapons, is typically placed on the police and the schools who create very narrow solutions ranging from hiring security personnel in schools, increased discipline, better teachers, relevant courses, zero tolerance, smaller classes, etc. These responses tend to de-contextualize violence in the wider community. Interestingly, the level of analysis evident in these changes remains at the interpersonal and organizational levels. Offenders and their respective reactors have become the foci while the following remain untouched: fundamental issues of inequality, the equivocation of law, the institution of the family, the nature of the educational system, the sensational media, the lack of political will in seeking genuine remedies, unemployment and under-employment, unequal opportunities, the under-funding of pre-emptive social services interventions, the manufacture and proliferation of drugs as well as weapons, the over-representation of minorities, and the pervasive culture of violence. For example, 21,597 murders were recorded in the US in 1995, 13% fewer than in 1991. The property crime rate fell by 1% to 12 million offences, the lowest number since 1987. US Attorney General Janet Reno and other law enforcement experts attributed the continuing drop in crime to various factors: a maturing, therefore less violent crack cocaine market; sharp increases in the number of police on the streets; improved coordination among federal, state and local authorities; and more prisons. And yet the US prison population exceeded one million for the first time in history (BJS, Department of Justice, 1995). In the last decade, the US prison population doubled on a per capita basis. During this period the incarceration rate doubled both for white and black inmates. There are well over 1500 black inmates per 100,000 black US residents and 203 white inmates per 100,000 white residents. According to the US Centres for Disease Control, firearms have replaced traffic accidents as the leading cause of injury-related deaths among young Americans. Gunshots now cause one of every four deaths among American teenagers, according to the National Centre for Health statistics. Fifty thousand children have been killed by guns between 1979 and 1991, a figure equivalent to the number of Americans killed in the Vietnam war, according to the US Children's Defense Fund report (*Toronto Star*, 23, 01, 1994: E5). The equivalent of a classroom of American children (approximately thirty) is killed every two days by firearms. Another thirty get hurt each day. In 1991 the number of American children younger than ten years who died from firearms was twice the number of Americans killed in the Persian Gulf and Somalia combined. An American child is fifteen times as likely to die as a result of gunfire as a child in Northern Ireland (ibid., 21, 01, 1994: A15). According to a 1991 American Senate

Judiciary Committee, the USA is "the most violent and self-destructive nation on earth ... the USA led the world with its murder, rape and robbery rates" (Report of the Standing Committee on Justice and the Solicitor General, 1993: 2). Every hour, approximately 200 Americans become victims of violence (ibid.). As Boyd (1988: 5) added:

> The United States is a less civil society than Canada. With a cult of individualism that makes confrontation almost inevitable, disparities of wealth that significantly exceed Canadian standards of fairness, and a culture that has made the right to bear arms into a national fetish, our good friends to the south have stacked the deck against themselves.

Clearly, Canada and the USA are among the most violent societies of the industrialized nations (*Toronto Star*, 16, 07, 1993: A15). In 1992 Los Angeles residents killed each other in record numbers; there were 1063 homicides, an increase of twenty-four over 1991 (*Toronto Star*, 5, 01, 1993: A10); in 1993, New Orleans had at least one murder a day. More recently, Gary, Indiana, a city of 116,000 near Chicago, finished in 1995 among the deadliest American cities with 130 killings. In general, the latest US average ranges from 50-80 per 100,000 a year (ibid.). The US murder rate dropped 8% in 1995. The crime fell in the USA in 1995 for the fourth straight year (*Toronto Star*, May 6, 1996: A10). As a quick aside, the metropolitan Toronto homicide rate was 1.79 per 100,000 in 1996 with 58 murders in 1996, the national average is 2.11, while Winnipeg's twenty-eight homicides, 4.12 per 100,000, accounted for the highest rate for a major Canadian city (*Toronto Star*, July 31, 1997: A22). More recently, 15% to 29% of murders and manslaughters in New York state are defined as capital crimes under the death penalty law. In 1993 there were 2386 murders in the state; New York City accounted for 81.5%, that is, 1946 deaths; Brooklyn, 718 or 30.1%; Bronx, 512 or 21.5%; Manhattan, 418 or 17.%; Queens, 273 or 11.4%; Staten Island, 25 or 1% (*New York Times*, March 8, 1995: B12).

These hegemonic accounts or constructions of crime are functional in terms of generating support for state sponsored agencies of social control. Alternatively, crime has emerged as a big business. Conservative estimates in the US indicate that for the fiscal period from 1990 to 1994, federal and state governments spent annually from $70-75 billion for criminal justice; this represents an increase of 22% since 1988 (*Toronto Star*, 16, 07, 1993: A15; Bureau of Justice Statistics, 1990a). The rates of imprisonment have been increasing, as Professor Jerome Skolnick noted: "They'll fill the prisons with geriatric prisoners who will be behind bars long after they pose any threat to society" (Clark, 1994: B4). Canadian prisons (provincial institutions) and penitentiaries (federal facilities) are overcrowded and thereby expensive to maintain in terms of human and financial costs. The cost of keeping an inmate—about $43,643 a year (1996-1997) —was up 3% from the preceding year (*Toronto Star*, Feb 18, 1998: A18). There are, however, on an average day (1996-1997) approximately 34,167 people serving sentences behind bars—the highest number ever—an increase of 382 inmates over the previous year (ibid.). One-third of inmates in provincial jails and 17% in federal prisons are doing time for property crimes; 25% of all provincial inmates are there for failing to pay fines; 12% for impaired driving. The average provincial inmate serves a one-month sentence while 25% of provincial inmates serve no more than two weeks of incarceration. (*Toronto Star*, Feb 18, 1998: A18). It costs the province $120 a day to incarcerate someone but only five to twenty dollars to keep them in the community (ibid.). In 1992 there were 28,163 persons employed in this growth industry. The hidden costs, such as insurance claims, the involvement of other security institutions, etc., bring the costs up to $14 billion annually. Besides the police and corrections industries, the legal profession has also exacted an exorbitant cost in serving to render a version of justice. Witness, for example, the growth of legal practitioners. In Canada, one in every 510 residents is a lawyer or a public notary. In Ontario there is one lawyer for every 900 citizens (*Lawyers Weekly*, 16, 09, 1994: 3). In the USA, there is one lawyer per 340 people, and one out of 8316 people in Japan (*Toronto Star*, 26, 08, 1993: A7).

Moreover, the business of crime also thrives on fear by motivating people to invest money in measures to reduce their vulnerability. The sale of weapons has proliferated. There are at least 290,000 federally licensed dealers in the USA (*Time*, 20, 12, 1993: 24). During the twentieth century, some 250 million firearms, excluding military weapons, have been manufactured in or imported into the US (Wright, 1993: 259). In fact, dogs are more strictly controlled than rifles and shotguns. On a more global scale, violence is equally profitable. The Congressional Research Service reports that the USA exported $14 billion worth of arms to Third World countries in 1991, compared to $4 billion in 1986. It supplies more than half of all arms sold to developing countries. In 1992 the Pentagon supplied arms and military aid worth $32.7 billion to 154 countries. Since the Persian Gulf war, the USA has sold Middle Eastern nations about $23 billion in arms

(*Toronto Star*, 24, 10, 1992: C5). At a time when Washington is discouraging the Russian arms sale, the USA has maintained dominance of the Third World arms market. Of the $30 billion in arms supply agreements signed by Third World countries in 1992, the American share rose 57% compared with only 13% five years earlier. In 1993 the American market share was $14.8 billion (*Toronto Star*, 5, 08, 1994: A22). The USA has taken over the arms market largely by replacing the former Soviet Union as a "gun runner" (tanks, jets, arms, etc.). Saudi Arabia paid $9. 5 billion for sweventy-two F-15 jets, following a personal plea by President Clinton to King Fahd to buy American. Kuwait paid $2. 2 billion for 256 battle tanks, a token of gratitude by the ruling al-Sabah family for restoring them to the lucrative throne after the Gulf crisis (ibid.). New orders are expected for Patriot anti-missile batteries. The French follow a distant second with 16% of the world's market, Britain with 10% and Russia 5%. As Alvin and Heidi Toffler described (1994: 27-30): "the way we make war reflects the way we make wealth." Throughout the 1990s a new form of warfare closely resembles a new form of wealth creation (ibid., 28-29) —dazzling, hi-tech forms of destruction that are for sale. The average number of yearly military conflicts since 1945 has ranged from thirty to thirty-five; in the last twelve months, there have been sixty-two wars—ensuring enhanced the profits for the American war industry. Examine, for instance, a few statistics concerning the nuclear weapons industry: currently there are 8380 strategic nuclear warheads in the USA; 9663 in the former USSR; 480 in France; 435 in China; 200 in UK; 200 in Israel; 50 in India; 15 in Pakistan (*Toronto Star*, 2, 05, 1994: E6). In 1992 there were 49,910 nuclear weapons down from a high of 69,480 in 1986 (ibid., 19, 06, 1994: F5). How can the American government expect its citizens to surrender its guns when it continues to be one of the world's leading dealer of weapons of mass destruction? In fact, the annual budget for national intelligence alone was $26.6 billion (US) for the 1997 fiscal year (*Toronto Star*, October 16, 1997: A40); 10 billion for tactical military intelligence; CIA gets 3 billion; National Security Agency 4 billion

Besides selling arms, the USA continues to rent its combat troops to perceived challenges. The world's most willing mercenaries, or what Chomsky (1992, 73) described as "rent a thug," continued a campaign of bombardment of Baghdad in 1993. The American missile attack was lawless, as was the invocation of Article 51 of the United Nations Charter, (a self-defence provision) that was similarly brandished by former Republican President Ronald Reagan when he ordered an air strike on Libya. With the latter, fighter planes were ordered to target Moammar Gadhaffi and his family in April 1986 under the pretext of attacking terrorist centres. The bombing sorties over Libya were never considered as state-sponsored terrorism because, as Cockburn (1993: A10) adds, "the US need not acknowledge no master." The 1993 bombings gave the President Clinton a political lift; he succeeded in garnering general support. Talking tough, President Clinton (ibid.) warned: "A firm and commensurate response was essential to protect our sovereignty, to send a message to those engaged in state-sponsored terrorism, to deter further violence against our people and affirm the expectation of civilized behaviour among nations."

The business of crime control requires the dramatized construction of images of evil, criminal or the dangerous especially concerning "those others". Moreover, pathologies are imputed for many reasons. The June 1993 American missile attack on Iraq's "intelligence headquarters" was conducted, according to President Clinton, in retaliation for the alleged Iraqi assassination attempt on former President Bush. For the USA, a brutal tyrant crosses the line from being an admirable friend to "villain" and "scum" when he or she commits the crime of independence (Chomsky, 1992: 51) as apparent in the hypocritical American treatment in the 1990s of Saddam Hussein of Iraq or Manuel Noriega of Panama—former friends of the State Department. For both Canada and the USA, Saudi Arabia and Kuwait are allies and friends and not perceived as corrupt feudal states run by monarchies that deny basic human rights to its citizens. Why was there no intervention in these two countries by Canadian and American troops on behalf of the same noble principles?

On the one hand, this crime text sustains conformity and stability, acts as a safety valve and re-affirms the significance of rules. On the other hand, these criminal accounts divert attention away from fundamental social problems as the following classic illustration suggests.

The social construction of crime: a case study

In Kai Erikson's study, *The Wayward Puritans* (1966), small and isolated seventeenth-century New England communities are examined to develop several ideas about criminal behaviour, to carefully map out novel theoretical directions and to demonstrate that the Puritanism of this setting has had lasting implications. In this study, the functions of crime are clarified. Crime serves to promote group solidarity and generate a common morality. Crime maintains boundaries that confine tolerable behaviour to a particular radius. Erikson notes, "each community draws a symbolic set of parentheses around a certain segment of that range and limits its own activities within that narrower zone" (1966: 10). The individual who moves beyond the margins is called to account for that vagrancy. The community declares how much variability will be tolerated and defines the nature of the appropriate confrontations. Today the media has replaced medieval public marketplace executions with information about the boundaries of acceptable conduct within communities.

Erikson analyzes three crime waves, that is, moments of excitement, alarm and a rash of publicity. These three confrontations include: the Antinomian Controversy of 1636-1638 or the Hutchinson Affair; the Quaker Invasion of 1656; and the witches of Salem in 1692. These events demonstrate how communities set up their boundaries and their identities, which become interchangeable. Certain occasions trigger crises that result in the re-alignment of power. Crime or deviance and conformity draw responses coterminously. That is, the most feared and the most respected, according to Erikson, mirror each other. Encounters in which the deviants or criminals are confronted by authority agents provide a forum for affirming control.

The first controversy involved a very religious, popular and respected Bostonian woman, Anne Hutchinson, who felt that New England Puritanism had departed drastically from early Puritan principles that emphasized the private nature of each person's covenant with God. New England Puritan orthodoxy maintained that God entered a covenant with the people of the colony as a corporate group and was only ready to deal with them through agencies or intermediaries such as congregations, government or civic administration. Evidently, this was a practice they fought against in England. Hutchinson's followers quickly increased; meetings were held at her home to discuss theological concerns, and the group agreed that the New England ministers were incompetent to preach the gospel. Eventually her criticisms irritated the church elders (ibid., 76, 80) who aligned themselves with the conservative founder of the community, John Winthrop. Conferences were held among all ministers of the colony. In 1636 political leaders crusaded against all insurgents. Hutchinson replied that the ministry was a political instrument and that her own religious calling set her above the government of ordinary men. Although no crime was committed, although all the arguments she raised were based in theology, Hutchinson and her supporters were charged with sedition rather than heresy. At her trial, Winthrop was the prosecutor and the judge, the ministers who were to be there as witnesses or spectators also participated as active prosecutors. This confrontation was a morality play, a ceremonial charade that disguised the power politics and levels of inequality. The public ritual declared plainly that the people who acted in this fashion had trespassed the boundaries of appropriate behaviour. To further chastise this deviance, Hutchinson was summoned before a church trial where she was asked to confess, revoke her opinions and accept excommunication.

The second crisis involved the arrival of the Quakers to New England in 1656. The Quakers felt that people should engineer their own relations with God and certainly did not need to submit their religious experiences to the review of any church official. John Endicott, chief magistrate, and John Norton, chief clergyman, quickly reacted in defence of conservatism. They treated the Quaker arrival like a military invasion (ibid., 116). Laws were immediately enacted against "those" heretics. Severe beatings and stiff penalties were directed at the Quakers. These new immigrants were treated like criminals and transported to the West Indies. The Vagabond Act was passed to deal with this threat. King Charles II of England intervened in 1661 and prohibited the use of corporal and capital punishment against the Quakers in New England. The Puritans eventually acquiesced and resorted instead to the Vagabond Act.

The third crisis, involving the witches of Salem Village, occurred when tensions were mounting between England and the colony. King Charles ll ordered New England, the bastion of Puritanism, to allow the establishment of an Anglican church in Boston. He also revoked the charter of New England and sent a royal governor to represent his interests in the colony. In 1692 many young girls were spending considerable time with Tituba, a black slave who belonged to Reverend Parris. These white girls displayed convulsions, unusual cries, lewdness, etc. Medical experts examined the girls and could not find any medical explanations. The clergy poured into Salem and diagnosed the phenomenon as witchcraft. These white offenders, however, were perceived to be victims. The most obvious candidate for "criminal" was Tituba, who was immediately implicated because she was black and knew something about voodoo (ibid., 142-143). Two other white women were eventually suspected—one because she was a pauper and another because she allowed a man to live with her before marriage. The trial of these three women was quick; they were found guilty from the testimony of other hysterical girls and quickly executed in public. Erikson suggests that they were on trial for all the disorder and suffering experienced by the colony. The general court continued to ask the girls to identify further witches. The governor appointed a special court of Oyer and Terminer to hear the growing number of cases. Even after twenty-two women were executed, the girls guided by the courts went into strange and unknown towns and singled out witches (ibid., 149). The girls finally got carried away and began accusing religious and political leaders, thereby eroding their sense of credibility. Consequently, many suspects were acquitted. It is remarkable how a few girls were exploited by the establishment to cleanse a community of any unsavoury figures who drifted around the edge of the community.

Erikson's study suggests that social control is calibrated to handle a steady flow of crime. Crime, difference or trouble is defined in a manner that invites considerable public participation; that is, crime becomes transformed as an elastic instrument of oppression. The persecutions in the colony moved from the individual to the groups; women were immediately criminalized or deviantized once they refused to obey the male-dominated political, social and religious rules. If we consider the implications of the study in relation to contemporary contexts, it becomes apparent that crime provides the much needed justification for keeping an extant policing industry busy. The powerful devise crime by manufacturing threats to the status quo. Perceived dangers and challenges to the security of the community are amplified to legitimate control and disguise the deviance of the powerful.

Erickson's study illustrates how crime is a public spectacle that serves many functions. Note contemporary parallels, such as the executions by beheading of eighty people in 1993 in Saudi Arabia for a variety of crimes where under Sharia (Islamic Law) rapists, murderers and drug dealers are beheaded while convicted thieves have their hands amputated (*Toronto Star*, 17, 04, 1994: C6). On the one hand, religion serves to hide indiscretions and on the other hand publicizes the dangers of difference. Throughout the 1990s media revelations continue to contradict the role of religion in ensuring conformity. For instance, how does one make sense of the behaviour of Catholic Bishop O'Connor in British Columbia who had been charged with a series of sexual assaults; the crimes committed by Christian lay brothers at Mount Cashel in Newfoundland; the twenty-eight Christian clergy charged with hundreds of counts of sexual abuse at Alfred (twenty former staff members) and Uxbridge in Ontario (*Toronto Star*, 12, 12, 1992: A3) and in Goleta, California? Again, how does one reconcile the self-righteous, viciously homophobic rhetoric of the Vatican newspaper (*L'Osservatore Romano*) in its attack against the European Parliament for moving towards a recognition of homosexual marriages, saying that these marriages could lead to the recognition of incestuous relationships and asking, "What if incest began to spread as an instinct, would that be marriage, too?" (ibid., 19, 03, 1994: B2). Alternatively, the Vatican has been slow in coming to terms with the large number of Christian brothers accused and convicted of countless sexual assaults and bizarre acts of degradation inflicted against children. In 1987 the Reverend Jim Bakker of the Praise the Lord (PTL) television ministry resigned because of an extramarital sex scandal that he claimed was "wickedly manipulation" by former friends. He was convicted on fraud and originally sentenced to forty-five years (Croteau and Worcester, 1993: 102). He was released in 1994 to a half-way house, after serving four and a half years for defrauding $125 million. The Reverend Jimmy Swaggart, a popular Pentecostal evangelist confessed to "moral failure" for his associations with a prostitute in 1988 (ibid., 477). At the urging of Reverend Jim Jones, 911 followers of the People's Temple were killed or committed suicide by ingesting Kool-aid and cyanide concoctions in 1978 (ibid., 99). In February, 1993, a firefight between US agents and Branch Davidians resulted in the death of four US agents and six Davidians. The Branch Davidian sect compound was burned to the ground in April, 1993 when US agents started bulldozing it to end a fifty-one-day standoff. At least eighty-five people died inside the compound. Apparently the above inconsistencies of prayer and practice are similar to the Church's condemnation of Galileo Galilei, a learned mathematician, astronomer and physicist, for asserting in 1633 that the Earth spins daily on its axis and rotates around the sun. Horrific atrocities were committed against Jews and Muslims in the name of Christianity during the Holy Crusades and the Spanish Inquisition.

Private morality plays are transformed into serious public declarations of war. The war image is exploited to muster support, mobilize resources and justify cleanup operations. The war on drugs, fighting crime, clearing the streets of prostitutes and the return to family values are vacuous and alarmist slogans designed to seduce and implicate an impressionable audience in supporting political interests. The pragmatic interests of the powerful are buried in the language of fear and security rehearsed in public trials. In turn, public perceptions frame, inform and fan state intrusions. Crime waves and moral panics are generated by self-appointed guardians of public morality who attempt to identify the emergence of a problem and suggest action to be taken (Taylor, 1981: 48-56).

Drug use has become increasingly associated with criminal deviance. The war on drugs has always provided a good excuse for state intervention. The US administration has spent more than 100 billion dollars on the drug war since 1981. Unsurprisingly, 70% of America's 1.4 million prisoners have drug problems, and yet less than 1% of federal inmates and about 15% of state prisoners receive adequate treatment (Kramer, 1993: 21). At the time when the American administration decided to wage the drug war, deaths from tobacco were estimated at 300,000 a year, with another 100,000 from alcohol. And yet, illegal drugs caused fewer deaths—over 3,500 a year (Chomsky, 1992: 83).

There are more than 330,000 Americans behind bars for violating drug laws (Nadelmann and Wenner, 1994). Interestingly, one-third of the inmates are incarcerated for drug-related crimes (Weinstein and Cummins, 1993: 44). In 1992, according to the FBI, 535,000 people were arrested for possession, sale or manufacture of marijuana. In six cases, life sentences were imposed. There is no evidence that this drug alone has ever caused a single death (Nadelmann and Wenner 1994: 24); marijuana had not caused any known deaths among 60 million users (Chomsky, 1992: 83). The war on drugs is absurd; there has been no reduction despite the interdiction of the Pentagon. This intervention cost taxpayers one billion dollars in 1991; this drug war has been efficient only in filling jails.

The USA appears infatuated with mandatory minimum sentences for drug possession (Steiberg, 1994: 33). In 1993, 60% of the 87,000 people in federal prisons were serving time on drug convictions, up from 22% in 1980. Interestingly, Michigan's "650 Lifer law" requires life sentences for possession of more than 650 grams of cocaine (ibid.). Mandatory sentences were originally designed to reduce sentencing discrepancies. Mandatory minimums are invoked more often with black defendants than white ones. Blacks make up 28.2% of the federal prison population and 38.5 % of the mandatory minimum defendants (ibid., 34).

Crime is easily commoditized as with every American democrat and republican national convention where speaker after speaker repeatedly highlight the return to conformist family values. Images indoctrinate thought through processes of propaganda but also succeed in distracting attention from the business of deviance and the politics of respectability.

The challenge of critical inquiries

No one book can hope to do justice to the enormous breadth and depth of crime. Even to catalogue salient ideas is an ambitious enterprise that suffers the dangers of trying to do too much while accomplishing relatively little. The corpus of existing texts provides too much reductionism that fails to transcend the local and situated politics to consider the relatedness of institutions and processes. Regrettably, many existing approaches include the following weaknesses: arguments are too inaccessible because of the excessive socio-legal jargon; the foci are too buried because of sterile and eclectic encyclopedic inventories of too many different perspectives; the evidence alludes to hackneyed, irrelevant and recycled illustrations; the layout demands little theoretic analysis as much as an acceptance of glossy or shallow, easy-to-follow cookbook recipes; readers are encouraged to adopt a single and simple theoretical approach that artificially weaves the fabric of loose thematic fibres; the tenor of the text is anti-intellectual in the omission of current and leading theoretical and applied struggles that incorporate culture, history and the Canadian political economy; approaches are far too Anglo- and Americancentric; arguments are overwhelmingly linear and neatly packaged with a "stir and mix" concoction of deviance and crime; arguments promote intellectual arrogance by trivializing critical pedagogy and ideological naivete by ignoring racism, misogyny and class concerns. A large number of conventional texts are reluctant to discover and analyze relationships of the taken-for-granted world, to question how the world actually hangs together and provide compelling evidence that moves beyond traditional logic. Accordingly, rules and the official statistics that form the foundations for hegemonic criminological narratives are seldom viewed as problematic and never treated reflexively.

In *Crime and Culture*, readers are advised to engage in an active reading; to develop an interrogative stance and to be informed by history and political economy in looking afresh at the familiar. Clearly, readers are asked to develop a sociological imagination (Mills, 1959) that links personal troubles with public or social issues; to connect patterns in their lives with the events of society; to appreciate the intersection of biography and history when approaching phenomena deemed to be deviant or criminal; to delve into the social sources, meanings and implications from various vantage points, using different analytic lenses, and to become more de-mystified and tentative in their traditional appraisals of crime and deviance. This book invites students of criminology or sociology of law to partake more fully in their own learning.

This text responds to past presentations. As Barthes (1975: 14) notes, the traditional text is a text of pleasure, grants euphoria, comes from culture and does not depart from it. The certitude of traditional texts demands intellectual servitude. *Crime and Culture* is a text of bliss that nonetheless "imposes a state of loss, the text that discomforts ... unsettles the reader's historical, cultural, psychological assumptions ..." (ibid.). As Wiseman (1989:

88) adds, challenging the modern text gives consciousness, new meanings and abolishes exclusions (ibid., 133). Traditional texts are separated from real experiences; they are written as "something apart from life itself, a separate world instruction, representation and truth" (Mitchell, 1989: 93). This book invites us to move beyond a rudimentary exposition of basic concepts to formulate fundamental questions about the nature of crime. We are invited to get "on the line" —resist and challenge commonsense assumptions. We are further urged to read between the lines—deconstruct official rhetoric and neo-liberal thought. By so doing, we link well-established narratives to various texts, subtexts and inter-texts that mediate the narratives with the lines. In other words we are required to become strangers, stand aside and witness our own traditions of conceptualizing crime. As we problematize relationships, we bring to the forefront questions that have been too conveniently ignored. The reader is asked to be courageous in deconstructing traditional canons by concentrating on the contradictions and closures inherent in conventional commentaries on crime. This book was not packaged to satisfy market conditions by journeying voyeuristically into the titillating worlds of the erotic or the exotic but rather to respond to the critical faculties of all students struggling with the phenomenon of crime. Readers are encouraged to document their experiences, consciousnesses, intentions, and their relational contexts especially when examining crime.

Besides clarifying the above processes inherent in learning, this book offers perspectival and substantive material. Admittedly, no perspective can be all things to all students. Any theory is a selective rendering of the world, a category of different realities. Different theories, however, address different sets of problems and produce different assortments of facts. Selectivity is inevitable.

Of course, this book will itself be deviantized for offending certain high moral grounds and for challenging conventional perspectives. To the threatened, the arguments herein will be easily discarded as rancorously polemical and controversially provocative—forever beating on rhetorical drums. As an expression of the dissatisfaction with extant texts, this undertaking will certainly be attacked, especially as readers decode the traditional text and relocate theoretical frontiers, i.e., as the traditional text becomes increasingly problematized. The loose forays of mainstream criminological cookbooks have failed to stimulate critical curiosities. Further, extant published empirical research on specific facets of deviance remains challenging and focussed but fails to provide an overview based on many critical readings and applications. Again, readers are implored to suspend, if not escape from, prevalent common sense assumptions about crime until they have, first, weathered fully the contradictions of culture and second, participated actively in interrogating complex problematic relationships. Readers are asked to situate themselves in the debates and struggles that characterize the study of crime, to ground their perceptions, to avoid self-incarceration, to empower themselves conceptually and to engage in open debate. Traditional texts obscure more than they reveal; the concept of power remains mysteriously hidden behind the magic of facile reductionism. This book is deliberately oppositional, challenging the unitary, polarizing and totalizing view of traditional models that refuse to defy the defining gaze of legal or legitimate authoritative definitions. We are constantly urged to move beyond the immediacy of the criminal moment to consider the backdrop of crime generally.

Clearly, *Crime and Culture* is a political project that invites readers to position themselves ideologically and historically. This gesture is typically carved in the legacy of Anglocentric privilege in order to display the origins of current North American values and practices. This book provides a variety of theoretical formulations that need to be fully appreciated and assessed for a more sound understanding of social order. The chapter topics were selected as the result of a careful and painful appraisal of many available texts addressing the contexts, conditions and consequences of crime from various levels of analytic inquiry.

Substantively, the study of crime is a fertile environment to question prevailing ideas and the cultural enclosures, not simply to debunk nor disparage orthodoxies. The sociology of crime "is a political observatory" (Foucault, 1979: 281) not a misfit zoology absorbed in the exhibitionism of the entertainment industry. Nor does crime solely belong to the confines of a juridic or legal narrative. A constricted definition of crime is also a meaningless exercise that forecloses any possibility of social justice that presumably must implicate such dynamic features as history and political economy. The ongoing official chatter, illusions and fascination with crime serve to mystify, trivialize and distract from a much needed public consciousness and debate. Crime is far too serious a subject matter to leave solely in the hands of such self-proclaimed crime experts as the police, lawyers or reporters. It is a subject matter that moves beyond the dubious celebration of sensational criminal investigations. Instead, the study of crime directly confronts the basis of social order, the nature of society and the interpretations of challenges.

As with many other sociological inquiries, the book is concerned with the quintessential questions: How is society possible? How is society made up? How is order reproduced? How is crime constructed? Since order is (per)formative rather than normative, it is important to explore and explain the problematic nature of official meanings and action; rules and the manner in which deviance designations are constructed and concretized; the consequences of these efforts to punish; the implications of power as criminogenic; and the legitimacy of authority. This book is but a modest attempt, a tentative guideline that seeks to better introduce readers to the world of crime by providing an accessible, progressive and an alternate framework. The defining characteristics of prevailing crime narratives must include such matters as the lack of coherence, ambiguity, fragmentation—these weaknesses are in effect the strengths of the discipline. Multiple subjectivities are mined. Equally, there are limits to texts especially as they become involved in moral struggles.

Texts, especially conventional studies, demand subservience (Itwaru, 1987) as they order interpretation. Texts and power, as Itwaru (1989b: 19) notes, are unities; they penetrate each other and succeed in re-directing attention. But no single text can do justice to the breadth and depth required in exposing cultural contradictions and the political economy of oppression. Even a catalogue of leading conceptual formulations is an enormously misleading and fruitless undertaking.

Although a general overview of the tradition is provided in this first part, this book strives to avoid myopic reductionism by interpenetrating or crossing boundaries immediately, i.e., by contextualizing the text's theoretical scripts. Explanatory paradigms—the normative, interpretive and conflict—are introduced. The reader is urged to evaluate ideas within the paradigms and search for continuities and convergences. The second part of this book develops a counterdiscourse, a more deviant text. Through advocacy and a commitment to reform, tensions are explored. Alternatives, informed by progressive writings, are sought in order to advance critical cultural perspectives that go beyond liberal styles of criminological reasoning that are so reflective of dominant ideologies. As we move towards the next millennium, one still remains quite impatient with the intellectual directions of criminology. Aside from the growing numbers of critical criminologists committed to both intellectual rigour and praxis, for decades the study of crime has been overwhelmingly silent, if not ignorant, in terms of the contributions of the Frankfurt school, Antonio Gramsci, CLR James, the French schools, the Birmingham school, etc. Empirical inquiries have also been too narrowly located according to the criteria of funding agencies. For decades, research centres have proffered only liberal accommodations to fundamental problems of inequality—racism, misogyny, classism and heterosexism.

Crime and Culture is more than a relative introduction to underlying contradictions in the political economy, that is, elements of social organization that are at the roots of inequality that usher crime-defining processes. As a generative idea, this book presents crime accounts as textures perpetually interweaving. The book per se is deviant, refusing to temper arguments and invoke quick-fix definitions that confuse. Instead, it succeeds even if only ideas are mobilized and readers politicized to think more subversively in empowering themselves.

Crime explanations intersect as sites, as historical subjects constituted in conflict. This critique confronts the politicality of accounts. Symbolically, thinking about crime reflects partisan interests. Crime, as a moral construct that produces and reproduces power relations, is examined from various analytic levels, from the very micro-world of everyday encounters to the macro realms of structural societal thinking. In piecing together the crime puzzle, we discover how culture not only contributes to diversity but we learn to appreciate how culture provides coherence to conventional consciousness. The overarching conceptual canopy that gives meaning to the criminalizing exercise is the ongoing confrontation with "order".

The ideological foundations of the criminological canons marginalize others. Crime as a discourse is a major device for interpreting the culture of control, powerful panoptic prisons and ideological hegemony. Crime is a constructed knowledge that pathologizes and devalues differences. What, for example, does it mean when a 1992 American study notes that the three Rs have been replaced by the three Ds—dishonesty, deceit and duplicity? Knowledge about crime is left to such social accountants as the media, consultants and functionaries of the criminal justice system, from trial lawyers to correctional officers. "Experts" have misappropriated commonsense, legalized moral language and celebrated possessive individualism leaving behind only mirrors and windows through which knowledge is framed. Juridic chatter has become an exaggerated social significance while the prestige of law continues to attract countless numbers. Law has become the language of official authority. But law, as the following chapters explain, is both remedial and coercive; a blessing for some and a curse for others. Law protects and punishes, imprisons and liberates. We will examine how the laurels of law can easily be transformed into its wreaths. The ideological contexts of conflict over the critical definitions of crime have led intrepid investigators to argue that official judgments are neither constant nor universal. In fact, there is no single and simple logic governing the claims of the powerful. As Mohr (1973: 49) admonishes:

> Trust, responsibility, care and love cannot be left to experts, whether in blue, black or white coats, nor can their opposites, since human qualities only grow by understanding and not by repression. There are risks involved.... We have long sneered at the law of the jungle; we may yet learn that this is a wiser law than the protective ones that we invent.

In general, the criminal justice system calculates the costs of crime and the value of appropriate sanctions. Ideological manipulations within the legitimation process makes crime more credible, by that making the label more adhesive. An objective frame of reference is the law. This justification of control provides formal images that distort rather than decode processes of crime, the meaningfulness of crime statistics, clearance rates or recidivism. The well-protected values of the privileged classes create illusions that demand deference.

Crime and Culture demonstrates that crime is a counter hegemonic cultural production. Resistance and struggle are central features in challenging deviance and the culture of domination. Accordingly, cultural criticism is essential in locating the marginalized other and in developing a liberating pedagogy. As bell hooks (1990: 8) elaborates:

> ... critical pedagogy (expressed in writing, teaching, and habits of being) is fundamentally linked to a concern with creating strategies that will enable colonized folks to decolonize their minds and actions, thereby promoting the insurrection of subjugated knowledge.

Before one can go on with alternate explanations of crime, it is important to have a fundamental understanding of well-respected assumptions that have informed early and contemporary perspectives that comprise the traditional texts. In the first part of this journey, emphases will be on:

1) the nature of crime and the sources of social definitions of conformity;
2) the formal and informal ways in which attributes and/ or behaviour of individuals, groups and communities come to be defined as criminal;

3) the social consequences of criminal designations and the pervasive role of conflict;
4) the problematic construction and imposition of standards, boundaries and criteria of appropriate norms, values and rules;
5) the constitution of the social within dominant ideologies.

The aim of this book is to explore the conceptual intersections of culture and crime by analyzing theoretical, substantive and methodological implications within the political contexts of coercion. The reader is expected to investigate major theoretical and methodological trajectories in the study of criminology and deviance. Additionally, the reader will be exposed to prospects and challenges of differing designs in order to advance an appreciation of praxis and ethics of interventive measures. Ultimately, the aim of this book is to confront contradictions in liberal thought. Liberal assumptions exacerbate the marginality already experienced by populations designated officially as criminal. Specifically, research on accommodation, resistance and struggle as generic features of survival are also studied in different sites. Interestingly, the dominant culture and attendant values are linked to forms of oppression. Qualitative methods for analyzing deviance and social justice within the critical ethnographic traditions are also developed to facilitate anti-racist, feminist and non elitist approaches in criminology or deviance.

Again, throughout this book, the organization of discussions seeks to move beyond the traditional texts. Conceptually, particular attention is given to law and authority relations which serve to reproduce order. Our inquiries into criminalization implicate social, political and economic struggles that reflect fundamental issues of inequality. Institutional forms are interrogated for their respective relationship(s) with the state, privileged interests in the political economy, law and cultural expressions. The behaviour of law or rules from moral creation to convenient enforcement, notions of consent, and invisible forms policing are investigated. The location of the acting subject and subjected actor within the control calculus are linked to ideological influences and hegemonic practices. Social conditions of criminality and deviance and informal and formal interventionist strategies warrant further analysis. Resource materials that will certainly help readers appreciate legal, political and cultural contexts are provided in the appendices.

Lastly, the social injustices of cultural reproductions are related to wider underlying structural and historical trends. In this book we will also study how moral entrepreneurs, like state agencies, maintain and reproduce social order by securing and protecting the legitimacy of continued accumulation of profit for the powerful, especially multinational corporations. Admittedly, this book reflects a commitment to the discipline, to the substantive subject, to those many undergraduate and graduate students from whom I have learned much about the disillusioning and de-politicized directions of the sociology of crime and deviance. This book is the product of many experiences over twenty years of teaching and learning at different sites: from the large university lecture rooms to the union halls, from community-based organizations to police cruisers, from factories to libraries, from parole offices and prisons to corporate suites. All these interactive trajectories identify formations and social reproductions as outcomes of cultural contradictions. *Crime and Culture* invites readers to be aware of the dominant other, the yardsticks by which the self is connected to the other, and to engage in the transformative potential of the self and to develop an active voice. Informed equally by both sociological principles and lived experiences, readers are asked to understand their own authentic location in the culture of criminal constructions and to move beyond traditional texts of conceptual paralysis towards more challenging critical catalyses.

The loose journeys of mainstream textbooks often fail to stimulate criminological curiosities beyond careerist aspirations. Processes (teaching and learning) involve commitment. As Ursula Franklin reminds us: "there is no teaching without learning; and, there is no learning without teaching." In reference to meaningful knowledge, Reverend Jesse Jackson once remarked, attitude not aptitude determines altitude. And yet unfortunately, we still suffer from boredom! The cure for boredom, however, is curiosity. But how does one exercise an atrophied muscle whenever analytic thinking is not in demand and whenever the traditional text is an analgesic, forever anesthetizing into complacency.

The struggle for change, therefore, is a challenge, a process that cannot be left to the benevolence of a handful of state sponsored actors bent on doing more good than concentrating on doing less harm (Rothman, 1980). Conscience extends a hand up rather than a handout, a characteristic model of convenience. Stated more vulgarly, the convenience inherent in the consumerist culture encourages citizens to remain lazy lap dogs rather than become vigilant watchdogs. In this regard we are mindful of the following Japanese and Chinese maxims, respectively: "the human mind is like an umbrella, it functions best when open" and "the willow that bends is stronger than the mighty oak that resists. " This book proposes an agenda that moves from human rights to social justice by undoing traditions and eradicating colonial discourses of the totalizing and commonsensical texts. Accordingly, authentic learning is risk-taking behaviour, challenging and confronting that which is so easily taken for granted.

Education as a major site of ideological reproductions (Althusser, 1971) shapes more than opinions of crime and rather frames consciousness. Conventional pursuits impose silence and inhibit the development of intellectual curiosities that challenge extant commitments. The morality of everyday life is taken for granted; prevailing moral rules are rarely problematized. Traditional models of teaching and learning continue to judge differences, colonize compliance and shackle the imagination. As Foucault (1979: 304) summarizes:

> We are in the society of the teacher-judge, the doctor-judge, the educator-judge, the social-worker-judge; it is on them that the universal reign of the normative is based. This carceral network has been the greatest support, in modern society, of the normalizing of power.

A more emancipatory and transformative potential of teaching/learning, grounded in struggle, is required. In other words, as Giroux (1983: 151) argues, the goal of developing an understanding of the immanent possibilities for a radical critique and a mode of social action based on the creation of a culture of critical discourses enhances a more developed conscientization. An empowerment of subordinate groups through a shared understanding of the construction and reproduction of dominant forms of knowledge has seldom been the program of socializing agencies. Empowerment and not just idle chatter about partnership will focus attention on the often-ignored structures and processes of inequality. Through a more critical education we will uncover our assumptions, learn more about our own learning, self-consciously challenge the dominant ethos and develop oppositional currents. To this end, this book has been deliberately oriented.

Crime as Normative

The study of crime enjoys a rich intellectual history. Traditional perspectives are replete with diverse theoretic tools that enhance our understanding of crime. This chapter presents a number of leading sociological and criminological writings which highlight the relationship between rule-violating behaviour and the dominant social order. Many of these well respected analyses maintain that crime is determined by structural forces. Moreover, norms form the consensual basis of society and thus are assigned considerable conceptual primacy in explaining the nature of crime. This chapter specifically assesses fundamental features of these normative accounts in reference to the following well researched substantive sites: anomie, strain, disorganization to subcultures, bonds and associations. Within this narrative, it is argued that the normative social order shapes the subjected actor, that is, the criminal actor is created by influential externalities. Subsequent chapters, however, will introduce alternate explanations in which the criminal actor is recast as an acting subject and where the concept of a dominant normative order is replaced largely with more interpretive and conflict oriented assumptions.

The social disorder of crime: the regulation of society—Emile Durkheim (1858-1917)

The impact of structure in the regulation of crime has been extensively examined within various normative traditions advanced by Durkheim, Merton, Parsons and the early Chicago school. The contributions of Emile Durkheim continue to advance the study of crime. This former chairperson of the Sorbonne was fundamentally concerned with the problem of social order, which he addressed by examining how diverse societies are held together. For Durkheim, society inoculates individuals from deviant pursuits ([1897], 1951: 241) by providing a pervasive belief system that preserves and protects social harmony. Social ties are integrating forces which constrain deviance. In routine encounters, shared social values are internalized, objectified and reproduced.

Durkheim's first major publication, *The Division of Labour in Society* (1893), investigates the processes of social change from primitive to more advanced societies. Durkheim was primarily concerned with discerning how highly differentiated societies secure social cohesion. He proved that various parts of society contributed to the maintenance of the whole. Specifically, Durkheim contrasts two types of integrating social orders— mechanical and organic solidarities. Briefly, mechanical solidarity is the moral and social integration associated with life in more simple or elementary societies. According to Durkheim, social integration refers to the quality and quantity of intimate affiliations. Within these undifferentiated societies, individuals are firmly anchored in extensive, close-knit networks that serve to maintain conformity. The process of moral integration, especially the sharing of beliefs, values and rituals reinforces conformity and promotes common conceptions regarding appropriate behaviour. Thus, a collective, dominant conscience based on similar social circumstances, feelings and interests directs individuals to internalize these collective sentiments. Analytically, the focus for Durkheim's investigation is social solidarity, rather than individual talents. This social solidarity is the basis of a common conformity that serves to keep a social order intact. For Durkheim however, all societies exist at any given moment in some stage of transformation from mechanical to organic structures. In time this mechanical solidarity ushers in organic solidarity.

Organic solidarity, evident in more contemporary, industrial and complex societies, is the natural outcome of relationships grounded in highly organized divisions of labour. Highly specialized roles and the diversity of functions result in a weakening of the collective moral conscience and a general decline in social integration. The division of labour integrated individuals by fostering interdependence. This division of labour replaced the collective conscience of traditional societies in ensuring harmony. Social differentiation promoted solidarity (ibid., 1933: 395-406) by creating an entire system of binding obligations replete with duties. The external mechanism of occupations, for example, not only integrates differences but also pacifies dissent by normalizing patterns of behaviour. The collective sense of morality diminishes as attachments are attenuated and competing values flourish. Complex differentiation within specialized institutions— economic, cultural, political—promote individualism, dependency and exchange. Deviance or rule-violative behaviour emerges whenever the power to constrain wayward members decreases. Laws enforce uniformity by repressing deviant instincts within mechanical solidarities whereas in organic societies laws regulate interactions of various social parts and provide restitution to aggrieved parties. Like law, deviance also assumes different functions in these emergent societal transformations. Within mechanical solidarity, deviance is normal in the sense that without deviance, society would be pathologically overbearing. In more organic forms, however, it is more likely that a pathological state, or anomie, creates deviance. Although Durkheim viewed the division of labour as a normal form of solidarity, he equally acknowledged several related problems. Commonly, a forced division of labour does not always produce a satisfactory standard of social consensus. To illustrate, merit or even occupations are seldom distributed according to talent. Alternatively, divisions of labour may fail to produce effectively functional contrasts between its members, and the activities of workers may be insufficient (1933: 354-355, 368) and too isolated to ensure conformity.

Durkheim (1893) introduces the idea of anomie to modern criminology to describe the conditions that persist in individuals and in society whenever norms are weak, absent or in conflict. Durkheim's conceptualization of anomie, derived from the ancient Greek word *anomia* meaning without law or lawlessness, designates the normlessness that leads to deviance. Accordingly, anomie or the absence of rules is an abnormal condition and a disruptive force especially since the natural state of society is consensus and integration. To repeat, this disruption of a collective order as a result of the absence or even conflicting norms causes intolerable, confusing and disorganized social conditions that lead to impaired moral regulations. For Durkheim, anomie is the outcome of historical forces that cause dysfunctions in the division of labour. The lack of appropriate economic controls, unregulated competition, conflict, meaningless attachments to one's labour and inappropriate work organizations produce tensions instead of solidarities (1933: 356, 375; Lukes, 1975). As people lose their links to one another, society suffers from anomie.

Durkheim's formidable publication, *Suicide* (1897), develops the concept of anomie more fully. Suicide, for Durkheim, is a dominant expression of anomie—the ultimate consequence of anomie. His painstaking research on suicide rates claims that a society with high levels of anomie—a lack of discipline and an absence of guidelines—risks disintegration. Theoretically, *Suicide* provided a clear sociological perspective on a substantive topic that could no longer be confined to biological or psychological explanations. Concerned with explaining the importance of a sociological orientation to deviant behaviour (suicide), this classic study emphasized social influences outside the individual. Suicide rates were attributed to features in the wider social organization of relations, that is, to levels of social integration and social control. As Durkheim remarks: "There is a relation between the way this regulative action is performed and the social suicide rate" (1951: 241). Conditions of economic prosperity, confusion and the breakdown of socially approved standards are related to suicide. Suicide is the product of failed restraints or, more specifically, the inability of the collective moral order to regulate aspirations or needs. Further, Durkheim sought to explain differential rates of suicide in terms of both inter- and intra-group variations. Briefly, he concluded on the basis of carefully scrutinized empirical evidence that rates were higher in urban areas than in rural settings, and more frequent in areas where Protestant rather than Catholic faiths flourished. The significance of Durkheim's *Suicide* goes well beyond the enormous contributions to the substantive sites and ideal typologies of suicide in pursuing an epistemology that became the foundation for modern criminology. But before we explore the theoretical contours of this narrative, it is instructive to clarify the specificities that ground Durkheim's normative claims in *Suicide*.

For Durkheim there are four ideal types of suicide, i.e., four consequences of differential degrees of social integration or regulation: altruistic, egoistic, anomic and fatalistic. Altruistic suicide occurs whenever a commitment to a group life is excessive—whenever levels of integration have become too extreme. The basis for existence extends beyond an individual's life. Group values overshadow the individual's interests. This over identification with a group leads to extreme forms of social integration believed to benefit others. For example, Durkheim found high rates of suicide in the military. Within military organizations, suicide rates were distributed unevenly—higher among officers than enlisted men. Besides rank, one's length of service contributed to a commitment and attachment to the group. Some contemporary examples of altruistic suicide include the activities of terrorists, patriots or even religious groups fanatically prepared to commit suicide for lofty social ideals or specific goals cherished by the group, movement, organization, institution or society. These goals are articulated within such celebrated expressions as the promotion of national security—"fighting for our flag", cheering for "our" team, or following "our" leaders—a return to fundamental family values, and the practice of keeping one's faith religiously. In this regard, the following correlation applies: the greater the social integration to a group or organization, the greater the likelihood of surrendering to that group's expressions of socially valued crusades.

Egoistic suicide, at the other extreme, follows from an insufficient identification with a group resulting in low levels of integration. Individuals in this category feel that they do not have a meaningful social basis for existence. They are extremely independent, and lack social ties that provide emotional support, especially in stressful situations. In this context, Durkheim found that single people had higher rates of suicide than those who are married, and childless couples more than married people with children. Concerning religious affiliations, there are marked differences between Protestants and Catholics. Suicide rates are higher for Protestants. According to Durkheim, Protestantism stresses the self-reliant and self-control nature of worship while Catholicism emphasizes ritual, strong group support and an organized authority upon which Catholics depend for redemption, especially within the confessional covenant. Similarly, Jews have lower rates of suicide than Protestants and Catholics because of the higher degree of social solidarity as evident in the significance attached to the family and community. Accordingly, the following correlation applies: the greater the social isolation, the greater the likelihood of suicide.

Anomic suicide results from a lack of regulation or insufficient rules (1951: 258). The regulatory function of the collective order breaks down whenever societies are in transition. A rapid and extreme change in society, in the individual's position, identity and in relations cause conditions of anomie. People are most content whenever clear and consistent goals govern their everyday lives. Whenever familiar goals are absent and expectations disappear, according to Durkheim, people's lives become more confused, meaningless and hopeless. Individual passions prevail without regulations (1897, 1951). More suicides are likely to occur in periods of unexpected severe economic depression (slumps) and prosperity (booms). When bonds are weak, individuals become more susceptible to sudden changes in society. Durkheim further examines the consequences of economic anomie—the breakdown of a normative framework that stabilizes expectations. These disturbances in the social equilibrium stimulate suicide. Whenever social forces fail to constrain, individuals are more likely to yield to suicidal tendencies (1951: 258). On the other hand, fatalistic suicide is "the suicide deriving from excessive regulation, that of persons with futures pitilessly blocked and passions violently checked" (1951: 276). As the polar opposite of anomic suicide, this fourth type is created for "completeness sake", since, as Durkheim noted, this type of suicide has little contemporary relevance and instances of it are difficult to find (ibid.).

In general, anomie provides an interesting interpretation of deviance, a conceptualization that promotes the social rather than individualistic accounts of rule-violating behaviour. For Durkheim, social determinants beyond the control of the individual were extremely influential in accounting for deviance. This normative epistemology maintained that rules provided the necessary constraints on individuals and their respective moral worlds. For Durkheim, only particular types of individuals commit crimes.

Nevertheless, deviance or crime can similarly contribute to social order. For Durkheim, crime is normal because it is bound up with the fundamental conditions of social life. A crimeless society is inconceivable. For Durkheim, the inevitability of crime is linked to social heterogeneity: people are different, behave differently in order to satisfy different needs. Crime, therefore, contributes to the survival of society by prescribing tolerable limits of behaviour, functioning to maintain social stability by informing people of the penalties attendant with rule-violative behaviour. Equally functional is the role of crime in providing the possibility of social change. Universal conformity, for Durkheim, stifles creativity and fails to draw attention to social evils. Increased and persistent deviance signals the need for adjustment or alternate methods for alleviating any further suffering. Durkheim used the example of the Greek philosopher Socrates who was considered criminal and put to death for corrupting the morals of youth. For Durkheim, Socrates was an altruistic criminal who offended the rules of society and yet sought social change (Nisbet, 1974: 220).

To fully appreciate Durkheim's impressive contributions, it is essential to locate his writings within a general theoretical context. Basically, Durkheim envisioned the social world as an objective social reality. Much like a physical reality, social reality is external and independent. Social reality can be studied as a given in its own right, *sui generis*. Society, as a social fact, is external to the individual; for example, note his first admonition, "consider social facts as things" (1938: 13), which suggests that the social world is to be treated as a natural world apart from the specific circumstances in which it is produced. Thus, Durkheim did much to advance a positivist sociology—a concern with the advancement of a scientific study of society. Positivism, as a philosophy of science, claims that the only things scientists should ask about are questions based on reason and measured according to criteria that demand systematic methods for collecting empirical data.

Further, Durkheim's analyses focused consistently on the strength of external forces. Social facts are not reducible to individual actors. The task of sociology, therefore, is to discover social facts that he operationalized as moral facts that determine social reality.

In general, anomie provides an interesting interpretation of deviance, a conceptualization that promotes the social rather than individualistic accounts of rule-violating behaviour. For Durkheim, social determinants beyond the control of the individual were extremely influential in accounting for deviance. An absence of crime or deviance suggests that the social structure is far too rigid in coercing similar behaviour.

Social structure and strain: Robert Merton (1910-   )

More than fifty years later in the USA, Robert Merton reformulated Durkheim's ideas in a general theory of deviance. Soon after he graduated from Harvard University in 1936, this distinguished Columbia University professor wrote his classic essay "Social Structures and Anomie" (1938). Revised in *Social Theory and Social Structure* (1957), this essay dominated deviance theorizing for decades. Like Durkheim, Merton emphasizes the significance of the social structure, especially the inadequacies therein, understood as discrepancies between objective social standards and conditions. Following Durkheim, Merton maintains that deviance is a normal response to a given situation. The strain towards deviance is remarkably similar to the pressure to conform. Deviance is a departure from well-established, appropriate and morally binding norms. Likewise for Merton, deviance is a characteristic feature of social structure and not simply a property inherent in the individual. Deviance occurs as an outcome of imbalances in the social system, that is, whenever the social structure fails to maintain control over individual aspirations. Again like Durkheim, Merton's social reality is an objective, independent and determining force, which for analytical purposes is dichotomized into cultural and social structures or, more specifically, culturally defined goals and socially approved means, respectively. Given the centrality of these critical components to Mertonian analyses, it is essential to detail more precisely how these elements interact in inseparable ways in modern society.

First, cultural structure is an organized set of shared values that govern the behaviour of members of a society (1957: 162). Merton argues that because of socialization individuals have a natural tendency to observe rules, follow norms and value several cultural goals. These culturally defined goals are legitimate objectives that frame aspirations. For example, Merton notes that contemporary society respects success, especially when operationalized as the acquisition of wealth. In general, Western cultures reward the pursuit of such values as possessive materialism, occupational prestige and consumerism.

Second, social structure is understood as institutional norms that define, regulate and control acceptable means for reaching cultural goals. Institutionally prescribed means for attaining success are resources that are not equally available, let alone accessible, to all interested candidates. Individuals vary in their location in the social structure; they are not equally positioned to capitalize on such opportunities as work, training and education. Since the capitalist economy, for example, is based on inequality, the pursuit of profit is exclusionary—only some and certainly not all individuals can attain culturally defined success. The structure of society, therefore, fails to provide the means necessary (1957) to realize much celebrated cultural aspirations.

According to Merton's central thesis, a discrepancy develops between the cultural goals and the legitimate means necessary to achieve them. This breakdown between aspirations and their corresponding regulating norms produces a strain towards both anomie and deviance. What are the implications of this malintegration of cultural goals with social structure for those who are disadvantaged? Oftentimes, individuals who have internalized the values of the prevailing culture and equally feel obliged to achieve them suffer from frustration. Consequently, regulatory norms break down as conformity becomes impossible. This strain leads to a search for different and often illicit means of achieving success. In explaining this state of anomie as a stressful situation in which norms lose their power to regulate, Merton, like Durkheim, concentrates not on the individual actor but on the social order. This breakdown in cultural structure occurs whenever there is an acute disjuncture between cultural goals and the socially structured capacity of individuals to act by them. As the social structure prevents what the culture encourages, normlessness emerges and individuals feel compelled to act against their conscience. In this way, integration of society becomes tenuous and anomie follows.

But the pressure to deviate is not felt equally by all members of society. Legitimate means are stratified across class and status dimensions. Those equipped with fewer resources will experience more difficulties in advancing towards success goals (ibid.). In less economically privileged classes, strain exists because socially approved avenues are blocked, if not completely closed. If individuals and groups are denied the means to achieve, they cannot attain valued goals to which they have been routinely exposed. Subsequently, this structured exclusion leads to deviance. This unequal access to socially approved means invites expressions of deviance, like crimes of theft and fraud. Merton, therefore, portrays the lower classes as more deviant-oriented, given the attendant anger, frustration and resentment that they experience in failing to achieve the trappings of success.

Strain, therefore, is unevenly exerted in society. Deviance is a direct response to this strain. What then, accounts for variations in behaviour? In his famous "typology of individual adaptations", Merton advanced a classification scheme that specifies five modes of adaptation according to the congruence of cultural goals with institutional means. Merton claimed that people may adjust to a situation in one of five alternate ways, depending on their acceptance or rejection of socially approved goals and the socially approved means of achieving them.

Adaptation 1, or conformity to both cultural goals and means, is the most common form of adjustment in a balanced society. Were this not so, Merton argued, the stability and continuity of society could not be maintained and society would cease to exist. Conformity or conventional role behaviour oriented towards basic values of the group is the rule rather than the exception. Conformists accept both approved goals and approved means.

Adaptation 2, or innovation, is the result of inadequate socialization. Conflict and frustration are eliminated by relinquishing the institutional means and retaining the success-aspiration. The individual assimilates to the cultural emphasis on success without equally internalizing the morally prescribed norms governing the means for its attainment. The actor accepts the goals but rejects the means. Moreover, the limitations of access to legitimate means create a strain towards more innovative practices. For example, when individuals desire luxuries but lack pecuniary resources, the resulting conflict forces them to adopt innovative solutions—they steal or cheat. The inescapable dominant demand to succeed prevails and places a significant burden on those who are more economically disadvantaged. In Canada, for example, considerable emphasis is placed on success, at the risk of minimizing the importance of legitimate routes. Additionally, the popular culture creates folk heroes of those who embezzle or cut corners illegally on their way to the top. This common form of deviance is pervasive and may be evident, for instance, in cases where students cannot make the grade but genuinely want to do well academically and to pursue professional training. Some actors resort to various forms of academic dishonesty, cheating and plagiarism. Likewise, a candidate who wants to win an election may select dirty tricks or gain the upper hand. A corporation determined to maximize profit may engage in unfair labour practices, fraud or tax evasion.

For Merton, a gangster like Al Capone typifies the triumph of illegitimate means when channels of mobility are closed or narrow.

Table 2. 1
MODES OF INDIVIDUAL ADAPTATION

Modes of Adaptation	Cultural Goals	Institutional Means
1. Conformity	+	+
2. Innovation	+	-
3. Ritualism	-	+
4. Retreatism	-	-
5. Rebellion	+/-	+/-

[+ = acceptance; - = rejection; +/- = rejection of prevailing values followed by substitution or acceptance of new goals and means] Source: adopted from R. K. Merton, *Social Theory and Social Structure*. Glencoe, Illinois: Free Press, 1957, p. 140.

With adaptation 3, or ritualism, the cultural goals are dropped as beyond one's reach, but conformity to the mores persists. Individuals realistically scale down their lofty goals of success and social mobility to the point where aspirations are satisfied according to rituals. By abiding by institutional norms, these individuals play it safe and derive pleasure from the practice of traditional ceremonies that are without a real purpose or goal. By playing the game, going along or doing time, the bureaucratic virtuoso, the bored student, the lazy professor, the inattentive but regular member of a religious organization, club or political party abandons goals as irrelevant but continues to impulsively accept the institutional means. This routine of ritualism represents the mildest form of deviance.

Adaptation 4, or retreatism, is the rejection of both goals and means. According to this least common form of deviance, retreatists are in the society but not of it. For Merton, they constitute the true aliens—pariahs, outcasts, vagrants, tramps, chronic alcoholics or drug addicts who have relinquished both the culturally defined goals and institutional norms. Defeatism, as an expression of retreatism, is an escape from the normal requirements of society. Conflict is resolved by escaping completely—

physically, emotionally and mentally. According to Merton, these losers withdraw from both goals and legitimate means to become double failures.

Adaptation 5, or rebellion, occurs when emancipation from the dominant standards leads to the introduction of a new social order. For example, one may reject the goal of personal wealth and the means of capital accumulation, substituting instead the goal of egalitarianism or revolution as a viable method. Rebels not only reject but substitute alternative goals and means; they subscribe to and act upon new value systems. Rather than adapt to conventions, they modify the social structure. Revolutionaries promote radical changes in both the culture and structure of society in order to create a better world.

For Merton the above framework provides an explanation of various ideal types of deviant expressions. As well, he links deviance and crime to success goals that control behaviour. But, his writings are not concerned with explanations of why particular actors commit deviant acts. Instead, he acknowledges the unjust distribution of legitimate means. Of considerable interest to students of social control is Merton's analysis of the sources of deviance, notably cultural and structural forces and not the social psychological or the pathological failures of the individual. Therefore, Merton is concerned with degrees of integration that contribute to social order. His usage of the term "dysfunction" suggests that certain elements of the social structure subvert the maintenance of social order (1957). Until the 1960s this paradigm dominated criminological theorizing for decades. In the USA, Mertonian approaches to crime continue to influence both liberal and conservative policies, research and criminological theorizing.

Systems and social order: Talcott Parsons (1902-1979)

Likewise, the contributions of the eminent Harvard University sociology professor Talcott Parsons, who studied at the London School of Economics and the University of Heidelberg, extended Durkheim's formulations within an analytic framework that incorporates both sociological and social psychological perspectives. Parsons's formidable contributions throughout the 1940s and 1950s have stimulated considerable dialogue and debate within orthodox criminology. Although it is impossible to do justice to his voluminous writings spanning over four decades, there are many recurring themes, especially as they relate to the sociology of crime, that warrant exploration.

Interested in the dynamic processes that contribute to the maintenance of social stability or integration, Parsons asserted sociology's concern with the analyses of interactions, forms of relationships and the variety of their conditions and determinants (1954: 68). Drawing on the work of Durkheim, Weber and Pareto, Parsons's theory of action on sociological thought dealt with the problem of relating agency (individual action) and social structure. In the *Structure of Social Action* (1937) and *The Social System* (1952), Parsons theorized that social life is regulated by common norms and values. Sociology should be attentive to interdependent sociological and psychological processes. The former foci—especially the social system—consists of the interactions of individuals (Parsons, 1952: 251). These interactions are mediated by common moral standards or norms which structure action. Norms maintain social order by patterning interactions, constraining actors and regulating conflict. All social action, for Parsons, is normatively oriented. Through such key mechanisms as socialization, interactions are institutionally integrated (1952) and subsequently internalized as bonds (1964). Standards are internalized, which in turn functions to secure conformity. Institutions serve to integrate. The individual as a member of society is under the social control of a prevailing moral authority.

In brief, Parson presented an analysis of social action that integrates interactional and structural levels—sociology and social psychology—as interpenetrating and interdependent. On the one hand, social order is internalized as part of one's personality; and on the other hand, personality connects the individuals to their social environments. As Parsons (1958: 82) elaborated:

> while the main content of the structure of personality is derived from social systems and culture through socialization, the personality becomes an independent system through its relations to its own organism and through the uniqueness of its own life experience.

Relying on psychoanalytic approaches, Parsons considers the personality, notably its ego, as socially structured. This ego is the primary site of interchanges between the personality and the outside world—the plurality of "alters" (1952: 249; 1954: 74). Together, the ego and its many alters internalize cultural values. The social system penetrates and determines personality. Therefore, deviance, as a contravention of institutional norms, occurs because of withdrawal, rebelliousness, compulsive performance or compulsive acquiescence and other psychological problems of adjustment. Deviance represents a disturbance of equilibrium within the personality and interactive systems (1952: 282).

Consistent with the above analysis of order is the Parsonian claim that resistance to normative expectations signifies a lack of integration. Disharmony occurs whenever an actor fails to fulfil expectations or is quite simply not exposed to role consensus. The sources of deviance include: a failure in the socialization process; strains arising out of difficulties of acting according to norms that then frustrate personality needs; and, strains arising when norms are ambiguous. In short, the failure to satisfy an ego's expectations creates strain. Simply, social control breaks down whenever expectations are not met (ibid., 1952).

Social functioning is contingent upon consensus. The dysfunctional nature of deviance is kept in check because of conscious and unconscious control mechanisms. Mechanisms of social control operate as secondary defences to combat deviance that, if left unchecked, would disrupt the much needed and well heeded social equilibrium and harmony. Deviance, or crime more specifically, is a fracturing or incomplete articulation of relations between people or institutions in change. The writings of Durkheim and Parsons maintain the position that conflicts are pathological phenomena, symptoms of a diseased social body. Norms, therefore, not only constrain the negative functions of conflict but are also important in enabling collectivities to predict integration.

The normative narrative encourages an investigation of conditions in the wider social environment such as social disorganization. The intellectual contributions of the Chicago School in attributing crime to the nature of the urban order have been impressive.

Urbanization and the Chicago School: the "community lost"

The relationship between urbanization and deviance has long been a major focus of sociological inquiry. According to many studies (Greer, 1962a; Greer, 1962b: 12; Carver, 1969; Lofland, 1973; Friedman and Wulff, 1975), an examination of the urban process is basic to an understanding of social order. Clearly, cities are special communities in which the "coordination and control of widely dispersed activities" occur (Tilly, 1974: 2). The organization, allocation and integration of tasks depend on the city's ability to maintain social order.

Urban sociology reflects a diverse appreciation of the phenomena of social order. An overview of the early contributions will yield some insights into the relationship between deviance and the city. Despite their differences, classical theorists of the nineteenth century were in no doubt as to the crucial impact of urbanization in transforming the structure of social relations.

In analyzing the qualitative experiences of new urban populations, the early writers were fundamentally attentive to the distinctions between traditional (rural) and modern (urban) communities. For example, simplicity and complexity, field and factory, *Gemeinschaft* and the more impersonal *Gesselschaft* (Toennies [1887], 1957) were contrasted. As noted earlier, Durkheim attributed the differences between mechanical and organic solidarities to the division of labour ([1893], 1933). Specifically, he studied the debilitating effects of urbanization. Forced forms of cohesion based on exchange relationships did not enhance commitment (Giddens, 1978: 22-27). As will be clarified in Chapter Five, the structure of social relations ushered in by urbanization was a blessing of dubious value especially for Karl Marx and Frederick Engels. Nonetheless, urbanization provided an indispensable environment—a necessary stage for the generation of a revolutionary force and consciousness (Engels, 1920: 122). Urbanization served to crystallize capitalist contradictions and irrationality (Mellor, 1977: xiii) by freeing millions from the "idiocy of rural life" (Feuer, 1959: 11-12). These same historical processes, however, transformed workers into appendages of the machine, making family life impossible by pushing working-class families into dense and squalid districts (Pahl, 1970b: 33). Under these conditions people did not perform as individuals but as personifications of economic categories, playing roles laid down by definite class relations. Marx stressed the de-humanizing effects of the workers' loss of control both over the products and processes of their labour (1969). Advances in productivity associated with industrialization and urbanization did not portend advances in humanity. The new industrial urban order with its contradictions, alienation and powerlessness was seen to be "criminogenic" (Gordon, 1973: 163), that is, deviance-producing. For Max Weber (1864-1920), the dissolution of the feudal order from rational and bureaucratic forces had produced a retrograde urban environment that obeyed its own laws. Weber's concerns with the negative effects of increasing bureaucratization were also articulated as expressions of alienation (Weber, 1958: 55; Giddens, 1973: 43). In analyzing the development of legal authority, Weber noted that domination becomes "impersonal and legalistic so that the institutional character of authority has largely, if not wholly, displaced the personal one" (Lloyd, 1974: 32). Pivotal to his discussion of this impersonal order is the coercive character of organizations whose primary task is norm enforcement (Weber, 1946). Unlike Marx, Weber associated power with the economic and non-economic forces of capitalism. Specifically, he maintained that power does not only originate from economic dominance. Classes, status groups and parties are also sources of power within a community (1946: 181), within the economic, social and legal orders, respectively. Weber observed that the "city often represents a locality and a dense settlement of dwellings forming a colony so extensive that the personal reciprocal acquaintance of inhabitants is lacking" (1958: 65). On the other hand, as Weber advised, the city encourages individuality, innovation and diverse lifestyles (Sennett, 1969: 6). Similarly, modern city life for Georg Simmel consisted of a rapid flow of events, dense living conditions and constant interactions that result in an overwhelming intensification of nervous stimulation. This in turn produces a blasé attitude, an impoverishment of creative drives, frustration and powerlessness (Simmel, 1969a: 51). Too many demands are placed on the urbanite. Appropriately, personal relationships emerge which are rational, functional, segmented, specialized and exchange-oriented. Underlying this social order of the city lies the ceaseless conflict and hostility of each person against every other. Simmel ascribed these traits to products of an urban condition that are essentially social psychological in nature. Despite these onerous constraints that produce estrangement, urban life for Simmel remains liberating. Formal controls such as the divisions of labour are more bearable than the coercive power of tradition with its overwhelming informal controls.

It is precisely within the Chicago School perspective, with its blending of insights derived from Emile Durkheim, Max Weber and Georg Simmel as well as the prevailing white male middle-class value systems, that the problem of deviance assumes exaggerated significance.

It is within this context that the early Chicago School sought to examine social processes that generate crime. The foundations of American sociology were built in department of sociology at the University of Chicago. The first large-scale research into deviance developed within the department of sociology at the University of Chicago in the 1920s. Researchers at the University of Chicago shifted the focus on pathology from the personal to the social. Adverse economic and social conditions, broken families, poverty, inadequate housing and increased immigration contributed to a form of disorganization that ultimately led to deviance. This social disorganization, the result of urbanization, was an immoral order and an expression of personal dislocation. As cities grew in size and density, impersonality, social distance and social disharmony increased. Adopting a monolithic conception of order, the Chicago School maintained that population increases were followed by competition and differentiation. The assumption that social disorganization produced deviance was related to a view of the actor as a passive recipient of basic drives and adverse social conditions.

As Robert Park asserted, "social control was the central fact and central problem of society" (Turner, 1967: xi). Transformations of society (Park, 1952; 1967), notably the rapid rise of cities and immigration, have altered the bases of social order. Accordingly, the dispossessed, rootless and "discordant medley of hundreds of thousands of individuals without any personal relations" (North, 1926: 233-237) threatened the existing social order. As conceived by Durkheim and Park, Louis Wirth (1964: 70) argued:

> The bonds of kinship, of neighborliness, and the sentiments arising out of living together for generations under a common folk tradition are likely to be absent, or at best, relatively weak in an aggregate, the members of which have such diverse origins and backgrounds. Under such circumstance competition and formal control mechanisms furnish the substitutes for the bonds of solidarity relied upon to hold a folk society together.

The city as "a relatively large, dense and permanent settlement of socially heterogeneous individuals" (ibid: 66) could not provide the much needed single normative order (Park, 1952; Wirth, 1964: 71; Suttles, 1972: 29-30). Consequently, the attenuation of primary ties necessitated the reliance on more formal controls to combat disturbances (Park et al., 1925: 107), that is, "irresponsibility and potential disorder" (Wirth, 1964: 74). For Wirth, new integrative and consensual mechanisms such as law, bureaucracy, segregation of land use, professional norms, organized interest groups and the criminal justice system are all inevitable features of urbanism.

For both Park and Wirth, divisions of labour shaped the nature of social relations. Specifically, these "impersonal, superficial transitory and segmental" secondary relations were based on simple specialized, functional or utilitarian roles (Wirth, 1964: 79). Predatory relationships, greater dependencies on formal organizations and punctuality of services have replaced personal relations as the basis for association in the modern city.

For Park and his contemporaries at the Chicago School, urbanization spelled a loss of community. However, Park also foresaw its progressive and liberative consequences. That is, the breakdown of tradition prepared the way for releasing new energies and ambitions (Park, 1925). Park argued that despite its many challenges, the city was still quite attractive.

A concern for social order coupled the relentless and romantic search for the pre-urban community. The early Chicago School analyzed the disintegrating relationships between individuals and their environment within a conceptual framework that interpreted the modern city as a pathogenic context. This pathological orientation, as Michel Foucault (1977: 175) later reminded us, serves to inspire a whole mythology, produces medical discourses of urban morbidity and places under surveillance a whole range of urban development, constructions and institutions.

For decades systemic indictments against city life proliferated. Cities were attacked for their physical growth and expansion that led to social and personality disorders (Burgess, 1926; Feagin, 1973; Fischer, 1976: 27). These new Sodoms and Gomorrahs were credited with debilitating moral orders; loss or decline of community (Hatt and Reiss, 1957: 13; Stein, 1960); and lack of attachments (Clinard, 1964; 1975; Banfield, 1974: 63; Morris, 1976: 14; Baldwin and Bottoms, 1976: 13). In contrast to rural areas, modern cities expressed higher rates of crime (Clark and Wenninger, 1962); greater mental illness (Faris and Dunham, 1939); sexual deviation (Kinsey et al., 1948: 455-458); incorrigibility (Ferdinand and Luchterhand, 1970); concealment (Goffman, 1959); and stimuli overload (Milgrim, 1970: 1461).

Within an essentially structural functionalist causation model, the theme of social disorganization prevailed. The inner city, conditions of density, deteriorating old houses, diversity of population and lack of social services were causally related to degrees of social deterioration, psychic disturbances and deviance. There is then a clear, albeit biased (Mills, 1943) and simplistic, image of the inner city as an area where misfits, dregs or the sediment of society live (Zorbaugh, 1929: 128-129). The behaviour of these unruly, predatory and unprincipled (Suttles, 1972) individuals was "never socially regulated; no life organization worthy of the name is ever imposed on them" (Thomas and Znaniecki, 1958 [1920]: 295). They were beyond society, free from middle-class values, alienated, without satisfying contacts and forever producing disequilibrium (Yablonsky, 1962). The inner cities as bailiwicks of disease, criminality, poverty and physical deterioration were perceived as contagious (Armstrong and Wilson, 1973: 67, 69) and hazardous to the inhabitants and passers-by alike (Brown and Howes, 1975).

Essentially, the work of the early Chicago School reflected a penetrating probe into ecology—the relationship between organisms and their environments. Accordingly, the term ecology in reference to crime highlighted the spatial and temporal distribution of deviance within a given city or neighbourhood. Robert Park and Ernest Burgess were the first sociologists to systematically apply plant and animal ecology to societal analysis (Vold, 1958). In their analysis of Chicago in the 1920s and 1930s, Park and Burgess employed the ideas of natural areas, symbiotic balances and deviance configurations within certain zones of the city. They focused attention on the community and its effect on the individual. Using an anthropological methodology of description, Park studied the ecology of neighbourhoods and isolated pockets of poverty and social problems. He was convinced that the certain areas in the urban environment fostered deviance especially in light of their harmful influence on families. Also, Park noted that socio-economic status varies with distance from the city centre. As migrants settle in old housing at the city centre, other groups enjoying higher status move outwards. Poverty combined with the exodus of the middle class from the city to the suburbs intensified deviance. Deviance as suicide, vice and illegal pursuits accompany urban congestion. According to the Chicago School, areas in which populations are unstable and composed of a variety of racial and ethnic groups have higher percentages of immigration and weaker neighbourhood controls.

In their book *The City,* Park and Burgess (1925) demonstrate that deviance varies with physical and geographic spacing. They developed a scheme of five concentric zones to analyze urban growth and its inherent social deviations: Zone 1, or "The Loop", consists of the central business district or the economic centre. Zone 2, or "The Zone of Transition", contains the rooming house district, underworld dens, brothels, Chinatown, Little Sicily and the ghetto. This zone of deterioration was originally residential, but business moved in and housing was made cheap. It was interstitial— neither business nor residential. Zone 3, or "The Zone of Working Class Homes", was characterized by multiple families, dense living quarters and in general by a large and stable labouring population. Zone 4 was the residential zone of apartment buildings, which included flats, residential hotels located on the fringe of the city's boundaries—dwellings occupied largely by single family dwellings. Zone 5, or "The Commuter's Zone", included areas with more respectable suburbs.

These zones were believed to be the result of ecological processes, urbanization and migration. For Burgess and Park, deviance was located within specified urban geographic and social areas, i.e., delinquency areas. Delinquency areas such as the inner city neighbourhoods exhibit economic uncertainties and the pressures of urban processes. Clifford Shaw and Henry McKay ([1942], 1969) also noted that official rates of delinquency varied in

Chicago and elsewhere. Rates of delinquency varied inversely in proportion to the centre of the city. High rate areas such as the "Loop" persisted over time; and even higher rates of delinquency were located in neighbourhoods experiencing rapid population changes, poverty and substandard housing. These localities lacked social stability, cohesion and effective social controls. Accordingly, areas adjoining the centre of the city and adjacent to industrial subcentres were natural sites for delinquent gangs. Juvenile arrests and truancy were commonplace. Despite the changes in ethnic and racial compositions of these areas over time, they continued to be high delinquency areas. The persistence of high rates of crime and delinquency is attributable to the constant transmission of delinquent values. Specifically, in these neglected neighbourhoods newcomers learned pre-existing cultural patterns in their ongoing interactions with local residents.

In brief, central to the work of Shaw and McKay (1969) was the notion that deviance emerges within the context of changing urban environments. Crime, manifested in social disorganization, was a product of decaying transitional neighbourhoods plagued by alien cultures and diffuse cultural standards.

All of the above assumptions about deviance as delineated by the Chicago School are grounded within a dominant normative paradigm that alludes unyieldingly to integration and consensus. Unfortunately, the problematic nature of deviance within the urban context was explored on the basis of police and court records. Zones of high delinquency may be the result of zealous police patrols and surveillance of slum dwellers who then face greater chances of arrest. Implicit in the logic of the Chicago School's formulations is the circular and certainly untenable reasoning that delinquency is caused by high delinquency areas.

Anomie, strain and disorganization: a critique

In general, strain theorists explain deviance according to unnecessary pressures. They assume that everyone is tied to the same conventional order—an encompassing common stability. For Durkheim, Merton and Parsons, three major structural functionalist writers, deviance is a consequence of a breakdown in social integration. For these contributors, deviance cannot be studied in isolation nor understood apart from an overwhelmingly binding collective belief systems. Consequently, deviance is defined normatively as behaviour that violates standards that are essential for social harmony. Consensus or general agreement maintains social order. Implicitly, a society characterized as too unitary, homogeneous and consensus-oriented with little or no room for conflict is perceived to be healthy. Deviance, therefore, only emerges in relation to the norms that actors are obligated to follow.

Although strain theory continues to survive, it has been subjected to many criticisms. Its internal logic, clarity, consistency and tenability appear inadequate. Additionally, the strain perspective suffers from some obvious sins of omission. There are many problems that this approach fails to address: strain theory retreats to a fixed image of human life caught between individual appetites and social necessities. Similarly, anomie is far too imprecise and leaves the reader with much confusion. As a quality of group life or as a striking feature of a social structure, anomie is not well supported in reference to individual or even collective acts of deviance. Societies or different elements of society vary in their respective degrees of moral and social attachments. And, one could argue that these variations do not necessarily render them more susceptible to strain. Despite the emphasis on structural aspects, strain theory does not even hint at let alone suggest a modicum of political, economic or social restructuring of institutions to safeguard against the inevitability of anomie.

The claim that deviance is disproportionately more prevalent among lower classes is clearly a distorted, class-biased model. Implicitly, this emphasis on stratification depicts lower classes as deviant. By implication, poverty, therefore, causes people to commit crime. Moreover, serious scholarship can ill afford to ignore crimes of the powerful. Many people with privileged access to legitimate means are criminals while most lower-class members with limited access to legitimate means do not necessarily engage in crime. Strain theory offers no explanation of deviant acts committed by actors in powerful social positions. Anomie fails to explain white-collar crime adequately.

Thus, anomie theory lacks internal consistency. It fails to explain why people with full access to legitimate means commit acts of deviance. It does not account for the behaviour of the wealthy who are inclined to cheat, embezzle or defraud. These criminals do not fit the poverty syndrome nor do they suffer from deprivation. Alternatively, the poor may not possess lofty goals and aspirations and thus suffer from anomie. Not surprisingly, their deviant acts may not alleviate frustration. As Taylor, Walton and Young (1973) cogently argued, the image of a meritocracy masks the advantages of the propertied classes. Instead of simply enhancing greater opportunities as remedies, a more convincing solution directs attention to efforts that would restructure society by promoting equality of condition. Merton's analyses fail to consider seriously the structural basis of capitalist societies that inherently promote the contradictions he so eloquently identifies. Who or what governs the values cherished in the broader social environment? The root of the problem is poorly investigated primarily because this framework offers very little of analytic substance in grappling with how the nature of society shapes the economic order and prevailing cultural values. Why is wealth so celebrated as a successful goal? In contrast, why is poverty perceived as a threat? How do the virtues of economic affluence get extolled?

Strain theory does not explain why people vary in their choice of deviance. Why, for example, do people resort to shoplifting rather than armed robberies? Concerning Merton's analyses, why do some people become innovators rather than retreatists? Retreatism lacks precision and trivializes many social problems like alcoholism, suicide, drug abuse and mental illness. The process of becoming an alcoholic is far more complex than simply retreating from a success goal. Drug addicts may not be only retreatists—abandoning the quest for success; they may be innovative risk-takers, ritualistic users of peyote or marijuana or rebellious crack users.

Admittedly, strain theory situates deviance within a conservative culture and not necessarily in psychological imbalances or the failings of an individual. Other factors that influence deviance cannot be so readily ignored. Many acts of deviance arise out of the process of interaction with others who serve as reference groups. Deviance, as will be elaborated later, may in part be due to the role expectations of significant others or to subcultural affiliations.

Strain theory ignores the process by which people are designated as deviant by others. This process involves a conflict of values between those who have power to label and those who are so labelled. Moreover, what is missing in strain analyses is any sense of the process by which structural reality is operationalized analytically on the level of interaction. The task of clarifying the micro processes of trouble, which should round off the above macro structural forces, falls to the labelling sociologists, to be discussed in the next chapter.

Anomie theory is limited because it neither explains why individuals lose their identification with the larger culture nor why the majority of persons exposed to approximately similar strains do not deviate. Strain perspectives that are culture- and class-bound do not challenge the legitimacy of prevailing moral standards. Because of its particular biases, strain theory overlooks the fact that people experience society differently, and therefore will have varying reactions to the normative standards by which they are governed. It is in this sense that assumptions made about the universality of norms and values become highly problematic. The collective conscience and the restoration of equilibrium, for instance, reflect particular rather than general interests. Furthermore, if norms are the machinery of equilibrium, who orders such norms as an equilibrium-restoring mechanism? On this question Parsons acknowledged that institutions enforce normative prescriptions through their powers to define and sanction undesirable behaviour. There is, however, no reference to the broader white, male, middle-class and heterosexual politics nor the contexts of privilege-reproducing institutions, such as the law.

Essentially, the assumptions inherent in the strain paradigm effectively obscure and frequently exclude structures and relations of power. At best, one discovers a glib and myopic acknowldgment that rules serve the best interests of all.

Parsons's theorizing consistently reflected an overwhelmingly conservative orientation. His evaluation of individual needs and behaviour is framed within an unquestioning normative orientation. For Parsons, social groups or collectivities have a system of culturally structured shared symbols accepted by most participants. Moreover, Parsons viewed social structures as enduring and interdependent in well-ordered societies. Simply, Parsons took the collective conscience for granted. His arguments revealed how deviance contributes to social order by explaining the strains of deviance. His analyses investigated how society provokes countermeasures to tighten institutional weaknesses while still enabling innovation. His strain theory is part of a grand theory of social action. Like all grand theories, Parsons's perspective on strain is remotely related to the empirical world. His rigid commitment to a single binding order fails to fully appreciate non-normative elements that influence society at both the interactional and structural levels. As sociologist David Lockwood admonishes in "Some Remarks on the Social System" (1956: 136), non-normative interests or motives must also be treated as independent categories in sociological inquiries. For Lockwood, the factual order consisting of the substratum of social action, systemic nature of conflict, the factual disposition of means which stimulate deviance such as productive processes, the organization of well defined social stratification, differentiation of competing economic interest groups, etc. must be also implicated. Lockwood notes that Parsons clearly fails to confront the problem of order in terms of relations of control—notably power.

According to the circularity of Parsons's logic, the behaviour of the system is explained strictly in terms of its needs. This structure is caused by the needs of the social order; causes are not distinguished from the functions of this system. Whichever deviance control system is adopted, it must, by definition, satisfy the needs of the system. Deviance, therefore, is evaluated in positive or negative terms.

Also, within Parsons's formulations the status quo is accepted uncritically (Tumin, 1965). The negotiative character of norms is completely discarded. Many of Parsons's theses generate no, or few at best, testable hypotheses. His ideas were not well linked to empirical operations (Mills, 1959). According to Turk (1967: 40), Parsons's theories are not logically consistent; terms and operations are neither well specified nor constant. His vague assumptions of social systems invite criticisms of a static bias. He foregoes logical consistency in favour of massive terminological structure or idiosyncratic word associations (ibid., 48). A form of "utopianism" (Dahrendorf, 1958a) characterizes Parsons's analysis. The amenability of theory to empirical validation procedures gives way to a fluctuating set of terms.

Processes of urbanization are related to the demands of the social order. But, as imputed by the classical writers, the conditions of urban life certainly do not necessarily follow from linking anomie, alienation and disorganization with urbanism (Cox, 1973: IX; Meadows and Mizruchi, 1976: 296). Much of this disorganization thesis involves a tendency towards circular reasoning in that the forms of behaviour explained by the conditions are used, simultaneously, to demonstrate the behaviour's existence (Carson and Wiles, 1971: 50). Simply put, conditions of living in the community explain social relations in that community (Mellor, 1977: 124).

Recently, more sophisticated analyses have endowed the concept of urbanism with wider meanings to include the existence of non-ecological factors as having consequences, such as socio-economic level, ethnicity, stage in life cycle, gender, values, age, etc. (Gans, 1972; Fischer, 1976). Rapid migration has not, for example, directly produced alienation, anomie or other symptoms of social disorganization (Berry and Kasarda, 1977: 377). Urbanism may be a factor, not a major cause, of certain social conditions to which systems of order and control respond. Attempts ought to be directed towards the examination of the relevance of the problems of the city, not merely the city as a locus of the problems (Hatt and Reiss, 1957), and towards considering the city as a constituent and dominant part of a complex society (Morris, 1968: XII-XIII).

Despite the voluminous literature connecting urban order and deviance, many findings remain fragmentary and inconsistent, stemming in part from confusing levels of analysis. Whatever the respective focus, "the quality of life in cities" (Gillis and Hagan, 1979), the resolution of conflict, collective consumption (Castells, 1978), the interrelationship of institutions and space (Hatt and Reiss, 1957) or mechanisms of change in cities (Stewart, 1977), the links between crime and the urban order are conceptually threadbare and often reduced to flawed normative orientations. The notion that urban life is composed of pluralities of different worlds is blurred, understated or covered up.

The above discussions have highlighted a number of significant contributions to the conventional text of deviance from diverse normative perspectives. Informed by the plethora of studies on anomie, strain and disorganization, deviance has been interpreted according to structural imbalances or systemic dysfunctions that are primarily attributable to a departure from prevailing norms, cultural values or traditions of solidarity. The following sections further this normative orientation by exploring more organizational or institutional foundations of deviance. Normative processes of socialization shape interpersonal relations designated as deviant. Such institutions as subcultures, families, school, media, work and the law control, contain and transmit "appropriate" a host of values that anchor conformity.

Social order is far too frequently decontextualized and too readily extricated from the larger processes of urbanization, industrialization, the attendant divisions of labour (Wellman and Leighton, 1978: 3), changing property relations or the transformation of space, which loom large in structures of social relations (Kahne and Schwartz, 1978: 474). Moreover, given the ceaseless conflicts over scarce resources (Schermerhorn, 1961: 14), social order as a general, vague and all-embracing frame of reference for identifying, arranging and interpreting the way things are remains relatively problematic (Berger and Luckmann, 1967: 96; Scott and Douglas, 1972: 3; Filstead, 1972: 3). Simply stated, social order emerges within a nexus of multiple involvements of networks promoting their own interests and concerns. What warrants further empirical investigation, therefore, is not only social order and its often neglected structural embeddedness but, more precisely, the nature of competing orders, inevitable intersections and structural linkages of communities in conflict or those simply different (Whyte, 1955; Jacobs, 1961; Gans, 1972; Sennett, 1970; Suttles, 1972). Towards this end of providing a better conceptual balance of urban contexts, the following section introduces some theoretical and methodological contributions of network analysis.

Chicago School: a critique

Great efforts have been directed towards modifying and, at times, refuting some observations of the Chicago School. For many, the much celebrated and nostalgically reconstructed images of normative social order of rural communities have been overestimated (Weber, 1958; Pahl, 1970; Meadows and Mizruchi, 1976: 222; Pearson, 1979: 200). This sense of solidarity was perhaps never available to the mass of men and women but only to a small elite of landowners and the propertied. Class stratification, status rivalry and intense social conflict existed in pre-urban, rural peasant environments. Moreover, this contrast of social orders may be a "fruitless and patently absurd exercise" (Greer, 1972: 15-16) for some people are of the city but not in it, and others are in the city but not of it (Pahl, 1970a: 101). *Gemeinschaft* may exist within *Gesselschaft*, and alternatively *Gesselschaft* within *Gemeinschaft* (ibid.).

The above portrayals of the social relations of urbanites were subjected to extensive empirical testing. Wirth's urbanism as "a way of life" has been recast to include "many ways" of life (Fava, 1968: 6). The mosaics of subcultures in the city fractionate a community-wide normative order into parochial varieties (Fischer, 1976a: 202), resulting in "ordered segmentation" within urban villages (Suttles, 1968: 164). Nonetheless, considerable order "underlies this supposed disorder of the city" (Tilly, 1974: 237). Routine interactions are not necessarily "haphazard, unordered and altogether non-existent" (Karp, et al., 1977: 101), even in the "world of strangers" (Lofland, 1973: 95; Melbin, 1978).

The bulk of ethnographic and survey research of this "community-saved" orthodoxy (Wellman, 1979: 1205) has discovered persisting, vigorous kinship and friendship involvements that provide vitality, sociability and support (Whyte, 1955: 147; 1974: 420; Jacobs, 1961; Gans, 1972; Liebow, 1967; Suttles, 1972; Wayne, 1974: 82; Fischer, 1976: 258; Bogdan, 1976: 204). But in their haste to rediscover well-established organizations and rich, complicated social relations within different communities or urban villages, studies of the community-saved tradition appear all too ready to dismiss pre-existing approaches. For instance, they are quick to point out that the communities studied "failed to mesh with the structures of society around" them (Whyte, 1955: 273). Given this concentration of local urban villages within self-contained personalized social environments, an element of the urban pastoral remains intact (Shulman, 1972: 23; Wayne, 1974: 87). Others have argued that the community-saved argument remains grossly inadequate for it unduly isolates the community from larger social structures

(Pahl, 1970a: 218; Smith, 1979: 171). The order of any local community is derivative of larger orders of society—the national land market, labour, capital and product (Greer, 1972: 7)—the whole economic and social order.

In critically evaluating the community-saved argument, sociologists may have also advanced an updated anti-urban tradition reminiscent of early writers. Accordingly, class structure and political economy, rather than degrees of urbanization, circumscribe patterned opportunities and constraints of modern city behaviour. Problems of quality of life become contradictions between capital and labour (Castells, 1978: 37). The urban community has become a politically defined area of conflict within which competing interests dispute the allocation of limited resources (Castells, 1976; Mellor, 1977: 6). The city appeared as a direct effect of the need to reduce indirect costs of production and consumption, thereby facilitating the rotation of capital, commodities and information. Ultimately, it becomes essential, according to this perspective, to understand relations between power and the city (Castells, 1978: 174). The above comments point to the legitimacy of connecting local community studies to wider societal concerns. The persistent weakness, however, lies in the general failure to distinguish problems that happen to occur in cities from those that are part of the urban process (Lithwick, 1970: 14); i.e., problems "in" the city from those "of" the city (ibid., 15). The above overview suggests that social order and its attendant controls exist within certain relational environments—notably the community. But the concept of community has been subject to endless and confusing debates (Gibbs, 1967: 14). In his review of the many meanings attributed to community, Hillery (1955) highlights three generally agreed-upon characteristics. They include the community as a spatially defined unit (Greer, 1972: 77); the community as common ties or modes of relationships where a prevailing normative value system characterizes a sense of belongingness, cooperation or distinctiveness (Dank, 1971: 195; Prus and Irini, 1980: 259); and the community as a social interaction (Siegal, 1977: 85-6). Essentially, many studies within the structural-functionalist tradition have failed analytically to move beyond the social and physical boundaries (Gross, 1967: 146) of this "multi-dimensional ordinal variable" (Effrat, 1974: 21). Network analysis arose in response to these *a priori* assumptions of community as necessarily grounded on locality or solid groupings (Mitchell, 1969: 1, 5; Pahl, 1970: 189; Effrat, 1974: 4, 18; Boissevain, 1974: 4-19; Fischer, 1976: 122; Bott, 1971; Tilly, 1974: 288-90).

Urbanization, therefore, is characterized neither by the withering away of primary relationships and the triumph of secondary relationships evident in the community-lost perspective of the early Chicago School nor by the persistence of localized, autonomous kinship, friendship or neighbourhood associations of the community-saved perspective apparent in the later Chicago writings of the 1950s and 1960s. More appropriately, a growth of specialized networks of social relations extending across wide areas that intersect, overlap or interact in various complicated ways accompany urbanization (Craven and Wellman, 1973: 2; Tilly, 1974: 29, 86). The lowering of spatial barriers and the increased freedom to choose social relations have led to a proliferation of personal communities consisting of networks of personal ties (Wellman, 1979), each more compatible and more supportive (Fischer, et al., 1977: 202).

Networks of social relations, especially those of kinship, friendship or mutual aid, are ubiquitous (Bott, 1971: 317), even in the most impersonal marketplace relations of advanced capitalist societies (Smith, 1979: 174). Cities contain many subcommunities with identifiable patterns of relationships both locally and non-locally based (Stewart, 1977: 32). Although they have their own organization, they are all tied together by a few large structures—labour, housing (Tilly, 1974: 3, 294) and other control markets.

Personal communities are based on interest, rather than residential proximity; they usually entail manipulations of several networks simultaneously (Craven and Wellman, 1973: 44). These communities are not immune from outside pressures or impingements from larger societal environments (Suttles, 1972: 178-179, 257). Communication and transportation facilities have changed the significance of space and locale for communities.

Control as normative: subcultures, bonds and associations

According to normative approaches, crime is the result of elements of anomie, strain and disorganization located within wider structural contexts. In this section we probe further into normative perspectives that establish crime as an organized response framed within institutional contexts. This discussion deals with the approaches and critiques of traditional canons that articulate subcultural perspectives, control theory, social bond, containment, differential association and neutralization. These approaches remain central to conventional criminological research in North America. Related to different contexts of deviant behaviour are the processes of learning appropriate adjustments. In contrast to the previous arguments, these perspectives seek to introduce the concept of agency, that is, the notion that deviant actors exercise free will and they subjectively determine options and learn to violate prevailing norms. We will observe not only how actors are forced to be deviant by social structures but also how these actors decide to disaffiliate.

Deviance is a product of social processes. Actors learn values and skills—they learn to identify their activities as different. The emphasis on social process, especially evident in the scholarship of 1960s, was a response to the inadequacy of structural models. In this section a growing appreciation of the relative nature of deviance and a gradual movement away from strict determinism are provided. All deviants do not necessarily suffer from strain; their activities cannot all be lumped together within a rigid framework. Like strain (structural) theories, subcultural perspectives incorporate many diverse levels of analytic thinking.

Reaction formations and status frustration: Albert Cohen

In general, "subculture" refers to an organized and recognized constellation of values that are different from and in opposition to prevailing dominant norms. In a fragmented and differentiated society, people contact and attend to the responses of others who share their distinct values. A collective wisdom emerges that serves to guide and validate perspectives and activities. The early subcultural approaches to deviance were reformulations of Merton's anomie theory. Specifically, these perspectives reflect Merton's view that the larger society maintains generally accepted goals of success, wealth and education, and that the means for acquiring these goals are not distributed equally among social classes. With an emphasis on the origins and development of delinquency, subcultural approaches argued that lower-class youths who lack access to appropriate means develop unique cultural values in supportive groups of similarly circumstanced others.

Informed by Merton's contributions, Albert Cohen, in *Delinquent Boys* (1955), shifted deviance away from the character of the actor to the character of the acts. According to Cohen, "subcultural group formations" are the result of successful attempts to collectively overcome the problems of conformity to existing norms. His study commenced with a review of how the dominant cultural order structures social existence (1955: 57). Within this normative orientation, human interaction is perceived to be governed by societal norms constructed by the people in authority, those who run politics, religion and education, i.e., the norms of well-respected individuals and groups symbolize conformity (1955: 86). These dominant middle-class norms reflect social consensus.

Cohen, like Merton, assumed that the members of the lower classes are likely to engage in deviance because the structures of society fail to fulfil their aspirations. Consequently, conflict emerges between lower- and middle-class cultures. On the one hand, Cohen charged that society encourages all classes to achieve status by internalizing middle-class success values. On the other hand, he pointed out that it is difficult for lower-class people to achieve success because they are ill-equipped to compete for opportunities. One site where the inequality of opportunity is particularly apparent is the school.

The school system ensures the failure of lower-class youths because it operates within a middle-class framework. Middle-class teachers reproduce middle-class values by rewarding middle-class achievements. For example, the middle-class school system prizes the following values: diligence, promptness, delays in gratification, industry, courtesy, respect for property, non-violence, to name a few. Cohen claimed that lower-class children are more likely to experience failure and humiliation. In brief, they are caught up in a game in which others are typically the winners, and they are typically the losers.

Cohen (1955) believed that lower-class boys are controlled by the norms and values of a generalized culture. Although they wish to be successful, these youths sense failure. Ill-prepared to live up to the "middle-class measuring rods" of respectable status holders, lower-class boys experience "status frustration" (1955: 25). Within this cultural conflict they suffer a deeply felt rejection. Consequently, they band together and create new and more realistic standards for themselves. The development of a subculture is not simply a function of class inferiority but a product of social and economic disadvantages.

A critical element in Cohen's analysis of the lower-class environment is the family. The relative position of a youth's family in the social structure conditions the quality of experiences. Cohen implied that lower-class families are incapable of providing the much-needed socialization of middle-class values. Because of impaired socialization, these youths are unable to impress authorities and measure up to the standards of teachers and prospective employers. They usually learn to adjust by adopting roles respective of a "corner", "college" or "delinquent" boy typology.

The corner boy role is the most frequent response to middle-class rejection. Although this boy is not overtly delinquent, he behaves in ways that are deviant. Contingent upon the levels of peer support, the boy hangs out at street corners, gambles or engages in truancy. Unable to achieve middle-class values, he retreats into the more comforting world of lower-class peers. The college boy, on the other hand, accepts and pursues middle-class values. According to Cohen, this boy's excursions into middle-class life are futile since he is ill-equipped academically, socially and linguistically to meet its standards. Finally, the delinquent boy, the primary subject of Cohen's analysis, adopts norms opposing middle-class values. Driven by a "status frustration", he returns to his respective slums and develops "delinquent subcultures" (ibid., 121) in which he can compete more fairly with his peers and achieve status within his more familiar worlds.

To deal with the conflict inherent in this frustrating dilemma, the delinquent resorts to a defence mechanism—reaction-formation. Reaction-formation is a process of repudiating and inverting middle-class criteria. The norms of the larger culture are literally turned upside down. Reaction-formation takes the form of irrational, malicious and unaccountable hostility to middle-class norms. In contrast to traditional standards of acceptability, the delinquent subculture values non-utilitarian, short-term hedonism, the destruction of property, the rejection of traditional taboos and violence. Delinquent boys are careful to maintain group autonomy and resist the controlling pulls of their family, school and other authorities. Status is gained by succeeding in delinquent pursuits within highly structured solidarities like juvenile gangs.

Like Merton, Cohen defined these boys as non-conformists. They create new means to achieve common goals of success. Unlike Merton, however, Cohen's boys reject traditional success goals. They do not aim to gain wealth by illegitimate means as Merton's anomie would predict. Instead, their delinquency is a protest, replete with anti-middle-class sentiments and behaviour

Illegitimate opportunities: Richard Cloward and Lloyd Ohlin.

Traditional normative explanations of delinquent subcultures were furthered by the efforts of Richard Cloward and Lloyd Ohlin who in their seminal study, *Delinquency and Opportunity* (1959), integrated the Chicago School tradition and Merton's concept of strain. Specifically, the concept of cultural diversity is combined with Merton's finding that deviance is a patterned product of differential access to conventional values. The following description explains Cloward and Ohlin's (1959: 167) indebtedness to and elaboration of Merton's theory:

> Apart from both socially patterned pressures that produce
> deviance, and from values, which determine the choices of

adaptations, the two aspects of Merton's theory we have outlined, a further variable should be considered: namely, differential unavailability of illegitimate means.

Here, the cause of deviance is clearly within Merton's strain—the differential opportunity to achieve success in legitimate ways. But deviance, Cloward and Ohlin reasoned, depends on the nature of all opportunities—including the availability of illegitimate means. The marked discrepancy between culturally induced aspirations among lower-class youth and the impossibility of achieving them legitimately results in the formation of delinquent subcultures. In other words, reaching out for "socially approved goals under conditions that preclude their legitimate achievement may become a prelude to deviance" (ibid., 85).

Delinquency for Cloward and Ohlin is a behavioural transaction which violates legitimate social expectations. Cloward and Ohlin subscribed to a consensual notion of social order that is similar to the normative approaches of Durkheim, Merton and Cohen. Deviant actors internalize dominant social goals; they want to conform to middle-class values, but they lack the means to do so. They therefore adjust to this problem of strain by seeking a collective solution—delinquency. But delinquency, a reaction to middle-class standards, is also influenced by the nature of illegitimate opportunities that are not always evenly distributed.

Also, delinquency involves the manipulation of mainstream legitimacy. For Cloward and Ohlin, lower-class youths neutralize and negate the norms of the dominant society, eventually becoming alienated from that society (ibid., 110). Essentially, these youths attribute their failure to the system; they respond to the latter's shortcomings by joining groups organized around specific activities and develop relationships that promote a group ideology that legitimates their respective deviance.

Delinquency is a gradual process of change. Initially, individuals question the legitimacy of existing norms. They align themselves with like-minded others who are also seeking similar solutions. Individuals internalize contra-cultural perspectives to justify their deviance. More cohesive subcultural supports gradually replace their initial guilt, fear and shame (ibid., 131).

A subculture does not exist in a vacuum, nor does it simply crystallize values that are fleeting or situational. Rather, a subculture is an opportunity structure that pre-dates the arrival of prospective members. Unlike Merton and Cohen, Cloward and Ohlin maintained that delinquent values are transmitted by means of both legitimate and illegitimate opportunities for success. The availability of these opportunity structures depends on the actor's position in the social structure. Neither legitimate nor illegitimate means are freely available. The legitimate avenue, as Merton noted, is inaccessible to those wishing to achieve society's success goals. But the more attractive illegitimate opportunity structure is also stratified. Not all lower-class areas are stable enough to ensure access even to illegitimate opportunities. Different social strata provide varying opportunities for the acquisition of deviant roles.

Cloward and Ohlin also developed Merton's concept of means more fully by incorporating both opportunity and learning structures. The latter refer to the environments that encourage the acquisition of values and skills associated with the performance of a particular role (ibid., 168). Individuals must learn appropriate perspectives and skills to be successful in deviant activities. Not everyone can become an embezzler, mugger, prostitute or con-artist. The opportunity structure, on the other hand, refers to the opportunity to discharge roles for which one has been prepared. The actor must have an opportunity to use the acquired skills. If denied access to illegitimate opportunities, actors are forced into ritualism or retreatism. Both the opportunities of learning and applying one's skills are rational activities. Choice depends upon the peer group and the attendant collective definitions of the delinquent solution. According to Cloward and Ohlin, variations in opportunity structures result in the formation of three types of delinquent responses—criminal, conflict and retreatist gangs. The criminal gang emerges whenever there are high levels of integration among different age levels of offenders and equally high integration of conventional and deviant norms. In these cultural contexts youths have the opportunity to learn from older delinquents. Successful hustlers—pimps, muggers, thieves, extortionists, con-artists—become role models to emulate. Criminal gangs are not just playgrounds, they are more importantly learning grounds for adult criminal careers. Knowledge and skills needed for success in criminal activities are communicated to neophytes. They learn to cooperate with mentors who teach them to regard the world with suspicion (ibid., 23). Typically, the criminal subculture is "devoted to theft, extortion and other illegal means of securing income" (ibid., 1).

But not all disgruntled youths enjoy this integration with pre-existing criminal lifestyles. They are not equally located in the social structure of the criminal world. Where integration is low and role models remain absent, the conflict gang emerges. Conflict results whenever youths lack access to legitimate and illegitimate opportunities. Control over violence is missing. These gangs generate in disorganized slums and neighbourhoods marked by transience and deterioration. These areas are unable to provide either legitimate or illegitimate opportunities. Appropriately, behaviour is more unpredictable and individualistic; crimes involve more violence and fewer financial rewards. Moreover, gang warfare is commonplace. Violent acts such as assaults, arson and vandalism are frequently justified in terms of protecting one's turf and demonstrating gang loyalty. Simply, they manipulate violence to win status (ibid., 1). For the conflict gang, the severe limitations in adjustments intensify frustration.

Lastly, the retreatist subculture rejects both criminal and conventional means. Similar to Merton's conceptualization of retreatism, the retreatist gang attracts individuals who are double failures. They are unable and unwilling to gain success either through legitimate or illegitimate opportunities. They have nowhere to turn and simply retreat. Merton's retreatists internalize the constraints in their use of illegitimate means. For Cloward and Ohlin, retreatists fail miserably in both worlds. The activity of this subculture revolves around a "consumption of drugs" (ibid.) or alcohol. There is usually some theft involved to maintain the drug habit. Not all double failures, however, become retreatists. Some boys decide, as Cohen's study illustrated, to become law-abiding, low status corner boys. To reiterate, Cloward and Ohlin contributed to Merton's study by distinguishing more clearly the concept of means according to learning structures and opportunity structures.

In summary, the early subcultural approaches pursue a problem-inspired approach oriented to the examination of the etiology and emergence of delinquent gangs. Rigid, limited and cohesive juvenile gangs are regarded as innovative and collective responses to socially created problems of status adjustments of lower-class boys living in a world dominated by middle-class values. The strain, injustice and repeated frustrations resulting from the uneven distribution of legitimate and illegitimate opportunities lead to deviance. These early subcultural reformulations of strain theory note that the environment of the school, for example, frustrates the goals and aspirations of youths. The contravention of normative middle-class patterns ranges from non-utilitarian, malicious, negativistic and hedonistic activities to more structured criminal, retreatist or conflict gang activities.

Control theory

Why do some youths decide to join deviant subcultures while others refuse such affiliation? Alternatively, one asks, why are there not more gangs? Why have we, as a society, not witnessed, let alone experienced, rampant criminality? For these and many other related questions we defer to the contributions of control theory. Consistent with the more social-structural aspects of deviance, control theory focuses on conformity rather than deviance. Again, conformity not deviance is problematic. Specifically, control theory asks: Why do people obey the rules of society? What causes conformity? Once the causes of conformity have been determined, then the causes of deviance may be easily ascertained. Control theory states that all people have the potential to violate rules, and modern society offers many opportunities for illegal activity. According to control theory, people are inclined to do both good and bad. People are naturally inclined to commit deviant acts and will do so under controlled conditions. People who refrain from deviance do so because they have a stake in conformity—an investment in obeying the rules of society. Control theory proposes that people who are least attached to social institutions are most free to violate rules. Deviance emerges when social bonds are weak. The presence of fragile or ineffective ties signifies an absence of social control.

Evidence to support control theory can be found in the works of Toby (1957), Nye (1958) and Briar and Piliavin (1965). Toby (1957), for example, introduced the concept of "stake in conformity" as a basic mechanism of control that regulates delinquent tendencies. All youths, he declared, are tempted to break the law. But, youths who do well in school risk being punished and jeopardize their future careers. Since they enjoy a relatively high stake in conformity they are more inclined to resist wayward proclivities. Although school performance is an important indicator of commitment, Toby cautioned that "in all fairness, it should be remembered that the basis for school adjustment is laid in the home and the community" (ibid., 14).

Hirschi (1969), in *Causes of Delinquency*, articulated a particular form of control theory—social bond theory. He cautioned that all individuals can commit deviant acts, but most people refrain from deviance because of their strong bonds to society. The strength and direction of ties with conventional groups and institutions like the family, parents, friends, peers, schools, teachers and employers influence deviance. According to Hirschi (1969), individuals bind themselves to society in four ways: attachment, commitment, involvement and belief. Whenever these four elements are weak, the individual is more likely to commit deviance.

An individual's bond to society is influenced most by attachment. Attachment refers to the sensitivity, affection and interest one exhibits towards others (ibid., 231). Social control results from one's attachments to the family, school, job and peers. The family, as a basic social control mechanism, socializes and disciplines. For Hirschi, commitment also shapes social bonds. Simply, commitment refers to the amount of time and energy one invests towards the achievement of societal goals. Commitment incorporates conventional types of behaviour such as getting an education, holding a job, developing skills, building up a business, studying and saving money. People who are committed to property, life and reputation are less likely to jeopardize their social positions. Those who do not have a stake in conformity or alternatively lack commitment are more predisposed to risk-taking and carelessness. In addition, social involvement inhibits deviance. According to Hirschi (1969), an individual involved in conventional activities does not have the time for deviant or illegal acts. Specifically, involvement in school, family and recreation insulates the youth from deviant temptations.

Finally, the decision to conform or deviate is influenced by the nature of one's belief system. Conformity is selected by those who believe in the moral validity of rules. And deviance is chosen whenever there is a breakdown or even an absence of conviction or beliefs that prevent deviance. The deviant, in other words, holds no dominant values nor moral obligations to conform and is therefore inclined to anti-social behaviour. The less one believes in conformity, the more likely one is to engage in deviant acts. As Hirschi concluded, "the less a person believes he should obey the rules, the more likely he is to violate them" (ibid., 26).

Containment theory

Walter Reckless (1967) provided yet another version of control theory— containment theory. In general, containment theory claims that society produces a series of pushes and pulls towards deviance. These are in turn counteracted by internal and external containments that help insulate the individual from criminality. Reckless developed containment theory in response to the failure of social theories to examine characteristics of individual offences. Essentially, he was concerned with addressing two questions: How is it possible for a person living in high crime, poverty area, to resist deviance? What personal properties insulate a person from deviance-producing influences?

Reckless (1967) hypothesized that external and internal controls act as defences against pressures and pulls that might otherwise lead to deviance. External pressures are adverse living conditions that influence deviant behaviour: relative deprivation, poverty, unemployment, minority status, limited opportunities, inequality, family conflicts and limited access to opportunity structures. The internal or psychological forces that affect behaviour involve such personal factors as restlessness, discontent, hostility, rebellion, mental conflict, anxieties and the need for immediate gratification. It is the psychological push within each individual that propels a person towards crime and delinquency. External pulls, on the other hand, consists of deviant companions, membership in deviant subcultures and such influences as the mass media and pornography. These social pulls are driving forces that remove the person from acceptable norms of social living.

Reckless (1967) contended that people caught up in these inner and outer forces have a strong tendency to violate social norms. However, besides the inner and outer forces that pressure individuals towards deviance, there are also inner and outer forces that protect and insulate against deviance or, more generally, contain deviant forces. Inner containments are strengths located within the individual that deter deviance. An individual with inner strength, for example, is one who has a good self-concept, ego strength, a well-developed superego, high frustration tolerance, high resistance to diversions, high sense of responsibility, goal orientation, the ability to find substituted satisfactions and tension-reducing capabilities. This inner containment is the product of internalization and develops throughout group socialization. On the other hand, outer containments consist of the normative constraints that societies and social groups use to control their members. They include the following: a sense of belongingness, consistent moral front, reinforcement of norms goals and values, effective supervision discipline and meaningful social roles.

If inner and outer containments are strong, people will conform. If either of these elements is weak, then conformity is moderate. Of the two influences, inner containment is more important primarily because individuals spend much time away from their "containing" families and other supportive groups. They must then rely on their own inner strengths to control deviant pushes.

Differential association

Interestingly, peer associations have also been developed by studies of differential associations. A social learning approach maintains that deviance is a product of learning appropriate values. As Vold (1958) noted, learning refers to habits and knowledge that develop as a result of the experiences of individuals entering and adjusting to an environment. Knowledge is anchored in experiences.

Historically, the social learning approach can be traced to Gabriel Tarde (1843-1904). This nineteenth-century scholar developed an innovative analysis of the "laws of imitation". Accordingly, individuals learn ideas in association with other ideas, and behaviour followed those ideas. The social learning approach to analyses of deviance represented the first attempt to describe deviance as a process of learning rather than as a product of biological or psychological factors. In the early 1920s Edwin Sutherland, a prominent American criminologist, developed a social learning theory known as differential association. He argued that one learns criminal behaviour in the same manner that one learns any other behaviour.

First introduced by Sutherland in 1924, differential association suggested that how we act depends on those around us. Accordingly, deviance is shaped by normal processes of social interaction and socialization. His theory consists of nine principles (Sutherland, 1939) intended to explain how individuals come to engage in criminal behaviour or deviance. The principles are:

1. Criminal behaviour is learned.
2. Criminal behaviour is learned in interaction with other persons in the process of communication.
3. The principal part of learning criminal behaviour occurs within intimate personal groups.
4. When criminal behaviour is learned, the learning includes: (a) techniques of committing the crime, which are sometimes very complicated, sometimes very simple; (b) the specific direction of motives, drives, rationalizations and attitudes.
5. The specific direction of motives and drives is learned from definitions of the legal order as favourable or unfavourable.
6. A person becomes delinquent because of an excess of definitions favourable to the violation of law.
7. Differential association may vary in frequency, duration, priority and intensity.
8. The process of learning criminal behaviour by association with criminal and anti-criminal patterns involves all of the mechanisms associated with any other learning.
9. While criminal behaviour is an expression of general needs and values, it is not explained by those general needs and values, since non-criminal behaviour is an expression of the same needs and values.

Sutherland's original theory of differential association has generated considerable research (Glaser, 1956; Burgess and Akers, 1968; Akers, 1985). Concurring with Sutherland's findings, these studies suggest that differential association produces criminality not directly but rather through an intervening mechanism. For Daniel Glaser (1956), this mechanism is differential identification, while for Robert Burgess and Ronald Akers (1968) this mediating device is differential reinforcement.

With an emphasis on the role-taking processes of individuals, differential identification stresses the way people select models of behaviour. The choice of appropriate models does not necessarily involve interaction with others in intense personal relationships, as required by differential association. Instead, "a person pursues criminal behaviour to the extent that he identifies himself with real or imaginary persons from whose perspective his criminal behaviour seems acceptable" (Glaser, 1956: 440). Burgess and Akers (1968: 146) elaborated: "criminal behaviour is learned in nonsocial situations that are reinforcing or discriminative and through that social interaction in which the behaviour of other persons is reinforcing or discriminative for criminal behaviour." The inclusion of non-social situations and the recognition that the environment per se reinforces criminality are equally important. For Burgess and Akers (1968), differential association is too broad; it fails to specify elements of the learning process. To further enhance differential association they suggested that differential reinforcement ought to constitute the substance of the learning process. Deviants will continue to behave in certain ways if they were to be rewarded for doing so, or discontinue a particular form of behaviour if they were to be punished for it. Thus, actors will continue to engage in crime only if they have been rewarded for doing so, for example, obtaining money for their efforts. From this idea, Burgess and Akers developed a law of differential reinforcement, they (1966: 310) noted specifically, "given many available operants, all of which produce the same reinforcer, that operant that produces the reinforcer in the greatest amount, frequency and probability will have the higher probability of occurrence." In other words, actors will choose the option that has been the most satisfying in the past. And, if crime has been more satisfying than conformity, it will in all likelihood be chosen.

In his later work, Akers (1985) presents a social learning theory that incorporates both differential reinforcement and differential association. Akers (1985: 58) adds that a great deal of learning occurs by observing the consequences of certain behaviour for other people: "Deviant behaviour can be expected to the extent that: (1) it has been differentially reinforced over alternate behaviour and (2) is defined as desirable or justified when the individual is in a situation discriminative for the behaviour."

Differential opportunity: a Canadian contribution

Maurice Cusson's (1983) *Why Delinquency?* invites us to take immediate stock of more recent conceptual and methodological advances in converging the above noted perspectives. This provocative Canadian study succeeds in stimulating considerable insights and intellectual adventurism by charting a theory of delinquency that draws on an array of disciplines from biology and philosophy to the social sciences. Beyond synthesizing diverse contributions, Cusson's concepts and propositions pay considerable tribute to cross-cultural sources.

Cusson's theory of delinquency is premised on strategic analysis. This innovative approach warrants careful examination because it is clearly and passionately developed and because it is based on a well-informed scrutiny of many competing trends in delinquency research. Strategic analysis places considerable emphasis on the notion that delinquent behaviour can be explained according to a model of a rational person furthering his or her interests and trying to achieve this goal by the most efficient means. The actor makes decisions, works out strategies and pursues goals. This theory, as Cusson accurately identifies, resembles Glaser's differential anticipation. Essentially, delinquency is explained by its consequences. A fundamental hypothesis of this theorizing suggests that whenever people wish to commit a crime, they select options that will have the greatest advantages at the least cost.

Simply stated, delinquency is determined by the results anticipated by offenders. Delinquent behaviour is premised on opportunities that are not only available but also yield the most benefits. According to Cusson, the rationality of delinquency is drastically limited because of unclear objectives, insufficient information and restricting circumstances. Delinquency, therefore, becomes a limited option as a result of a crucial variable—the immediate environment, as expressed in the family, school, work or friends. Upon cursory reading, this analysis appears quite convincing, though more clarification is warranted regarding the process of limiting rationality and the factors that influence differential commitment to these results.

Cusson's solution to the delinquency puzzle is presented in two themes—goals and opportunities. Goals are the "results" that actors mean to achieve by their acts (1983: 25). Four types of objectives are advanced: action, appropriation, aggression and domination. These goals, however, seek to satisfy basic human needs. That is, delinquency is a means of achieving that which most people are looking for: excitement, possession, power and defence of essential interests. But, he admonishes: "To say someone steals to solve problems is of no help because many people in the same situation do not resort to stealing" (ibid., 26).

The second related component of his ends and means scheme accounts for the above discrepancy. Cusson employs the concept of opportunity and endows it with considerable explanatory power. Opportunities dictate freedom (ibid., 103), limit scope and determine the choice of goals and methods for achieving them. Opportunities indicate prerequisites for affecting a delinquent solution; prerequisites that depend on outside circumstances and personal abilities. Simultaneously, opportunities are resources used to take advantage of these circumstances to realize certain goals. The very core of this opportunity theory is expressed as follows: the greater the legitimate opportunities that arise for someone, the less the inclination to choose delinquent activity. This proposition certainly reflects a curious blend of Hirschi's control theory and the more classic opportunity theorizing by Cloward and Ohlin.

It is, however, in his analysis of the concept of "presentism" that encouragingly bold theoretical contributions are made. Presentism is defined as the lack of perseverance in the pursuit of long-term projects, a lack of persistence and the extremely limited temporal horizons of delinquents. According to Cusson, this presentism is a major stimulus or determinant of delinquent activities. Two factors are isolated as the root of juvenile restlessness: lack of parental discipline and repeated failures. For Cusson, this immediate pleasure cannot go hand in hand with respect for one's obligations. He concludes that a presentist is neither a person of duty nor a person of his or her word. It is the delinquent's Achilles' heel standing in the way of efficiency not only at work but also in the chosen field. Presentism pervades all the delinquent's interpersonal relations.

Cusson argues that peer associations contribute to opportunities. Peers furnish the newcomer with a means of achieving certain ends. He adds: "It does the opposite of what occurs in school or in the labour market: rather than blocking opportunities, it opens them up" (ibid., 151). Cusson claims that youths select friends according to their affinities; a theme reminiscent of the "dangerous disaffiliations" which characterized the early Chicago Schools.

The influences of opportunities are mediated by decisions. The problematic relationship between goals pursued and available opportunities, for example, are resolved at the level of subjective meanings, i.e., in the social construction of action.

According to Cusson's analysis, presentist opportunity and subcultural marginality occupy a central place in the lives of troublesome youths. Presentism, as an expression of the delinquent's identity and world vision, is a viable conceptual device for investigating the process of delinquency; he argues that "the more an adolescent commits crime, the less he is involved in establishing a career" (ibid., 125). In Cusson's work, presentism is essentially a procedure the individuals use to make sense of their delinquency. Presentism, however, remains part of a larger, ongoing process of self-indication or self-validation. Presentism is one of many fundamental expressions used in building and maintaining symbolic worlds constituted by the skills of the actors, reactions of others and self-identity.

A more interpretive perspective suggests that presentism is continually evolving during interaction. Presentism is supported by the actors' interpretations of opportunities, however defined. Delinquency is a social accomplishment in which actors stage their activities, skilfully play many roles and construct appropriate strategies that ensure a certain passage. Presentism must be seen as one of these strategic interpretations.

Presentism cannot be strictly operationalized as a consequence of failure. Social failures are not necessarily coterminous with the actor's self-image. The logic of Cusson's model presupposes that once an actor has failed at school, he begins to move in the direction of a generalized failure. Delinquency research, however, cannot be limited to such pre-ordaining or converting notions of failure. Failure is not necessarily incremental nor consequential as Cusson's examples seem to indicate.

Cusson depicts actors as defining and legitimating their presentism in reference to given norms of the family, school and work. He argues that delinquents do not succeed in school either because they are not interested or because the school is not interested. According to Cusson, school means work, and given the contempt for work youths opt for objectives consistent with this failure.

One of the most interesting and difficult questions facing modern criminology and sociology concerns the relationship of schooling and work. The role of schooling in easing the orderly transition from adolescence to adulthood remains well-documented in the literature. To ensure the rules of passage, the school system and its attendant socialization of values are also related to the institution of the family in a complex and tightly interwoven manner. One cannot overlook the plethora of extant perspectives on success and failure or conformity and deviance. This concept of presentism is valuable precisely because it is linked to internal matters such as self-image, felt identity and changes. On the other hand, it is related to social identities and the dialectics of socialization such as conformity and failure. But in his discussion, Cusson comes very close to marshalling thinly disguised deterministic propositions about school failure and delinquency. He reluctantly adopts a view that would allow him to address structural factors generating delinquency. The wider contexts of delinquency are treated as unproblematic. Presentism, delinquency or failure as instances of marginality also warrant exploration. Marginality as an intervening variable is of great analytic utility in directing delinquency research to both the immediate context of relations and the wider structural contingencies. Many of Cusson's subjects are not committed fully to delinquency nor to prevailing conforming values. The concept of marginality provides a major clue for predicting how susceptible these youths are to presentist ideologies. Their location in the general social structure can condition opportunities. Delinquency research may presumably be made more conceptually complete and considerably more comprehensive by addressing presentism as a function of marginality rather than simply a reflection of failure.

In brief, *Why Delinquency?* seriously revisits opportunity theory in an attempt to clarify correctional impulses that dominate normative approaches. The sociology of this text, however, remains committed to an understanding of the significant interpretations of youths, especially with reference to the importance of the moment.

In summary, people learn social behaviour by operant conditioning. Accordingly, behaviour is controlled by subsequent stimuli. Social behaviour is acquired through direct conditioning and modelling of other people's behaviour. Behaviour is reinforced whenever positive rewards are gained or penalties are avoided. Behaviour is discouraged by negative stimuli and loss of reward. People learn to evaluate their own behaviour in interactions with their significant others. For Akers, the principal behavioural influence, therefore, consists of those groups that both control an individual's major sources of reinforcement or punishment and expose him or her to behavioural models and normative definitions. Again, social learning approaches argue that social behaviour is the result of direct conditioning and modelling (Akers, et al., 1979).

Neutralization approaches

David Matza and Gresham Sykes, like Sutherland, regarded the process of becoming a criminal as a learning experience. However, beyond this fundamental premise the two perspectives differ. Specifically, Sutherland was concerned with learning techniques, values and attitudes necessary for performing criminal acts. Sykes and Matza, on the other hand, maintained that most delinquents hold conventional values and attitudes. The focus of their neutralization theory concerns techniques that are learned which enable individuals to neutralize their values and drift back and forth between legitimate and illegitimate behaviour.

Neutralization focuses on the learning of crime-producing rationalizations in reference to norms as "qualified guides for action" (Sykes and Matza, 1957: 666). This is consistent with the position that delinquents do participate in normative culture and do not necessarily hold values that are diametrically opposed to dominant values. As Sykes and Matza (1957) point out, delinquents express a sense of guilt over illegal acts. They respect and admire honest, law-abiding persons, and they defend and revere parents, sports figures and teachers. In fact, delinquents draw a line between those they can victimize and those they cannot.

Finally, delinquents are not immune to the demands of conformity— they participate in family, school and church. Given their connection with a law-abiding culture, delinquents must develop a distinct set of justifications for violating conventional norms. These neutralization techniques allow them to temporarily drift and participate in subterranean activities. A state of drift (Matza, 1964) is used to describe those adolescents who are in limbo between conventional lifestyles and criminal lifestyles with no strong attachment to either. Drift specifically refers to the process by which an individual moves from one extreme of behaviour to another, behaving sometimes in an unconventional, free or deviant manner and at other times with constraint and sobriety. Delinquency is not an alien phenomenon but rather a "disturbing reflection or caricature" of social values (Matza and Sykes: 1961: 717). Drift precedes delinquency and functions to loosen the mechanisms of control.

How specifically do Sykes and Matza account for deviance? Unlike strain, neutralization theory does not support the claim that criminals or delinquents reject middle-class values. In fact, they share some values and participate in conventional pursuits. Accordingly, deviance unfolds because of the neutralization of accepted social values. To elaborate, illegal behaviour is framed within a set of conventional rationalizations. Techniques of neutralization are extensions of general impressions and judgments prevalent in the dominant culture. Specific techniques may be subcultural in origin; they exist among certain groups and are learned in association with members of a subculture through the process of differential association. Motives are derived directly from conventional society. These justifications minimize the influence of moral constraints by that facilitating deviant pursuits.

There are five techniques of neutralization: denial of responsibility, denial of injury, denial of a victim, condemnation of the condemners and appeals to higher loyalties.

When individuals deny responsibility they claim that they cannot be held liable or faulted for unlawful acts. The perpetrator would argue that these acts did not occur through his or her fault. Individuals deny personal responsibility for their actions. They maintain that the crime was an accident or equally assert that it was caused by factors well beyond their control— such as negligent parents, broken homes, poverty, minority status or failure in the economy. This technique is commonly used to deny white-collar crime and political corruption, for example, former President Nixon denied committing a crime during the Watergate Scandal in the 1970s. And throughout the 1980s many tele-evangelists were prosecuted for crimes ranging from fraud to sexual assaults; they denied responsibility by claiming that their indiscretions were not their fault but rather the successful work of Satan. Throughout the early 1990s, local politicians continually defaulted to global economic recession as an explanation of extremely high unemployment rates. Also alcohol and drug abuse are often invoked as the culprits thereby minimizing the responsibility.

With denial of injury individuals claim that their actions do not really harm anyone. They rationalize illegal behaviour by simply dismissing it as a prank or mischief. Individuals declare that even if their behaviour were technically deviant or criminal, no one would have been hurt. Offenders assert that certain victims of a mugging, a burglary, vandalism or even arson can well afford the loss. Additionally, these victims can recover the losses suffered through their respective insurance companies. Thefts from large corporate interests are not viewed as criminal because of their respective profits or wealth. Similarly, car thieves may justify their offences by saying they were only borrowing the car temporarily, as in the cases of car-jacking. Gang fights are also presented as private quarrels that do not really concern others. Again, these and other crimes are justified as socially useful rather than injurious.

The denial of a victim involves the process of ignoring the rights of an absent or unknown victim. Here invisibility precludes respect or sympathy for the target. One might further rationalize one's actions by arguing that the victim was offensive, that is, in some way he or she had it coming—as often happens with typical homophobic and anti-lesbian bashing, misogyny, racism, etc. There are no victims, some would argue, because their prey is viewed as offensive. That is, victims are transformed as offenders, people who are out of place and deserve to be punished. This rationale has been used conveniently in campaigns of ethnic cleansing or genocide characteristic of the treatment of Jews by the Nazis, the exclusion of Aboriginal people or the ethnic struggles in the former Yugoslavian republics, Rwanda, etc.

Those who use the technique of condemnation of the condemners view the world as corrupt and hypocritical. They depict authorities as dishonest. For example, this perspective considers the police to be on the take, teachers bent on favouritism, lawyers as practising liars, corporations as thieves and politicians as prostitutes, etc. Given this cynical logic, it is ironic, if not inappropriate, for authorities to claim a right to condemn deviance. Now, blame is shifted to others whose motives are condemned or classified as equally derisive. Accordingly, authority figures are viewed as deviants in disguise and ought to be condemned for their corrupt, brutal or self-serving behaviour.

Finally, an appeal to higher loyalties typically describes situations where offenders are caught in a dilemma between competing loyalties. They are required to make choices, for instance, between their respective reference groups or societal norms. Here, one weighs the demands of society and its laws against the needs of smaller groups. When one uses this technique, the needs of the peer group are usually given precedence over the rules of society. But, the deviant activities especially of the small group are couched eloquently according to higher loyalties. The RCMP justified its illegal activities in the 1970s according to threats against the national security. Patriotic slogans are often used to incriminate any foreign aggressions. For example, the Canadian military involvement during the Persian Gulf crises, the bombing of Baghdad in 1993 by American missiles and the policing of Somalia were clearly phrased in terms of peace initiatives and humanitarian concerns. Likewise, the Ku Klux Klan and other supremacist organizations repeatedly allude to higher loyalties. Law and order are often appropriated as justifications for further state intrusions into civil liberties. Similarly, terrorists depict themselves as freedom-fighters just as often as states continue to wage war in the name of peace.

In summary, neutralization is a social psychological perspective used by offenders to justify their deviance according to more morally and socially acceptable standards (conditions, contexts or qualifications).

Subcultures, bonds and associations: a critique

A major limitation of traditional subcultural explanations proffered by traditional subcultural perspectives relates to the inadequacy of the conceptual framework which defines away both inter- and intra-subcultural conflicts. As operationalized in studies by Cohen, Cloward and Ohlin, the concept of a subculture suffers from gross simplification and too often becomes equated with the gang or other highly exaggerated structural formations. Hirschi (1969), for example, rejected the implied notions that delinquency is a relatively permanent attribute of the lower class and refuted the assumption that delinquency is a regularly occurring event among these youths. Also, the fact that most delinquents eventually become law-abiding citizens does not bode well with this static portrayal. The finding that delinquency results from intense frustration is inconsistent with the large number of lower-class youths who are conformists. More recently, a proliferation of studies endowed the idea of a subculture with wider meanings to include the existence of non-locality based factors (Wiseman, 1979; Lee, 1980; Cohen, 1990). In addition, subcultures are loose, permeable and changing structures (West, 1978; Corrigan, 1979; Brake, 1980; Willis, 1980) and not necessarily restricted to working-class adolescent males. The much celebrated and nostalgically reconstructed image of a normative order is recast to include a plurality of relational environments or, more specifically, multiple social realities. With a few exceptions, subcultural research has been slow in considering various outside impingements that regulate behaviour.

Subcultural norms, rules and roles set conditions but do not necessarily determine social action. A subculture is not a neatly articulated response packaged according to shared values and constraints. A subculture emerges as a social construction caused through the characteristic interplay of self-definition, reaction and interaction. In other words, a subculture is not only a consequence but a context of ongoing meaningful interpretations. A more comprehensive approach to subcultures moves beyond fixed, static and self-maintaining systems. Clearly, subcultures are fluid, loose and continually emerging webs of interaction. Shifting membership, limited involvements, role discrepancies, norm ambiguities, incomplete rules and change are just as much part of subcultures as stability or cohesively integrated structures. As Braithwaite (1989: 25) argues, knowledge is largely preserved and transmitted by loosely structured subcultures. Nonetheless, the process of acculturation, that is, the learning of "new ways and meanings" from subcultural involvement (Rubington and Weinberg, 1987: 200), offers a collective solution to the social strains. These values provide a symbolic framework for the development and maintenance of a collective identity as well as individual self-esteem (Murdock, 1973: 9). Brake (1980: 9) reiterates that subcultures provide group standards, behaviour and values that have meaningful symbolism for the individual actors involved.

In Hirschi's explanation for crime and deviance, there is a failure to explain the more powerful, higher status, sophisticated crimes of adults. It does not explain "upperworld" crimes like tax evasion, price fixing and fraud. Furthermore, the deviance or conformity dichotomy provides a very simplistic view of social control. For instance, the theory does not adequately address why some youths who lack conventional commitments fail to deviate. Or alternatively, why do people committed to conventional values deviate. As Gary Marx (1981) suggested, the above perspectives on social bond fail to implicate social control as a cause of deviance. These approaches reject the social structural sources (social, economic and cultural forces) that motivate law-breaking activities. Similarly, the notion of attachment is problematic in that it ignores the significance of attachments at different stages of one's life cycle. In addition, the manner in which different institutions intersect and subsequently impact upon social control is not delineated. For example, what are the effects of conflicting loyalties? As with strain, anomie, disorganization and early subcultural approaches, one cannot assume that we all subscribe equally to the moral values of the dominant culture. Deviance is not only learned phenomenon but is also the result of different institutional controls. Social control, therefore, instigates deviance.

For Reckless, the conceptual and methodological approaches involved too much ambiguity regarding the definition and measurement of the central notions of pushes and pulls. For example, explaining delinquency by internal controls often generates a circular or tautological argument in that it is extremely difficult to separate actual internal states (the cause or independent variables) from the measures of delinquency (effect or dependent variables). Furthermore, Schrag (1971) contends that containment theory does not lend itself to empirical testing. Specifically, no hints are provided concerning the relative measures (strengths or weaknesses) of inner and outer containments. The nature of inner or outer control and the process by which this control is exercised remain unclear.

There are methodological difficulties with differential association. For example, defining an excess of definitions favourable to violations of the law over definitions unfavourable is problematic. What does "excess" mean? What are the structural origins of these definitions? Testing the above proposition is extremely demanding given the large number of poorly operationalized variables. Conceptually, the theory is too simplistic. It oversimplifies the process by which deviance is learned. Furthermore, it falters in explaining why people have the associations; it fails to account for how friends influence our behaviour and teach us to deviate, and it refuses to address the issue of why delinquent friends exist in the first place. If attachments lead to deviance, what then causes the deviance of friends? What explains the sources of these deviance-inducing relationships? Some strong criticisms have also accompanied the above revisions of Sutherland's work. For instance, Sutherland's key ideas of frequency, intensity, duration and priority of criminal or non-criminal influences are not well operationalized (Stebbins, 1970, 1987). Short (1957) attempted to test the theory by asking groups of delinquents whether they considered their friends to be delinquent. Although supportive of differential association, he concluded his study by calling for a restatement of the theory of differential association into a series of verifiable propositions from which verifiable predictions may be derived. The high level of abstraction found in differential association renders it difficult, if not impossible, to test empirically (DeFleur and Quinney, 1966: 21).

Sutherland stressed the social processes of cultural transmission, focusing on external variables while underscoring the individual's definition of the situation. Accordingly, differential association treats people as though they were equally influenced by stimuli of one kind or another. In reality, however, each person has different reactions to different stimuli.

Neutralization: a critique

Finally, neutralization theory has also been subjected to many revisions and criticisms (Ball, 1966; Hindelang, 1970; Taylor, Walton and Young, 1973). Hindelang (1970) found that delinquents and non-delinquents supported different values. Matza, for example, did not indicate why juveniles continue to engage in delinquency over time nor does he suggest why they are drawn into it in the first place. Additionally, the rewards of delinquency are not specified. Furthermore, the evidence is weak concerning the invocation of these justifications. Are they used before, during or after the commission of illegal acts?

Neutralization implies that people who are committed to crime are more likely to resort to these accommodating techniques. The relationship between the practice of neutralizing excuses and the subsequent deviance exists only for those experienced individuals who had previously committed acts of deviance and not for those who have never deviated. Neutralization only develops and is employed in anticipation of negative imputations attendant with being caught, that is, after the act of deviance. But, Matza and Sykes argued that these techniques precede deviance, they exist as a readily available repertoire of excuses.

Concluding comments

In brief, the traditional literature on subcultures or oppositional cultures tends to support highly elitist claims that lower-class youths tend to engage in delinquency. The deviance of so-called middle- or upper-class youth is overwhelmingly ignored. Authorities seem to notice lower-class youths more frequently. These youths hang out more publicly since they frequently lack the protection of property or privacy enjoyed by their equally deviant but largely ignored middle- or upper-class counterparts. The latter group's deviance is hidden and therefore more privileged. For England (1960), middle-class youths display such cultural straits as irresponsibility, hedonism towards sex, drugs, thefts, search for thrills and immediate gratification. According to his study of 1639 youths, Edmund Vaz (1966) discovered that despite the benefits enjoyed by the wealthy, these youths engage in many crimes like gambling, drug abuse, violence, vandalism and theft. Richards and Berk (1979: 12) argued that middle-class youths develop cultural responses to their boredom attendant with affluence. More recently, O'Bireck's (1996) analysis of affluent and working-class youth cultures demonstrated the importance of collectivities in resolving several problems. Youth cultures reproduce and consume middle-class stereotypic values. Delinquency provides moments of escape, artificial excitement and the acquisition of material objects. Teenagers seek each other out for survival and recreational purposes. Ralph England (1960: 539) argued that youths are too controlled according to paternalistic criteria; conventional controls ranging from the more punitive juvenile justice legislation to the more compassionate social welfare protections evident in compulsory education, child labour laws, the proliferation of an industry to protect the rights of children and youths are always justified according to their best interests.

Culturally, children and youths are treated as chattel, as the property of adults and not as persons in their own right.

In this chapter we have also discovered the significant influences peer associations, interactions and bonding contribute to delinquency. The frequency and quality of peer associations influence attitudes and behaviour. Deviant subcultures, disaffiliation and associations are cultural contests within controlled contexts. In contrast with early sections relating to deterministic notions of anomie, strain, social disorganization and subcultures, this latter discussion introduced the concept of agency. That is, actors choose to violate the law and are not strictly forced to do so by social forces located on the social structure. Crime, it was demonstrated, is a product of the interplay of values learned, the skills acquired and the availability of opportunities. This chapter analyzed normative conceptions of deviance and explored perspectives that introduce more relativistic features. The following chapter, however, highlights more exclusively the other end of the spectrum—the more dynamic and process-oriented interpretive models of deviance.

CHAPTER

Crime as
Performative

Introduction: "constructing" crime as differentiated cultural realities

In response to the deterministic propositions specified in the previous chapter, interpretive perspectives have explored the nature of the self-conscious individual who does not merely act but reflects on the meaning of action. In this chapter we review a select number of traditional texts within the interpretive paradigm that are particularly relevant to analyses of crime and deviance, namely Blumer's symbolic interactionism, Lemert's secondary deviation, and Becker's labelling theory, with a more cursory consideration of dramaturgy, phenomenology and ethnomethodology

In contrast to the normative explanations of crime, this chapter details elements of the interpretive models that directly confront the fundamental nature of reality. Simply, reality is an interpretation that is socially constructed. Interpretive approaches abandon the problematic practices of predefining or predetermining causalities of crime, trends so evident in the previous chapter. Presuppositions of the self as a passive object determined by external forces are replaced logically with arguments about the active, subjective and arbitrary nature of deviant designations. Accordingly, social life shapes and is shaped by the nature of structures.

From an interpretive perspective, crime is viewed as a social accomplishment, constructed and negotiated (Wilson, 1970) in ongoing interactions with various social agents. Definitions of crime are problematic because of their emergent character. This interpretive paradigm challenges the normative characterization of social reality as given and static. In brief, normative approaches consistently argue that social reality is constructed by external forces (beyond the control of the individual) that propel criminal behaviour. Fixed sets of norms and values set the boundary by which crime is defined. Within the interpretive model, actors are presented as creators of their environments. They engage in a continual process of meaning construction in relation to their social realities. As agents, they actively and reflectively shape their experiences and the experiences of those with whom they routinely interact. Through interaction, individuals collectively define situations. Participants, therefore, negotiate and reconstitute meanings.

For the interpretive perspective, social order is problematic. Reality remains inexhaustible, and knowledge, existing in the interaction of the subject and object, is equally tentative. The interpretive process examines how people control their own behaviour and that of others through the social construction of meaning and its application in interaction (Ericson, 1975). This paradigm calls for a sociology characterized by what Max Weber (1969) called *verstehen*—an empathic and interpretive understanding of the subjective meanings which actors attach to social action. The only way to contextualize social action is to know the subjective meanings of actors. Actors take into account the actions of others and are guided by these subjective meanings. Action incorporates all human behaviour to which the acting individuals attach subjective meanings (ibid.). The individual actor, therefore, becomes the basic unit of analysis, and the process by which meanings are assigned become a focal point of inquiry. Action, in the sense of subjective understandable orientation of behaviour, exists only as the behaviour of one or more individual human being. Both for sociology in the present sense and for history, the object of cognition is the subjective meaning-complex of action. In addition Weber (1947: 88) defined sociology as: "a science that attempts the interpretive understanding of social action in order to arrive at a causal explanation of its course and effects."

Symbolic interactionism: Mead, Cooley and Blumer

The social world is constructed out of shared symbolic universes. Within this world, human beings have the capacity to represent themselves symbolically because of their unique ability to use words and language. Interactionism emphasizes the way(s) in which individuals share symbols and the significance of these symbols in shaping interactions. The meaning of symbols, learned through interaction, is very important in appreciating behaviour.

Again, the social world is constructed by actors in complex interactions that occur in concrete situations. In turn, social interaction affects the interpretation of individual experiences and future behaviour (ibid., 1975).

This emphasis on the construction of social action requires a concern for the situation. We cannot know why people do what they do unless we clearly understand what the situation means to them. Towards this end, the study of symbolic interactionism becomes particularly fruitful.

Symbolic interaction refers to the peculiar and distinctive character of interaction as it takes place between human beings. The peculiarity of symbolic interactionism claims that human beings interpret or define rather than merely react to each other's actions. These actions are based on their concomitant meanings. Thus, symbols mediate human interaction. This mediation is equivalent to inserting a process of interpretation between stimulus and response in the case of human behaviour, that is, strategies of learning the meaning of one another's action. Mind, self and society are dynamic processes continually created and re-created. Symbolic interactionism highlights the processual and dynamic nature of definitions of self, others and situations. Humans act in a world that is interactively defined. Interaction, therefore, is the primary organizing unit of analysis.

Symbolic interactionism goes back to the ideas first presented by George Herbert Mead (1863-1931) and later elaborated by his student, Herbert Blumer (1900-1987) who coined the term. For Mead, social life is a dynamic, continuing social process governed by interactions among mind, self and society. He argued that mind, self and society are not static, acted-upon entities but are instead continually created, changed and re-negotiated. There can be no self "apart" from society. Social structure is the patterned expression of ongoing processes of social activity. The self is "essentially a social process" (1934: 178) occurring within social situations. Clearly, the individual is both object and subject. For Mead (1934: 173), the "essence of the self is cognitive; it lies in the internalized conversation of gestures that constitute thinking." Role taking is the act of entering into the perspective of others to become aware of one's own perspective (ibid., 254). The self emerges in reference to others, in projections and rehearsals of roles. As Mead (ibid., xxv) noted, the "individual constitutes society as genuinely as society constitutes the individual." In other words, Mead (ibid., 182) added:

> The "me" and the "I" lie in the process of thinking and they
> indicate the give and take which characterize it.... There would
> not be an "I" ... if there were not a "me"; there would not be
> a "me" without a response in the form of an "I".

In this regard the "me" represents experiences in which the individual is an object to himself or herself, the generalized other. The social product or "social-ness" of being an individual in society controls the "I". The "I" is the unpredictable and uncertain element of freedom and initiatives of immediate impulses. The "I" responds to the attitudes of others, the impulsive manifestations of the human natural needs (ibid., 174). The "me" for Mead is the organized set of attitudes of others which one assumes. These are the internalized norms and values. The attitudes of others make up the organized "me" while reactions to the situation frame the "I".

Charles Horton Cooley (1864-1933), a student of John Dewey, argued that humans have a capacity for self-consciousness that emerges out of interaction with others. Communication is the mechanism through which human relations exist and develop (Cooley, 1956: 61). He noted the significance of primary groups in making the individual human, in instilling ideas and developing sentiments and feelings of right and wrong. Consequently, actors have the ability to see themselves and recognize themselves as objects. The group gives meaning to the individual. Therefore, the self never exists alone but in interactions. Cooley saw society as an organic whole composed of interrelated parts and of individuals who make up those parts.

Charles Horton Cooley (1902) maintained that society is a mental phenomenon, a relation between personal ideas. By examining the human capacity for self-consciousness that flows from social interaction, Cooley stressed the indissoluble relation between self and society through his looking-glass self concept. Specifically, Cooley (1902) insisted that individuals come to regard themselves as others see them. This perception of self is analogous to the view in a mirror or looking-glass. Images people have of themselves are reflections of meanings assigned by the primary groups. The self does not exist in isolation, but always remains directly connected with others (1902: 84-87).

Influenced by Weber, Mead and Cooley, Herbert Blumer (1969) reiterated the significance of the subjective meanings of individuals. Blumer advanced a perspective that was sensitive to the capacity of humans to construct social worlds by arguing that no comprehension of human behaviour and social life can be obtained without taking account of the process of forming and transforming the self. Blumer stressed the importance of considering the subjective experience, behaviour and observable conduct of actors. He portrayed people not as passive recipients of societal norms but as active creative beings. In this sense, it was Blumer who refined symbolic interaction within a more sociological orientation (Adler and Adler, 1980). Humans interact, that is, they interpret and define the actions of one another, as Blumer described (1969: 2):

> symbolic interaction rests in the analysis of three simple premises. The first premise is that human beings act toward things on the basis of the meanings that the things have for them.... The second premise is that the meaning of such things is derived from or arise out of social interaction that one has with one's fellow. The third premise is that these meanings are handled in and modified through an interpretive process used by the person in dealing with the things he encounters.

Meanings, therefore, are social constructions that serve to anchor, orient and indicate action to the self.

For Cooley, Mead and Blumer, the self as the foundation of interactionism is a construction of consciousness continuously created and re-created. The individual appreciates his or her self in interaction with others. The self is made possible by the symbolic community of the individual with significant others. Thus, the self is not fixed immutably, but emerges through interactions in routine situations. Individuals make choices and construct actions that shape the self. Actors reflect upon their activities and upon the relationship of such activities to their identity. The views of the self are not given by simple self-reflection, they are acquired from others. Society and the individual are created in interaction.

Symbolic interactionism stresses the importance of others in shaping self-concept and draws attention to the central role of self-evaluation in the development of self-conception (Drakich, 1986). This reference to others is strongly influential in validating and sustaining one's self-concept; it is the audience in which an actor claims his or her self-worth. By attending to others, for example, the actor learns both favourable definitions of self and guides for interaction. The interactionist concept of "joint action" refers to the collective unit, the fitting together of different participants. As Blumer described (1979: ix): "The acts of others constitute the social for one's own act, serving to initiate, to inhibit, to temper, and to guide one's own line of action as one takes note of what others are doing or are likely to do." This frame of reference aids in organizing experiences. This clarification of individuals as actors is a process of "self-indication, a moving communicative process in which individuals note things, assess them, give them meaning and decide to act on the basis of the meaning" (Blumer, 1962: 181). Self-indication is central to the idea of human agency; the actor is an active agent bestowing meanings on every situation. Moreover, interpretations are communication processes through which action is constructed.

In reference to crime and deviance, the writings of Mead, Cooley and Blumer are particularly significant. As symbolic interactionists, their contributions highlight the way(s) in which individuals construct and share symbols that in turn generate definitions of crime or deviance. The insights of Mead, Cooley and Blumer understood crime or deviance as a learned meaning that is shared and defined differently. Meanings are learned in social interaction and, therefore, the definitions of crime and deviance are dependent upon the societal contexts in which interactions occur. It was the application of symbolic interactionism to crime and deviance that succeeded in advancing labelling theory.

Symbolic interactionism represents a departure from traditional approaches to the self, identity and relationships. Interactionist thought has influenced the labelling perspective in criminology and deviance theorizing with the following kinds of concepts: stigma, secondary deviance, sequential processes, master status, moral entrepreneurship and career contingencies. This perspective introduced a social space that respected the constituting capacities of the subject as a social agent. To further explicate the nature of crime, we will now examine elements of the interpretive approach in reference to labelling perspectives.

Labelling perspectives

> "Sticks and stones may break my bones but words will never hurt me"
>
>   Nineteenth-century proverb (Hyman, 1993: 278)

Although Frank Tannenbaum (1938) wrote about the "dramatization of evil" in the 1930s, labelling perspectives did not fully emerge until the early 1960s—marking the beginning of a substantial revision of criminology's parameters. Labelling theory attempts to resolve a whole set of new issues related to old questions that the disciplines of sociology and other social sciences have been raising for some time. The important difference is that before labelling theory, traditional criminology had rarely, if ever, considered them relevant. For example, one is encouraged to ask the following questions. First, how are designations of deviance constructed and applied to individuals and practices? Second, what are the origins of these designations and how have they become institutionalized? And third, what is the process by which agents of the criminal justice system attach official designations?

The labelling perspective directs attention away from the causes of crime and deviance, focusing instead on the relationship between people who have the power to label (Schur, 1971; 1980) and those who are unable to challenge the social repercussions of this stigma. Crime and deviance come to be defined specifically as processes of interaction between at least two kinds of people: those who commit or are said to have committed a deviant act and the rest of society. These two groups are complementary and cannot exist without each other (Becker, 1964: 3). Central to the labelling perspective is a concern with interactive processes of typification and designation (Fleming and Visano, 1983). What becomes central to this process is the reaction of some towards others. As Kitsuse (1962: 253) noted, it is the response to deviance that transforms people into deviants or criminals. Definitions are reactions to deviance or crime articulated within the backdrop of a shared universe of symbols. There are two analysts who are particularly well-known for their work in this labelling tradition—Edwin Lemert and Howard Becker.

Secondary deviation: Edwin Lemert

As a result of this emphasis on the application of labels, we see a shift in the sociology of criminology or deviance—a move away from a highly deterministic etiology of crime and deviance to a more comprehensive investigation of the problematic nature of societal reactions.

Edwin Lemert's (1951) inquiry into primary and secondary deviance represents a formidable analysis of societal reaction. Although one of Merton's strongest critics, Lemert has acknowledged fully the relevance of original causes of deviation or primary deviation. He did not entirely deny the validity of structural factors, especially in his discussion of primary deviation. Primary deviation refers to "initial behavioral deviations from modalities in human behaviour" (ibid., 23; 32-33). In Lemert's terms, primary deviance is situational: "The deviations remain primary deviations or symptomatic and situational as long as they are rationalized or otherwise dealt with as functions of a socially-accepted role" (1952: 75).

Essentially, primary deviation is a differentiated form of behaviour that occurs prior to a reaction. It is caused by a variety of factors and arises in a variety of social, cultural and psychological contexts (ibid., 1967: 17). Lemert's initial stages of deviance follow Durkheimian and Mertonian models of social reality in which reality is held to be independent of the actor's consciousness. This conception of reality allowed Lemert to appreciate as unproblematic notions of action as modal or as deviating from the mode. Thus, Lemert's concepts of reality and "behavioral modalities" provided him with a standard—a shared normative system against which action can objectively be evaluated by an independent scientific observer. This model of reality considers causes of deviance in terms of a series of external factors, i.e., forces that exist independently of the actor's consciousness.

Lemert reasoned that primary deviation is only applicable to original and not effective causes of deviation because problems resulting from one or several polygenic factors are handled within the realm of already established relationships. Although acts under this category may be socially recognized and defined as deviant and undesirable, they are observed and acted upon through a normalization process by which the deviant act is seen as a variation of normal behaviour in relation to a common problem of everyday life. The other basic responses to primary deviation include functional and administrative controls. These mechanisms do not significantly stifle nominal social interaction nor prevent further repercussions on either the deviant actor or the societal response to his or her acts.

Lemert highlighted the distinction between primary and secondary deviance to delineate two types of methodological approaches. One of these approaches, which seeks to discover how deviant behaviour originates, had been investigated by Merton. But the second approach is specifically related to a processual or social control explanation, emphasizing both how deviant acts are symbolically attached to persons and the effective consequences of such attachment for subsequent deviation for the person.

Unlike Merton, however, Lemert did not narrow the definition of deviance to norm violation. It is precisely in Lemert's analysis of secondary deviation that we witness a radical reappraisal of deviance. For Lemert, social control leads to deviance. As the following statement suggests, the process of negative reactions creates negative role engulfment: "When a person begins to employ his deviant behaviour or a role based upon it as a defense, attack, or adjustment to the overt and covert problems created by the consequent societal reaction to him, his deviation is secondary" (1951: 76). In effect, the original causes of the deviation recede and give way to the central importance of disapproving, degradational and isolating reactions of society. The sequence of interaction leading to secondary deviation is roughly as follows: (1) primary deviation; (2) social penalties; (3) further primary deviation; (4) stronger penalties and rejections; (5) further deviation, perhaps with hostilities and resentment beginning to focus upon those doing the penalizing; (6) crisis reached in the tolerance quotient, expressed informal action by the community stigmatizing the deviant; (7) strengthening of the deviant conduct as a reaction to the stigmatizing and penalties; and, (8) alternate acceptance of deviant social status and efforts of adjustment on the basis of the associated role (1951: 77).

Lemert's perspective is concerned with actors moving from primary to secondary deviance based on societal reactions. For Lemert, when a person begins to employ his or her deviant behaviour or a role based upon it as a means of defence, attack or adjustment to the overt and covert problems created by the consequent societal reaction to him or her, his or her deviation is secondary. Lemert (1967: 40) elaborates: "The secondary deviant, as opposed to his actions, is a person whose life and identity are organized around the fact of deviance."

Secondary deviation, then, is a product of the interaction between primary deviation and negative social reaction. As he suggests, secondary deviation is a special class of socially defined responses people make to problems created by societal reactions to their crime or deviance. Deviance, therefore, is an ongoing accomplishment rather than captured. Secondary deviance is a social construction that results from processes of adjusting to and coping with primary deviation. Thus, societal reactions are the processes that create, maintain and intensify stigma. Lemert's (1962) analysis of paranoia is a classic example of secondary deviance.

Similar to Tannenbaum's dramatization of evil, which segregates an actor, secondary deviation traumatizes the self-concept and encourages the continuation of criminal or deviant acts. Dramatization of evil, in other words, traumatizes the individual. He (1938: 19) wrote: "The process of making the criminal is a process of tagging, defining, identifying, segregating, describing, emphasizing, making conscious and unconscious.... The person becomes the thing he is described as being." Within Lemert's sociology of secondary deviance, there is evidence of a clear move in the direction of an interpretive paradigm. While Lemert proffered this orientation, he explicitly continued to retain a number of deterministic tenets in his theory. To clarify this point it is necessary to emphasize that the first stage of Lemert's theory is indeed dominated by normative assumptions of a deterministic perspective. Evidence of a shift towards the assumptions of the interpretive paradigm did not appear until the second phase of his theorizing—secondary deviation.

Clearly, Lemert's theory suggested that we are all engaged in deviance, but only certain actors are singled out or labelled, and only certain individuals encounter contingencies that lead to confrontations with defining agents. In other words, only some individuals are pushed towards secondary deviations. Interestingly, Lemert points out that there are no perfectly uniform and static rules that apply to all situations. Rules do not exist detached from meanings; rules apply to specific people at different times. There is, for Lemert, a sliding scale of norms: what is deviant or criminal at one moment may easily be an acceptable norm at another time. Just as official rules shift, cultural norms also change over time and so do people who violate them. Thus, the individual who violates a norm a second time may be qualitatively different from the person who broke the rule in the first place. The causes of rule-breaking behaviour change over time. Accordingly, Lemert advised that when the differences are extreme, it may be useful to distinguish between primary and secondary deviation and to recognize that the societal reaction to the original offence may also change the nature of the later offence. Moreover, societal reaction expresses the responses of the community to an act designated as deviant or criminal. Again, this reaction is not necessarily uniform.

The other as the "outsider": Howard Becker

Like Lemert, Becker's (1963) early theoretical formulations confronted traditional approaches to crime and deviance by placing an emphasis on rule-breaking behaviour. He asked, for example, why do conventional people not act on criminal or deviant impulses. Like the control theorists discussed in the previous chapter, Becker highlighted the increasing commitment to conventional norms as a check on criminal or deviant impulses. Lacking conventional commitment, criminals or deviants not only participate in supportive subcultures but also neutralize their crime or deviance.

More importantly, however, are the ways in which Becker's theoretical contributions politicized Lemert's conceptions. Specifically towards this end, Becker's work addressed the following: the nature of labels, the power of some to impose labels, and the acceptance or rejection of labels by the affected targets.

In *Outsiders*, Becker (1963: 8) provided us with the principal element of the labelling perspective—crime and/or deviance as a creation of society. His (ibid.: 8-9) classic statement on the labelling perspective suggested that the nature of deviance is to be discovered in the social reaction of the community:

social groups create deviance by making the rules whose infraction constitutes deviance, and by applying those rules to particular people and labelling them as outsiders. From this point of view, *deviance is not a quality of the act the person commits, but rather a consequence of the application by others of rules and sanctions to an "offender".* The deviant is one to whom that label has successfully been applied; deviant behaviour is behaviour people so label. [emphasis added]

In other words, he (ibid: 163) argued:

We must see deviance, and the outsiders who personify the abstract conception, as a consequence of the interactions between people, some of whom in the service of their own interests make and enforce rules which catch others who in the service of their own interests have committed acts which are labelled deviant.

Still working with elements of a normative orientation, Becker (1968: 1) added that the outsider is created by forces of law or traditions:

Social rules define situations and the kinds of behaviour appropriate to them, specifying some actions as "right" and forbidding others as "wrong". When a rule is enforced the person who is supposed to have broken it may be seen as a special kind of person, one who cannot be trusted to live by the rules agreed on by the group.

Likewise, Kai Erikson (1964: 11) pointed out that:

Deviance is *not a property inherent* in certain forms of behaviour; *it is a property conferred* upon these forms by the audiences which directly or indirectly witness them. The critical variable in the study of deviance, then, is the social audience which eventually determines whether any episode of behaviour or any class of episodes is labelled deviant. (emphasis added)

From the above excerpts, we discern that crime and deviance are politically and dynamically interactive processes. Definitions of crime and deviance are arrived at and constructed in negotiations between deviants and politically powerful audiences, thus directing attention to the understanding of welfare measures, police practices and ideologies as vital components of an understanding of crime and deviance. Differences in the ability to define crime and deviance are inherently power differentials, the relative power of groups involved and their channels of publicity. Becker urged readers to ask questions about the very nature of rules. Further, he suggested that institutional practices and related ideologies reinforce power differentials. Becker (1974: 60) elaborated cogently: "Elites, ruling classes, bosses, adults, men, Caucasians—superordinate groups generally— maintained their power as much by controlling how people define the world, its components and possibilities, as by the use of more primitive forms of control."

Becker developed the concept of moral entrepreneur to refer to persons or groups who attempt to criminalize or deviantize certain acts and individuals by influencing law-makers and law-enforcers. Consequently, socially distant or marginal people are treated in a way that exacerbates and exploits their vulnerability. These people have little or no power and few resources to resist powerful deviant or criminal labels (Gove, 1980: 11). Moral entrepreneurs affix stigmatizing labels to those who threaten the normative conceptions of societal good.

Stigmatization has extensive consequences for an individual's self-concept. A label once affixed by powerful interests not only crystallizes identity but remains so sticky that it becomes difficult to remove. Specifically, labels generate new definitions of self for the particular person, his or her reference group and the larger societal audiences. Furthermore, when these individuals fail to shed the designation, they often personalize or internalize the labels by organizing their lifestyles around the assumptions associated with the labels. A "master status" emerges and overshadows all other aspects of identity.

In the context of a strict interpretive framework, Becker's statements may prove to be troublesome. Admittedly, the nature of crime or deviance is created by the namer or labeller. However, within an interactionist perspective, the essence of deviance is both definitional and interpretive. Congruent with Becker's formulations, deviance is not constituted through an interpretive process, but is rather a consequence of the application of rules by others. The nature of response is restricted to the application of rules, i.e., rules that are independent of both the labelling and labelled actors.

However, in the second part of *Outsiders*, Becker articulated a conceptually more persuasive approach to labelling. He moved outside a deterministic approach to rules by examining crime and deviance as constituted by actors in an active process. Becker's actor is involved in producing and developing patterns of behaviour in an essentially interpretive process. He developed explicitly two features essential to the negotiation process: consciousness and intention. The process of becoming a secondary deviant, the steps by which a person moves from primary to secondary deviation, is related to the notion of career (to be discussed shortly). Here Becker has made particularly significant contributions to the study of labelling by clarifying career sequences and by conceptualizing crime and deviance as an equation in which the previously overlooked definitional power of rule-creators and rule-enforcers constitutes an integral part of the phenomenon.

Critiques of labelling perspectives

While the labelling perspective provides a theoretical framework from which social constructions of deviance are examined, it has been subjected to many criticisms. Jack Gibbs has characterized labelling merely as a conception rather than a coherent theory. Causality herein is unclear and imprecise (Gibbs, 1966). The concern with the application of labels during social reaction presents highly relativistic moral statements. For example, Gibbs (1966: 12) argued that this orientation fails to specify the conditions that must exist before an act or individual is labelled deviant. Specifically, labelling approaches fail to ask why people commit the initial deviant act and do not deal adequately with personal decision-making in the crime or deviance process (Akers, 1968: 463). According to Akers (ibid.), there is only an over-emphasis on the importance of official labelling:

> One gets the impression from reading this literature that people go about minding their own business, and then—"wham" —bad society comes along and slaps them with a stigmatized label. Forced into the role of deviant, the individual has little choice but to be deviant.

Within this context, labelling assumes an exaggerated sense of equivalence, i.e., once labelled, similar consequences are felt by all transformed offenders.

Furthermore, what is important yet often downplayed is that much crime or deviance goes undetected and is never labelled. That which appears as criminal or deviant tends to be class specific due to visibility, vulnerability and the lack of resources enjoyed by certain communities. The overstated character of official labelling has, however, been noted by Edwin Lemert (1971: 16):

> Unfortunately, the impression of crude sociological determinism left by the Becker and Erikson statements has been amplified by the tendency for many deviance studies to be preoccupied with the work of official agencies of social control, accenting the arbitrariness of official action, stereotyped decision-making in bureaucratic contexts, bias in the administration of law and the general preemptive nature of society's controls over deviants.

Labelling approaches fail to consider the general deterrent effects of social control on deviance. For Schur (1972: 14), labelling theory is far too narrow. It fails to explain differences in crime rates and ignores the onset of deviant behaviour.

In a more general sense, the assumptions of labelling theory do not fully address more macro sociological concerns. For example, labelling theory examines how the deviant responds to the label applied, but fails to address the process by which the larger society has come to define him or her as deviant. The deviant in this instance is portrayed as a submissive, passive victim of a one-sided process (Piven, 1981). What needs to be developed is an interrelated typology of subjects, situations and societal sanctions in order to predict the outcomes of the labels. Also, in its theoretical orientation, labelling theory does not examine the historical foundation upon which the labels were constructed. Again, labelling approaches neglect issues of social structure and class. For example, labelling theory ignores the crimes or deviance of powerful corporations (Chambliss, 1969). Similarly, Alvin Gouldner (1968) has shown that the attacks on the discriminatory or discretionary practices of social control agencies have served in some measure to effectively divert attention from the fundamental underlying disparities in the social structure.

By overemphasizing the causal aspects of labelling, the social reaction approach creates a somewhat insidious role inversion that promotes an "ideology of the underdog" (Gouldner, 1968) within a liberal ethos. The difficulty inherent in the classical labelling perspective, as suggested by Howard Becker, is its tendency to reject, expressly or tacitly, a normative definition or orientation of deviance (Clinard, 1974). It has also been observed that persons commit criminal or deviant acts because of social circumstances or particular contingencies. Many crimes go unreported, let alone detected. Thus, many crimes occur despite the label. Becker's (1963) argument suggests that deviance does not exist until it is constituted or recognized, while simultaneously allowing for the possibility of secret or unlabelled deviance. And yet, there are normative overtones to assumptions of the early labelling approaches that remain inconsistent with the theoretical foundations of interactionism. Assuming that rules are consistently applied by actors to define crime or deviance, Becker has unfortunately compromised processes of interpretation. He has "filled in" the process of interpretation by describing it as the "application of rules" instead of attempting to "catch the process as it occurs in the experience of the acting units which use it" (Blumer, 1962: 190).

Likewise, Kitsuse (1964) has suggested that the critical feature of the criminal- or deviant-defining process is not the behaviour of individuals who are defined as criminal or deviant, but rather the interpretations others make of their behaviour. He viewed the process of interpretation and defining acts or individuals as criminal or deviant as extremely problematic. Unlike Becker, he argued that the perspectives of those who define and interpret behaviour must be explicitly incorporated into a sociological definition of crime and deviance. In this respect, his discussion on societal reactions strongly supports the interpretive approach in developing a sociology of deviance. Kitsuse's (1964: 88) conception of deviance provided a stronger adherence to a more naturalistic orientation:

> Deviance may be conceived as a process by which the members of a group, community, or society (1) interpret behaviour as deviant, (2) define persons who so behave as a certain kind of deviant, and (3) accord them the treatment considered appropriate to such deviants.

A few lines later, his empirical questions indicated an obvious symbolic interactionist methodology: "how do they interpret such behaviours, and what are the consequences of those interpretations for their reactions to individuals who are perceived to manifest such behaviour" (ibid., 90)?

Working within a symbolic interactionist perspective, Kitsuse recognized actors as they are, namely, persons constructing individual and collective action through an interpretation of the situations that confront them. Kitsuse

(1975) rejected Becker's assumption that before the act of labelling, the independent observer can determine a classificatory scheme based on a set of pre-formulated rules without confronting the labeller's perceptions and interpretations of a situation. The labelling process may be tentatively described as interactional and interpretive in which actors construct particular classifications with specific or vague meanings based on their interpretations of other actors' words, gestures or what Goffman terms "presentations". The process of constructing social categories is also significant for subsequent action. Anslem Strauss (1967: 326) remarked:

> The naming of an object (or person) provides a directive for action, as if the object were forthrightly to announce "You say I am this, then act in the appropriate way towards me". Conversely, if the actor feels he does not know what the object is, then with regard to it his action is blocked.... An act of classification not only directs overt action, but arouses a set of expectations towards the object thus classified.

Regrettably, the early labelling theorists neglected to provide a rigorous and critical analysis of the processes involved in having a particular definition (label) maintain its credibility and legitimacy. Undoubtedly, this type of analysis would have confronted the politicality of social interaction, the process under which definitions are imposed on particular members of society and why social control agents are considered legitimate and credible classifiers. A more disciplined scrutiny of the political nature of deviant phenomena must be undertaken if the sociology of crime and deviance is truly committed to understanding the nature of social order. It can be respectfully submitted that a failure to analyze the politicality of social interaction may invite the charge of a conservative bias, which is in ideological agreement with existing arrangements of political order.

Appropriately, the focus of theory and research should shift from the forms of criminal and deviant behaviour to the processes by which persons become defined as criminal or deviant by others. Such a modification requires that sociologists view as problematic what they generally assume as given, namely, that certain forms of behaviour are criminal or deviant per se and are defined by the conventional members of a group (Kitsuse, 1964, 1975). By addressing the processing of crime and deviance, both normative control mechanisms and interpretive insights can combine to support a more holistic world view distinguished by a more humane and voluntaristic view of the individual caught up in, yet aware of and reacting to, such social processes. Herein, the concept of a career eases this shift in focus.

The concept of "career" as an analytic tool

The concept of career refers to the progression of related experiences and identity changes through which one moves during his or her working life. As Becker noted (1963: 24), a career is a socially recognized process involving a relatively orderly "sequence of movements". This constellation of behaviour and values serves as a framework for interpreting action (Hughes, 1937) and for charting identities (Rock, 1979: 140). Within the interpretive paradigm, a career, therefore, is not only a way of being but also a way of knowing. Careers consist of forms of sociation which impose some intelligibility on the actor's world.

Using the concept of career, we are able to focus on the processes of, and stages in, choice, development and transformation. We are led to discern major components and relations; to investigate both formal and informal links between stages; and to specify various contingencies affecting the nature of interactions located in these stages.

Career stages are characterized by identifiable and organized sets of relations and social meanings. As they emerge from social interactions and as they are subsequently interpreted as meaningful, career stages provide actors with a set of perspectives. In other words, actors construct knowledge of their different worlds by assessing situations and assigning meanings to the activity and to others as classificatory schemes. Consequently, staging a career becomes an ongoing process of self-indication and self-validation. Stages are essentially procedures that individuals use in making sense of their immediate situations. With increased and continued interactions, these career categories evolve so that stage identifications follow and are considered by others in future encounters. These categorizations establish routine rules for interaction and serve as directives for future involvements.

Rules are not independent of actors, but are constructed by actors who define social reality because a belief in the objective facticity of various sets of rules. Rules are objectively established through interpretive processes and not by simple reference to a body of culturally given norms. Activities and the careers with which they are associated are often attached to institutions that enjoy powerful codes of conduct, fixed discipline and reward structures. The social organization of careers consists of various forms that typically plot biographies and relationships. They include different features of: (1) the initial "getting connected" or "becoming" stage, which involves various aspects of exposure, exploration, entry (recruitment or induction), trial and initiation, or training and apprenticeship; (2) the "staying connected" or "being" established in roles that concerns the maintenance of identity, achievement, stability and clarification and also advancement, promotion or specialization; (3) the "disconnecting" or decline stage of a career pursuit characterized by graduation, expulsion, termination, retirement as well as transformation, conversion or greater induction into another orientation (Visano, 1987).

Actors create stages that in turn are used to justify degrees of involvements. Passing through these stages is not an automatic process. Participation in and commitment to a career stage depend upon several specific adjustments. These contingencies appear both as conditions and consequences of interactions. At each stage a number of tightly interwoven contingencies operate and assume different meanings. They do not operate "simultaneously" (Becker, 1963: 24) but become important to the actor during different stages of his or her commitment to a career. Instead of leaping from one stage to another (Ericson, 1975: 84), actors experience "contingencies" (Goffman, 1961: 135). Three related factors are fundamental in building and maintaining the symbolic worlds of careers: constituting skills of actors, reactions of others and self-identity.

First, movement within a career is conditioned by the acquisition of skills, knowledge and resources. Rewards are maximized by the ongoing development and application of knowledge. Aspirants' interest alone is not sufficient to qualify them for mobility. They must learn a stock of beliefs, values and ways of acting that will ensure continued participation. They may be expected to interpret the rewards offered and their chances of realizing them. Rational choice requires information that they would presumably channel within different stages (Becker, Geer, Hughes and Strauss, 1961). This may be influenced by the individual's interpretation of several immediate conditions: abilities or qualifications, specific occupational information, orientation to the specific work life and social relations. In addition, there are the unexplicated features of settings of interactions that promote and permit the exercise of the actor's capabilities.

The second factor that affects acting units is the action of other acting units (Blumer, 1967). This reference to "previous significant others" (Gerth and Mills, 1953: 93) aids in securing access to services and information. More significantly, associations with similarly circumstanced others serve to "validate" (Lemert, 1972: 81) and sustain a convenient self-concept. By attending to the reactions of others, the actor learns favourable definitions of experience and self that, in turn, guide new strategies of interaction. Actors acquire their roles by interpreting the roles of others and by reacting to how they think others conceive normal action in a situation. As Blumer (1979: ix) noted: "The acts of others make up the social setting for one's own act, serving to incite, to inhibit, to temper, and to guide one's own line of action as one takes note of what others are doing or are likely to do." Actors interpret and define the actions of others. They do not simply react to the responses of others. The responses of significant others will be framed by the career that is extrapolated for the self (Rock, 1979: 137). This frame of reference aids in organizing perceptions and experiences.

The third pivotal condition affecting career advancement is the acquisition of techniques for constructing appropriate self-concepts. Actors establish and situate meaningful identities for themselves and for others at different stages (Goffman, 1961: 125). The influence of an individual's self-concept has received considerable attention in studies of vocational choice. Traditionally, the self-concept has been studied in terms of normative theories of congruence (Holland, 1973). Vocational development is the process of carrying out one's self-concept. Personality orientation is the overriding factor in selecting an occupation (ibid.). Research within this tradition specifies that choice is made consistent with one's self-image only for those who have high self-esteem. Those who score low in self-esteem are less likely to make choices that are congruent with their self-image.

An interpretive framework, however, suggests that participants are actively involved in shaping their identities with others with whom they interact. Self-concepts are negotiated, assumed and discarded. The developmental perspective of the knowing self is fundamental to the career process. It is, however, mediated by the actor's interpretations of contingencies such as the actor's own definitions of social reality. Actors define stage expectations in socializing associations. Consequently, their moral characters and their relationships to rules and to others are continually evolving during the course of interaction. Socialization simplifies the learning and maintenance of an appropriate self-concept by specifying the necessary world view, skills and knowledge. Interestingly, these products are based upon, but are not coterminous with, the actor's image reflected in interaction with others (Lemert, 1972: 78).

The logic of this developmental model does not presuppose that once actors have begun to move in the direction of a certain career, they will inevitably go through the entire range of stages. Rather, the premise of this model suggests that there are a number of situational and subjective contingencies which the actors confront, interpret and select at various stages in the sequence. These contingencies are not objectively given. A career study, therefore, is not limited strictly to "affinities" which preordain actors nor to "affiliations" which convert them (Matza, 1969: 119-121). Shifting relations and meanings emerge in order to cope with these affinities and affiliations. An actor may enter at any stage only to move forward, backwards or out of the process completely. At each stage, the actor accomplishes the necessary skills and identities to respond to the various career challenges, however constructed. The nature of the relationships is significant in affecting the next stage he or she will pursue in advancing, maintaining or abandoning his or her career. It is not guaranteed that once all the stages have been experienced, the actor will have secured a career.

Stages often involve varying degrees of overlap, negotiation and compromise (Miller and Form, 1951). For Lemert (1972: 79) an analysis of recurrent or typical contingencies awaiting someone who continues a course of action is a more meaningful inquiry. It becomes necessary to specify the precise mechanisms of learning and patterns of interactions that allow for the development of contingencies integral to one's becoming, being and changing orientation. The "theoretically best choices" and "points of no return" or "turning points" warrant exploration (ibid.).

An interpretive perspective recognizes that many unrelated encounters occur at different stages of a career which are neither incremental nor consequential (Rock, 1979: 140-1). Likewise, there are "objectified" elements of a career of which actors are no longer conscious and which are beyond their control (Ericson, 1975: 39).

From the social action perspective (Weber, 1946; Blumer, 1967: 143), careers are viewed as emerging accomplishments of actors in their daily encounters. The process by which meanings are assigned to routine activities with and among fellow participants is the focal point of inquiry. This perspective highlights the need to consider the meanings and negotiations of definitions behind the formation and coordination of career stages and their attendant contingencies. The common everyday properties of work, interaction and social identity become the subject of sociological examination.

A career is an enterprise developed and articulated against a backdrop of significant meanings. The social organization of careers—status, roles and stages—enter action only to the extent that it shapes situations in which people act and it provides symbols that people use in interpreting these situations (Blumer, 1967: 146). The career as a meaningful concept is ordered reflexively by social actors into a human enterprise. Career stages, therefore, are presented as the outcomes of the actors' consciously applied skills. Emphasis, however, is on the coping and problem solving aspects of interaction (Hughes, 1971; Becker, 1963; Matza, 1969; Lemert, 1972).

In analyses of crime and deviance, the concept of career is valuable precisely because of its two-sidedness (Goffman, 1959: 127-69). On the one hand, this concept is linked to internal matters—the individual, the image of self, felt identity and its shifts. On the other hand, it is related to social identities, to the public, the significant society with which the former interacts. A career study provides an examination of this dialectic in terms of the socialization process through which an individual acquires a set of values, rules and language. In orienting his or her behaviour to that of others, the actor encounters a number of contingencies. The actor often interprets these experiences by attending to the accounts of others. This reference to his or her experience and the experience of others becomes classified according to stages that in turn assume meaningful designations.

Influenced by his association with Hughes, Becker suggested that within this processual dimension, careers flow out of differential experiences that actors undergo (1963: 31-34). The experience of social reaction becomes a significant determinant of career development. Non-institutional careers are subject to the typing and control process of institutions with which actors interact. Being caught, branded or even rescued has important consequences for one's social participation and self-image (ibid.; Matza, 1969; McIntosh, 1974: 58). A criminal or deviant designation may serve to facilitate a pattern of crime or deviance and fit an appropriate self-image. A criminal or deviant career develops in order to cope with and manage the problems of adjustment arising from the overriding stigma of a newly assigned criminal or deviant status (Lemert, 1972; Goffman, 1973: 79).

This interpretive framework downplays the notion of careers as fixed, static and self-maintaining systems constrained by strict rules. Instead, this perspective emphasizes the fluid, loose and continually emerging qualities of career, the ongoing dynamic reorganizations and changing webs of interaction among its members. Shifting memberships, limited career involvements, role discrepancies and ambiguities, incomplete rules, conflict and change are just as much part of careers as stability and consensus. There are, however, other traditional perspectives within the interpretive paradigm that warrant mention—dramaturgy, phenomenology and ethnomethodology.

Dramaturgy

Dramaturgy, informed by symbolic interactionism, similarly emphasizes the self as the focal point of analysis. Dramaturgists, like Erving Goffman (1922-1982) believe that social actions are theatrical performances enacted for the purpose of creating shared symbolic and eliciting good self-images. Goffman maintained that human beings are active and knowing agents who stage their respective worlds through symbols (1959; 1961; 1963).

Dramaturgy is predominantly concerned with analyzing appearances, especially that which can be seen in public places. Dramaturgists believe that appearances are carefully managed—acted or presented, to get the right billing. In other words, these theorists believe that performances must be managed interactionally and actors must support each other's presentations in order to produce favourable consequences. As Goffman analyzed (1963: 24), every society appears to come under strict normative regulation, producing a kind of communicative traffic order. Public order deals with normative regulation. Rules of interaction maintain a noticeable order (ibid., 1963, 1963a). Body movements, rules of interaction, rituals, deference exchanges or civil inattention follow certain codes and are scripted within frames. Goffman's theatrical model is a methodology used to conceptualize social order as everyday events. Interpretations of public order and an awareness of rules (1967) are ritualized like religious practices. It is not a matter of learning rules but rather understanding normative assumptions that govern forms of encounters, an understanding of micro-processes of social interaction.

Phenomenology

Phenomenology is yet another sociological perspective identified within the interpretive tradition. In contrast to normative orientations, phenomenology is a sociological perspective that critically examines the notion of social order by challenging culturally learned beliefs, values and ideas. Phenomenology, as a philosophy, owes much to the writings of Edmund Husserl (Giddens, 1976: 25), which encourage analysts to describe and question underlying forms of experience and objects of consciousness. For Husserl, intentionality consists of, first, the intentional aspects of consciousness, the "noesis" (for example, I deviantize)—the building up or constitution of consciousness. And, second, intentionality incorporates the objective component of consciousness, the "noema" (for example, that which I deviantize). Specifically, phenomenology asks us not to take the notions we have learned for granted, but to question them instead, to question our way of looking at the world in order to study how people define their social situations once they have suspended or "bracketed" their learned cultural notions (Armstrong, 1976: 252; Gurwitsch, 1966).

Generally, there are two related methodological imperatives built into phenomenological orientations: (1) to give correct representation to the phenomenon under study; and (2) to show how the phenomenon is constituted or built up. The descriptive form of the constitutive is examined. In other words, facts are reduced to phenomena, that is, facts are interpreted as events and analyzed as phenomena.

Specifically, phenomenology stresses that the mind is a conscious active process. Activity is to be studied by means of a subject's intentionality. This social investigation diverts attention away from deterministic theories towards intentional action. The meaningful constituting activities of the subject ground knowledge.

The goal of the phenomenologist is to correctly represent the phenomenon under study by emphasizing the subjective experiences and perceptions of relevant social actors. Understandably then, in relation to deviance, phenomenology rejects perspectives that attribute the application of a deviant designation to external forces impinging upon the individual. It is more concerned with how individuals construct meanings of things for themselves in their own respective consciences. Accordingly, the process by which a social world is available to us or constructed for us is a problematic object of inquiry. Consequently, we suspend belief in the existence of that world as an objective social reality and question our everyday worlds (Schutz, 1964).

Phenomenologists focus on the actor's account of an event. An account is an actor's personal interpretation of a situation as it is announced to others in interaction. Given the subjectiveness of this process, previously taken-for-granted notions of deviance can be interrogated. That is, traditional conceptions of deviance acquired through socialization can be suspended as individuals begin to dispute the normatively imposed deviant labels attached to certain actions or behaviours. As an example, consider the occurrence of drug use. It has traditionally been characterized as a deviant act. However when upper-class, "respectable" individuals partake in the consumption of illegal substances, the action can take on a different, more positive connotation such as a form of recreational activity. The intricate process by which deviance is defined is directly related to the ways in which behaviour and experiences are constructed by social actors. Several types of sociological analyses can be incorporated within a phenomenological perspective. In the present context, only two will briefly be reviewed—the naturalism of Matza and Garfinkel's ethnomethodology.

Matza (1969), for example, maintained that only the deviants themselves can provide a true account of the nature of deviant phenomena and how they come into being. Towards this end, the major theme in his work is naturalism: the constant attempt to remain true to the phenomenon one is studying. In *Becoming Deviant*, Matza (1969) explained how beliefs and actions are related in the mind of social actors via the process of constructing meaning. He alluded to the naturalistic perspective, a methodology that provides an accurate and truthful presentation of phenomena in their own right rather than a description or explanation in order to correct, reform or eradicate them (correctional perspective.

In studying deviant phenomena, particularly in relation to delinquent formations, Matza rejected subcultural theories discussed in the previous chapter on the grounds that they characterized delinquents as holding to a system of values which were "an inversion of the values held by respectable society." Matza insisted that these descriptions represented an over-antagonistic view of the relationship between delinquent values and those of the larger society. Matza claimed that in reality delinquents are committed to values that are ultimately linked to those of the wider society. The adolescent is not involved in a rejection of conventional morality, rather the adolescent neutralizes the normative bind of society's legal order.

The emphasis on the similarity of delinquent values and those of the larger society has led Matza to replace the notion of a delinquent subculture with the idea of a subculture of delinquency, which exists in a subterranean fashion in normal society. If carefully examined, one discovers that many apparently delinquent values closely resemble those embodied in the leisure activities of the dominant society, that is, there is a similarity of larger societal values and delinquent ideologies. This insistence on more accurate representations of the phenomenon under study steers Matza's naturalistic methodology towards a more phenomenological orientation.

Ethnomethodology

While one can argue that Matza's work was moving gradually towards phenomenology, it was Garfinkel's (1967) ethnomethodology that contributed to the tradition's most eminently authentic approaches. Garfinkel looked into the commonsense knowledge that emerged in the everyday interpretation of social reality. He too treated as problematic that which was taken for granted in order to more fully appreciate everyday commonsense interpretations that govern social realities (ibid., 1967: 6). He focused on rules that make everyday life meaningful thereby juxtaposing deviance and conformity.

Ethnomethodology studies and analyses everyday activities, i.e., the construction of meanings that actors account for their activities. Ethnomethodology asks how does the constituted world present itself as if it were external or independent. How do we go about seeing and describing a situation, any social action? For many, the world is presented as an objective fact. According to Garfinkel (1967: vii), ethnomethodology encourages an orderly and artful way of making sense of the objective reality of social facts as ongoing daily accomplishments of concerted activities. Ethnomethodology is not merely an extension of everyday life, rather it scrutinizes society from a viewpoint that will show how members build procedures to accomplish events. Also, ethnomethodology is concerned with the processes by which rules are invoked, taken for granted and used for interpreting situations. Garfinkel (ibid., 76) stated that the term ethnomethodology refers to the investigation of the rational properties of indexical expression and other practical action. Everything has a context and every item of significance is an index for which there is meaning. Ethnomethodology is concerned with how everyday social life is accomplished, i.e., how social order of a situation is possible for its members. Briefly, ethnomethodology is the study of the construction of the meanings used to characterize and account for activities. Practical knowledge is isolated and seeks to explain how the social constitution of knowledge is mediated by methods. Accounts are not independent of the socially organized character of their use (1967: 4). Again, social situations are not independent of lived experiences. The context is salient; scripts or texts are not pursued. Garfinkel (1967) stated cogently that ethnomethodology is an organizational study of members' knowledge of their ordinary affairs, of their own organized enterprises.

The world is experienced inter-subjectively as a world common to all. Language and other gestures, for example, are indexical—they contain taken-for-granted elements. Meanings of situations are embedded within larger contexts of meanings. Indexicality requires a documentary method of analysis for the actors and the analysts. This necessitates the treatment of actual appearances as "documents of" presupposed underlying patterns.

The accomplishment of meaning on the part of the actor is paramount. Meanings are contingent; they are not known in advance. Additionally, the concept of reflexivity, the notion that every act is at once both in the setting and simultaneously creates the setting. Reflexivity refers to the social activities whereby members create and maintain the very situations in which they act (Churchill, 1971: 185; Shearing, 1973), to the constitutive process in which neither the parts nor the contexts are independent of each other. The process of constitution is reflexivity. The examination of experiences enables the ethnomethodologist to realize the lived experiences and the organization of meanings for the actors. This inquiry recognizes individual consciousness only as an essential plane of social reality. What is understood is never fixed, and meanings are always fragile in interactions.

Ethnomethodology concentrates on face-to-face interactions. Social interactions are analyzed in terms of processes of sociation. Cicourel's (1968) study on juvenile justice is an explanation of rules and background expectations that authorities like the police employ in negotiating appropriate labels for the subject. Cicourel's thesis is that rates of juvenile delinquency are constructed by organizations. He investigated the procedures in which labels are applied—the contexts of definitions—and explored how the community and its representatives decide what is delinquent. The meanings available to the actor and the researcher, the encounters, reports etc., are researched to understand the creation of official documents on delinquency. Cicourel (1968: 8) argued that the concern is with how the observer decides what he knows and how the actor accomplishes this task.

Ethnomethodology contributes to the sociology of deviance by examining precisely the relationship between beliefs and action. But, in rejecting general statements and concepts until they are limited to members' consciousness, ethnomethodology has been criticized for reducing all meanings to those held by the studied individual actors. Also, ethnomethodologists maintain that nothing is really fixed in the world, that the social world is merely an ongoing practical achievement of its members. But is it? People create society, but not always in circumstances of their own choosing. Theoretically, ethnomethodologists deny both the totalities in the world and the completeness of individuals. They reject the reality of structured values. Experience and perceptions are very important to the analyst. Actors' accounts are to be explained in terms that must be reducible to the actor's meanings and intentions. However, this perspective remains extremely subjective and descriptive, and does not always address the importance of social structure in sociological analyses. Ideas like class, deviance, alienation or anomie are secondary. From a phenomenological perspective, these concepts represent constructions removed from typifications. Specifically, they neither have reference to nor are they reducible to everyday, taken-for-granted, practically constituted and intentionally created phenomena.

Conclusions: interpretive as (per)formative and generative

This chapter examined the reasoned ontology of symbolic interactionism while highlighting an emergent conceptual orientation. Interactionism encourages theoretical pursuits that directly confront the time-honoured distinctions between process and structure. In general, the priority of micro-social constructions acknowledges elements of social structure. Interactionists, however, have moved judiciously in unravelling macro-conditions from the plethora of their detailed observations (Lyman, 1984). More recently, there is a growing tendency in interactionist writings to develop more formalistic directions of social inquiry. Processes of group life are articulated as generic (Couch, 1984) and alternatively recast within socio-historical influences (Rock, 1979; West, 1981; Denzin, 1984; Saxton, 1987; Hall, 1987).

Clearly, there is no single overarching conceptual canopy that integrates process and structure. Presently, attention will be directed towards providing clues for linking the concept of self to cultural reproduction. It is argued that the situation, as a site of cultural reproduction, mediates the tensive and creative foundations of micro and macro sociologies. Informed by Simmel and Blumer, this discussion emphasizes the development of generic forms and processes in an effort to appreciate the nature of group life. Specifically, the research question asks: How does culture influence the negotiation of identities and relations? Ultimately, the social construction of reality is analyzed in terms of wider issues—the reproduction of dominant values.

To fully appreciate an interactionist analysis of structure, it is appropriate to clarify the analytic structures of interactionism. This endeavour requires a discussion that goes beyond routine stock-taking of past theoretical accomplishments. The adequacy of such sensitizing concepts like generic processes in discovering "forms that universally display themselves" (Denzin, 1970: 15) must be demonstrated rather than simply stated.

Clearly, interactionism defies systemization. But, the subject of recurring regularities within diverse temporal and spatial domains has emerged as a more heightened focus of study, especially in reference to generic concepts. The generic concept is a panoptic tool that imposes order on diverse findings. Generic concepts are abstract categories or invariant properties of human life (Blumer, 1969: 86; Couch, 1984). Dimensions of social life are illuminated by ongoing comparisons of different research sites. The task for interactionists, therefore, is to delve into universal forms of processes which make group life possible. This commitment to formalism is shown in the repeated admonitions of interactionists. According to Lofland (1976: 31): "To scrutinize a situation generically is to seek out its abstract, transcendent, formal analytic aspects." Likewise, Wiseman (1985) argues that generic concepts reflect complex social forms that are not limited to specific settings, populations or relationships.

The development of formal theory (Glaser and Strauss, 1967: 90) incorporates a higher order of meaningful generic forms that are grounded in localized interactional discourses and symbols. Forms, as properties of conjoint activities, are related to the reproduction of social order. The unity of society is derived from forms of sociation—conflict, domination, competition, exploitation, isolation, segregation, hierarchy—or symbiosis—consensus, cooperation, sociability and intimacy (Wolff, 1950). In *Soziologie,* Simmel studied group processes and structural forms, adding that "the sociological process remains, in principle, within personal interdependence and does not result in a structure that grows beyond its elements" (Simmel, 1950: 126). According to Simmelian insights, these forms are experienced as reified objects that debilitate and/or enhance choice. Social life, however, is not simply a truncated constellation of inexorable forms. Rather, forms of sociation inhere in unfolding processes that are structured within routine interpretive activities.

Generic processes extend grounded theorizing by focusing upon interactions that are similar despite variations in situational contingencies. Basic social processes are generic theoretical constructs (Bigus, Hadden and Glaser, 1982: 251), which capture "forms in action." Some germane and problematic features of group life include: information management, reputational control, interpersonal manipulation, negotiation, promotion of loyalty and institutional response. Generic processes of comparable situations are located within complex master forms. On-site processes are concatenated to organizational and structural contexts.

In reference to generic concepts, an investigation of self, situation and culture facilitates the exploration of more critical directions. As will be elaborated, the self and culture are closely implicated in the medium of the situation. Logically, structure inheres in the processes of group life.

The self is the crucial concept in interactionist inquiries. Although the self is the lens through which social worlds are refracted (Rock, 1979: 146), the self exists ontologically before the situation. Actors constitute situations by making them meaningful. Actors structure situations by "materializing" them, i.e., by assessing, producing and locating experiences according to immediate concerns.

The self is not only situated (Charon, 1979: 82; Weigart, 1983) in immediate encounters but it is also a generic process that transcends the plethora of diverse daily routines. The self presents itself as spontaneous and voluntaristic in concretized symbols and interactions. The self is linked to processes of interpretations. Additionally, the self signifies a cumulative consciousness which renders a host of political and economic determinants of relations more visible. The self is a conscious product mediated within careers of subjectivity (Visano, 1983). The dialectical relationship between the more mediating and situated self and the more developmental and mediated self serves to project objectified forms—identities and activities— amenable to social validation. The social environments of the self, such as situational contingencies, condition the interpretive methods available to actors.

Grounded in situations, actors develop typologies for interacting with others. The unfolding of these experiences acquires an obdurateness that extends beyond the immediate situation. According to the social action perspective, meanings are assigned within the careers of activities, identities and relations. To reiterate, the concept of career refers to the constellation of meanings that link the situated self to larger dimensions of group life. Careers are organized according to identifiable perspectives from which actors evaluate their respective social worlds. Participation in the generic stages of becoming, being or disconnecting depends on a number of contingencies. The development and maintenance of symbolic worlds of careers involve three fundamental contingencies: self-concept, skills and reactions of others. First, self-identity and motivation shape the interpretation of situations that are at different stages of involvement or relationship. Secondly, the learning of a stock of beliefs, the application of knowledge and the acquisition of skills ensures continuity. Lastly, the perspectives of others are important in validating claims of self-worth and in certifying favourable responses to experiences. These contingencies reflect both subjective and objective elements of situations.

These contingencies are constructed in conjoint activities and expressed intersubjectively through such referents as linguistic, symbolic and interactional structures. Situations become objectified to manage a discourse that frames respective lived experiences more meaningfully within the minds of others.

Actors adopt classificatory schemes of self-other relations validated in concrete routines within diverse milieux. Projected images and values are congruent with the attributed meanings of similarly circumstanced others. Therefore, meanings are stabilized through negotiations and inter-subjectivity, and cognitive activities are institutionalized as objectively established, collective typifications. It is precisely within the concrete situation or materialist present (MacLean, 1986) that subjectivity emerges as objective empirical reality. The primacy of the materialist situation objectifies the self and anchors contingencies.

Contingencies are anchored in situations confronting actors. These situations are structured according to the corpus of interpretive practices that are themselves formed in reference to the currency and criteria of institutionalized experiences. Loose and fragile ensembles of situations have frequently become the foci of contested definitions. Consistent with prevailing normative notions about the imposition and compliance to rules, interactionists have courted the politics of interactions. For example, Becker (1963), Lemert (1967) and Lofland (1969) have examined the promotion of partisan interests in deviant designations. Collectively they suggest that institutional practices and related ideologies reinforce certain hegemonic realities.

In problematic situations that accompany organizational processing, contingencies are also negotiated commodities. The generic process of negotiation reflects features related to specific encounters as well as properties of larger social orders (Strauss, 1978; Ericson, 1981; Warren, 1983; Regan, 1986). The weight of economies, culture and politics on interpersonal exchanges is well documented (Vaughan and Reynolds, 1968; Collins, 1979; Este and Edmonds, 1981; Stryker and Craft, 1982; Rank and Lecroy, 1983; Tomlinson, 1985). In general, the influences of wider forces are always mediated by more localized (situated) organizations (institutions). That is, they enter into action by shaping situations in which people act and equally supply fixed sets of symbols people use in interpreting their situation (Blumer, 1969).

The above discussion of interpretive approaches highlights the significance of agency, intentionality and subjectivity. The actor is an active creature, not a passive determination of external and pre-given forces. Also, all knowledge is grounded in the meaning-constituting activity of the knowing subject. Meanings are negotiated. In this world of meanings, actors create their social environment, which in turn conditions them. Interactionism mediates and opens space for the hitherto neglected subject, the constituting capacity of the social agent. To reiterate, social order is a social accomplishment. Interactionism, with its emphasis on the emergent self, fails, however, in exploring more fully the grounding of these accomplishments. Despite their differences interpretive approaches have been criticized as too liberal, too relativistic, too voluntaristic and too easily accommodating to state interests. The de-politicized elements of labelling, for example, have been appropriated by the state. In discussions of human agency of the deviant, these approaches ignore structural features of class crimes and state reactions. The traditional text of labelling reduces too much to actor-reactor relations lodged in the interactions at a micro-level of inquiry. The textured language of agency forecloses an examination of more global political struggles.

The Conflict Paradigms and the "New" Criminologies

Introduction: "constructors" of crime

Within the study of crime there are well-established traditions that foster different accounts of social reality. Normative approaches to deviance, detailed in chapter two, provide a consensual view of society—a perspective that highlights fundamental agreements on rules and values that determine social life. The previous chapter delineated interpretive accounts that reject these deterministic or a priori assumptions. And in this chapter we examine the conflict perspectives; approaches that, for example, extend a view of social relations that underscores the centrality of social conflict and change in shaping political, social and cultural institutions. Contemporary conflict approaches to the study of deviance emerged especially when labelling perspectives were gaining in popularity. Both approaches flourished in a social climate of unrest, disillusionment and protest.

Specifically, during the 1960s and the early 1970s, the proliferation of social movements expressed a genuine drift, discontent and despair with the prevailing social order. The 1960s were marked by unparalleled large-scale widespread demonstrations by the women's, gay, lesbian and anti-war (peace) movements. Peaceful protests within the Civil Rights Movements (for example, the Washington march of hundreds of thousands in 1963) and the counter-cultures of the hippies and yippies (Woodstock Music and Art Festival in August, 1969 was attended by 500,000 people) also highlighted the growing confrontation with the conventional rules. But the violence of this decade, especially inflicted by traditional authorities, resulted in a general cynicism towards law and its distant sibling, justice. Notably, the disturbances of the 1960s brought the much needed public awareness to the systemic deprivation of so many fundamental rights. Along with prison and race riots throughout the USA and the UK, there were countless political trials, violent labour-management discords, the separatist campaign in Quebec, student activism (notably the Students for Democratic Society), protest movements (Canadian Party of Labour), nuclear testing, groups like the Black Panthers, the Weathermen in the USA and the FLQ in Canada, etc. The state responded to all these challenges with unabashed violence. Witness the following: Canada's Liberal government under Prime Minister Pierre Trudeau imposed the draconian War Measures Act in peace time; National Guardsmen fired into a crowd protesting against the American and South Vietnamese invasion of Cambodia at Kent State University killing four students on May 4, 1970; the East Germans built the Berlin Wall in 1961; the Soviets invaded Czechoslovakia in 1968; a savage war continued in Vietnam; in the My Lai massacre of March 1968, a US infantry unit killed more than 300 unarmed Vietnamese civilians; the American sponsored military coup of General Augusto Pinochet Ugarte in Chile overthrew a democratically elected government and killed the legal and legitimate head, President Salvador Allende in 1973, etc.

Besides state sponsored violence on local and global scenes, authorities have never hesitated in engaging in wholesale deceit and cover-ups as with the Watergate scandal in 1972 and the complicity of American President Richard Nixon. Internationally, Fidel Castro overthrew Cuban President Fulgencio Batista and seized American assets in 1960; the imprisonment of Nelson Mandela; Congo and many other African countries were engaged in liberationist struggles to secure independence from their colonial masters throughout the 1960s; Mao Zedong launched the Great Proletarian Revolution in China from 1966 to 1969. Even now in the 1990s the assassinations of President John Kennedy on November 22, 1963, Malcolm X on February 21, 1965, the Reverend Martin Luther King on April 4, 1968, Senator Robert Kennedy on June 5, 1968, all remain mysteries. Many questions about the role of government agencies and corporate interests in these horrific acts of brutality are still unanswered. All these events noted in this lengthy overview drew attention to the uneven distribution of resources, and, more specifically, these crises increased awareness of the fundamental inequalities within the criminal justice system.

There are many areas of continuity and convergence within labelling and conflict approaches, notably the interest in the sociology of law, structures of discrimination and the processes of collective rule-making and enforcement. Consistent with labelling perspectives, conflict theorists conceptualize criminality in reference to power differentials. Specifically, that which is criminal becomes a "definition applied by individuals with the power to do so, according to illegal and extra-legal, as well as legal criteria"

(Turk, 1969: 10). Similarly, both perspectives examine crime control agencies according to actual practices rather than stated or expected ideals. However, for many scholars writing within the conflict tradition throughout the 1960s and 1970s, labelling approaches were too timid analytically to grapple with fundamental social relationships. Despite the sensitivity of labelling to the role of social definitions, this perspective offered little more than a sensitizing orientation to questions of structure and dominance. Thus, it was left to the conflict perspectives to develop more fully the theoretical and empirical relationships between crime and deviance, social control and power.

Conflict theorists concentrated on the power relations inherent in the criminalizing and deviantizing process. Informed by general theories of social conflict that directly implicate the dominant social and political processes structuring crime and deviance, contemporary conflict approaches scrutinized more closely those mechanisms that routinely reproduce extant inequalities. Conflict moved beyond viewing crime and deviance as a consequence of social definitions created and applied by those in power. This politics of crime and deviance framework compelled researchers to interrogate diverse political sites and to ask the following questions. In whose interest is crime or deviance created, maintained and punished? How do those in power use crime and deviance to protect and promote their respective interests? Who makes the rules? What rules get enforced? How are certain conceptions of crime or deviance accepted and legitimated? In short, crime or deviance is examined as a politically charged phenomenon shaped by conflict. Again, the designation of deviance is the result of power relations.

Within this tradition, a recurring theme emerges regarding definitions of crime and deviance. This research has demonstrated that deviance is not shaped by moral consensus but by the relative power of groups who use scarce resources to impose their moral preferences. Conceptions of social order focus on the social control of the weak by the powerful, rather than social control by consensus. An essential requisite for the maintenance of power is the legitimation of one's interest and the corresponding de-legitimating of competing claims. Legitimacy is often persuasively achieved through law, culture (education, religion, morality, media) and politics. For example, although legal definitions and decisions represent special interests, they are invariably disguised according to criteria propitiously invoked to protect monolithic notions of public morality, justice, order or even national security.

Contemporary conflict approaches: Sellin's cultures in conflict and Vold's contexts of power

Contemporary conflict approaches to crime can be traced to the works of Thorsten Sellin (1938), George Vold (1958) and Ralf Dahrendorf (1958a, b; 1959). In his study *Culture, Conflict and Crime* (1938), Thorsten Sellin argued that cultural conflicts cause crime. In agreement with the early Chicago School, detailed in chapter two, Sellin claimed that the consequences of urbanization, especially social and cultural diversity, contribute to crime and deviance. Crime and deviance are related to the attenuation of moral bonds, the disintegration of the community and the social disorganization that create conflict. For Sellin, people are caught between conflicting cultural rules.

In general, cultural conflict refers to competing norms and values that lead to conflict and ultimately result in crime or deviance. Specifically, two particular forms of cultural conflict influence crime and deviance: primary and secondary conflicts. Primary cultural conflicts occur when residents of culturally diverse areas are exposed to an environment that is different, ambiguous and in disagreement. These clashes reduce social controls and generate stress that contributes to crime or deviance. Secondary cultural conflicts emerge because of differentiation and inequality in the parent culture (Sellin, 1938: 105-107). Traditional norms, especially among ethnic minorities, are in conflict with contemporary or dominant values upheld by law enforcement practices. Crime, therefore, is a consequence of the conflicts between cultures (inter-cultural).

Informed by Sellin's contributions to culture conflict, George Vold produced the first criminological text on social conflict, *Theoretical Criminology* (1958). Vold's conflict theory outlined the social circumstances that frame crime. Social relationships contribute significantly to crime especially within the group situation. Vold shifted attention away from individualistic law violations to an appreciation of a more group conflict orientation. He argued that in any society, people in similar situations group together to secure their interests. The needs of groups are served through collective action; these groups are constituted to serve their members' interests. For Vold, society is depicted as a constellation of groups held together in a shifting and dynamic equilibrium of opposing interests. Groups are in conflict whenever expectations or goals clash (1958: 208). People are constantly struggling to promote the interests of their respective groups and strive to further ensure access to resources for their groups. The result is a continuous state of group conflict or more appropriately, social struggle.

Conflict for Vold was an essential social process upon which the ongoing of society depends (1958: 204).

Conflict arises whenever groups compete in the same field of interaction—a conflict of interests among different groups. Social groups gain advantage and repress others by means of political processes. The group with the political clout controls the resolution of differences. For example, when one group has the power to express its values in laws, it has the power to criminalize or deviantize those who disagree. Crime or deviance is manipulated by vested interest groups who enjoy considerable access to political resources that enable the imposition of sanctions on subordinate groups.

In brief, crime for Vold can be explained by social conflict. Laws are created by politically motivated groups who seek the assistance of the government to protect their interests. With enough support, they succeed in creating laws that crush opposition groups. As Vold (1958: 209) described:

> the whole political process of law making, law breaking and law enforcement becomes a direct reflection of deep-seated and fundamental conflicts between interest groups and then more general struggles for the control of police power of the state .... those who produce legislative majorities win control over the police power and dominate the policies that decide who is likely to be involved in violation of the law.

In this context, crime or deviance can be understood as cultural conflict. Those in power translate their cultural norms into laws, i.e., differential enactment of laws.

While Vold's model is useful for highlighting how criminalization reflects different degrees of political power, it is limited to situations in which individual acts flow from the collision of group loyalties. It falters in explaining impulsive or irrational acts outside the context of, and unrelated to, any group interest. Lamentably, deviance or crime outside of intergroup clashes is not well addressed.

Class and class conflict: Dahrendorf (1929-   )

The scholarship of Ralf Dahrendorf has contributed enormously to modern conflict perspectives. In *Class and Class Conflict in Industrial Society* (1959), Dahrendorf provided a challenge to the dominant social consensus theories by analyzing conflicts over authority in society. For

Dahrendorf, "every society is based on a coercion of some of its members by others" (1959: 161). He (ibid., 165) added: "in every social organization some positions are entrusted with a right to exercise control over other positions in order to ensure effective coercion; it means, in other words, which there is a differential distribution of power and authority." Towards explaining "effective coercion", Dahrendorf (ibid., 166) adopted Weber's definitions of power and authority:

> the probability that one actor within a social relationship will be in a position to carry out his own will despite resistance regardless of the basis on which this probability rests; [whereas] authority is the probability that a command with a given specific content will be obeyed by a given group of persons.

Comprised of a plurality of competing interest groups, Dahrendorf viewed society as organized into associations in which relationships comprise two groups—those who dominate and those who are subject to authority. Authority is the central source of conflict; classes are defined by relations of authority. In this context, people act in reference to their position in a pluralistic society wherein a range of authority-subject relationships directs action.

Authority-subject relations: Turk

Informed by Dahrendorf's writings, American criminologist Austin Turk provided an influential conflict theory of crime in *Criminality and Legal Order* (1969). This study developed an insightful appreciation of criminalization—the processes, conditions and consequences of defining actors as criminal. Turk asked, for example, under what circumstances do those who violate norms become criminalized. Central to Turk's thesis is the argument that social order in modern societies is based on the relationship of conflict between authorities (the dominant decision-making category responsible for the enforcement of norms) and subjects (subordinates affected by the imposition of cultural and social definitions). Power is a critical dimension in the determination of authority-subject relations. The degree to which any individual or group acquires, controls and mobilizes power resources will affect the outcome of these relationships (1976a: 280). Essentially, power is the control of the following resources: first, the means of direct physical violence—war or police power; second, the production, allocation and/or use of material resources—economic power; third, decision-making processes—political power; fourth, definitions and access to knowledge, beliefs, values—ideological power; and fifth, human attention and living—time-diversionary power (ibid.). These social, political and economic resources are mechanisms that allow individuals or groups to maintain domination over the powerless.

Within the above contexts, criminality is the result of social conflicts between authorities and subjects. Conflict is an ongoing process that emerges in interactions between individuals or groups competing over scarce resources. This ubiquitous struggle is intrinsic to the creation, maintenance and extension of behavioural and relational patterns that maximize the life chances of individuals or groups (1966, 1976b: 285, 1977). For example, as different groups seek to protect and enhance their life chances, as defined by both material and non-material criteria, conflict is inevitable. The source and locus of conflict exist in the structuring of social life.

Turk (1969: 25) defined criminality not as a biological, psychological or even a behavioural phenomenon but a social status defined by the way in which an individual is perceived, evaluated and treated by legal authorities. Criminality occurs within the interactions among various parties—all kinds of norm makers, interpreters, enforcers and violators (ibid., 53). Rather than focus on the causes of crime alone, Turk's theoretical reformulations of criminalization seek to discover how people come to acquire a criminal status. He suggested that the acquisition of a criminal status is largely due to the legal authority's definition of the person as criminal.

Criminality as a social process involves a system of sanctions. As he highlighted, the key factor in criminalization is the ability of some people to announce and enforce legal norms (1969: xi). Conflict leads to criminalization under certain conditions. For instance, Turk maintained that the greater the cultural differences between authorities and subjects, the greater the probability of their conflict and subsequent criminalization. Criminalization will occur whenever: one, authorities consider a law highly significant; two, law enforcers find the subject's legally prohibited behaviour to be greatly offensive; three, the power differentials are great in favour of authority; and four, the moves of the parties are more realistic (1969: 67-75). Rather than adopt a social psychological model of the internalization of criminality, Turk proffered a sociological theory of interactions that highlights a learning process based on power. He asserted that authorities and subjects learn and re-learn to interact with one another as occupants of superior statuses and inferior statuses who, respectively, perform dominating and submitting roles (1969: 41). "Criminal" is a status accorded to norm resisters whose realism and sophistication are inadequate to anticipate the results of their actions. Interestingly, law is both power and authority. While every legal relationship has the power at the core, it also has some grounding in mutual acceptance of the terms of the relationship (1986: 499).

The social reality of crime: Quinney

Along with Turk, Richard Quinney's earlier studies on the social reality of crime (1970) blended the interactionism of Lemert and Becker with the conflict perspectives of Dahrendorf and Vold. In *The Social Reality of Crime* (1970: 15-24), Quinney developed a conflict theory of crime that contains six proposition, the first of which addresses a definition of crime. For Quinney, crime is a definition of human conduct created by authorized agents in a politically organized society. Thus, agents of law, representing segments of a politicized society, are responsible for formulating and administering criminal law. Clearly, crime is created. This focus avoids the clinical perspective which concentrates on the quality of the act and assumes individual pathology. Crime is not inherent in behaviour but is a judgment— a perspective developed by the labelling approaches.

The second proposition concerns the formulation of criminal definitions. Criminal definitions describe behaviours that conflict with interests of the segments of society that have the power to shape public policy. Criminal definitions are formulated according to those interests that have power to frame public policy—an obvious manifestation of conflict. Indebted to Vold and acknowledging Turk's contributions, Quinney argued that the greater the conflict in interests between segments of a society, the greater the probability that the power segments will formulate criminal definitions.

The third proposition deals with the application of criminal definitions. Criminal definitions are applied by the segments of society that have the power to shape the enforcement and administration of criminal law. Citing Vold, Quinney viewed crime as a political behaviour, and the criminal becomes a minority without sufficient support to dominate the control of the police power of the state (1970: 18). The probability that criminal definitions will be applied varies according to the degree to which the conduct of the powerless conflicts with the interests of the powerful. Criminal definitions are influenced by the following community and organizational factors: community expectations of law enforcement; the visibility and public reporting of offences; and the occupational organization, ideology and actions of legal agents to whom the authority to enforce laws is delegated.

The fourth proposition involves the development of behaviour patterns and criminal definitions. Behaviour patterns are structured in segmentally organized society in relation to criminal definitions, and within this context persons engage in actions that have relative probabilities of being defined as criminal. Derived from Sutherland's differential association, Quinney noted that all persons—whether they create criminal definitions or are the objects of such definitions—act according to normative systems learned in relative and cultural settings. Persons whose behaviour patterns are not represented in the formulation and application of definitions are more likely to act in ways that will be defined as criminal. Behaviour that is likely to be defined as criminal depends on the structure of opportunities, learned experiences, interpersonal associations and identifications, and self-conceptions. Those who are defined as criminal often conceive of themselves as criminal and play what Lemert refers to as the role of the criminal. Fifth, Quinney formulates a proposition regarding the construction of criminal conceptions. Conceptions of crime are constructed and diffused in the segments of society by various means of communication. Social reality is a construction— created and believed according to the kind of knowledge actors develop, the ideas to which they are exposed and the manner of interpreting conceptions they have selected. People behave according to social meanings attached to experiences. Conceptions are constructed by both personal and mass communications. The most influential conceptions are those held by the powerful.

The sixth proposition incorporates the social reality of crime. The social reality of crime is constructed by the formulation and application of criminal definitions, the development of behaviour patterns related to criminal definitions and the construction of criminal conceptions. Figure 4. 1 represents Quinney's theory.

For Quinney, an absolutist definition of crime is replaced by a more relativistic legal conception. His theory of crime is specifically based on a dynamic perspective that incorporates the notions of process, conflict, power and social action. Process is a dynamic aspect of social relations. These social phenomena include a continuous series of actions, complex network of events, structures and underlying processes. Conflict is an inevitable (ibid., 9) and normal consequence of social life. Power is a basic character of social organizations. It is inextricably linked to conflict. Clearly, the differential distribution of power produces conflict. Social action is

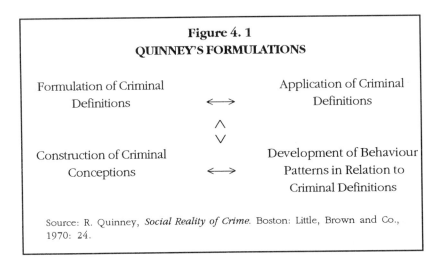

Figure 4. 1
QUINNEY'S FORMULATIONS

Formulation of Criminal   Application of Criminal
Definitions   ⟷   Definitions

                                    ∧
                                    ∨

Construction of Criminal   Development of Behaviour
Conceptions   ⟷   Patterns in Relation to
                                           Criminal Definitions

Source: R. Quinney, *Social Reality of Crime*. Boston: Little, Brown and Co.,
1970: 24.

consistent with the conflict-power conception of society. A social action
frame of reference maintains that actions are purposive, intentional,
meaningful and goal-oriented. The social reality of deviance or crime is the
product of coercion and conflict in an unequally structured society. In
applying his theoretical perspectives to a variety of situations, Quinney
notes how institutional orders define the content and direction of interests.
These orders include: 1) the political order which regulates the distribution
of power and authority in society; 2) the economic order which regulates
the production of goods; 3) the religious order which regulates the
relationship of people to a conception of the supernatural; 4) the kinship
order which regulates sexual relations and family patterns; 5) the educational
order which regulates the formal training of society's members; and 6) the
public order which regulates the protection and maintenance of the
community and its citizens.

Conflict approaches, which analyze how the powerful segments of
society impose criminality on the powerless, have been criticized for trying
to explain too much—ranging from the more trivial forms of deviance and
non-political indiscretions to more violent consensus crimes such as sexual
assault, burglary and murder. Another criticism directed at conflict
perspectives is its fundamental assumption that all laws reflect the interests
of the powerful. This conspiracy orientation leads us to believe that offenders
are all victimized and harmless products of a damning criminalization process.
It is naive to assume that violent acts will disappear once the power to
criminalize is removed. Moreover, although conflict perspectives highlight

the oppressive nature of law, they fail to develop more fully a much-needed structural analysis that would simplify an inquiry into the crimes of the powerful, the nature of social inequality and an agenda for action.

The above group culture or pluralistic conflict approaches were important in forging new directions in theorizing about crime and deviance. Although they highlighted the centrality of coercive authority relations, they failed to analyze fully the historically based contexts in which conflict exists. However, the schools of radical, critical or new criminology do assign considerable priority to historical and structural analyses in identifying the political economy as the source of criminality, as is evident in the work of William Chambliss, Taylor, Walton and Young, and Richard Quinney.

Radical and "new criminologies"

As British analysts Taylor, Walton and Young (1973: 265-266) admonished: "To say, as group conflict, law is in the hands of powerful interest groups, does not go far enough." Powerful interests share a common framework that is often glossed over by pluralistic conflict theorists. Moreover, the contexts in which power struggles occur are ignored. The radical or new criminologists argued that the mode of production, for example, influences all social relations. Organized social relations are disturbed whenever one class gains and maintains superiority by controlling the economy and by exploiting the less fortunate. Consequently, individuals no longer participate in the collective production of the economy. Instead, individuals are compelled to compete with each other for economic advantage. This structural inequality leads to conflict—the social control of the dominant class over the working classes.

Law, order and power: Chambliss

The political economy of crime has been extensively studied in the USA by William Chambliss. As he stressed in his article "The Saints and Roughnecks" (1973), criminality reflects the political organization of law enforcement and the social class power distribution of the economic system. Chambliss and Seidman (1971: 4), in *Law, Order and Power*, noted:

> It is our contention that, far from being primarily a value-neutral framework within which conflict can be peacefully resolved, the state is itself the principal prize in the perpetual conflict that is society. The legal order ... is in fact a self-serving system to maintain power and privilege.

The legal system serves to support the existing economic order that only benefits the rich and powerful. In *Whose Law? What Order?: A Conflict Approach to Criminology* (1976), Chambliss and Mankoff detailed how criminal law comes about as a result of the struggle between the ruling economic class and the ruled. They (1976: vii-viii) described the aims of radical conflict approaches by noting that

> conflict approaches are not content to re-analyze and improve upon theories concerned with the question of why people become criminals. They have taken a step beyond this by going to the history of law to learn by what criteria societies have differentiated criminal offenses from normal behaviour. They have recognized that the legal system "created" crime and criminals by its arbitrary categorization of certain human behaviour as illegal.

Chambliss and Mankoff (1976: 8) outlined five functions of crime for society: 1) crime allows the capitalist class to create a false consciousness that advocates that the interests of the ruling class and the ruled are identical; 2) crime reduces the surplus labour by creating employment for criminals and non-criminals, jobs are created, for example, for law enforcement agencies, welfare workers and professors of criminality; 3) crime diverts attention of the working-class population, shifting attention away from their own exploitation towards other members of their own class rather than towards the capitalist class or economic system; 4) crime increases the capitalist control over the proletariat, the working class is coerced into submission; 5) crime is a reality that exists only as it is created by those in society whose interests are served by its presence. The state intervenes, acting as if it were a neutral party while legitimating the interests of the capitalists. The criminal justice system is essentially class-based and biased in favour of the ruling class (Chambliss, 1975). Laws, as tools of oppression, are manipulated by the economically advantaged to punish those who challenge their security.

Concerning causality, Chambliss defined crime as a reaction to the life chances of a person's social class. Crime is the result of the proletariat reacting to their life circumstances—exploitation and oppression (1975: 152). A more comprehensive appreciation of the etiology of crime requires an analysis of the structure of capitalist societies. Accordingly, Chambliss and Ryther (1975: 56-67) provided six conflict principles: (1) economic forms shape other institutional forms; (2) a particular economic form or mode of production dominates a given time or place; (3) each economic form has inherent contradictions that produce classes and class conflict and may produce its own destruction; (4) class conflict shapes other social institutions; (5) social change arises when the needs of the weaker class are being met less through the dominating instituting patterns; and (6) contradictions lead to radical transformation.

Throughout the 1980s Chambliss formulated a more explicit political economy of crime model. In *Exploring Criminology* (1988), Chambliss presented a structural contradictions theory of crime. Every society in every historical period constructs means of survival and creates contradictory forces and conflict (1988: 201). In capitalist societies, labour and capital seek to maximize their respective share of surplus. Workers demand better working conditions and more wages, while capitalists resist these efforts. Labour and capital advance their own interests—the latter protects the status quo and the former attempts to change it (1988: 308). Attempts to resolve conflicts between labour and capital exacerbate the situation precisely because fundamental contradictions remain untouched. Two contradictions contribute to crime: the "wages, profit and consumption contradiction" and the "wages-labour contradiction" (ibid.: 309). With the former contradiction, owners, on the one hand, violate health and safety provisions, breach exchange practices, defraud the stock market etc. On the other hand, workers pilfer, supplement their wages, deal in drugs, illegally strike and so on. Although the state is caught in the middle of these conflicts and is influenced more by the pressure of the owners, it cannot allow these struggles to destroy the economic system; therefore, laws are passed.

In reference to the second contradiction, the wages-labour contradiction, Chambliss argued that capitalism maintains a surplus labour force to keep wages low and to keep a supply of labour which capital draws upon whenever workers threaten profits. Typically, workers are fired and new labour is hired. These new workers cannot consume but are socialized into consumption. Crime is a solution to this underclass who earns through illegitimate means (ibid.: 309). In addition, contradictions create conditions under which there are opportunities for state officials to violate criminal laws. In his study of state organized crime, Chambliss reminds us that crime is a political phenomenon that must be analyzed accordingly (1989: 204). These crimes, to name only a few that continue to be unchallenged, include piracy, smuggling, assassinations, illegal spying and terrorism.

The new criminology: Taylor, Walton and Young

At the root of any criminological inquiry, therefore, are the problematic interrelationships among criminality, social structures and political economy. In *The New Criminology: For a Social Theory of Deviance* (1973), Ian Taylor, Paul Walton and Jock Young advanced a comprehensive review of different theories of crime. This powerful critique of traditional criminology challenges the work of group and pluralistic conflict perspectives. Traditional conflict approaches concentrate on the plurality of interests while ignoring too blithely the alliance of interests between capitalism and the state. As they noted in a subsequent interview with Robert Mints (1974: 39):

> ... the most important thing about *The New Criminology* is the attempt to do a criminology which takes account of *the total society*. It's not microsociological, like symbolic interactionism, labelling theory and so on, and it's not crude either in its view of social conflict. It is at least an attempt to do a Marxist criminology.... So our problem is to go back to Marx—and not simply to take isolated sections of Marx.... We see crime as an authentic form of consciousness, we take it seriously, and we try to relate that back to the total structure and avoid the impasse that characterizes microsociological accounts.

This new criminological perspective "would be free of biological, psychological assumptions" (1973: 268) and social positivistic explanations of crime. In exploring the social origins of deviance, the authors insisted that the fundamental processes of social life need to be more fully incorporated. The basic elements that define a society include specific mode(s) of production and the resultant contradictions. In the context of capitalist societies, the most basic contradiction is expressed in the relationship between the superstructure (ideological-juridical apparatus of the state) and the infrastructure (individuals' material conditions within the social system). The former imposes values and norms that are incompatible with the latter conditions. Taylor, Walton and Young supplied a political economic explanation of deviance and crime in which capitalism is singled out as the main criminogenic factor.

The New Criminology is a structural critique of the way in which individuals are handled, with the way society handles itself and the forces in society that process and produce that handling (Mints, 1974: 40). The elements of this comprehensive theory include, on the one hand, political economy of crime, social psychology of crime, the social dynamics surrounding the actual events and, on the other hand, a social psychology of social reactions to crime, a political economy of social reactions, the consequences of social reactions and the criminalizing or deviantizing process as a whole. Antagonistic contradictions between the individual and society cause crime and deviance. Although Taylor, Walton and Young accept individuals as both determined and determining (ibid.: 157), crime and deviance must ultimately be viewed as predetermined by structured inequalities and ideologically enforced (ibid.: 169). Their approach is a consideration of all the above relationships and processes together. Specifically (Mints, 1974: 40):

> If you are going to study "crime", there's no point in trying a causal, let's say a social reaction analysis, without situating that specifically—the specificity historically of that kind of behaviour, the reasons for that kind of behaviour, the motives of the individuals engaged in that behaviour, the motives of those that bring the force of law to bear on that behaviour, and so on ... but all situated historically, yet hanging together as a total process....

In effect, *The New Criminology* responded to the crisis in theorizing about crime and deviance. This critical text represented a reconciliation of criminology with sociology and politics. Taylor, Walton and Young (1973) called for the creation of a society "in which the facts of human diversity, whether personal, organic, or social are not subject to the power to criminalize" (ibid.: 282). "The task," they insisted, "is not merely to penetrate these problems, not merely to question the stereotypes, or to act as carriers of alternate phenomenological realities." Rather, the task is to forge a commitment to be revolutionary rather than side with oppression. Criminology must be committed to the abolition of inequalities of wealth, power, property and life chances (ibid.: 281). The politicization of criminology is imminent. *The New Criminology* succeeds in both moving the study of crime into the sphere of political economy and in interrogating the bases of economic, political and social orders that constitute the culture of capitalism.

Capitalism and the legal order: Quinney

Moving away from his earlier liberal, group-conflict paradigm, Richard Quinney revised his theoretical perspective in a way that is more consistent with the radical philosophies and criminological explanations of Taylor, Walton and Young (1973). He attacked pluralistic conflict approaches as inadequate, misguided examples of bourgeois academic enterprises that serve the existing capitalist order. In *Critique of the Legal Order: Crime Control in Capitalist Society* (1974), Quinney directly assailed capitalism as criminogenic. Specifically, he contends that the criminal law is used by the state and ruling class to secure the survival of the capitalist system. And as capitalist society is further threatened by its own contradictions, criminal law will be increasingly used in the attempt to maintain domestic order (1974: 16). Quinney's later scholarship (1977: 33-34) furthered the examination of the relationship between capitalism and crime, specifically grappling with the following fundamental question: "What is the meaning of crime in the development of capitalism?" According to his model of the political economy of crime, those who own and control the means of production (the capitalist class) attempt to secure the existing order through various forms of domination, especially crime control. Crimes of domination, which reproduce the capitalist system, include crimes of control (authorities like police committing crimes), crimes of government (political terrorism), crimes of economic dominance (corporate crime, price-fixing, environmental social injuries), racism, sexism and class elitism. In spite of the presence of a few laws directed at the crimes of the powerful, laws protect capitalist interests; the crimes of the dominant class are seldom brought to public attention. Instead, with the assistance of social scientists and the mass media, attention remains focused on lower-class crime, i.e., on the crimes of those who do not own and control the means of production. This especially includes the capitalist working class, which accommodates to and resists, in various ways, forms of capitalist domination (1977: 60). These crimes of accommodation—predatory, personal and resistance (sabotage, rebellion)— are the responses of lower and working classes to the opportunities and options available in capitalism (1977: 54-55). Given this context, Quinney suggested four areas that require analysis: the development of capitalist political economy; systems of domination and repression; forms of accommodation and resistance; and, lastly, the dialectic relationship of accommodation and resistance to the overall conditions of capitalist political economy, wherein one discovers the creation of both crimes of accommodation and crimes of domination.

In essence, Quinney's (1977) work produced an excellent account of how and why the legal system serves the interests of the elite. He accentuated the variety of complex processes and structures that enable the law to act as an instrument of the state and the ruling class in order to maintain and perpetuate the existing economic and social order. Furthermore, by criminalizing the powerless the powerful preserve social inequalities. Crime control is simply a means for checking threats to the existing capitalist order. As a response to this serious scenario, Quinney called for a revolutionary consciousness that will end the oppression of the powerless by the powerful (1974: 16). That is, only a socialist vision will allow people to work towards a form of life beyond the oppression of capitalism.

Radical reformulations: Schwendingers, Platt, Sykes and Spitzer

There were many theorists who continued to work in the new criminological traditional, including Schwendinger and Schwendinger (1979), Platt (1974), Spitzer (1975) and Michalowski (1985). Julia and Herman Schwendinger investigated the relationships among law, crime and the state, asserting that "every comprehensive system of laws is essentially determined by class factors" (1977: 6). As a response, they advocated a radical commitment consisting of practical critical activity and participation in ongoing political struggles. More specifically, the Schwendingers (1979) defended the following five claims. First, legal relations secure the economic infrastructure that centres around the capitalist mode of production. The legal system is designed to guard the position of owners at the expense of workers. Second, legal relations maintain the family and school structure in order to secure a labour force. Third, the class interests that underlie laws of the land are based on conditions that reproduce the class system. Laws, in other words, are designed to secure domination. Fourth, the legal system may, at times, secure the interests of the working class, e.g., protective or collective bargaining. Fifth, due to contradictions, all laws differ from the stated purposes of justice. The legal system not only highlights the ethos of individualism but also perpetuates a class system. The Schwendingers argue that legal relations secure an economic infrastructure that centres on capitalist modes of production. The legal system protects positions of privilege at the expense of the disadvantaged. All laws secure and reproduce a class system. Despite the appearance of justice in law, and despite their articulated principles, laws inherently maintain the dominant hegemonies.

Anthony Platt (1974) charged that mainstream liberal criminologists sustained repression with their constant focus on the poor, invisible and visible minority criminals. According to Platt (1974), criminology must redefine its goals. In the past the discipline was woefully constrained by legal definitions of crime that restricted analyses and ultimately facilitated the control of only legally defined criminals. We need, Platt elaborated, a more humanistic definition of crime, one that exposes the reality of a legal system based on power and privilege. To accept a legal definition is to accept the fiction of a neutral law. A human rights' definition of crime frees us to examine imperialism, racism, sexism, exploitation and other political or economic systems that contribute to human misery and deprive people of their potentialities. For Platt (Currie, 1973: 28),

> We are just beginning to realize that criminology has serviced domestic repression in the same way economics, political science, and anthropology have greased the wheels and even manufactured some of the important parts of modern imperialism. Given the ways in which this system has been used to repress and maintain the powerlessness of poor people, people of colour, and young people, it is not too farfetched to *characterize many criminologists as domestic war criminals.*

Correspondingly, Sykes's (1974) Marxist theory regarded the criminal law and criminal justice system as vehicles for controlling the poor. The criminal justice system helps the powerful to: first, impose their morality and standards on all; second, protect their property and physical safety from the have-nots; and third, extend the definition of crime to encompass those who challenge the status quo. The poor may or may not commit more crimes, but they are arrested and punished more often. Moreover, Sykes (1974) argued that the poor are driven to crime because the rules imposed from above are irrelevant to the culture of the poor. In addition, a natural frustration exists in a society in which affluence is well-publicized but not attainable. He concluded by arguing that a deep-rooted hostility is generated towards a social order in which they were not allowed to shape or participate.

Unlike the instrumental Marxist interpretations, which tend to view the relationship between law and capital as unidimensional, structural Marxists reconsider the law in terms of its relationship with all classes; law is not an exclusive domain of the rich (Siegal, 1998: 239). If laws were designed just for the rich, why then are there numerous laws controlling corporate practices? For the structuralists, laws secure capitalism interests; any individual or organization that threatens capital will be controlled. Spitzer's writings represent a formidable contribution to structural Marxist explanations of crime. In his influential article "Towards a Marxian Theory of Deviance," Spitzer (1975) asked "why are problem populations criminalized." He maintained that criminalization depends on the degree to which problem populations are perceived to be threatening; the size of the population; its degree of political organization; and the effectiveness of alternate forms of social control. Criminals and deviants are selected from groups who create problems for those who rule. Although they victimize their own classes, "their problematic quality ultimately resides in their challenge to the bases and form of class rule" (1975: 640). Criminalization occurs when any one of the five following features of capitalism challenge: 1) capitalist modes of appropriating the product of human labour—when the poor steal from the rich; 2) social conditions under which capitalist production takes place— those who refuse or are unable to perform wage labour; 3) patterns of distribution and consumption in capitalist society—those who use drugs for escape and transcendence rather than for sociability and adjustment; 4) the process of socialization for productive and non-productive roles—youth who refuse to be schooled or those who deny the validity of family life; 5) the ideology that supports the functioning of capitalist society—proponents of alternate forms of social organization (1975: 642).

Problem populations are constructed from two sources: directly from the fundamental contradictions in the capitalist economy and indirectly from the contradictions or disturbances in institutions of social control. An illustration of direct influences is the existence of surplus labour populations. These populations support capital accumulation by providing a pool of labour that may be conveniently manipulated and drawn into the wage labour market. This population must be controlled to ensure profits for the owners. Both a large proletarian class and a surplus population hinder the advances of capitalism. Indirect creations of problem populations, for example, include the failure of the educational system to indoctrinate, discipline and prepare youths for wage labour. Youths who drop out, or alternatively students who develop insights critical of capitalism, are vulnerable to the processes of criminalization.

According to Spitzer (1975), there are two kinds of problem populations within capitalist economic orders: social junk and social dynamite. Social junk populations are relatively harmless to society, but their control exacts a substantial cost. They do not participate fully in the capitalist marketplace. Examples include the differentially abled members of society for whom institutional support is provided—physically, mentally or emotionally "disabled", alcohol or drug dependents, the elderly, and so on. The social dynamite category consists of those who have the potential to "call into question established relationships, especially relations of production and domination" (ibid.: 645). This group represents a political threat to the capitalist class and includes groups like the alienated, youth, politically volatile associations and the Communist Party.

How are these criminals or deviants controlled? Two strategies are employed in responding to challenges—integrative and segregative approaches. The integrative approaches are control efforts, such as probation and parole, ostensibly designed to integrate offenders into the community—efforts designed to bend the mind. Segregative approaches remove the troublemaker from the community if all else fails in order to inflict maximum punishment by breaking the body in warehouses of punishment. Likewise, Louis Althusser discussed structural Marxism in terms of the concept of social formation, which he describes as "a totality of instances articulated on the basis of a determinate mode of production. Social formations refers to the many 'structures within structures' that exist in any society; a 'totality of instances', different actions that occur within these spheres, which are ultimately based on the dominant mode of production—capitalism" (Resch, 1992).

Order, law and crime: Michalowski

In *Order, Law and Crime* (1985: vii), Raymond Michalowski suggested that the underlying elements of social organization—"particularly the production and distribution of economic, political and cultural services—largely shape the perception of what constitutes unacceptable social injury." It is the social construction of harm that gives form and character to the processes of law and injustice. He outlined four postulates about the nature of crime and its relationship to social order (1985: 14-17). First, social order precedes and shapes the nature of law and the definition of crime. Second, economic organizations shape and interact with other elements of social life in fundamental ways. Third, the study of crime should not be limited solely to those acts defined as criminal by the law, but should incorporate an analysis and comparison of officially designated crimes with other forms of socially harmful behaviour not designated as criminal. Fourth, criminal and other socially harmful behaviours emerge, for the most part, as individuals attempt to create meaningful lives as defined by their view of the world and the real and perceived alternatives for action that exist in a given economic, political and social context. Michalowski developed a compelling innovative framework within which to study crime. This model is divided into four units: modes of production, state law, individual characteristics and individual behaviour.

The mode of production in any society consists of three basic components: the elements of production, the relations of production and the dominant consciousness. The elements of production consist of a society's material base, its technology and its division of labour. These elements circumscribe the range of possibilities for producing the material required for social survival. The relations of production are the associations or the social component of the elements of production. These relations are shaped by the patterns of ownership of, and access to, the means and elements of production. Control over the elements of production governs access—the right to use and distribute wealth. Lastly, consciousness—ideas and concepts that explain the meaning of action—is characterized by the ways of thinking about the world taken for granted by most people in the society. Societies are characterized by a dominant consciousness—ideas rooted in the actual organization of society. A given group or class of people derive benefits from creating and maintaining interpretations of the existing mode of production, an interest in creating an ideology that explains the existing order as natural, appropriate or inevitable. Ideology establishes the dominant way of thinking. The goal of the dominant class in any society is to achieve a position of ideological hegemony, i.e., to dominate the everyday consciousness in adhering to the beliefs and activities associated with the dominant mode of production (Michalowski, 1985: 27-28).

Law-making is based upon political power. Access to law is shaped by society's mode of production and limitations on state action emerging from the dominant consciousness. Nonetheless, law protects the social order (ibid., 30). Law-making and law-enforcing institutions largely reflect the ideologies and exigencies of capitalist societies.

Individual characteristics consist of biology, constitutionality, cognitive and emotional processes, acquired skills and objective relations. The previous chapters have highlighted features Michalowski's model addresses. It is, however, the objective relations that warrant attention, especially since social relations locate the experiences and responses of actors. Variables like poverty, class, race, education and gender are manifestations (ibid., 37) of material relations. Objective relations demarcate the kinds of experiences which contribute to self-formation.

Three options exist for human behaviour: acts of adaptation, acts of rebellion and acts of personal or interpersonal maladaptation. For

Michalowski, the political economy defines what is adaptive, rebellious or maladaptive. In modern state societies, the institutions of state and law control rebellious and maladaptive forms of behaviour (ibid., 38). Throughout this model, Michalowski argues that the state takes on a capitalist form not because of simple conspiratorial designs among decision-makers, but more significantly because institutions themselves reflect capitalist economic relations. Clearly, capitalist institutions protect the capitalist economy and define what constitutes crime. Government investigations of corporate crimes are negligible in order to divert attention from corporate misbehaviour and skew public opinion away from practices which are significantly more threatening that common crimes.

Critiques of conflict: from liberal to radical indictments

Both conflict and radical perspectives have been subjected to considerable criticism. The following represents the litany of charges. First, for Gibbs and Erickson (1975), the central tenet of the conflict approach— that the powerful enact and impose laws for self-serving reasons—is nothing more than tautology. By definition, the powerful obviously control resources and the propositions that follow tend to be circular. Second, the causes of crime and deviance are never fully analyzed. It is appropriate to argue that criminalization is a consequence of the imposition of definitions, values and rules. But, does conflict theory apply to all kinds of deviant behaviour? According to Akers (1985: 27), conflict theory "is less appropriate to the analysis of the behaviour of those involved in many types of common-law crimes, usual deviations, and vices." As Hagan (1991: 130-131) reiterates, group conflict theory fares best in explaining types of crime about which consensus is minimal. Similarly, some laws are based on a consensual model of society, that is, supported by societal consensus (Gibbons, 1979: 188). Rules are not always expressions of powerful interests. Laws are often compromises. Rock (1974) charges that conflict theory is far too simplistic, leading to a naive understanding of the following: the complexities of law; the constraints of law even upon law-makers and law enforcers; the accommodative aspects of law rather than just the overwhelming emphasis on the coercive dimensions; and the multi-dimensional, relational and dynamic character of law. Third, as Pfohl (1985: 343) notes, pluralist conflict theory fails miserably in examining the historically based structural contexts within which power struggles occur. Fourth, as Taylor, Walton and Young (1973) describe, subordinates are too simplistically presented as cultural dopes all too compliant and passive. Turk, they insist, fails to explain how authority relations are linked to wider systems of social stratification. Similarly, Pfohl (1985: 343) admonished:

> Despite its analytic utility, Turk's theory is little more than a disruption of the way in which contemporary social life is hierarchically structured. Turk falsely equates the way things are with the way things naturally have to be. He fails to realize that social structures are historical creations.

Equally, radical criminology has been severely criticized. Textbooks and journals are replete with vituperative attacks, especially from more mainstream liberal and conservative criminologists. Interestingly, throughout the 1970s one easily notices the obvious exclusion of articles oriented towards a radical criminology in leading conventional publications. Also, in James Inciardi's *Radical Criminology: The Coming Crisis* (1980), contributors like Toby, Akers and Klockars engaged in a scathing review of radical criminology. For example, in his article "The New Criminology is the Old Baloney," Toby concluded: "The New Criminology was far from being new; rather, he continued, the new criminology is the explicit assertion of a relativism and a sentimentality that is as old as sympathy for members of the oldest profession" (1980: 131). Maintaining a similar level of enlightened candour, Carl Klockars (1980: 115) suggested:

> By presenting itself as ideal and as inevitable, of inexorably moving towards a relatively crime-free, unexploitive, unrepressive, unoppressive future, Marxist theory relieves itself of all responsibility, corruption, crime, and human abuse which has been and continues to be perpetrated in its name.

Similarly, Akers (1980: 138) concluded with the polemic, as a blueprint for the good society, the Marxist ideal was not reliable. Socialist societies have been unable to deliver on the promise of classlessness and economic equality.

Although mainstream liberal and conservative criminologies are disturbed with the ideological tenor of radical criminology, they fail to see how their own assertions, hyperboles and prognostications are loaded with bias. The most serious criticism directed at radical criminology concerns its lack of objectivity and scientific rigour. The new criminology has been dismissed as visionary, utopian (Nettler, 1974), fantasy, empirically shallow, biased, scholastically bankrupt (Inciardi, 1980: 8) and virtually non-falsifiable (Erickson and Gibbs, 1979). For Turk, the inherently dogmatic and partisan rhetoric of this perspective is politically rather than scientifically decided (Turk, 1979). Radical criminology is frequently condemned as inauthentic and righteous. For Hagan (1977), these writings are used as a catalyst for a classless society. In addition, Hagan (1991: 138) and Liska (1987: 205) argued that the above conflict propositions are difficult, if not impossible, to test.

Beyond judging and discarding the methodology of radical criminology as invalid according to the orthodoxy of positivism, mainstream designs and natural science criteria, the substance of radical criminology has also been criticized by Marxist social commentators. Just as Klockars (1978: 498) challenged the class bias of criminal justice systems, Greenburg (1975) questioned the uni-dimensionality of radical criminology. Throughout the 1970s, radical criminology had paid considerable attention to the links between law and the state, trying to move away from the instrumentalist Marxist position. Within an instrumentalist perspective, the structural relations between the ruling class and the state promote dominant capitalist interests. Accordingly, law is interpreted as a mechanism for reinforcing the affairs of the ruling class by state officials. Those who own and control the means of production, the capitalist class, secure the existing order through forms of legal domination. The legal system, like other forms of oppression, is viewed simply as a tool of the bourgeoisie. This instrumentalist stance risks exaggerating the unity of the ruling class. Also, it ignores the actual and rhetorical claims of relative independence of the state. Capitalist actions, however, do not necessarily involve the direct capture of the state by a single class (Pearce, 1978; Pashukanis, 1978). The capitalist state emerges out of capitalist relations, economic and non-economic. Within these collectivities, there is a "circulation of elites" (Bottomore, 1964: 42).

Beyond crime: law, conflict and the state

Additionally, when discussing the behaviour of law, it is unnecessary and misleading to capitalize simply on the courts, police and administrative bodies which grind out rules every day. Laws frequently originate as trade-offs or compromises, with the written word poorly reflecting those social forces that have the upper hand. Social forces may have different influences at different levels of legal acts. The legal system, in other words, need not mirror society itself. The interests that institutions, associations and corporate entities enjoy depend on what power, direct and indirect, can be marshalled behind them.

Analyses of historical origins and transformations of law show not only the deliberate ambiguities of sanctions but also the conflicts waged by powerful organizations to secure their respective interests. Many well-documented histories describe how law is pliant to the needs of powerful interests or influences (Hay et al., 1975; Hall et al., 1978; Donzelot, 1979; McMullan and Ratner, 1983). Miliband (1969: 49) conceptualizes the state as a system composed of diverse interacting institutions—polity, government, legislatures, political parties, bureaucracy, military, criminal justice and political elites. For Marx, the state arose out of contradictions. On the one hand, the state furnishes an illusory communal life based on customs and language. On the other hand, the state is the product of a social division of labour that further conditions the classes and makes one class dominant (Marx and Engels, 1947). In general, the state has been defined as an instrument for class rule, the executive committee of the ruling class. Despite these structural ties between the state and the dominant social class (Poulantzas, 1974), the state has advanced interventionist strategies promoting welfare infrastructures. Liberal welfare provisions continue to be directed towards disenfranchised populations. The state, therefore, must be examined beyond instrumental notions of creating conditions favourable to capital accumulation to include efforts designed to harmonize and reduce potential trouble.

The capitalist state fulfils two basic and often contradictory functions—accumulation and legitimization. For Panitch (1977) and O'Connor (1973: 6), the extended reproduction of a capitalist economy requires the increased intervention of the state in financing those services and facilitates which are too costly and unprofitable for private enterprise. This movement involves the expansion of state functions, of gaining legitimation in an imaginative and progressive manner in order to implicate the interests of the subordinate. Through state assistance the state represents itself as a neutral body, a benefactor of interests and a recipient of wholesale gratification. This regulation of consensus, although not directly related to capital accumulation, serves to maintain order. This pacification, in turn, creates a multiplicity of socio-political guarantors that foster public participation and encourage private or self-help initiatives. The impact of this brokerage role obfuscates conflicts and contests that result from asymmetrical relations and masquerades the political and ideological character of interventions. The logic of benign liberal welfare, supported by vocabularies of support and care, has transformed the social landscapes of social services.

Undoubtedly, the state is allowed to expand its social terrain and simultaneously promote private arrangements. This discourse "in the name of individuals and of civil society" (Pasquino, 1978: 44) emerges as a simple and therefore a more seductive theme that disguises the need to "subject, intern or banish everything that opposed its advance along the royal road of accumulation and proletarianisation" (ibid., 42). As Procacci (1978: 56) noted:

> We have rediscovered in the insane, the beggars, the paupers, the criminals, the women and children, the heretics ... the multiplicity of social islands to be dealt with on a local level, of modes of behaviour to be combatted, encouraged or promoted.

For example, interventionist legislation governing the poor "never went beyond the aims of protecting the labour market, disencumbering the taxpayer or generalising wage labour as a means of subsistence" (ibid., 58). In liberal society morality has been grafted on economics (Donzelot, 1979). Relief measures, as expressive features of liberalism, implicate and integrate disenfranchised citizens in the existing order through a series of ad hoc, incoherent and short-term responses. The participation of this largely marginalized constituency in the activities of state appendages is a poor substitute for the redistribution and equalization of resources. Subsidized housing, education, health and a growing sensitivity towards affirmative action have not, however, prevented current privatization trends in these and other areas. Harmony or cohesion enables the state to relinquish or reclaim historically acquired benefits. The War Measures Act, compulsory back-to-work legislation, wage restraints, means tests and the dismantling of trade unions attest to the unlimited control of the state and the elasticity and refashioning of liberalism. The criminal justice system maintains this ideology by focusing specifically on individuals who have been pathologized as social parasites to be feared and thereby diverts attention away from the crimes of the powerful (Reiman, 1979).

This political and cultural hegemony based on the ideology of possessive individualism strives to secure the consensus and participation of diverse stakeholders. The working class is held back from its own achievements. For instance, formal education instils relatively little awareness of subordinate positions and their inability to compete. As Karl Marx (1956: 78-79) clarified:

> The ideas of the ruling class are, in every age, the ruling ideas: that is, the class which is the dominant material force in society is at the same time its dominant intellectual force. The class that has the means of material production at its disposal, has control at the same time over the means of mental production, so that in consequence of the ideas of those who lack the means of mental production are, in general, subject to it.

A culture of marginality conveniently conformist and conflictive permeates legal, religious, educational and work institutions and "can be understood only in relation to a whole complex of other social activities" (Hook, 1933: 41). Marx (1956: 74-75) further explained:

> The production of ideas, conceptions and consciousness is at first directly interwoven with the material activity and the material intercourse of men, the language of real life. Representation and thought, the mental intercourse of men, still appear at this stage as the direct emanation of this material behaviour. The same applies to mental production as it is expressed in the political, legal, moral, religious and metaphysical language of a people.

In brief, during the development of a radical criminology the instrumental Marxist approach was predominant. Milovanovic (1990: 70) commented that during the 1980s the structural Marxist perspectives had become much more accepted.

Conclusions: behind conflict traditions

Notwithstanding their obvious weaknesses, conflict and radical approaches offer a sound framework for grappling with macro and micro processes of inequalities. Where do we go from here? Having reviewed the salient features of conflict and radical criminology, especially the relationship between crime and features of the political economy, culture and the state, we still remain puzzled. It is difficult to ascertain which conceptual path(s) to follow unless we become familiar with traditions and destinations. It is equally difficult to ask questions unless we can assess the analytic strengths and weaknesses of current texts. Hence, radical criminology has become increasingly reformulated incorporating anarchist, Marxist, feminist, left realist, post-modernist, peacemaking and eclectic interpretations (Milovanovic, 1990: 8).

In Canada, we too have witnessed in the 1980s a proliferation of progressive publications informed by the contributions of radical criminology (Taylor, 1983; West, 1984; Fleming, 1985; MacLean, 1986; Brickey and Comack, 1986; Ratner and McMullan, 1987; Caputo et al., 1989). In her incisive review, Snider delineates four major themes that have preoccupied critical criminologists in Canada in the past decade: the Canadian response to the crisis of capitalism, the role of ideology, the presence or absence of state autonomy in the operation of criminal justice system and critical feminist studies (1991: 141-2). In a brilliant essay written in 1985 entitled, "Inside the Liberal Boot: The Criminological Enterprise in Canada," well-respected critical criminologist, Robert Ratner warned against walking "lockstep inside the liberal boot" (ibid., 26). He suggested

> that much nurturing of the counter-hegemonic potential remains to be done before a truly radical criminology can unfold in Canada. For the moment, the possibility of such a development taking root institutionally is not encouraging. Segregated from the exercise of power, radical criminologists in Canada face problems of small numbers ... geographic dispersion, funding scarcities, and problems in attracting recruits, given the meagre resources at their command. Since universities and government ministries cannot be expected to provide either moral or material support, a broad left organization must be sought—one in which links are forged between academics, feminists, natives, prisoner's rights groups, radical lawyers, social workers, and civil liberties associations.

Finally, DeKeseredy and MacLean (1993: 364) have more recently restated a theme so prominent in early Canadian critical criminology, a theme clearly evident in Ratner's earlier admonitions—the need for inclusivity within the pedagogy, praxis and scholarship of Canadian critical criminology.

In the early 1980s Gord West and his colleagues at the Ontario Institute in Studies in Education, University of Toronto, collaborated in promoting well-attended critical ethnographic seminars designed to confront social justice concerns. Students, faculty and the wider community participated in incorporating strategies to overcome fundamental inequalities perpetrated by misogyny, class elitism, racism, homophobia and anti-lesbianism (Visano, 1982). Notably absent during these formative years of Canadian radical criminology was the participation of left liberals and well-funded state sponsored criminological consultants. Moreover in 1989, with the inaugural

issue "Critical Criminology in Canada," *Journal of Human Justice* editor
Brian MacLean (1989: 2) summarized the agenda, direction and commitment
of critical criminology in Canada:

> The struggle for justice, a struggle in which critical
> criminologists are engaged, is a class struggle that transcends
> the boundaries of the criminal justice system, transcends the
> limits of criminological discourse, and transcends the state
> as the only object of analysis.

The Human Justice Collective was committed to the broader study of
social justice in Canadian society within a collectivism, an orientation that
encourages the development of networks and alliances in the struggle for
justice (DeKeseredy and MacLean (ibid., 365). Critical criminology in Canada
fully realizes, perhaps more than its American counterpart, that analyses
that move beyond the ethnocentric bias of criminology in English-speaking
countries are long overdue. Much effort is needed in incorporating the
contributions of practitioners, scholars or revolutionaries from Africa, South
America, Asia and Mediterranean Europe. Also, the Journal of Human Justice
and in general Canadian critical criminology have remained vigilant and
prudent in not allowing the petty arrogance and self-serving careerist
intentions of a few destroy a rich tradition. Admittedly, the collective in
Canada has never subscribed to a single normative script, but neither should
it render itself vulnerable to shallow divisive politics. Surely, the left
recognizes dangerous contradictions inherent in appropriating the language
of praxis by rogues who easily surrender to state sponsored initiatives in
order to aspire to lofty heights through prolific writings, mercenaries who
seize every opportunity to include those who have been historically silenced
in order to speak on their behalf, to sacrifice the seductive glamour of a
short-lived media blitz that forge, instances of self-aggrandizement. Critical
criminology is well aware of these limitations and strives to be accountable
if not collegial to wider constituencies. Critical criminology in Canada enjoys
a very robust and distinguished tradition that cannot be so whimsically and
carelessly dismissed as a fad or as fashionable, as one sociologist argued in
a paper read at an annual learned conference of sociologists and
anthropologists in Winnipeg in 1986. In the 1990s such claims still resonate
rudely among the more privileged academicians. Besides the obviously
solid contributions of the *Journal of Human Justice*, few inroads were
made in other Canadian-based, non-criminology oriented journals advancing
an equally critical examination of the state, culture and law.

Throughout the 1980s and continuing into the 1990s, there is an increasing appreciation of a return to the writings of Marx and Engels. To improve the quality of theoretical inquiry, a closer reading, truer to Marxist thought is encouraged. The benefits are many. From Marx's dynamic social theory we soon realize: the importance of culture, which has frequently been ignored in criminology; heightened attention to ideological issues; the movement beyond a static economic determinism; the significance of human agency in the historical constructions, to name only a few.

The Contributions
of Marx and Engels

Introduction: crime and culture in context

Radical criminology would be incomplete without an introduction to the writings of Karl Marx (1818-1883) and Frederick Engels (1820-1895). Traditional texts on deviance and crime mistakenly portray Marxism simply as a substantive variant of conflict theory. These texts are too easily satiated with glossy encyclopedic overviews of neatly packaged and sterile descriptions of Marxist contributions. Likewise, Marxist analyses are often juxtaposed against Weberian explanations. However, the contributions of Marx and Engels are far too influential to be dismissed as irrelevant or reduced readily to a conflict theory of deviance or crime. As Hinch (1989: 7) compellingly argued:

> The bottom line is that Marxism is not a conflict theory and treatment of it as such in the textbooks deprives students of the opportunity to ask and seek answers to different questions than those that can be derived from conventional theoretical models. The treatment of Marxist criminology as just another variant of conflict criminology domesticates it.

Subsuming the scholarship of Karl Marx and Friedrick Engels under the radical or conflict paradigm risks trivializing the importance of their writings. The challenge, therefore, is to ensure a more balanced exposure to Marxian analysis (ibid., 8).

Marx and Engels are not customarily associated with analyses of crime or deviance; nor, as many commentators have noted, was deviance or crime ever a central focus of their inquiries. Nevertheless, their writings continue to supply invaluable conceptual tools for probing the intersections of crime and culture by detailing the significance of capital and its attendant ideologies. By unravelling and clarifying historical trends contextualizing substantive issues like crime and deviance, Marx and Engels provided a systematic history, sociology and political economy of order in industrial societies. These approaches do not just encourage structural and historical perspectives, but they also provide a substantive account of specific social practices.

In general, the theoretical perspectives of Marx and Engels continue to make profound contributions to sociological thinking. Their work is remarkably significant because of the unquestionable depth and breadth of their ideas, and because these views have stimulated, and continue to encourage, intellectual responses and practical agendas for action. Unequivocally, an appreciation of the relevance of Marxian analyses to the study of crime or deviance demands that prudent attention be paid to political economy. That is, even at a modicum level, efforts to incorporate conceptually the production of wealth in relation to the activities of the state are long overdue. This centrality of political economy is explained in the following review of more specific themes—the Marxian conception of history, the primacy of class analysis, alienation and ideology. As noted in the previous chapter, radical conflict approaches moved beyond the close-minded canons of conventional texts and strove to capture some enormous insights of Marxist ideas. And yet, mainstream liberal as well as conservative criminology continue to ignore these insights while blithely favouring a cornucopia of barren illustrations that accommodate vulgar voyeurism, infectious lethargies and ill-informed scholarship. In addition, research exercises supported by crass corporate commercialism or state sponsored funding grants of institutes, commissions and projects promote the study of deviance or crime in a way that vilifies Marx and Engels.

The previous chapter presented various strains of contemporary conflict analyses of deviance. Moving beyond these insights, this chapter begins to bridge the limitations of orthodox approaches by more systemically considering the writings of Marx and Engels.

One cannot investigate specific actors and activities (conformist or deviant) without fully locating them within their wider social, historical, political and economic contexts. Marx and Engels succeed brilliantly in addressing generic processes and structures that clarify the social organization of society, the conditions and consequences of historical forces and changing economic orders. Towards this end, the writings of Marx and Engels are catalytic in stimulating further critical inquiries.

Marx's understanding of history

Marx argued that phenomena cannot be understood as things, *sui generis*, in terms of their inherent attributes, but more importantly they must be analyzed according to their social relationships. Consequently, it may be conceded that Marx's conception of history generally falls within the rubric of historiography. Marx's historiography understood and depicted the concrete nature of human societies and the changes which they have undergone as well as the many interrelated concomitants—class organizations, modes of thought, technology, politics, economics etc. Marx was a modern historian who searched for laws of motion, recognizing dynamic processes in which each moment is new in the sense that it possesses creative characteristics. One of his greatest abilities as an historian was his perspicacious appreciation of "totality." As Marx (Ryazanoff, 1963: 170) described:

> If we ask ourselves why a given principle made its appearance in the 11th century, or in the 18th century and not in some other, we shall find it necessary to study with close attention what people were like in the 11th or in the 18th century, as the case may be ... what does the study of all these questions mean but to write the actual and everyday history of the people of each century.

Like Georg Hegel (1770-1831), Marx started from a conception of a world ordered by rational laws of nature. Marx conceived history as a process of evolution of humanity; he aimed at discovering the laws thereof (Marx and Engels, Vol II, 1962: 273). Briefly, societies are defined by the way they produce; relations between people are defined by the way they develop their productive forces (Marx and Engels, 1947: 7). In social production, people enter relations that are determined by but independent of their will. These relations are determined by the evolutionary phase of the forces of production. All these relations form the economic structure of society. The manner in which people relate to one another while producing their material means of life support shapes consciousness.

Material, therefore, is foundational. For Marx the materialist conception of history begins with the premise that all of human history is the existence of living individuals. Action is, in part, the product of the material world outside the individual and, in part, a result of the actor's own knowledge of how to control the material world—which she or he gets through experience. The history of being, therefore, determines the history of thought.

Gradual quantitative transformations in the characteristics of a particular order of relations lead to a change in the quality of these relations. New methods of production appear as old ones disappear. Every society has a set of economic institutions and social relationships allocating the production, distribution and consumption of goods. The notion that economic institutions constitute the critical variable in social organization is highlighted in Marx's historical materialism. Changes in material factors determine the direction of historical change for the whole society. According to this "materialist doctrine" (Fromm, 1961: 18-19), change is due to the contradictions between productive forces and existing social organizations. History is characterized by these ongoing struggles. Unlike Hegel, Marx employs practical and concrete forms in his transition to the materialist conception of history. When a mode of production or social organization hampers given productive forces, a society will choose such forms of production which fit the new set of productive forces and develop them.

In *Marxism and History* (1973), Helmut Fleischer provided a lucid, succinct and analytic examination of three Marxist approaches to the theory of history in order to carefully reconstruct Marxist philosophy as a "humanist-emancipatory philosophy of practice." These three approaches—history as a whole (anthropological), history as laws (nomological) and history as practice (pragmatological)—are certainly complementary and ultimately constitute Marx's "theory of history" (ibid., 361).

In the *Early Writings of 1844*, Marx outlined a general, two-stage anthropological definition of the meaning of history: history as the unification of existence and being and "history as the humanization of the ape" (1973: 14-18). Concerning the first stage, the concept of history evident in the *Paris Manuscripts* presented history as a "totality with a definite trend, combining past and future in a living unity." It is also presented as a "uniform process with a recognizable beginning and an end knowable in advance," a goal towards which the endeavours of the whole community in history were directed (ibid., 16). In this process, individuals are characterized as total and self-aware actors (ibid.). Years later, Marx and Engels discussed the second state, a return to humanization in a more "naturalistic" context (ibid., 17-18), and a discussion of the genesis of a new species. Essentially, the prehistory of human society concludes with the bourgeoisie, the last socially antagonistic form of economic development. According to Engels, humans finally depart from the animal kingdom by the conscious organization of social production, in which production and distribution are planned (ibid., 19). Anthropologically, the transition to socialism meant that individual struggles for existence ceased. Humans thus grapple with conditions as humans and not as animals; they will consequently make history with full consciousness and live harmoniously united with themselves (ibid., 20). There is no direct link between advances in productivity and advances in humanity, for increased productivity almost invariably implies increased destructivity (ibid., 77).

As outlined in the introduction to the *Critique of Political Economy* and in the introduction to and epilogue of *Capital*, history was construed as a process of change in the structures of social relations that occur in adherence to certain definite laws. This approach had produced a view of history as highly material and as a process of cumulative developments of the productive force and productive relations governed by objective laws and social relations that were not influenced by human intentions (ibid., 29).

Furthermore, history evolves as a natural process. Under the conditions of capitalist production, people do not act as individuals but as personifications of economic categories, fulfillers of roles laid down by definite class relations and interests. In the *Outlines of a Critique of National Economy 1844*, Engels wrote that the law of competition was purely a natural law, a law that depended on the lack of consciousness of those involved (ibid., 32). Thus, natural growth inherent in social processes like capitalism existed above human circumstances, that is, external to people. People were products of traditional social relations, and since their social behaviour followed certain patterns, they were calculable like natural physical processes.

In the *Theses of Feuerbach*, and other writings of 1845-46, another historical perspective was put forward that is self-critically directed against earlier ideas of 1844 (anthropological) and sets fundamental limits to the later references regarding the underlying laws in historical processes (nomological). Essentially, the *Writings of 1845-46* provided the following propositions of the order of historical process. First, history is represented not as a closed program but as an open process of continuing synthesis in a unique situation (ibid., 23). Second, the central theme is not the idea of any process or the form that it takes but the subjective activity of human beings, their production, the meaning of their products to them and their further stimulated activities. Third, the accountability of the activities of human objects or individuals is concentrated on the idea of the wants and interests transmitted to them in practice by existing subject-object relations, as well as inter-subjective relations (ibid., 24). The Marx of the *Theses of Feuerbach* assumed a standpoint of practical subjectivity and at the centre of this subjectivity were human needs. This discussion of the practical approach to the philosophy of history highlighted the impulses or driving forces behind historical changes. Conducive to, and perhaps imperative for an intelligent discussion of a "subjective driving force" was an articulation " in practically relevant fashion of the self understanding of those active in making history" (ibid., 38). What leads or motivates activities must be located at the dynamic centre—the human subjects, from the view of their active impulses and their relations both to objects and other subjects that share in their activities or oppose them.

How then should history be studied? First, it must be understood that history occurs under definite, empirically demonstrable conditions, and that "individuals are productively active in a definite way and accordingly, enter into definite social relations" (ibid., 21). In their analyses of history, Marx and Engels acted as "empirical observers" (ibid., 23).

The above three diverse but not mutually exclusive approaches assist the reader in moving away from any over-simplification of history. Marxist historical knowledge involves the imputation of meaning and not simply a barren prosaic chronicle of determinism. Historical inquiry can be of the utmost value in furnishing concrete, accurate and discriminating data for understanding experiences and social development as they are created and modified by the interactions of various types of institutions, forces and struggles.

The primacy of class analysis

In *Capital*, Marx perceptively used the concept of socio-economic class as a tool for historical analysis. Particularly, he maintained that class inequality is central to the understanding of capitalist societies. Classes are defined by the social relationships that incorporate political, ideological and material influences. But a more compelling definition of social class includes the modes of production. These dominant modes of production include social classes. Correspondingly, there are many modes of production—primitive communism, slavery, feudalism, capitalism, socialism and communism. Under capitalism specifically, there is a basic class struggle between those who own capital—landlords, capitalists, industrialists etc.— and the working class. Additionally, there is the lumpenproletariat, described by Marx and Engels (1969: 442) in the following excerpt:

> Alongside decayed roues with dubious means of subsistence
> and of dubious origin, alongside ruined and adventurous
> offshoots of the bourgeoisie, were vagabonds, discharged
> soldiers, discharged jailbirds, escaped gallery slaves,
> swindlers, mountebanks, lazzaroni, pickpockets, tricksters,
> gamblers, brothel keepers, porters, literati, organ-grinders,
> rag-pickers, knife grinders, tinkers, beggars—in short the whole
> indefinite, disintegrated mass, thrown hither and thither, which
> the French term la boheme. . .

Essentially, this group is comprised of the unfit, the unwashed, classless idlers, predators and reactionary mercenaries.

Briefly, economic class is determined by one's economic position within the given mode of production. The economic structures determine relations. People have made themselves by their own labour, using intelligence and creative talents to dominate by a process of production. The process of production is a collective effort, not an individual accomplishment. But, the ruling class owns the means of production. As explicated in *Capital*, the mode of production consists of: (a) means of production—technology, labour, monetary system, land tools, machinery—the raw materials for producing commodities; and (b) social relations of production—the many ways in which members of society relate both to the possession of the means of production and to the distribution of commodities (Marx, 1969). Within the capitalist mode of production, there are essentially two classes who are engaged in struggle, those who own the means of production— the ruling class or the bourgeoisie—and those who work for the owner or the proletariat. The bourgeoisie profit from the exploitation of workers through poor working conditions, low wages, long hours and never sharing any profit. The bourgeoisie, represented by a minority of individuals, enjoy the profits and re-invest it in the business to yield further profit. Members of the proletariat must sell themselves; they live as long as they find work. In reality, these individuals are commodities like every other article of commerce—exposed to the fluctuations of the market (Marx, 1978: 479). Because the bourgeoisie own and re-invest profit, modern labourers sink more deeply below the conditions of existence of their own class (ibid., 483). The working class, which possesses nothing but its power to labour, sells it to capital in return for subsistence. Whenever the worker does not secure the surplus that the capitalist desires, he or she is discharged (Tucker, 1978: 205). A "commodity exchange value" (Tucker, 1978: 208) characterizes the relationship between the worker and the capitalist. Their interactions are shaped by "economic relations" (ibid., 203) and they need each other in order to survive (ibid., 210). As Marx (ibid.) described:

> The interests of the Capitalist and those of the worker are therefore, one and the same, assert the bourgeoisie and their economists. Indeed, the worker perishes if Capital does not employ him. Capital perishes if it does not exploit labour power.

In *Capital*, Marx demonstrated that the form of production in capitalist society is hierarchically structured—serving the needs of private capital at the expense of labour (Marx, 1965: 443). The tendency of capital is always directed towards the accumulation, maintenance and reproduction of profit (ibid., 1965: 709). Capitalism can only be presented in market terms, in the spheres of unequal exchange, unequal competition and class conflict (ibid., 1969: 1-9). In such a system of exchange, where humans enter into determined relations of production, the social relations of individuals are transformed into relations of material things. The development of industrial capitalism has led to increased human misery, the uprooting of peasants and the dehumanization of workers through the introduction of technology. On the one hand, processes of mechanization have expanded private capital, while on the other hand, these same processes have pauperized the working class.

Clearly then, the social function of capital is coercion. Relations between labour and capital are antagonistic. Capital supervises while labour expands production for profit; and, capital maintains a constant supply of labour while reducing the costs which in turn forces the greatest amount of labour out of the production process. As Marx ([1859] 1969, 503-504) noted in the preface to the "Contribution to the Critique of Political Economy":

> The sum total of these relations of production constitutes the economic structure of society, the real foundation, on which rises a legal and political superstructure and to which correspond definite forms of consciousness. The mode of production of material life conditions the social, political and intellectual life in general. It is not the consciousness of men that determines their being but on the contrary, their social being determines their consciousness.

In capitalism, production is not planned by the producers themselves but by those who own and control the means of production. Workers execute the tasks, all of which have been planned in their absence (Marx, 1965: 449). The underlying principles of capitalist system consist of the maintenance and perpetuation of a class society through the power of capital. With the division of labour, the workers' own deeds become transformed as alien, oppositional and controlling forces (Marx and Engels, 1969: 35, 39).

Alienation

What then are the effects of capitalism? The ways and conditions of labour affect the minds, bodies and social relations of workers. Central to Marx's concept of human character are his perspectives on alienation. A person's psychology is inseparable from his or her material well-being. Three concepts explain this integration: labour, the social person and species being. Although labour is a physical activity in which actors accommodate to their physical and social circumstances, labour also involves mental aspects. By acting upon their environments, actors also engage in a dynamic process of changing their social realities. Marx (1973: 102) noted: "At the end of every labour-process, we get a result that already existed in the imagination of the labourer at its commencement." For Marx, people are social beings developing consciousness of themselves through interactions and labour. The essence of the person is not an abstraction, "the real nature of man is the totality of social relations" (ibid., 83). In effect, reality is socially constructed. Lastly, Marx indicated that it is through labour that people become conscious of their species being. Through an imaginative appreciation of one's work, the worker realizes his or her own nature. To reiterate, "life is not determined by consciousness but consciousness by life" (Marx, 1973b: 47). But as expected, labour cannot be appreciated by actors when they are themselves alienated from it. Labour becomes simply a means to an end, an objectification of both physical and mental activities. Therefore, Marx's theory of alienation incorporates many categories—exploitation, degradation, etc. Marx often spoke of alienated life as a condition in which human beings fail to affirm, confirm or actualize themselves. Alienation is an estrangement from, a disharmony and a dissatisfaction with the human essence. Individuals are far from being considered as species beings; instead, they occupy a space external to their original independence (Marx, 1978: 43). Alienated workers are actors "robbed of all actual life content," rendered "worthless and devoid of dignity, degraded and enslaved" (Wood, 1981: 9).

Alienation is a condition that emerges from "the kind of work that destroys a person's individuality and transforms him or her into a thing" (Fromm, 1961: 48). In general, the essence of one's humanity is one's capacity to labour. Through labour, therefore, one gives expression to one's very essence. When that capacity to labour—when that which makes the individual truly human—is bought, sold or taken away as with the division of labour, individual character is lost (Marx, 1978: 479). By becoming appendages of the machine, people are forced to become proportionately less human. This dehumanizing process is particularly evident under capitalism. Human labour is reduced to a relatively cheap commodity. During this process of exchange, labour loses its unique and humanistic quality and simply becomes a means to an end. For the capitalist, the end is making profit, while for the worker the end is simply survival. Whenever labour is redefined and actualized as only a means to an end rather than an end in itself, alienation emerges and false consciousness is created.

It is in reference to Marx's discussion of private property that one appreciates alienation as economically determined. As Marx (1848 [1965]: 44) analyzed:

> the essential condition for the existence, and for the sway of bourgeois class is the formation and augmentation of capital. In bourgeois society, capital is independent and has individuality while the living person is dependent and has no individuality.

Private property is the source and consequence of alienated labour (ibid., 79). It is both the product of alienated labour and the means by which labour alienates itself. Private ownership prevents workers from expressing socially their creative abilities. The enslaved worker is subjected to forces beyond his or her control or understanding. Succinctly, alienation is the context: the worker is alienated from the object he or she produces; the labour product is confronted as alien, as a power independent of the producer. As workers produce more, they move even further from their inner selves (ibid., 1978: 72). For Marx, there is the alienation of the worker's product and the alienation in the activity that produces it (ibid., 74). The product of one's labour, the object produced, is no longer part of the process of creating. The object of labour is in fact the objectification of one's species life (ibid., 77). Estranged labour removes the species life, transforming the human advantage over animals into a disadvantage. To the extent that people are deprived of relations to sources of life, their interactions with fellow workers are also alienated. For Marx (ibid., 75), this activity does not belong to the worker—it is a process which acts in opposition to him or her. Workers and their work belong to someone else. The social conditions of work prevent human beings from realizing themselves. Clearly, workers lack access to self-activity and self-expression. Reflexivity, therefore, is difficult.

Freedom from alienation requires a fundamental transformation in the domain of work—the abolition of bourgeois property. Bourgeois property is the final expression of producing and appropriating products based on inequalities—the exploitation of many by a few. Consequently, bourgeois property, as a meaningful expression of the social power of capital (ibid., 485), would have to be eliminated. As clarified by Marx (1978: 717):

> The proletariat seizes the public power, and by means of this transforms the socialized means of production, slipping from the hands of the bourgeoisie, into public property. By this act, the proletariat frees the means of production from the character of capital they have thus far borne, and gives their socialized character complete freedom to work itself out. Socialized production upon a predetermined plan becomes henceforth possible. The development of production makes the existence of different classes of society henceforth an anachronism. In proportion as anarchy in social production vanishes, the political authority of the state dies out.

To repeat, workers do not own the means of production. Instead, they sell their labour power in return for wages. This system of labour displays four relations that are at the core of Marx's theory of alienation. First, workers are alienated from their productive activity, that is, they play no part in deciding what to do and how to do it. Second, workers are alienated from the product of this activity—having no control over what is made and what happens to the product. Third, workers are alienated from other human beings as competition and indifference replace cooperation. And fourth, workers are alienated from the distinctive potential inherent in being a human being. Alienation is, therefore, ideologically reinforced. Alienation is related to the prevailing economic conditions and the attendant prevalent ideas.

Ideology

Marx and Engels made impressive strides towards understanding the nature of ideology by highlighting how systems of ideas are both illusory and socially regulating. Ideas are historical products (Marx, 1930). One first gains an appreciation of what constitutes ideology by recognizing that labour has both a material and mental component (Marx and Engels, 1962). One's mental labour, or the production of ideas, is structured by one's material conditions. Specifically, for Marx and Engels, all manifestations of ideology—morality, law, religion, art, metaphysics and corresponding forms of consciousness—no longer retain the semblance of independence (ibid., 47). These moral codes comprise a society's superstructure, the glue that binds together the economic base or substructure of that society (Allahar, 1986: 610). Since the mental is governed by the material, the division of labour as "a productive alienative structure" results in both the objectification of the products of man's labour and the reification of consciousness and thought itself (Carlsnaes, 1981: 43).

Ideological manifestations of mental labour become illusory when individuals purport that ideas, rather than being determined by material conditions, exist independently of them. When ideology is relegated to a sphere beyond the world of human praxis, it takes on a distorted dimension; workers and "their circumstances appear upside down, as in a camera obscura" (ibid., 47). Marx and Engels move beyond a discussion of the nature of ideology towards a consideration of its functions by analyzing class. Note the following analysis:

> The ideas of the ruling class are, in every age, the ruling ideas: that is, the class which is the dominant material force in society is at the same time its dominant intellectual force. The class which has the means of material production at its disposal, has control at the same time over the means of mental production, so that in consequence the ideas of those who lack the means of mental production are, in general, subject to it. The dominant ideas are nothing more than the ideal expression of the dominant material relationships, the dominant material relationships grasped as ideas, and thus of the relationships which make one class the ruling one; they are consequently the ideas of its dominance (Marx and Engels, 1962: 93).

As this quotation shows, the ruling class is extremely influential in the production of ideas. Because the ruling class has a monopoly over the means of material and mental production, it will regulate the production and distribution of ideas in a way that is consistent with protecting its own interests in the field of material production. Anton Allahar (1986: 617) clarifies:

> ruling class ideologies set limits to the consciousness of the ruled classes, or stated differently, they create false consciousness. Since ruling class ideologies are linked to practical political and economic interests, they will portray those interests as universal. To maintain social order and stability, it is important that those who benefit from such order and stability, those with a direct stake in maintaining the status quo, convince the less privileged that the system works to the mutual benefit of everyone in it.

For Marx, ideology is viewed negatively as a set of beliefs that serves to justify and legitimize the rule of the few over the many (Allahar, 1986: 610). In effect, the prevailing ideas of the dominant class function to sustain class interests and to encourage silence.

The concept of the dialectic

Intimately connected with Marx's materialist approach is the dialectical perspective to the study of history. Emerging from the works of Hegel and Marx, the dialectic represents a world view that is distinguished by a many salient characteristics. First, it focuses on the concrete, phenomena which are embedded in a social world characterized by contradictory relationships and interactions. Accordingly, the concrete constitutes an ongoing process of struggle—one of movement, development and change. This approach does not reduce everything to matter; rather, in opposition to idealism, matter is not a product of the mind but mind is the product of matter. Laws governing matter are not mechanistic but instead dialectical. These laws are the transformation of quantity into quality, and, conversely, the law of penetration of opposites and the law of negation—the reconciliation of contradictions producing fresh contradictions.

In *German Ideology* [1845], Marx identified the relationship between people and their environment as dialectical. For example, Marx claims that "circumstances make men just as much as men make circumstances" (Marx and Engels, 1947: 59). Likewise in the *Eighteenth Brumaire* Marx ([1853] 1969b: 13) wrote: "Men make their own history, but they do not make it just as they please; they do not make it under circumstances chosen by themselves, but under circumstances directly encountered, given and transmitted from the past." For Marx there is a dialectical relationship between structure and agency. Man is both determined and determining. As he described, "men are the producers of their conceptual ideas ... as they are conditioned by a definite development of their productive forces" (Marx, 1973b: 47). Consistent with the early humanist conceptions, Marx believed that actors create social structures which in turn shape them. Informed by Hegel, Marx maintained that each system produces within itself seeds of its own destruction. Within this dialectic, there is a tendency, a thesis in the social world; and there is a counter-tendency, antithesis, which will overcome the thesis. Elements of the two combine to form a new third tendency—a synthesis. In the course of history, as the dialectical method unfolds, "what the bourgeoisie produces are its own gravediggers. Its fall and the victory of the proletariat are equally inevitable" (Marx, [1848] 1965: 38).

Dialectics, in its broadest sense, is the scientific method applied concretely, consistently and comprehensively; a method for revealing what Engels called the interrelatedness of things. "Wherever the dialectic method is applied, it presupposes not the attitude of contemplation but of action ... only in practice (praxis) can problems be solved" (Hook, 1933: 38). In the present context, the notion of the dialectic is significant for two reasons. First, it allows one to recognize the subjectivity of persons. Specifically, by adopting a dialectical way of thinking, one can more fully appreciate the importance of individuals in all phases of social life. They are not simply objects which are routinely acted upon. Rather, as beings embedded in society, persons play a crucial role in all dimensions of social transformation. Their real-life experiences constitute moments in a continuous process of societal development and change. Concomitantly, the notion of the dialectic provides the underlying philosophical foundation of the concept of praxis.

Praxis is more than simply political involvement. It represents the informed action or behaviour of individuals emerging from the dialectical relationship between practice and theory. Practice is the concrete context within which social experience is created. Theory is the critical analysis of actions or ideas emerging from social experience. Praxis occurs when individuals, after critically reflecting upon some action, consciously engage in specific forms of behaviour with the goal of initiating social change.

The *Communist Manifesto* is a vivid incorporation of this new philosophy of history. In its introduction Marx's message is clear regarding the lessons of history: "The history of all hitherto existing society is the history of class struggle" (Marx [1848] 1965: 13). Throughout the manifesto Marx re-iterated a central theme—capitalism is not a permanent state but simply the latest phase of historical development. Essentially, Marx ([1848], 1965: 54) argued that "the history of all past society has consisted of the development of class antagonisms, and antagonisms that assumed different forms at different epochs." The manifesto demonstrated that class war depends upon social and economic relations; the struggle of the proletariat is a necessary phenomenon within history, just as the struggle of the bourgeoisie was in the earlier days. The proletariat, as the agent of change, must confront the economic and political power of the bourgeoisie. The transition from one economic state to the next level of production demands a re-arrangement of the entire society. As Marx urged ([1848], 1969a: 54):

> The first step in the revolution by the working class, is to raise the proletariat to the position of the ruling class, to win the battle of democracy ... the proletariat will wrest all capital from the bourgeoisie, to centralize all instruments of production in the hands of the state.

Additionally, he suggested: "When the worker cooperates in a planned way with others, he strips off the fetters of his individuality and develops the capabilities of his species" (Marx, 1967: 447).

Marx and Engels on crime

Beirne and Messerschmidt, in *Criminology* (1991: 344-349), assembled a rich review of the claims of Marx and Engels in reference to crime and criminalization. Although a formal theory of crime is absent in the writings of Marx and Engels (Hirst, 1972), there are several observations that warrant attention. For Marx, economic relations determine the manner in which state institutions structure order. Because of the prevailing inequalities, social control is manipulated. The ruling class (Tucker, 1978: 78), as a whole, can organize non-economic institutions as well, such as the law and the criminal justice, with coercive and persuasive devices. Law and its attendant ideological framework are tools of the bourgeoisie in perpetuating illusions of neutrality, fairness and equality (Marx [1868], 1969). The promise of law is a persuasive bourgeois accommodation invented to disguise coercion. As will be argued in Chapter 6, the law tenaciously alludes to promises of freedom and equality in a limited mythological sense.

In his article "Capital Punishment" ([1853], 1956: 230), Marx suggested that crime is produced by fundamental anti-social conditions. That is, instead of glorifying the hangman who executes many criminals, there is a "necessity for deeply reflecting upon an alteration of the system that breeds these crimes" (ibid.). As Beirne and Messerschmidt (1991: 345) pointed out:

> Marx and Engels' sociological analysis of the links between crime and capitalism contained three roughly separate dimensions: criminalization as a violation of natural or human rights, crime and demoralization, and crime and primitive rebellion.

In his empirical work, "The Condition of the Working Class in England in 1844," Engels said that the economic position of the working class was instrumental in generating crime. Since the proletariat was not allowed to pursue their aspirations and were constantly prevented from enjoying the benefits of the economic order, they would strike out at the brutality of the bourgeoisie. Again, the conditions of capitalism—exploitation and pauperization—lead to demoralization that in turn leads to crime (Engels, [1845], 1975). Also, Marx and Engels reiterated that the abolition of private ownership would witness the disappearance of crimes.

In the "Productivity of Crime," Marx noted that the most important function of crime in society is its contribution to temporary economic stability in an economic system that is inherently unstable. Marx (1969b: 375-376) wrote:

> A criminal produces crime.... The criminal produces not only crimes, but also criminal law ... the criminal moreover produces the whole of the police and of criminal justice, constables, judges ... and all these different lines of business.... The criminal produces an impression, partly moral and partly tragic ... and in this way renders a "service" by arousing the moral and aesthetic feelings of the public.

From crimes of capital to carceral cultures

Throughout the bourgeois culture, the masses of people are educated in ways that encourage an acceptance of their own subordination. Moreover, the prevailing culture of capitalism hinders the development of class consciousness. As Marx advised: "Your very ideas are but the outgrowth of your bourgeois production and bourgeois property" (Tucker, 1978: 487).

This dominant culture is replete with illusions that enhance alienation. Alienation, a condition of the material environment, denies creativity and restricts choices.

The prevailing values of liberal democratic cultures are fundamentally material. Culture surrenders to the material; material productive forces shape cultural values. As Hook (1933: 41) explained: "Marx realized that every culture is a structurally interrelated whole, and that any institutional activity, say religion or law, can be understood only in relation to a whole complex of other social activities." Specifically, in our society the dominant culture is expressed through material consumption. Materialism is not simply the product of socialization but, more importantly, materialism is an imperative of the economic order. The conditions of materialism constitute concretized forms of existence. Materialism, as a ubiquitous feature of our culture, speaks on our behalf; that is, our sense of self emerges from material dependence. It is used as a code to guide and classify the ways in which we display our experiences, imagination and consciousness. As a condition, materialism subjugates, enslaves and binds. Much effort is invested in conforming to the ways we appear, what we possess—fixated through materialism, resulting in self-enclosure. Thus, identities and self-worth are carved by an enslaving materialism. As a society, Canadians invest heavily in carving out conformity as measured according to material possessions. Fixation becomes self-enclosure; materialism overwhelms as it mediates mental, emotional and social expressions. Although people living in advanced capitalist societies are not forced to be material, they consent to be acquisitive. Materialism is personal to the extent that the dominant culture celebrates possessive individualism. Materialism manipulates especially as actors are expected to display an insatiable appetite for material gains. Those who do not have great material goods feel responsible for their frustration and sense of failure.

Materialism is individualized—assessed in reference to individual efforts. The sanctity of the marketplace symbolizes advanced capitalist societies. Within series of exchanges in the marketplace of social relations, people treat each other as objects with prospective material value. Society is atomized as people are respected as individualized, independent, self-reliant—as winners or losers competing for more material. Wholesale consumerism objectifies the individual who is shaped according to material results of production and reproduction. Individuals are transformed into objects allied to products. Consequently, relations of production quantify the individual.

Culture is a function of underlying productive structures. As demonstrated earlier, Marx maintained that materialism impacts on consciousness. The private worlds of mental productions suffer from estrangement. This is evident in the unequal access to cultural capital—socialization into the cultural heritage, language facility and knowledge in general. Cultural capital refers to literature, science, religion, art, language and all symbolic systems (Dawson, 1983: 35). As Marx (1969a: 304) described:

> The political, legal, philosophical, literary, and artistic developments rest on the economic base. It is not the case that the economic situation is the sole active cause and that everything else is merely a passive effect. There is, rather, a reciprocity within a field of economic necessity which in the last instance asserts itself.

Socio-cultural processes occur within environments that assign currency to reproductive practices. Whether in the world of state propaganda, the projects of profit, or the limits of knowledge, culture situates and is situated according to material differences. The text of exclusive cultural enterprises succeeds in deviantizing outsiders by limiting the discourse to certain appropriate modes of thinking. Inevitably, a culture of impoverished ideas triumphs. Conceptual imperialism distorts, alienates and coerces into compliance an already susceptible general consciousness. Dominant modes of mental production divide, invade and colonize according to basic imperatives of capitalism. Differences that challenge or ideas that really make a difference are tortured into submission. Equally, only those ideas are celebrated which can be calibrated and re-routed successfully in terms of a market-driven logic of materialism.

The state maintains favourable legal conditions which privilege the manipulations of profit by devaluing, deviantizing and criminalizing others. Intrusions are not only state sponsored but ideologically legitimated. Embedded at all tiers of domination and unequal relations are cultural mythologies (law, justice and morality), cultural colonizers (the experts) and cultured consent (vulgar co-optation and generalized manufactured consensus) that succeed in further marginalizing the disadvantaged. Despite the roles played by the law and criminal justice system in protecting individual rights and the rights to property, major cultural institutions like religion, family, education, silence the helpless and dispossessed through a dubious benevolence of dependency. The following section, informed by Marxist contributions, sets the tone for moving beyond the text by charting a critique of culture.

From Marx Towards Critical Cultural Approaches

"The real voyage of discovery consists not in seeking new lands but in seeing with new eyes"

Marcel Prevost (Held, 1996: xiv)

Introduction: crime, culture and capital

The previous chapters presented various strains of contemporary conflict analyses of crime. Moving beyond these insights, this chapter bridges the limitations of orthodox approaches with the challenging prospects and promises of a cultural or critical social analyses of crime. One cannot, for example, investigate specific actors and activities (conformist or deviant) without fully locating them within their wider social, historical, political and economic contexts. The writings of Marx and Engels succeed brilliantly in addressing generic processes and structures that clarify the social organization of society, the conditions and consequences of historical forces and changing economic orders. Towards this end, the writings of Marx and Engels are catalytic in stimulating further critical inquiries.

In this chapter, forms of thought are pursued which express conceptually the experiences of the deviantized, penalized or criminalized. By claiming that crime is constructed and normalized in relation to privilege, this chapter analyzes the nature of social relations, various discursive practices of the state and the role of culture in positioning certain kinds of subjects as outsiders. Culture, it is argued, produces a particular knowledge, the corroborative evidence used to compel coercion. The cultural resources of power will be fully investigated in understanding the social location of crime. Likewise, this chapter examines the construction or reconstruction of definitions of crime, meanings of threat or social identities. These ideas about crime and their corresponding symbols are manipulated and deployed as resources.

Crime and its subsequent responses are related to the constitution of order. Equally, any appreciation of crime and control encourages us to ask the following: How illusory is the mastery of propaganda and the logic of popular consciousness? How does ideology, for instance, interpolate individuals as subjects? In the discussion to follow, we will analyze discipline—various panoptic sites of surveillance and control. Given that exploitation is ubiquitous, what is the social organization of dependency relations? How is authority experienced, objectified and resisted? How does the individual actor relate to wider structures? How is agency structured? What is the role of culture in mediating inequalities? How is the text of authority narrated? By whom and when? What are the forces of change? How does the discourse of crime fit within wider configurations of power? Where is the law and its very distant sibling, justice? In this chapter we are moving away from the stereotypic traditions of criminology towards the development of a more critical, emancipatory and reflective analysis of crime as culturally mediated. In these chapters, we are informed by a number of compelling oppositional currents to the privileged criminologies of the past—the racist, misogynist, heterosexist and class-elitist texts.

The study of crime is an ideological exercise in discredit, an inquiry into confrontations with cultural conformities. Earlier, our review of traditional texts introduced readers to the challenge of crime. Admittedly, the plethora of these perspectives provided various vantage points, lenses through which one may appreciate the conceptual frames, strengths and limitations of different accounts. We are now afforded opportunities, however, to move beyond an encyclopedic inventory in order to piece the crime puzzle together in light of more current theoretical reformulations of Marxist, feminist, post-structural, post-modern, cultural, critical cultural studies, New Left and constitutive inquiries. Recently, the study of crime has produced a remarkable number of rich and critical analyses. The enterprise here, therefore, invites a more intrepid, circumspect and perhaps a more ambitious interrogation of our familiar, traditional and common-sense interpretations in forging more critical social analyses of crime.

With many conventional texts, critical thinking is not usually in demand. Students are simply asked to comply with what they perceive as irrelevant, alien and dogmatic modes of inquiry. Consequently, students are drawn more easily into the more familiar, less threatening and seemingly fascinating worlds of the exotic, erotic and erratic. But crime is, as the following review demonstrates, a serious substantive site for investigating often overlooked fundamental issues of inequality, for unravelling the connectedness of concepts and applied practices and for questioning dominant modes of discourse.

A number of issues remain unresolved despite the proliferation of different texts. Notably, in the sociology of crime, the quintessential debate concerning the relationship between structure and agency looms large in all our discussions. To what extent does structure shape and, in turn, is shaped by the nature of human agency? Contrary to conventional texts, we are not supporting the fallacies of either determinism or subjectivism—an emphasis on the duality of objects and subjects. This binary method of analysis erroneously reduces subjects (actors) to objects (structures) or, alternatively, objects to subjects. Instead of bifurcating the phenomenon of crime in an either/or framework, a priority of agency or structure, it is conceptually more fruitful to examine, as Marx suggested, the "totality," the interconnectedness of events and activities, the intersections of history, culture and political economy. Throughout Marxist writings, there is no attempt to deny the capability of the human agency in intervening in events. Clearly, structure emerges out of social interactions. Since interactions are social, they are essentially interconnected and conditioned. Just as the processes of interrelationships among actors constitute structures; structures simultaneously constitute agency. In other words, structures and processes are shaped conjointly, as indicated by Marx (1956: 74-75) in the following excerpt:

> The production of ideas, conceptions and consciousness is at first directly interwoven with the material activity and the material intercourse and thought, the mental intercourse ... still appear at this stage as the direct emanation of their material behaviour. The same applies to mental production as it is expressed in the political, legal, moral religious and metaphysical language of a people.

People, for Marx, are the producers of their conceptions, ideas etc. —real active agents, as they are conditioned by a determinate development of their productive forces, and of the intercourse which corresponds to these up to its most extensive forms. Marx's analysis focused on real, active and creative beings, who "from their real life process show the development of the ideological reflexes and echoes of this life-process" (ibid.).

More precisely, interactions originate between subjects through meaningful relationships with objects of their environments. In other words, actors and activities are situated within certain identifiable settings which contextualize relations and encounters. Unfortunately, traditional texts typically de-contextualize both specific and generic conditions of crime. According to these myopic accounts, crime is advanced as habitualized or institutionalized, assuming a life independent of its constituent elements. A more circumspect approach, however, suggests that crime is a condition and consequence of relations of control. Crime, as a localized script, is written within a larger narrative on the appropriateness of control. In fact crime is a challenge that signifies subversion—a defiance of normative and integrative efforts ostensibly designed to conform actors, groups or communities. Alternatively, control shapes crime. Crime represents symbolically the rationalization of control. Crime is conveniently incorporated within a discourse that supports intrusions of the more powerful. Power ultimately exploits images of crime. Witness, for example, the local crusades against prostitution, lyrics in rap music, as well as more global campaigns such as Operation Desert Storm in the Persian Gulf crisis, the struggles in Bosnia, Operation Restore Hope in Somalia, the belligerence of the South African state, the failed coup in the Soviet Union, the provocative gestures of the American intelligence community and the corresponding adventurism of the USA military. These projects involve much more than the maintenance of tolerable boundaries of diversity by moral entrepreneurs. These declarations of crime succeed in manufacturing excitement, hysteria and crime waves that are then used to justify further interventions.

Social control is not only calibrated to contain crime but, more importantly, to create public outrage within a morality play that enhances the legitimacy of power. Rhetorical devices appeal to national security and a sacred morality. Interestingly, crime is manipulated. Observe, for instance, the dramatically contradictory types of responses of the American government vis-à-vis the overthrow of the Allende regime in Chile in the early 1970s, the support generously provided to Boris Yeltsin's regime in Russia in the early 1990s, the American support for the Contras in Nicaragua, or the drive-by bombings on Libya authorized by American President Ronald Reagan in the 1980s. Slogans about democracy and freedom conceal cultural contradictions.

In problematizing the relationship between crime and culture, the following questions need to be addressed. What are the mechanisms through which the dominant class maintains its hegemony? How do actors consent, resist or accommodate, that is, make sense of power relations? Informed by Marxist writings, we analyze the context of crime by examining the content of culture in reference to political economy and the state on the one hand, and subjectivity and consciousness on the other. Crime is the manipulation and commodification of aspects of a given culture, (general and specific, temporal and spatial). Let us briefly turn to a discussion of culture.

Culture is a central aspect of society. Social life is conditioned culturally. Clearly, culture pervades society. Culture, as will be argued, is an ideological superstructure that is reflective of socio-economic structures. Also, as a social accomplishment, culture is rooted in history and expressed in action, consciousness and change. Culture, simply put, is the channel through which social relations are conducted. As a set of shared meanings, expectations and understanding, culture is manifested in symbolic communication—language, customs, myths as well as material artefacts. Culture consists of ideas that are selectively communicated, believed and legitimated often as knowledge. Oversimplified threats or exaggerated claims of harm are manipulated to dismiss, counter or even create convenient ideas. Material consumption also operates in the realm of ideas, thereby depoliticizing explosive class relations.

Ideas are appropriated and distributed by dominant class interests. Within the cultural sphere, there is considerable deference to social engineers who, as experts, translate and advance appropriate material needs. Credentials, technology and corporatism generate informational capital and cultivate a general consumption that depends on the compliance of the less vigilant. Essentially, everyday life is colonized by corporate capitalism. Corporate capital propagates consumption, narcissism and material fetishes not as a reward in affluent societies but essentially as continued investment in a consuming and producing force. The consumer culture is directed by those who profit. Consequently, materialism transforms social relations. Figure 6. 1 schematically depicts the dynamic relationships that structure crime.

Figure 6. 1

Political Economy* <<<>>> State** <<<>>> Ideology***

* = class interests, privilege, production, property/profit, ideology, state and history.
** = law, coercion, history, bureaucracy, effectiveness, criminal justice, ideology and political economy.
*** = culture, morality/justice, violence, materialism, inequalities (race, gender, class, sexual orientation), popular images, law, political economy, state and history.

Cultural reproductions are integrally related to political economy and the state. Culture, organized on hegemonic principles, is crucial to the political economy. As previously indicated, political economy and the state influence social relations. Political economy depends on instruments of authority to maintain control over capital and profit. The state hegemonizes by responding to challenges with repression and terror. The state tolerates trouble as long as crime can be absorbed into existing political-economic structures. Culture provides the reason, the modus operandi, by setting up a series of non-thinking values; by developing subtleties of crime as pain or pleasure; by advancing mythologies regarding justice and morality; and by creating panics which restore standards of conformity. Typically, the unsuspecting actor seldom thinks about other ways of thinking. Instead, she or he is encouraged to think like the reproduced others, to obey ritually shared symbols. Norms are inherited and passed on for generations without any critical debates.

As noted above, culture is a social production that is inextricably tied to political and economic power. As will be elaborated later, culture serves the existing social order through ideology and hegemony. It is precisely because the content of culture is material that it becomes so easily appropriated. Material assigns meaning to culture and provides an embodiment, a medium of communication that overwhelms.

Interestingly, materialism demands deference and loyalty; moreover, materialism becomes personalized and possessed. All mainstream institutions are implicated in reproducing this morality of materialism. The cash nexus is the essence of material fixation. Normative notions about conformity and crime are protected emotionally and are transformed as moral catechisms. Emotional judgments are required in defence of this pervasive value system. Emotionally charged normative beliefs are used to define the appropriateness of identity and behaviour. Of considerable importance in contemporary Western societies are cherished beliefs about private property, individual rights, family values, and law and order.

Emotions are used to justify and privilege ideas. On the one hand, certain ideologies are used as filters through which people are encouraged to make sense of everyday routines. On the other hand, ideologies are conceptual canopies under which control is constructed. For example, the ideology of liberalism highlights private and public distinctions and avoids any analyses of the political aspects of institutions outside of government (Adamson, 1987). Even a failure to impersonate, let alone accept values rewarded in the dominant culture, invites serious repercussions—deviantizing practices.

Antonio Gramsci: hegemony and ideology

To fully appreciate the importance of culture in social relations we now turn to the intricate investigations of Antonio Gramsci (1891-1937) who developed an extremely perceptive awareness of ideology as a constitutive dimension of structure and agency. While incarcerated and suffering from poor health, he read voraciously and wrote brilliantly. He was far ahead of his time in offering theories of culture, politics, art, history etc. His scholarship remains extremely relevant especially at a time of widespread retreat from traditional Marxist positions. Briefly, Gramsci was detained in 1927 to await trial by the Fascists in Italy. His trial, which began on May 28, 1928, was a political showpiece in which Gramsci and twenty-two others were charged with organizing an armed insurrection. The public prosecutor declared that "For twenty years we must stop this brain from functioning" (Hoare and Smith, 1976: lxxxix), and demanded an exemplary measure of punishment. On June 4th, he was sentenced to twenty years. As a result of his poor health he was released to a prison clinic in 1935. He was to be released officially from prison on April 21, 1937; he was too ill to leave the clinic and died on April 27, 1937.

In the *Quaderni del Carcere* [prison notebooks] (1971) Gramsci accredited cultural facts, cultural activities and cultural fronts as necessary alongside the economic and the political. He attributed considerable significance to facts of culture and thought in the development of history. Culture complements force, ideological struggles are historical driving forces. Culture is a site of domination and resistance. Gramsci injected a compelling sense of agency into Marxist writings. For Gramsci, the human actor is conceived as an historical bloc of both subjective and material elements, enjoying the capacity to will, potentiate and develop herself or himself. A key to the improvement of society was the transformation of thinking, the liberating potential of culture, the expression of creative capacities and the formulation of a new class order. For example, one's will and consciousness play fundamental roles in changing attitudes. This logic provides a sustained critique of economic determinism (Wolff, 1989), characteristic of a particular dogmatic Marxism. Gramsci's heterodoxy restores a sense of subjectivity and places significance on the intervention of human actors, not brute economic forces, as the primary movers of history (Nteta, 1987). Class rule in advanced capitalism is based on ideological-cultural hegemony within a civil society (Pontusson, 1980). Gramsci provided a theory of political action in which a popular form of Marxism is possible.

Let us now focus more fully on Gramsci's inquiries into hegemony—a concept that is central to the deviantizing process. Answers to the following questions may be found in the Gramscian concept of hegemony. How is crime constructed? What explains the cohesive nature of the deviant label? And, why do those deviantized, especially the oppressed, accept passively disparaging designations?

In 1926, Gramsci re-formulated the dynamic concept of hegemony. According to Bocock (1986), the concept of hegemony was the most original idea in Gramsci's social theory and philosophy. Hegemony, the key element of political thought (Luksic, 1989), is a condition that secures the consent of the exploited. Hegemony is a process in which the ruling elite either absorbs rival groups or serves the interests of the entire society. The latter prospect is only possible for the working class and not the ruling class (Benney, 1983). Through hegemony the ruling class institutionalizes values and goals. Hegemony is the equilibrium between leadership based on consent and domination based on coercion. It is a form of cultural, moral and ideological rule based on force and consent over subordinated groups. In examining hegemony, the interests and tendencies of the groups subordinated need to be studied (Gramsci, 1988: 211). Hegemony is constructed, renewed and re-enacted through a complex series or process of struggle (Hall, 1988: 54). General and dominant views become acceptable, reproduce themselves and become hegemonic. Not only do views become accepted but are fiercely defended as part of one's common sense. Thus, the coercive aspects of hegemonies tend to remain hidden.

Gramsci identified procedures such as elections, collective bargaining and the courts in resolving conflict. Stated differently, hegemony means moral and philosophical leadership attained through the active consent of major groups in society (Bocock, 1986: 11). Hegemony influences people's perceptions. The concept of hegemony is leadership based on the consent of the ruled, consent secured by the diffusion and popularization of ruling class views. Consent of the ruled to their ongoing exploitation flows from the capitalists' hegemonic practices in all institutions of state and civil society. Hegemony, achieved through institutions of civil society, is the predominance of one class over other classes through consent rather than force. This consent is manifested through a generic loyalty to the ruling class by virtue of their position in society. This position also entails that the ruling class uphold the prevailing traditions and mores of the period. The ruling class developed this hegemony through a level of homogeneity, self-consciousness and organization. Thus, hegemony is based on economic, ethical, social, philosophic and political interests. Hegemony meant the permeation throughout society of an entire system of values, attitudes, morality or beliefs that are supportive of controlling class interests. This prevailing consciousness is internalized and becomes part of a "common sense".

Mouffe (1988: 103), in discussing the Gramscian hegemonic principle as the articulation of demands coming from different groups, explores the two ways in which demands can be articulated. One is hegemony by neutralization—a process in which demands are considered to resolve antagonisms without transforming society. Second, there is expansive hegemony, a process that links demands with other struggles to establish a chain of equivalence while respecting the autonomy and specificity of the demands of different groups. In other words,

> Hegemony is an order in which a certain way of life and thought is dominant, in which one concept of reality is diffused throughout the society in all institutional and private manifestations, informing with its spirit, all tastes, morality, customs, religious and political principles and all social relations, particularly in their intellectual and moral connotations. (Merrington, 1968: 21)

For Gramsci, hegemony cannot be purely ideological since it must have as its foundation the domination of a particular social bloc in economic activity (Hall, 1988: 54). Hegemony not only fulfils a role that brute coercion could never perform but also justifies deprivation and encourages passivity. This dominant value system and its integrative effects penetrate everyday practices—all aspects of the social order. Hegemony is secured in religious groups, the law, education, the media, in everyday events. Gramsci cautioned, however: "though hegemony is ethico-political, it must also be economic, must necessarily be based on the decisive function exercised by the leading group in the decisive nucleus of economic activity" (1988: 211-212). As Jackson argues, controlled groups have difficulties in trying to locate the source of their unease, let alone remedy it. Consent for Gramsci involves a complex mental state, a "contradictory consciousness" mixing approbation and apathy, resistance and resignation (Jackson, 1985: 590).

In his humanistic reading of Marx, Gramsci defined hegemony as a political and cultural predominance of the working class and its party aimed at securing the compliance of other groups. Hegemony, the rule of consent rather than force, is the legitimation of revolution by a comprehensive culture (ibid.). Gramsci also articulated the hegemony of a proletariat, a consciousness of its own identity. Hegemonies rise and fall in their abilities to solve problems of conflict. But why then do people and communities consent to their own exploitation? Why, for example, do people generally acquiesce to harmful economic, legal and social policies and applications? Simply, and within a more interactionist model, how do we explain the deference to control especially by those individuals or groups who have been singled out or designated as deviant? The process of imposing definitions of crime is directly related to the maintenance of hegemony.

Crime signifies disturbance, a challenge to hegemony and a clash with authorities. By subverting structural relations and resisting ideological integration, crime is oppositional. Dominant power blocs struggle to maintain domination by absorbing crime and rendering it useful without disrupting the status quo. Whenever institutions of authority perceive real or symbolic threats, the dangers of crime are immediately constructed.

Ideology, as a system of ideas manifested in all aspects of social life, performs powerful policing functions. As a cultural form, ideology legitimates social control. Ideology directs cognition, evaluations and ideals. With its links to political economy and the state, ideology encapsulates by distorting material conditions and privileges. For example, the dominant ideology incorporates and displays features from other ideologies. For instance, liberty and freedom have become powerful instruments of domination. From challenges made under Canada's Charter of Rights and Freedom to the invasion of foreign sovereign states, the ideology of freedom has been appropriated conveniently. It is interesting to observe how the Canadian state selectively applied this rationale in providing support to the reform movements in the former Soviet Union or Eastern Europe in the early 1990s and not to the struggles of our own Aboriginal people.

Ideology is a signifying system. It manipulates and creates new discourses. But, a dominant discourse must be expressed in the lived experiences of subjects in order to establish consent through common sense understandings. Common sense is established to serve state and economic bloc interests. Ideologies, therefore, are discourses flowing through subjects who use them to construct their self-identities. Common sense, as Hall (1988: 55) clarified, is itself a structure of popular ideology, a spontaneous conception of the world; thoughts sedimented into everyday reasoning. Ideology becomes part of the knowledge. The dominant sectors not only transmit that which will legitimize their interests but also deprive the dominated sectors of access to knowledge. The dissemination of information is sufficient to satisfy elementary levels of popular curiosity. Resistance remains limited. The ideological hegemony of the ruling classes is received by the masses as common sense, which blinds them to their own experiences (Counihan, 1986). Belief becomes intellectualized as ideology affects social behaviour; ideology functions cognitively as a mode of self-interpretation. Interestingly, ideology overwhelms in its persuasion rather than in its prescriptions. This complex normative belief system, according to Gramsci, is both an independent and a related factor in the maintenance of state power. As Szymansky (1978: 176) described:

> [F]ew people ever challenge the fundamental assumptions of capitalism and the state structure. People usually accept the basic "rules of the game" and judge the system to be fundamentally just and legitimate even if they see many specific failings. Such a high level of voluntary acceptance of the system does not occur spontaneously. The state must work very hard to produce such sentiments and reinforce them once they are created. The capitalist state maintains the legitimacy of the capitalist state through propagating procapitalist values and attitudes in schools.... This positive mechanism is supplemented by repressive measures designed to check the spread of anticapitalist and anti-state consciousness.

It is naive to assume that ideology is simply an external conspiracy of repressive institutions of control. Following Gramsci and Foucault, one could argue that the dominant ideology cultivates helplessness by acting more locally through the consenting and docile individual. That is, ideology is inscribed as the social control of common sense. Consequently, ideology contributes to the construction of consciousness. Ideological hegemony creates and homogenizes a self that enhances opportunities for control. An intriguing complement to Gramsci's "consent" is Foucault's (1979) "docile body," that is, "a body that may be subjected, used, transformed and improved" (Foucault, 1979: 136). The individual is a reality fabricated by institutions of power (ibid., 194). Ideology enhances a panoptic form of control; the construction of perceptions that guide action. As Foucault suggested:

> We are in the society of the teacher-judge, the doctor-judge,
> the social-worker judge; it is on them that the universal reign
> of the normative is based. This carceral network has the
> greatest support, in modern society, of the normalizing of
> power. (1979: 304)

As Habermas (1974) indicated, the meanings and symbols of the
dominant ideology prevent critical thinking by penetrating social processes,
language and individual consciousness. Ideology transforms the self into a
subject—individuals adopt versions of the truth for themselves. But, as a
sophisticated means of domination, the dominant ideology succeeds in
creating processes of self-subordination. The actor learns to repress, deprive
and deny self-autonomy by projecting a billiard-ball or assembly-line
conception of self. This advances the vulnerability and credulity of the
individual. The whole concept of individuality also warrants exploration.

As noted earlier, the dominant liberal ideology forever talks about the
language of individuality—a disciplined or conformist subjectivity. Liberal
assumptions about society impede the development of a theoretical analysis
of law and the practice of criminalization. The liberal state is dependent
upon notions of individualism and the relationship of the individual to the
state. Individual liberty, therefore, becomes abstracted from social relations.
A Marxian critique rejects liberal assumptions about equality and the claim
that individuals ought to be rewarded on a competitive basis (Lakoff, 1964:
196). As Marx (1956) wrote, we are not abstractions, rather we are the
totality of social relations. In other words, we are all connected. Liberalism,
with its emphasis on egoism and self-fulfilment, must be juxtaposed against
the history of human inequality. Liberal discourses repeatedly avoid equality
and accessibility to resources while stressing the individual's relative freedom
of action. Equality is an anathema to capitalism let alone liberalism especially
since equality is a collective accomplishment. Only on rare occasions have
the twin concerns of equality and democracy been advanced in substantive
Canadian studies of crime (Mann and Lee, 1979; Clairmont and Magill, 1983).

As mentioned earlier, the dominant ideology monopolizes the means
of mental production. Within post structuralist analyses, the objective
dimension of self—the me—consists of mass-mediated images and the "I"
arises through the process of meaning deconstruction and reconstruction,
that is, signifying practices (Kristiva, 1976). The self is a productive entity
occupying a space between dominant discourses. The dominant discourse
in the popular culture, however, is consistent with official conceptions.

Elements of the culture industry—the media, education, arts, entertainment etc.—legitimate the interests of advanced capitalism. As Adorno and Horkheimer noted, the "stronger the positions of the culture industry become, the more summarily it can deal with consumers' needs, producing them, controlling them, disciplining them ... " (1989: 181). The culture in which we live is, as Itwaru (1989a: 2) clearly clarified,

> an escalation and fusion of technology and capitalism—technocapitalism—whose hegemonizing momentum produces deception in a delirium of vertiginous frenzy in the deepening of its control over. its human subjects who have in many ways been persuaded they are in the age of the nirvana of progress.

The culture of capital, filtered through an ideology of liberalism, rewards corporate power and privileges the ethos of possessive individualism. The prevailing materialist culture destroys the dignity of those individuals, organizations and communities deviantized as the others. Moreover, crime is constructed within a framework of sophisticated surveillance, characteristic of industrial and post industrial societies. This ubiquitous regulation is legitmated by institutions that promote a peace that safeguards privacy and property. Typically in our society, privacy and property are articulated within a well-respected utilitarian framework of liberalism. Although the liberal prophet John Stuart Mill stressed the importance of acting in ways that advance the greatest good for the greatest number, the foundations of liberalism consist of an unquestioned acceptance of the compatibility of capitalism with democracy (Simon, 1988). Clearly, individualism and materialism have become interchangeable. In Canada, as we will argue, profit, privacy and liberty are interconnected conceptual projects that define basic social relations. The fabric of order as envisioned by liberalism is woven together by a wide assortment of different but equal fibres constituting the liberal democratic quilt. Another liberal British political theorist, John Locke, argued that society as a patchwork was loosely formed by the unanimous agreements of its members who make up the community. Individualism is at the centre of this universe. The source of legitimacy is the sovereignty of culture that defers to capital. The right to property is seen as sacred, a right closely linked to notions of liberty and freedom. Accordingly, this right implies that each individual has an equal chance or opportunity to accumulate as much as he or she wishes or is able (White, 1986: 27).

An appreciation of the contributions of Thomas Hobbes and John Locke is central to an understanding of the foundations of liberal democratic societies. Specifically, Thomas Hobbes (1588-1679) developed a political theory of individualism. In *Leviathon* ([1651], 1946: 80), Hobbes writes: "Nature hath made men so equal in the faculties of the body and mind." Men want power and yet lack power; in this they are all equal. He contrasted the state of nature and the social contract (covenant). The natural state is a "war of all men against all men;" men are so possessed by the will to power that they will ravage person and property. For this competition to be meaningful it must be mediated by a rule-maker. Hobbes creates a ruler who derives his authority to make law from the consent of those who will have to obey. Power is given to the sovereign by the people. Society emerges as an association. Liberal notions of individual rights and freedoms support ideologically the prevailing social order. For Hobbes disagreed that the state of nature—war of all against all—does not exist in civil society.

The writings of John Locke (1632-1704) provide concrete expressions of liberalism. In *Second Treatise of Civil Government* (1690), Locke was primarily concerned with the free individual and freedom from external restrictions. Like Hobbes, he gives primacy to the ideas of individualism and equality. For Locke concepts of natural law and natural rights were significant in highlighting the natural order and its consequences in terms of violence. Locke emphasized the nature of man as creator or maker of things, the right to self defence and the right to property. The ruler cannot violate the natural law, which is a method not a code. This theory of natural law led to the creation Magna Carta, the US Constitution, the British Bill of Rights, the Canadian Constitution (refer to the Appendix).

Locke's freedom is permissive—it comes from the state. Individualism must always be bulwarked by political recognition of this inherent right. He wrote (*Second Treatise*, [1690]:

> The state of nature has a law of nature to govern it, which obliges every one; and reason, which is that law, teaches all mankind who will but consult it, that being all equal and independent, no one ought to harm another in his life, health, liberty, or possessions (paragraph 4).
>
> The great and chief end of men's uniting into commonwealths, and putting themselves under government, is the preservation of their property (paragraph 124).

For Locke there is a difference between right and privilege. Governments must be limited but still strong to secure the rights of individuals. It has been traditional to associate with Locke's arguments a possessive conception of property (Macpherson, 1964). Locke urges governments to preserve property. This plea forms the basis for limited government and the creation of a minimalist state. For Locke capitalism in England and America became synonymous with unbridled acquisition and capitalism. Some regulation of property was needed to protect the public interest. In his 1993 paper, "Can Locke's Theory of Property Inform the Court on Fifth Amendment 'Takings' Law?", Oren Levin-Waldman explores the relationship between Locke's needs of government to regulate on behalf of the public interest and its need to preserve a tradition of property rights. Locke, the ultimate libertarian, sees property as the ultimate bulwark between individuals and the state (Levin-Waldman, 1993). This theory of property asserts that one should be able to reap the benefits of one's property because one's labour. Property is an extension of the individual self, infringements upon property are taken to be infringements upon individual liberty. For many, Locke's theory of government meant that individuals had a right to unlimited acquisition of money and wealth, a virtue in the establishment of the liberal agenda of competitive individualism (ibid.). Locke exhorts governments to preserve society (Glendon, 1991). This logic promotes unrealistic expectations, heightens social conflict and inhibits dialogue; moreover, it fosters "a climate that is inhospitable to society's losers" (ibid., 14). In short, Glendon argues that America is the land of the "lone rights bearer," the "helmetless and free on the open road" (ibid., 46). In North America rights are held as entitlements and ultimate weapons. Through the generic notion of rights, Americans conceptualized property as the prototypical natural right—"the cardinal symbol of individual freedom and independence" (ibid., 24). It is within the context of the North American culture that this devotion to individualism and liberty must be appreciated.

The culture of capital

What then is the relationship between the state and capital? Governments seek strategic alliances with business especially in the form of multinational investments. In fact, countries are tripping over each other trying to make their respective resources attractive to capital. Politicians typically offer many sweeteners in order to tempt business (*The Economist*, August 14, 1993).

The Trilateral Commission, which was initially funded by Rockefeller, has broadened its financial base to include the world's most powerful corporations. This force has shaped public policy not through overt mass mobilization of resources but through pressure on select arenas of world power and appeals to a small attentive public of elite world decision-makers. At the core of this influential group is a vast array of banking interests. The Group of Seven Industrialized (G-7) Nations and their multinational banking interests endorsed a $24 billion (U.S.) aid package for Russia in early 1992 in an effort to create a more comfortable economic climate; that is, an environment suitable to the capitalist projects of investing, appropriating and accumulating more profits. During the 1993 Vancouver meeting, President Yeltsin was promised $200 million from Canada and $1.62 billion from the USA. Aside from obvious personal connections and loyalties, the relationship between business and government is far more structurally rooted. Evidently, corporations are given a free reign in capitalist economies. Examine, for instance, how in 1992 governments, laws and the banking systems have come to the rescue of Olympia and York Developments (O&Y), which owed $14 billion. O&Y filed for bankruptcy protection to restrain creditors from seizing assets or forcing it in the hands of a receiver. Under Canada's Companies' Creditors Arrangement Act, O&Y had months to put together a plan to restructure its debts on more than ninety different loans. The American Chapter Eleven of the Federal Bankruptcy Codes goes even further by providing an infusion of new capital on the security that these lenders will be first in line for repayment. Interestingly, in these cases, company's owners still maintain control; management remains unchanged, and repayment to lenders is conducted in an orderly manner. In other words, the courts protected the assets of O&Y from various creditors. The law protected the world's largest real estate developer irrespective of the reaction on the markets, which included a two percent drop in the dollar, a fifty point dip in the Toronto Stock Exchange and a general wipeout of bank stocks, but only for a very brief period. Court protection may signal some loss in corporate leverage. Accordingly, the state attempts to project a neutral role, claiming this is a private sector concern. But, the possibility of loan guarantees still exists for this multinational corporation. In the interim, small businesses and consumers will end up paying for loan losses which banks had expected from the O&Y real estate empire. Banks had tightened loan policies for small firms struggling to stay in business. Analysts have argued that the prime interest rates are at least a quarter-point higher than they should be. Canada's new Bankruptcy Act emphasizes reorganization rather than liquidation. This act provides struggling companies court protection from creditors as they draw up plans to remain in operation, similar to Chapter 11 of the Bankruptcy Code in the US. Large corporations cam also use another statute, the Companies Creditors Arrangement Act to secure the same protection. Likewise, throughout the 1990s Donald Trump had to go through Chapter 11 bankruptcy proceedings to retain privileges and legal protections regarding debts of $2. 5 billion in the USA, and Robert Campeau's take-overs also created a $12 billion debt. Moreover, Campeau had even taken his own company to court to demand extravagant retroactive salaries. By comparison, imagine if you will, how quickly the banks come to the assistance of the average Canadian defaulting on a loan.

Governments and businesses incestually protect and reward each others interests. What efforts has any Canadian revenue minister ever made to hunt the countless billions of dollars in unpaid delinquent corporate taxes? The culture of capitalism generates widespread inequalities. Some individuals, groups and communities are treated as commodities to be rented, sold and discarded. As noted in Chapter Five, under capitalism workers are forced to sell their labour, which in turn is used to accumulate more capital and maximized profits (Singer, 1980: 45). The worker is compelled to perform for the interests of the corporate other. Kropatkin and Kusserow (1986: 8) note the importance of social forces such as the emergence of commercialism, industrialization and the attendant dehumanizing influence of capitalism in alienating labour and valorizing capital.

Interestingly, ideological banners of capitalism have always been waved zealously by Canadians. For example, three-quarters of Canadians believe that competition leads to excellence. Interestingly, more Canadians than Americans maintain that the profit motive teaches the value of hard work and that only a few would strive to do their best if private enterprise were abolished. According to Fletcher, author of a federally funded study entitled, *Canadian Attitudes Toward Competiveness and Entrepreneurship*, "the picture that emerges is of a people who greatly value individual achievement, and believe in the benefits of competition" (Enchin, 1992: B1). Canadians tend to be complacent or, alternatively, admire generations of entrepreneurs. This logic falls essentially within a Gramscian analysis which highlights the role of the state in having people believe in and accept responsibility for what is presented as their failure or success. In general, the dominant culture encourages ignorance by diverting public attention away from fundamentally problematic relations between the state and profit. Much of what Canadians know about the political economy is determined by what is read and heard in the media. But, as suggested in

Chapter Five, the media is primarily in the business of making profits. What Canadians read and hear is very similar; these messages are sanitized and particular versions of the truth are manufactured. Not only do the mass media share similar ideological commitments to profit but many of these sources of knowledge are concentrated in the hands of a few powerful corporations. For example, note how Canada's print medium is controlled: the *Financial Post* is 60% owned by the *Toronto Sun*, which in turn is 61.8% owned by Maclean Hunter—publisher of both *Macleans* and *Chatelaine* and 30% owner of C. T. V. (Winter, 1992: 33). Maclean Hunter Ltd. has revenues of $1.74 billion. Its assets include Canada's fourth largest cable company with 690,000 subscribers in Ontario and 534,000 in the USA; one television station and twenty-one radio stations; publishes 191 periodicals as well as sixty other publications. In addition Maclean Hunter owns fifteen plants in Canada and the USA; operates radio paging, trade and consumer shows; book distribution and direct-mail services (*Maclean's* 21, 03, 1994: 39). The Southam corporation runs seventeen dailies, and Coles Bookstores while the Thomson corporate interests own more than one-third of the dailies in Canada, including the *Globe and Mail* (ibid., 34). Rogers' Communication, with revenues of $1.34 billion, enjoys the following assets: Canada's largest cable television company, with fourteen cable systems serving 1.8 million subscribers; video stores; and nine AM and eleven FM radio stations. Its assets also include CFMT TV and YTV as well as a 25% stake in Viewers Choice; 32% interest in long-distance company Unitel Communications; 80% of Rogers Cantel Mobile Communication with 500,000 subscribers and a paging service (*Maclean's* 21, 03, : 40). In 1994 Rogers launched a take over of Maclean-Hunter. How then is all this permitted? Where is the freedom of expression when news appears to be monopolized by a handful of companies? The freedom to inform has become the freedom to monopolize. Media ownership is highly concentrated. Chain ownership carries the danger of homogenized content (Hackett, Pinet and Ruggles, 1992: 11). Nine Canadian newspaper groups in 1990 enjoyed 82.8% of the national newspaper circulation (Holmes and Taras, 1992: 349).

The media, language and culture: crime as a crass capital commodity

From popular and seemingly innocuous televised cartoons to more sober newscasts in mainstream media, certain versions of the truth are learned. All aspects of the dominant Canadian culture project a complex set of shared knowledge, beliefs and customs that in turn frame conventional thinking. Everyday practices are replete with significant ceremonies, signs, symbols, cues and clues that pattern gestures, rituals or performances that in turn stage degrees of cultural affiliations. Social membership or a binding way of life constitutes and is constituted by the interplay between specific behavioural circumstances and powerful ideologies that structure society. Institutionalized behaviour, identity and thought have become naturalized such that crime becomes framed according to very familiar common-sense notions. But how is this sense of knowing something about crime acquired?

Crime is constructed in reference to well-established, even if poorly understood, impressions grounded in the canons of orthodox ideas and common experiences. Within all societies, coated images and coded representations of knowledge, personified categories and empirically verifiable facts of crime are always circulated. These interpretations, respected as self-evident truths, succeed in disciplining understanding by compelling comfortable, if not convenient, compliance. How does the dominant culture control what is defined as criminal? How do individual and collective insights that moralize, pathologize and criminalize emerge?

In this chapter we also examine the role of an array of extraordinarily persuasive moral campaigns by entrepreneurs, an industry of inter-related agencies obsessed with regulating differences and punishing defiance. One such powerful force repeatedly highlighted here is the media. The media conceal as much as they reveal about crime. Because of the pervasive influence of the media, the general public is made to feel both content and competent in talking about crime. Without interrogating the sources of knowledge, this general public is encouraged to cite trite truths or glib gospels according to newspapers, television and radio accounts and learn to participate as crime experts well-nourished by media illusions, deceptive bits and biased fragments. Media crime talk satisfies basic consumption needs (O'Neill, 1985: 91-117).

By manufacturing morality plays, the media reduce crime to a juridic and analgesic chatter of crime news. This convenient obsession with crime news by the corporate media that have become the new social philosophers, engineers and theologians, alludes to customary meanings of morality. But, crime news is a problematic discourse that obstructs meaningful explanations. Crime as an extreme expression of deviance is celebrated opportunistically as a forum for public commentary and as a mechanism for solidifying the approbation of a consensually oriented society. Images of crime predominate as cultural markers designed to mirror a generic deference to the authority of law and the morality of traditional customs. A more prudent discussion of the presentation and brokerage of crime news, however, summons a critical analysis of the influences of culture, political economy and history. As will be argued here, the dominant order scripts crime as a commodity that is marketable and profitable for those who have a stake in conformity. Crime news, as an exercise of control, is linked to privilege. Accordingly, we ask the following: Who, for example, benefits from the reported incidence of crime? What does crime news produce and re-produce about existing hegemonic imperatives? What elements of the dominant culture define the appropriateness of conformity? To what extent are crime stories contextualized culturally, mediated politically and articulated legally? What cultural capital is gained by these distorted tales, revered myths and absolutist monologues? According to one of the news industry's well-respected newscasters and veteran of CBS and ABC news, CNN anchor Bernard Shaw, who argues:

> Our daily overdose of crime and violence has become a blunt instrument against the very interests, attention, and sensibilities of our listeners and viewers.... An orgy of the worst has become an endless night especially on local TV news programs.... Shootings, murders, abuse, verbal and physical, have so numbed us that real suffering, real tears, real death and even the sight of real blood can no longer shock us as they once did.... Viewers are becoming less informed despite the wealth of news programming.... Are we too intoxicated with bottom line billions from advertising sales, services and programming?... It's a dilemma. It is driven by the hot breath of competition. It is driven by the race for ratings and revenues.... There are times when people take principled positions. Rare. But there are times. Sometimes people in journalism are cowards. (*Toronto Star*, Oct 22, 1997: B4)

Interestingly, the mainstream print and electronic media disguise themselves as authoritative knowledge brokers, bringing together the collective conscience of a community (a normative moral consensus) by concentrating public attention on their definitions of disrepute, deviance or crime. Through processes of exclusion the media purport to explain a view that re-creates a "one-dimensional mind" (Marcuse, 1964: 10). By mythologizing, by publicizing a particular narrative of crime and by promoting moral recipes, the media mediate knowledge and indoctrinate values. Inevitably, electronic colonialism triumphs. The media not only establish dependency relationships but also succeed in socializing thought by inculcating a set of foreign norms, values and expectations (McPhail, 1981: 20). Sets of interrelated beliefs used for buttressing a particular social order are projected. Symbols are manipulated to control the definition of situations for readers who are perceived to be ill-informed and analytically lazy citizens. Knowledge is filtered through self-serving organizational lenses that demand deference. The media as a vehicle of cultural incarceration not only seek to deliver messages but more importantly sustain dominant elitist values.

The freedom of the press, for example, is nothing more than the freedom to monopolize. As Altheide (1976: 173) notes:

> events become news when transformed by the news perspective, and not because of their objective characteristics ... the way newsworkers look at the world was shown to be influenced by commercialism, political influence, technology, and scheduling demands.

Irrespective of the media's own publicly stated commitments to inform, the media primarily strive to generate dividends attendant with increased circulation and enhanced revenues from advertisers. Of interest to the media are stories that are unusual, that is, "eccentricities rather than the routine" (Martin, 1947: 57). In this regard, crime stories are especially attractive and easy to sell. As Skogan and Maxfield (1981: 142) contend:

> media coverage of crime emphasizes violence.... Television in particular devotes a substantial proportion of its total news coverage to crime, while the newspapers report a number of stories of violent crime in every issue....

Images of crime create a contagion, an infectious public thirst for even more sensational spectacles to be found in the pages of newspapers, the newscasts of culturally well-tailored reporters or in the proliferation of popular radio phone-in, television talk-show programs and televised tabloid newsmagazines. They include: *Current Affair, Cops, America's Most Wanted, Court TV, Inside Edition, Unsolved Mysteries, Real Stories of the Highway Patrol, American Journal Patrol, People's Court, Hard Copy, A Current Affair, Top Cops, 48 Hours, American Justice, Dateline NBC, Geraldo, Sally*

Jessy Raphael, Maury Povich, Oprah Winfrey, Shirley, Ricki Lake, Montel Williams, Jerry Springer, etc. Crime news has become the new circus, a public spectacle parading tragic events as advertised entertainment. These news carnivals deliver the magic of illusions and a cornucopia of delectable images that render readers or viewers even more vulnerable targets of manipulation. Additionally, technology has further improved this voyeurism with instant, banal and simplistic social messages that delineate the good and the bad to captivated audiences. The audience, as spectators or witnesses, is encouraged to focus attention on the personae of slick celebrities, commentators or crime experts who are all too mindful of the dazzle of their respective side-shows, advertisements and commercials. Witness, for example, the media lust for uninterrupted coverage of the following throughout the 1990s: OJ Simpson, William Kennedy Smith, Woody Allen, Mike Tyson, Michael Jackson, John Wayne Bobbett, Paul Bernardo, Lady Diana, Bill Clinton, etc.

Readers and viewers have become fixated in their fascination with the new clown, trapeze or animal acts in the form of bombastic, crude and shallow crime stories that plague both the electronic and printed media. Spectacles persist and become even more tantalizing with court ordered publication bans. Despite, for example, the 1994 Ontario publication ban imposed by the trial judge for Paul Bernardo-Teale or even the Los Angeles deputy district attorney's ban on a public disclosure of the audio evidence of the 911 telephone calls in the OJ Simpson case, issues of justice, fairness and even a modicum of concern for the victims' families were dismissed in favour of immediate sensational coverage of sordid details. With the former case, the media argued on the basis of the public's right to be informed; from the Atlanta-based *CNN,* ABC's *World News Tonight, Newsweek, The Washington Post* to the *Detroit Free Press,* the case was nonetheless reconstructed to attract the curiosities of the reading and viewing public.

Television watching, for instance, is a favourite form of entertainment and pastime. The vast majority of Canadian households (97. 5%) own at least one colour television set (Statistics Canada, 1992). Canadians watched 24.2 hours per week on average (Statistics Canada, 1987) and were subjected to over 25,000 commercials per year (De Rooy, 1994: 15). Many children spend one-third of their waking hours in front of their television screens. Statistics Canada noted that the average child watches eighteen hours of TV a week, or a little more than 2.5 hours daily (Brown, 1994: 78). The average American spends 7.5 hours each day watching television; the

TV has become the greatest consumer of leisure time (*USA Today*, 19, 08, 1994: 11A). But this amusement is troublesome given its deliberate inculcation of distorted values. The fascination with crime, the appetite for violence and the delirium of the moment disguise the ongoing media deceit. This susceptibility to the socialization of media-generated values is unsurprising considering the American Psychological Association's finding, the average child watches 8,000 murders and 100,000 other acts of violence on commercial television by the time he or she leaves primary school (*Toronto Star*, 1, 07, 1993: C7). According to author Miriam Miedzian, author of *Boys Will Be Boys: Breaking the Link Between Masculinity and Violence*, by the time children reach their eighteenth year, they will have watched 26,000 murders on the TV screen (ibid., 27, 03, 1993: K2).

The products of television, information dissemination and entertainment are shaped by commercial interests. The fundamental product of TV's fascination with crime in popular network programming is the audience, which is manufactured by corporate interests. The audience then is sold to advertisers through the market share process, upon which cost of air-time for commercials is based (Clarke and Blankenburg, 1973; DeRooy, 1994: 19). Since air time is expensive, advertisers are careful to present commercials that can only capitalize on their investment. Besides regular programs, viewers are drawn into commercials that are also designed to "attract and persuade" (Schietz and Sprafkin, 1978: 69). Commercial television and television commercials sell distorted messages. Messages are communicated (Denisson and Tobey, 1991) that manipulate the insecurities and curiosities of the individual, making the viewer feel incomplete without particular products. Clearly, advertising requires the communication of values—consumerism. Because of this insecurity, individuals see the product as a need to survive and succeed (Moog, 1990). Commercials produce the wants that need to be satisfied. Commercials reinforce consumption and create new appetites, fetishes or needs measured as the product.

This medium, however, is used to project many different kinds of messages (O'Sullivan, 1990). Since viewers are less aware of the negative effects of this medium, they are made to truly believe that reality is being portrayed. Notice, for example, while reading the following captions one's own reaction or even the response of others to the assumptions implicit in the following headlines that appeared on the front pages of newspapers and magazines.

Front Page Headlines

Metro Crack Capital of Canada: RCMP
Toronto Star, 30, 05, 1989
Police Death Sparks Metro Gun Outrage
ibid., 18, 06, 1994
Canned Juice charged in two murders, Simpson surrenders after long, slow chase
Toronto Sun, 18, 06, 1994
Karla Shielded, defence cries: Deal With the Devil, Bernardo hearing
ibid., 06, 06 1994
Sun Exclusive New Photos from Paul and Karla's wedding
ibid., 31, 03, 1994
Time's Up For Teen Killers
ibid., 2, 06, 1994
Concert Security How Safe Are You
Rolling Stone, 15, 04, 1993
Drugs in America
ibid., 03, 05, 1994
Murder Next Door
Maclean's, 18, 04, 1994
On the Trail of Terror
Time, 4, 11, 1993
An American Tragedy
ibid., 27, 06, 1994

What conclusions about crime are we as readers expected to draw? What images are manipulated? And how? In addition, viewers are called upon to participate in fabricating a fantasy. The various media discipline by producing consent and by enjoying a virtual monopoly over information.

Approximately 95% of Canadians learn about the criminal justice from the media (Simmons, 1965). Surette (1989: 5) also noted more recently that the media accounts for 95% of the information the public receives about crime. The media have become more than just social mirrors; more accurately, they provide the only windows available through which largely eager constituencies hope to catch even a glimpse of events, individuals or relations designated as deviant. Likewise, Reiman (1990: 117) suggests that this is "a distorted carnival mirror." According to Surette (1984: 16) the media perpetuate negative stereotypes:

> Media images of crime and criminals are contained within
> numerous formats, including news reporting, documentaries,
> features, and entertainment programming. The images are
> often inaccurate and are uniformly fragmentary, providing a
> distorted mirror reflection of crime within society and an
> equally distorted image of the criminal justice system's
> response to such behaviour.

In particular, the media reward consumers and deviantize social actors who are actively engaged in interrogating the fundamental ethos of passivity, individuality and consumption. The subliminal seduction manipulated (Key, 1981: 40) by the corporate, profit-oriented media—television, radio, newspapers, magazines and film—cultivate the dominant ideology, mould mindless ways of understanding and homogenize everyday life experiences. (Holmes and Taras, 1992: 4) noted that the media "reflect the interests and ideology of their owners rather than the needs of the communities they serve. The audience is little more than a commodity that is sold to advertisers."

This practice of producing audiences as a commodity for which advertisers pay to communicate messages to selected demographic segments affects not just the content of news but also its form (Goldman and Rajagopal, 1991: 16).

The mass (crass) media play a significant role in transforming the individual into a compliant consumer. The critical faculties of the viewer or reader have been dulled. There is little escape from images of appropriateness with which we are relentlessly bombarded. These images become increasingly real as we develop relationships between ourselves and the items we see, hear and read. In fact, we are encouraged by the images; necessity of that which is produced by the media. In fact, we emulate the images and engage in mindless and mimetic gestures of conformity as we become what we purchase. The central political and economic role of mass culture in manipulating through propaganda and thought control destroys reason, literacy. The society of the spectacle distracts, stupifies and paralyzes the public. Instead of political action, the public is captured by the text of spectator sports, advertising, film and other mass cultural forms (Lazere, 1977). For Chomsky (1989), a careful scrutiny of the subtext reveals that illusions are necessary to maximize the profits of corporate interests. In Europe, TV ads alone are expected to double to $36 billion by the end of this decade. The Pacific Rim's newly emerging TV market is already reaching $14 billion. (Lippman, 1992: A21). Instead of political action, the public is captured by the text of spectator sports, advertising and other mass cultural forms (Lazere, 1977). These distorted views may stem largely from public ignorance or false consciousness, supported by the media. Stories about increasing crime rates sell newspapers (Cohen, 1973: 28-40). Billions of dollars are earned in horrifying and titillating the general public. Violence is a commodity sold to generate attention, secure funding, especially for the criminal justice system and its armies of consultants, and maximize a profit for the film industry. Images of violence are always manipulated.

Monopoly media are inherently commercialized to the extent that even watching the news requires little or no involvement except the promise to consider the products advertised. As noted in Chapter One, broadcasting, for example, is financed through advertisements. Television is an incredible power resource especially since we are dealing not only with a captive audience but also with programs that are deliberately addictive, reflecting romanticized notions of escape under the guise of entertainment. Television requires little literacy but much faith. This "new religion" (Gerbner, 1978: 47; DeRooy, 1994: 40) cultivates images fitting the structure of social relations (ibid.). This contrived TV reality shapes moods, dreams and fantasies. This alleged friend of the family assumes many roles. Not only does television entertain but it also preaches through programs, newscasts and advertisements. Solemn sermons from distant corporate offices are miraculously delivered instantly in simple, attractive and of course colourful formats. Messages are stacked or layered according to the requisite levels of compliance. Commercials, per se, divert attention away from authentic reflexivity towards cultivating followers through indoctrination. The television sets the apolitical agenda, the mindless recipe for success and the formula for fitness according to foreign criteria. As the distinguished analyst and former newscaster Peter Trueman (1980: 169) noted, television news is a "stolid acceptance of the status quo." By mirroring the viewer and establishing intimacy, television seeks to extend its control by extending its net or web of control widely. Viewers are besieged with appropriate appetites and personalized products. All aspects of the human condition are inspected from personal hygiene to horrific atrocities on sensational talk shows. Personal privacy has been appropriated by corporate greed. The viewer's body has been refashioned while the mind remains idle. The viewer has been held captive; television annihilates the present lived moment by enabling viewers to enjoy experiences beyond time and space.

These hostages view images on the screen—often new and improved images of themselves (sanitized, homogenized and, of course, colonized).

Television is the most popular medium. The French, for example, spend more time watching TV than working (ibid.). On average, each household in the USA has a TV set on almost fifty hours a week (Meyrowitz, 1992: 218). In general, television programs are a major USA export, worth $2.3 billion annually. There are more than one billion television sets worldwide, and worldwide spending for television programming is $65 billion and growing by 10% annually (Lippman, 1992: A21). Cable Network News (CNN), a global TV news channel available in at least 140 countries, is an American cultural enterprise. Annually, the USA exports more than 120,000 hours of TV programs just to Europe. In Japanese homes TVs are more common than flush toilets (Parker, 1994). In Canada and the USA, 98% of households have televisions (Holmes and Taras, 1992). In 1993 Canadians spent an estimated $1. 6 billion to rent or buy movies for home video (*Toronto Star*, 4, 01, 1994: A1). The USA has the most televisions with 815 for every 1,000 people, followed with Canada with 641 while at the other extreme, China has 31 per 1, 000 (*Globe and Mail*, 1, 01, 1994: D3).

Sporting events, especially the performances of athletes on the playing fields, and the behaviour of spectators clearly demonstrate the inherent culture of violence. Revelry, celebration and patriotism inoculate the frenzy of violence, vandalism and mischievous behaviour. Note briefly the following aftermaths of successful sporting events: on June 9, 1993, after the Montreal Canadiens defeated the Los Angeles Kings to win the NHL Stanley Cup, there were 168 people injured and 115 arrested, 10 million dollars in damages; on June 20, 1993, after the Bulls won their third NBA title in Chicago, three people were killed, dozens injured, 700 arrested for shootings, burglary, disorderly conduct; on January 9, 1993, in Dallas, as the NFL Dallas Cowboys won the Superbowl there were 26 people injured, 25 arrested for looting and fighting; on June 14, 1990, seven people were killed, hundreds injured and 140 people arrested when the Detroit Pistons won their second NBA title (*Sports Illustrated*, 5, 07, 1993: 34).

The world of soccer has certainly experienced the ravages of riots and hooliganism. In Bogota, Colombians took to the streets after the national team defeated Argentina to win a World Cup slot in 1993. Revellers ran amok at least 154 people were killed in this celebration (*Time*, 20, 09, 1993: 12). In 1994 Colombian soccer player Escobar was assassinated by fans because he mistakenly scored against his own national team during the World Cup matches. This defensive act gave the margin of victory to the USA team. Soon thereafter, three men and a woman accosted him, hurled insults for his slipup, two men drew handguns and as he was shot twelve times one of the assailants reportedly said, "Thanks for the own goal, you son of a bitch" (*Time*, 11, 07, 1994: 38). For example, the following summary suggests that a large number of soccer fans have been killed or injured because of the fanaticism that accompanies sporting matches.

Casualties at Soccer Matches

04/ 5, 1902, Glasgow, Scotland: 25 fans were crushed to death;
03/ 9, 1946, Bolton, England: 33 fans were crushed;
05/ 25, 1964, Lima, Peru: 301 people killed in a riot between fans
   from Peru and Argentina;
06/ 23, 1968, Buenos Aires, Argentina: 73 fans killed in a riot;
01/ 2, 1971, Glasgow, Scotland: 66 spectators crushed
05/ 1985, Brussels, Belgium: before a match between Liverpool
   and Milan, 275 people were injured and 39 spectators killed.
04/1989, Sheffield, England a large drunken mob fell against the
   barricades crushing hundreds; 95 people were killed.

Source: *Maclean's*, 13, 12, 1993: 63; Visano, 1985: 32-33

Music and film also create passivity. Whatever gets aired on the radio has been carefully appraised by radio stations attentive to their respective corporate sponsors and advertisers. The mainstream aired music is not creative, critical nor confrontational. Rather, the criterion of conformity triumphs; a conformity or perfect fit between profit and consumption is met. For instance, only a select representation of rap music deemed to be functionally and financially beneficial will enjoy official recognition.

Billions of dollars are earned in horrifying and titillating the general public through film. Violence is a commodity sold to generate attention, secure funding for the criminal justice system and maximize a profit for the film industry. Images of violence are always manipulated. Violence as killings, drive-by shootings and street fighting accompanied the premiering of such movies as *Juice, Boyz 'n' the Hood, Jungle Fever, New Jack City, Ricochet* and *Trespass*. The popularity of both adventure/action and horror films attest to this fixation. Note, for example, the incredible popularity of violent, vigilante, and macho-avenge films that pretend to portray a sense of popular justice. With a wide array of aggressive heroes and type-casts played by Segal, Schwarzenegger, Bronson, Eastwood, Norris, Stallone, Van Damme, Willis, etc., Hollywood recycles, promotes and delivers themes of violence in the following films and their sequels: *Die Hard, Death Wish, Terminator, Out for Justice, Lethal Weapon, Double Impact, Rambo, Rocky*, etc. Violence has no longer been restricted to mindless horror films like *Friday the 13th, Doctor Giggles, Nightmare on Elm Street, Child's Play, Halloween,* or even to the suspense films like *Cape Fear* or the 1991 Academy Award winner *Silence of the Lambs*, but violence continues to be embedded in comedies like *Home Alone, Hot Shots,* which boasts that it contains the most killings of any movie. The top moneymaking films in the USA for 1992 (*Toronto Star,* 1, 01, 1993: D10) were: *Batman Returns* ($163.7 million), *Lethal Weapon 3* ($144.6 million), *Basic Instinct* ($117.2 million), *Home Alone 2* ($110.1 million), *The Hand that Rocks the Cradle* ($87.5 million), *Patriot Games* ($82.5 million), *Dracula* ($79.8 million). Of all time Hollywood top-grossing films *Home Alone* earned $285 million; *Terminator Two*, $204 million; and *Lethal Weapon Three*, $144 million (*Time*, 28, 06, 1993: 39).

The North American culture has moved from the acceptance of crime as normal to more immunized or anaesthetized complicities in routines of violence. A violent society is prompted by the inaction of governments and an overwhelmingly de-politicized commercialism. The reactions of North Americans to the horrific murder rates run the range from complacency to paranoia. What does it mean when Clinton declared that we must fight violence with values? Whose values are represented?

The media influence the public's perception of crime. These impressions, however, are also the result of the socializing influences of traditional education. Consciousness is constricted, advocacy muted and inequalities legitimized within these cultural codes. Beyond sports and film, television newscasts are especially effective in capturing our attention and then hold us captive to edited accounts of reality slotted between commercials. The audience gets close to the action, believing it knows immediately what is happening through the cultural intervention of a newscaster impeccably attired to conjure up further images of integrity. In turn, the audience is self-absorbed and consumed with trying to identify itself with the messenger's so-called objective accounts or self-evident truths. As Foucault (1979: 194) argued: "power produces; it produces reality, it produces domains of objects and rituals of truths." The media, therefore, discipline and pass judgments. Ultimately, the audience is watching itself and the reproduction of dominant values without any discrimination of the misinformation. Through commercials, the economically powerful corporations hit hard in demonstrating that their consumerism will improve the quality of life for the audience. A record $900,000 (US) was paid for each thirty seconds of commercial time during the 1994 SuperBowl between the Buffalo Bills and the Dallas Cowboys on NBC, a game that proved to be a predictable rematch of the 1993 contest. The National Football League four-year television package is worth $4.3 billion; the National Basketball Association has a four-year television contract worth $1.1 billion with NBC and TNT; the NCAA (Basketball tournament) is worth one billion dollars with CBS; Molson National Hockey League contract is worth $330 million over the next five years (*Toronto Star*, 21, 12, 1993: E1; 2, 02, 1994: E1). The audience buys the message and is programmed to believe that purchasing more products enhances success, sociability, physical attractiveness, etc.

Newscasters cannot simply be viewed as representing their personal and organizational interests; they are also cultural workers reproducing dominant ideologies. These cultural managers share class interests and associations with state and business managers and other privileged sectors (Chomsky, 1992: 93). To serve the interests of the powerful, the media must present a tolerably realistic picture of the world. And professional integrity and honesty sometimes interfere with the overriding mission. The media represent only parts of a larger doctrinal system; other parts are journals of opinion, schools, universities, academic scholarship and so on. These shepherded audiences of viewers, readers or listeners are simply required to follow orders. Essentially, they are the real targets. This doctrinal system serves to divert the unwashed masses and reinforce basic social values: passivity, submissiveness to authority, the overriding virtues of greed and personal gain, lack of concern for others, fear of real or imagined enemies, etc. The goal is to keep the bewildered masses even more bewildered. It is unnecessary for them to trouble themselves with what is actually happening in the world. In fact, it is undesirable. If they see too much of the reality, they may set themselves to change it (ibid., 95). This shared consciousness promotes laziness and silence. These homogenizing influences feed into components of a larger social machine (Meyrowitz, 1992: 230). News media especially offer disciplinary and normalizing discourses, intextually related to each other and to other disciplinary and normalizing institutions (Ericson, Baranek and Chan, 1992: 235).

As noted in Chapter One, the media succeed in fostering paranoia, a fortress mentality where the only comfort zone is in front of the television set in our homes. The market provision of security generates its own paranoid demand (Davis, 1992: 224). The media generally exploit and manipulate in the interests of power and self-preservation by conveying socially sanctioned messages about the consequences of unacceptable conduct. But this personal prison, incarcerated self or colonized will is fundamentally related to discursive practices. Structures of conformity are constituted through these disciplines. The media evade the most urgent and essential social issues. Narratives are designed to reproduce control, to confer object-like realities to crime. Privilege channels thought within conformist boundaries (Chomsky, 1989: vii). As a mode of discourse, the patho-centric script of crime objectifies challenges by invoking existing codes. Legal, scientific and professional discourses dominate the language of control. As professionals follow a privatized and bureaucratic recipe language, a cornucopia of meaningless technical terms and illusions emerges. Meanings are degraded, debates remain limited and rituals that exalt privilege are rewarded. Moreover, specialized vocabularies mystify the services rendered to deviants and justify further interventions. Many linguistic devices— rhetoric, jargon, cliches or commonsensical sayings—provide the appearance or the form that glosses over content and meaning. Cultural hegemony felt in the media and other institutions insidiously syphons off class affiliation by using a language replete with well-established words, a hypnotic-style that negates identity by forever erecting strict materialist conceptions of reality. Language is symbolic of this cultural obsession with materialism.

Language, a central expression of all cultures, is both ideological and illusory. Language commoditizes control by structuring dependency relations. The content and morphology of language as well as vocabularies are anchored in particular histories that circumscribe acceptable expressions and marginalize differences. In other words, both spoken and written languages reflect limitations. Only when the actor surrenders to a depersonalized recipe language is he or she considered both in and of society. Even the everyday chatter of familiar banter fails to move beyond the cultural script. Language objectifies, stultifies and disciplines expressions of self-awareness. The regularization of language is culturally necessary if talk is to be meaningful. Nevertheless, these normative dimensions assign privilege to stereotypic language. More recently we are witnessing the impoverishment of vocabularies and the domination of the technical, the efficient and the objective. Language presupposes a context of rules that cannot be contradicted (Gellner, 1959: 56). For Barthes (1973), language contributes to myth making; language politicizes myths by claiming reference to signifying signs; and the clarity of language is misleading. Language is a performance; the more articulate is more legitimate and therefore more knowledgeable. Irrespective of its legal outcome, the following case captures the culturally mediated language of trouble, the social amplification of crime and the manufacture of a sensational spectacle. In this surreal, media-hyped crime story, violence is perpetuated within the dazzle of technological marvel. Images shape a shallow chatter of criminology, forensics and justice. The following Simpson case mirrors a moral crisis in a culture that demands unfettered entertainment by unleashing a thirst for more vulgar Hollywood productions of villains and victims.

A case of media frenzy: sporting a symbolic spectacle as a commercial commodity

In *US Today* on July 18, 1994, the headlines read "The OJ Frenzy: Media Slip Up in Dash to be First." Throughout the summer of 1994 news executives pushed hard to secure record-setting ratings through the construction of the Simpson spectacle. This story made for great gossip and speculation transforming viewers into overnight social commentators. Despite its distant geo-political contexts, this tragedy touched many lives in North America. The unfolding of this drama was a classic media production that exploited sensitivities for commercial gain. In fact, 95 million Americans watched the 96-kilometre journey; twice the typical Friday night audience watched this freeway drama (*Toronto Star*, 24, 06, 1994: A21). This surreal chapter in the history of journalism was carried by every local TV station in California, CNN, ESPN, major Canadian and American television networks and radio stations. Millions watched the chase, easily interrupting NBC's television coverage of the fifth game of NBA finals.

The circus as a tragedy: the ritual of a police chase

Simpson's failure to surrender himself at 11AM on June 17, 1994, a failure to honour the agreement he and his lawyers made with the police, caused authorities to contact police agencies and issue an all-points bulletin. After five hours of searching, the police spotted a white Ford Bronco carrying the wanted O. J. Simpson. At 6.25 PM on June 17, 1994, Chris Thomas and Kathy Ferrigno spotted this vehicle described on the radio, minutes later Orange County sheriff's deputy Larry Pool saw a car that matched. The licence plate checked out and the chase began with the California Highway

Patrol joining the Orange County sheriff's department. The police were followed by a KABC TV traffic helicopter that captured the bizarre chase on TV. The white Bronco was followed by more than a dozen patrol cars along three different freeways. Cruisers with emergency lights flashing pursued in a slow speed chase until the Bronco parked inside Simpson's mansion. Al Cowlings, a lifelong friend of Simpson, was the driver of the Bronco, he called 911 saying:

> This is A.C. I have O.J. in the car. Right now, we're all, we're okay. But you get to tell the police to just back off. He's still alive, but he's got a gun to his head. He just wants to see his mother. Let me get back to the house.

As helicopters buzzed overhead, Simpson sat alone at the back of the Bronco, cradling two pictures of his family, a rosary and a gun (ibid., 19, 06, 1994: A6). Police made no attempt to force the car over or position a roadblock. Instead, they followed close behind, lights flashing and sirens set. In this regard Los Angeles Police Chief Willie Williams denied that Simpson was given any preferential treatment. Compare for a second the treatment of Rodney King who was viciously beaten by an LA police after being pulled over for traffic violations. In this instance, Simpson, a suspect to a double murder, failed to surrender to the police as negotiated, held a gun to his head possibly endangering himself, his driver and other motorists. A suspect who at that time was possibly facing California's death penalty was escorted by the media and dozens of cruisers to his mansion. This courtesy does not appear to be extended to many individuals suspected even of minor infractions.

The main attraction: celebrating a cultural icon

Orenthal James Simpson was a football legend. He was a powerful running back for the Buffalo Bills, for whom he set a single-season NFL rushing record with 2,003 yards in 1973. Earlier, in 1968, he had won the prestigious Heisman Trophy. Throughout the chase the very large viewing audience listened in on dialogue from the police radio broadcasts, teams of newscasters and network anchor persons commenting on Simpson's suicide note learned about the gun he held to his head and his failure to surrender himself to the police earlier. But many onlookers were not prepared to consider their hero a murderer. For decades, Simpson was an icon of the North American popular culture—he appeared in TV commercials for the Hertz Co., starred in comedies, commentated for a major network during football matches. Consequently, thousands of California freeway commuters stopped their vehicles in traffic lanes, dashed between cars to wave fondly and scream at the passing Bronco. Signs surfaced everywhere: "We love you, OJ", "Be strong brother", "Go OJ Go". Large crowds of gawkers lined up for miles along the freeways and also at his home to cheer him along. Even the US Senate got into the chorus. In chamber on Friday, the Senate chaplain offered a prayer for O. J.: "Our hearts go out to him. Our nation has been traumatized by the fall of a great hero" (*Time*, 4, 07, 1994: 27).

During the nationally televised preliminary hearing, all major networks suspended regular programming while outside the courtroom Simpson supporters continued to gather to take in this media frenzy. Some entrepreneurs were even selling "Free OJ" T-shirts. While in jail Simpson received 3,000 letters a day (*US Today*, 18, 07, 1994: 2). Sadly, a woman told the *New York Times* "My husband used to hit me ... I left Louisiana to get away from him ... OJ must not have been so bad. This woman couldn't leave him alone" (Bruning, 1994: 11). Throughout this preliminary hearing it appeared that he was not guilty by reason of celebrity (*Time*, 18, 07, 1994: 44).

Stay tuned: more high drama of cultural capital

The preliminary hearing, a routine presentation of evidence to show probable cause that the defendant should be tried for murder, turned into a made-for-TV mini-trial replete with intrigue and suspense. At one point in this hearing a mysterious envelope was given to the judge. His lawyers were also worth viewing—high powered, premium-brand attorneys. They included Robert Shapiro, Johnnie Cochran, Harvard Law professor Alan Dershowitz and F. Lee Bailey. Afternoon ratings continued to soar 24% above the usual levels. While detained awaiting trial, Simpson (inmate 4013970) enjoyed a number of privileges. He did not endure communal showers, wait in long lines to use the pay telephone or spend many hours locked in his cell. He exercised twice a day on an exercise bike in the "7000", a unit in LA County Men's Central Jail. The jail's other 6, 500 inmates bunk more than one to a cell; eat together in the cafeteria, 50 to 60 at a table; take communal showers; and wait long lines to use the phone. (*Toronto Star*, 25, 07, 1994: A2)

The invisible victims of violence

Ronald Goldman, an aspiring actor and waiter, and Nicole Brown were found outside her residence, both stabbed on June 12, 1994. Clearly, throughout the above drama the victims were invisible in the media coverage. In a June 1994 edition of the *Newsweek*, sixteen pages covered OJ's "trail of blood" while only seven paragraphs were dedicated to wife battering. Much was written on this fallen hero and role model. On the other hand, the media referred to Brown as "O. J. Simpson's ex wife," as if she had no other identity independent of the superstar. Alternatively the media cast her as a former homecoming princess when she was an eighteen-year-old waitress (*Maclean's*, 27, 06, 1994: 49).

Orenthal James Simpson divorced Brown in 1992 after a seven-year marriage. While still married she called the police in 1989 saying she feared he was going to kill her. She had been punched, slapped and kicked by Simpson who pleaded no contest in the case.

In a letter written in June 1994, Simpson explained:

> I took the heat New Year's 1989 because that's what I was supposed to do. I did not plead no contest for any other reason but to protect our privacy and was advised that it would end the press hype.... (*Toronto Star*, 18, 06, 1994: A3)

According to 911 tape recordings, distraught Nicole Brown sought police assistance in 1989 and 1993. She had called 911 eight times with assault complaints. At one point she was beaten so severely that she required hospital treatment. On October 1993 Brown made a call to the police as OJ was threatening to bash her door down (ibid., 24, 06, 1994: A21). He broke the door down of her house in a rage triggered earlier when he spotted the picture of an old boyfriend in her photo album. In a shaking voice Nicole Brown is heard on tape saying: "He's O. J. Simpson, I think you know his record. Could you just get someone over here?" He is heard shouting and swearing. Earlier in 1985 police were also called after an argument between them during which he smashed the windshield of her car with a baseball bat. Though he admitted responsibility, he insisted that it was a private matter. No charges were laid (*Time*, 4, 07, 1994: 27).

This immortalized sports figure had a lot of help denying the problem. Originally his conviction was downplayed by friends, teammates and sponsors. This violence was accepted as a private or family matter. In turn, she was unable to get help because as she said, "who would believe me?" (*Toronto Star*, 1, 07, 1994 D1). Throughout this tragedy the media attention had been misdirected, concentrating on his public accomplishments on the field and in film. Noticeably absent were comments and questions about how OJ learned to be violent (Robinson, 1994: A19). These issues were as relevant to the legal case as his much paraded celebrity status.

Greed, at its worst, accompanied the proceedings. During the selection of the jury, Vidmark Entertainment released *O. J. Simpson: Juice on the Loose*, priced to sell for $14. 99, a video about a 1974 sports documentary. MPI released *A Question of Evidence: The O. J. Simpson Hearing*, a court TV production that edits Simpson's preliminary hearing down to fifty-one minutes of highlights for about $25. A sensational book entitled *Nicole Brown Simpson: The Private Diary of Life Interrupted*, written by Faye Resnick, who claimed to be a close friend of the deceased Nicole Brown, was released in October 1994 during the jury selection. The book exploits the tragedy by detailing the affairs of Simpson's former wife. In Los Angeles, stores sold halloween masks of the suspect OJ Simpson and of the deceased Nicole Brown as well as costumes featuring a blonde wigs, prosthetic slit throats; the blood soaked football sweater of the former athlete went on sale in California. These appalling practices are all designed to capitalize on prurient and mercenary interests. As noted in Chapter One, violence is commoditized and customized as entertainment.

The Olympics revisited: misogyny and money

The absurdities of the 1994 Winter Olympics are revealed when professionalism was overshadowed by a media produced morality play that pitted two American women skaters against each other. On the one hand, there was the delicate Nancy Kerrigan, depicted as the innocent, attractive all-American girl determined to compete for her country despite an early injury suffered from a physical blow to her body inflicted by forces loyal to her competitor Tonya Harding. Kerrigan quickly became one of *People's* "50 Most Beautiful People" in 1993; she appeared on the cover of *Life*, won endorsements from Northwest Airlines, Seiko and Campbell's soup (Sullivan, 1994: 82). And on the other hand, Tonya Harding was cast as deviously bold and courageously callous—the obvious villain who refused to admit to any complicity in harming Kerrigan. Harding was transformed from a talented figure skating champion to the world's most visible villain. To this socially constructed monster went alleged offers by *Playboy* magazine while to the former—the embodiment of American ideals—went exorbitant offers by the Disney corporation and numerous television commercials. Within this soap opera, the mud wrestling of Snow White Nancy Kerrigan versus the Wicked Witch Tonya Harding was valorized while the contributions of all women skaters were once again trivialized. The international media sensationalized the relationship between the two as a nasty spat. More than 500 reporters and photographers appeared when Harding and Kerrigan took to the same ice. At what was billed as the real showdown, *Time* described Kerrigan as: "Often depicted as a fragile blossom ... she insisted on wearing the white costume in which she was attacked (*Time*, 28, 02, 1994). In a special section on the Olympics, *USA Today* (25, 02, 1994: 6E) devoted a full page to the skaters. In reference to Kerrigan, the newspaper presented two articles: one headline read "She knows how to be a leader now" and the other caption, "Kerrigan's costume on trial". In the former article Kerrigan is described as having the "mental defense mechanisms" to be a leader. In the latter article, the story begins by noting that

> the world will hold its breath as Nancy Kerrigan goes for her gold. But perhaps no one will be more nervous than Vera Wang. The New York designer and former skater will be praying the $13,000 costume she designed for Kerrigan doesn't split, snag or ride up.... Kerrigan will skate wearing Wang's ice couture creation, smothered with 20,000 Austrian crystals.... The costume is actually a short version of a gown originally designed for actress Sharon Stone. (ibid.)

In the piece on Harding entitled, "Troubled Tonya," considerable attention is paid presenting her off-ice troubles:

> After she returns to her Portland Ore. home, Harding must deal with a US Figure Skating Association panel that asked the skater to appear for a March 10 disciplinary hearing. The request stems from the panel's determination that Harding might have known about a plot to attack fellow US skater Nancy Kerrigan. A similar hearing called by the US Olympic Committee was cancelled this month after Harding filed a $25 million lawsuit. The lawsuit was then dropped. (ibid.)

The United States Olympic Committee and its business partner CBS paid $295 million to broadcast the games to North America, recognizing fully that the Harding-Kerrigan confrontation in Norway would produce a ratings bonanza (Sullivan, 1994: 114). Tabloid TV, especially *Inside Edition*, took the lead, buying exclusive rights to interviews with Harding for (reportedly)

$300,000; *Current Affairs* was paying $175,000 for Harding's associate Jeff Gillooly's insights; *Hard Copy* paid Smith and Stant $60,000 for their appearances. Likewise, Kerrigan's performance rights were sold to Disney for two million dollars as part of a larger deal that included a TV movie, televised skating special, theme park appearances, a children's book, etc (ibid.).

In March 1994, Harding pleaded guilty to helping cover up the attack against rival Kerrigan. According to Harding's plea bargain, she was given three years probation, fined $100,000 and ordered to resign from the US Figure Skating Association. Tonya Harding was convicted of conspiring to cover up the plot to attack her rival, Nancy Kerrigan, and in a plea bargain before an Oregon court she was ordered to pay $220,000 in penalties, perform 500 hours of community service, undergo psychiatric examination and remain on probation for three years. Typically, the pains of competition, the ethos of individualism, the politics of corporate sponsorship and the culture of material success were completely ignored in favour of mindless entertaining drivel that focused on pathologies, cosmetics and public relations.

More Olympics: racializing the offender

Sprinter Ben Johnson presents an interesting case study of the treatment of black athletes. Ben Johnson was stripped of his Olympic gold medal and 9.79 second, 100-metre world record on September 26, 1988 after testing positive for anabolic steroids. At least 122 athletes have been suspended for drug use since 1975. Many athletes use performance-enhancing drugs. The incredibly negative backlash directed at sprinter Ben Johnson for being disqualified as gold medalist for steroid use during the Seoul Olympics suggests the exploitative nature of sports. Bob MacDonald wrote under the caption, "The Aftermath":

> It's only natural to feel betrayal, shame and even rage....
> Sport for sport's sake is long gone. The Olympics are big
> business. Politics and greed have won. Only an all-out war
> against drugs can save it. (*Toronto Sun*, 28, 09, 1988: 180)

In a shameful society in which cheating is endemic and accepted, why the shock? How then was Johnson depicted in the media? With Johnson's picture on the full front page, the caption boldly read on September 27, 1988,

"Why, Ben?" with a bold underlined caption below, "Canada's shame". In this issue there were thirteen pages devoted to this story. They included: "Canada's Shame: A Sad, Sad Day" (*Toronto Sun*, 27, 09, 1988: 64); "Canada's Shame: Stripped of gold Johnson loses it all" (ibid., 2). The lead article quoted people of Toronto's streets who were shocked, angered, saddened, depressed, [and] bewildered. Opinions in the column included: "This is one of the lowest days in international sport," while another reported, "He has shamed the whole country." In London, England, the following headings appeared: "Cheat!" (*Daily Mirror*); "Fool's Gold" (*Daily Star*); "Johnson facing Olympic shame" (*The Times*). In the USA the *New York Post's* headlines read: "Hundred metre dashed. Ben Johnson stripped of gold after flunking drug test." In Canada the reactions were brutal. The *Globe and Mail* ran the following stories: "Johnson still silent under siege": "Police surround sprinter, hold media at bay" (*Globe and Mail*, 28, 09, 1988: 1). Not to be outdone by any newspaper, the *Toronto Sun's* first page asked: "Is Ben to Blame?", with a picture of a worried Johnson (*Toronto Sun*, 28, 09, 1988: 1). In this issue there were twelve pages of articles and columns devoted this story. Throughout the following week The *Toronto Star* ran a series of articles.

The overwhelmingly hostile scrutiny and hysterical denunciation in the headlines appear to be misplaced. Compare this reaction with the apathy or occasional curiosity felt by the Canadian public to the ongoing atrocities of workplace deaths, violent crimes, corporate fraud or political corruption. In the above sensational newspaper headlines, cartoons and editorial commentaries, Johnson's indiscretion was treated as an act of treason. Why was Johnson so quickly criticized? The type of media coverage of war criminals or even mass murderers pales in comparison with the above portrayals. What rendered Johnson so vulnerable and what incited the public rage? Compare this media reaction with the relative silence that accompanied the discovery by the Liberal government in 1993 of the politically motivated myth of the then outgoing Conservative government, perpetrated by finance minister Mazankowski, that the economy was enjoying a healthy rebound in employment and a that there would be a $27.5 billion decline in the deficit by 1998. Instead, this exaggeration left a curious endowment—the largest deficit in Canadian history. That is, the Conservative finance minister erred and left $13 billion more than the target he set for in 1993 (ibid., 31, 12, 1993: A16). This economic distortion is felt by all Canadians and yet quite interestingly there has been no severe criticism by the media.

A culture of exclusionary practices

Bigotry is commonplace in Canadian history and contemporary culture. The popular culture viewed, for example, Canadians or Americans of Italian extraction as "excitable bricklayers and passionate Carmens who when not gulping down spaghetti, are addicted to knife-slinging crime" (Sturino, 1978: 71). Typically, the media relies on the prevailing folklore of the dominant culture in celebrating certain preconceived views. The notion of the Italian-ness of crime, proclivities to organized crime and dangerous social tendencies are linked to what the late Professor Harney (1978: 55) termed "Italphobia." An article written in *Popular Science Monthly*, entitled "What Shall We Do With the Dago?" (Alba, 1980: 7), reinforces time-honoured stereotypes blatantly perpetuated in the entertainment industry with movies like *The Untouchables, Good Fellas, Raw Deal, The Godfather, Married to the Mob, Scarface, Mobsters, The Firm*, etc. With the conviction of John Gotti in New York, Murray Kempton (1992: 52) of *The New York Review* wrote: "we shall have lost the last grand personages who had been our dependence for supporting the myth of the Mafia as a force in current history. Organized crime will no longer be a crude euphemism for fascinatingly disreputable Italo-Americans." On July 5, 1994, following Italy's wins in the World Cup, CFRB talk show host John Oakley insulted Italo-Canadians by his comments about Italians sporting "cement shoes" and boasting "soccer balls" (*Toronto Star*, 10, 08, 1994: 94: A6). And yet, the Canadian media conveniently overlooked the fact that during World War II approximately 17,000 Italo-Canadians were branded as enemies of the state and required to report monthly to military authorities. Another 700 were interned for up to three years. In 1992, Prime Minister Mulroney apologized on behalf of the Canadian state, saying that these Canadians endured "brutal injustice" in time of war (ibid., 29, 03, 1993: A16). The 1927 state execution by electrocution of Nicola Sacco and Bartolomeo Vanzetti in Massachussetts for crimes they did not commit is replete with bigotry. The punishment was not solely directed at the alleged anarchists but equally launched against Italians.

Take, for example, the case of twenty-eight-year-old mother of four Angelina Napolitano who, on Easter Sunday 1911, killed her husband Pietro, a steel mill labourer. As Pietro lay asleep in bed, she entered the bedroom and struck him near the neck four times with an axe (Iacovetta, 1993: 12). She did not run nor hide; instead she informed her neighbour and on her own surrendered to the police. She spent three weeks in a local detention facility, and was tried with inadequate legal representation. Within two days she was found guilty and sentenced to death by hanging. The date of the execution was delayed in order to provide sufficient time for the pregnant Angelina to give birth. Angelina was a desperate woman who was repeatedly abused by her husband. She was stabbed nine times with a knife by her husband Pietro who was charged with assault but only given a suspended sentence (ibid., 13). On the evening of his death, he insisted that she prostitute herself; he threatened that if she did not have money for him when he woke up, he would beat her. At the brief trial, the judge refused to consider Pietro's assault against her as admissible evidence. James Curran, the prominent editor of the *Sault Ste Marie Star,* a bigot (Iacovetta, 1993: 13) who referred to southern Italians as "hot-blooded" foreigners and who believed that "Italians are all too ready as it is to use the knife, the pistol, or any other weapon that lies at hand, as a means of redressing real or fancied wrongs." In essence, Curran maintained that Angelina deserved to die because she was immoral. Nevertheless, Angelina received considerable public support from Northern Ontario-feminists, Suffrage Movements, compatriots, Italian liberals and socialists throughout the USA, UK and Italy. The enormous support was a surprise to federal authorities. On July 15, 1911, clemency was granted and her sentence commuted to life imprisonment. She was paroled in December 1922. Her four children were all taken away from her and placed in foster homes. It is obvious that at that time the law expected Angelina to remain quiet and suffer the abuse alone.

Immigrants are perceived as job stealers, welfare bums or criminally oriented. These immutable qualities are invariably assigned to immigrants (Mourbese, 1994: A17). In terms of the links between criminality and immigration status, much of the passionate talk and unsubstantiated claims have been sparked by events in 1994. In Toronto two events were used to make this faulty connection. First, there was the "Just Desserts" killing by Oneil Grant who had been ordered deported, appealed and was allowed to remain. Oneil Grant, who had several convictions for assault and drug-related offences, had been ordered deported in 1992, but the decision had been stayed by the appeal division of the Immigration and Refugee Board. He was granted a second chance by a member of the board. He had been charged with the April 1994 manslaughter of ViVi Leimonis in a Toronto cafe, Just Desserts (*Toronto Star,* 17, 06, 1994: A19). Second, in 1994 Constable Baylis was killed with a stolen handgun while on community patrol. Clinton Junior Gayle, a twenty-five-year-old living in Metropolitan Toronto was ordered deported in 1991 to Jamaica following convictions on nine charges; he was convicted on another five charges after the deportation order was issued, most of which were drug related. He was to be deported in 1992 after his appeal was turned down, but authorities lost his case and through bureaucratic errors he was never deported.

But these two men came to Canada as children—Grant at the age of twelve and Gayle at age nine. They were not recent immigrants. Moreover, the current system of citizenship requires that an individual reside legally in Canada for three years. If the person commits a crime in the fourth year one's immigration status cannot be used. Oddly, if the person fails to apply for citizenship and commits a crime even after a decade in Canada they will be considered as immigrant (Mourbese, 1994: A17). Part of the anti-immigrant sentiment is related to the fact that both victims were white and both accused are black (ibid.).

Reactions to the tragedies in the media and the public sentiment were based on deeper pathologies in Canadian society related to the colour of one's skin. Simplistic knee-jerk solutions to complex problems pander to the more basic instincts. This public outrage further sowed the seeds of racism. For example, in the year prior to the Baylis killing, two other officers were killed in Ontario: one in Minden in July 1993 and one in Sudbury in October 1993. Both the accused are white. Where was the public outrage? Where were the media? Why were the flags not at half-mast at Queen's Park for these two officers?

In part, this popular misconception linking immigrants and criminality has been an element in Canadian folklore dating back to the Chinese, Japanese, Italians and more recently the Jamaicans. Every major study has debunked this myth, including the 1994 the federal immigration department's own study. The immigration department studied 21, 399 criminals convicted of serious crimes and sentenced to more than two years (12,000 in jails and the rest out on conditional release. This study found that the foreign-born were "very significantly under-represented" among criminals—about half of their percentage in the population. Not only are they under-represented, the foreign born commit fewer murders and rapes. Their rate of recidivism is lower than Canadian-born residents. These conclusions were similar for 1989 and 1991, and hold true for all regions. But, two groups wound up in jails in numbers greater than their proportion in the population: 18 out of every 10,000 Caribbean-born people and 14 out of 10, 000 Latin-born, compared with 10.55 for Canadian-born and only 5.5 for all immigrants. As for Caribbean-born inmates, a large number are from Jamaica and Haiti. There are many explanations, according to this report, most arrived illegally and sought refugee status or endured underground for years. The report indicates that many inmates who came legally were sponsored by single mothers engaged in low-income domestic work toiling long hours with little time to attend to teenage children. High unemployment, low incomes and low rates of home ownership need to be implicated. The report concludes that immigrants in general commit fewer crimes; there is a correlation, however, between crime and education or income, but not between crime and race, crime and ethnicity, crime and geography (*Toronto Star*, 23, 07, 1994: B2).

PLACE OF BIRTH* AND CRIME

Place of Birth	% of Prison Population
18,003 born in Canada	88.25
2,396 foreign born	11.75
420 Caribbean	2
240 Jamaica	1.1
70 Haiti	.3
239 Latin America	1.1
230 UK	1.1
204 Italy	1
199 USA	.97
92 Germany	.45
92 India	.45
85 Portugal	.41
68 China	.3
49 Hungary	.24
Total: 20,399	100

Source: The Foreign Born in the Federal Prison Population; *Toronto Star*, July 23, 1994: B2; Visano, 1994

IMMIGRANTS AND CRIME (1991)

Immigrants as	% of Total Population	% of Criminals who are Immigrants
Canada	20.2	11.9
Ontario	29.7	20.1
Visible Minorities	8.5	6.3

Source: The Foreign Born in the Federal Prison Population; ibid., July 23, 1994: B2;

Despite the above immigration bashing based on notions that immigrants are job stealers and "welfare bums," recent statistics also reveal that immigrants are more productive and better educated than Canadian-born and that immigrants provide proportionately more of our managerial and professional classes. In *Canada's Changing Immigrant Population,* a sixty-one-page Statistics Canada Report released in 1994, based on 1991 census and comparative data going back forty years, the following findings were discovered. It was demonstrated that despite what is perceived publicly as a high intake annually of 250,000 people, the percentage of immigrants in the overall population remains virtually unchanged. In 1951, it was 15% now it is 16%—4.32 million immigrants. Notwithstanding public and media complaints about the illiterates, immigrants who arrived from 1981 to 1991 were more educated than those who arrived earlier. In 1991, 17% of the 1.24 million immigrants who came to Canada between 1981 and 1991 aged fifteen and over held a university degree, compared to 9% for those who came before 1961 (*Toronto Star,* 14, 07, 1994: A24). According to the findings 84.1 % of immigrant men between ages of forty-five and sixty-four were working in 1990, compared with 79.2% of Canadian-born males.

The media and policing authorities have perpetuated stereotypes about the incidence of black crime, ethnic crime and crimes committed by refugees and illegal immigrants. American network news does not report on black Americans. It reports most often on a stereotype called "the black" or "the Negro" (Effron, 1971: 144). The media typically attribute increased crime rates on an unruly black underclass (Cashmore and McLaughlin, 1991: 3). In the wake of violent crimes committed by non-whites in various cities across Canada and especially following the fatal shooting in 1994 of Georgina Leimonis during a robbery at Toronto's Just Desserts restaurant and the fatal shooting of a police constable also in 1994, the media were engaged in creating crime waves. Carolyn Strange of Carleton University noted:

> it [the Leimonis shooting] tapped into underlying fears, tensions and anxieties that were certainly bubbling beneath the surface ... it became a volcanic explosion of hatred. It unfolded as a drama of racial hatred and intolerance. (Mitchell and Abbate, 1994: A1)

Throughout history criminals were always considered to be "those outsiders" —Jews, Japanese, Chinese, Italians, Jamaicans, etc. More recently, nonwhite immigrants have been demonized. Culturally they were cast as dangerous villains existing in the margins and not fully belonging to the host society. More recently, in the sensational case involving Susan Smith of Union, South Carolina was charged in 1994 of murdering her two children. She reached into the available nightmares and constructed a case that demonized African Americans. On October 25, 1994, she explained to the police that she was on her way to visit a friend at about 9:00 when she stopped at a red light and encountered her attacker. A black man in his twenties wearing a plaid jacket and jeans and waving a gun, out of breath as though he had been running, jumped into the passenger seat and said: "Shut up and drive or I'll kill you. Sixteen miles out of town he ordered her out of the car, a 1990 burgundy Mazda Protege. She told the police that she begged him to let her take the kids, he replied: "I don't have time but I won't hurt them." The town reared in horror. Police, state troopers, FBI gents and thousands of volunteers searched the 1,330 sq. km county. Sketches of a black suspect flooded the area. The national press showed up. On November 9, 1994, Smith broke down during questioning and told the police where the boys could be discovered (*Time*, 14, 11, 1994: 62-63). In 1989 in Boston, Charles Stuart, a white furrier, claimed that a black stranger had leaped out of his car as he and his wife were returning from a natural childbirth class, forced them to drive to a remote location, robbed and shot them both. It was Stuart who killed his pregnant wife then shot himself to make his story credible. The Boston police bought the lies, rounding scores of black men and further polluting the racial atmosphere (Lacayo, 1994: 62). These inventions of the black culprit are commonplace. On the other hand, we have also witnessed the crass manipulation of colour as in the Simpson case. Johnnie Cochran, one of Simpson's lawyers, suggested that Christopher Darden has been assigned to the prosecution team because he is black. Los Angeles District Attorney Gil Garcetti denied that he added a black lawyer to the team to curry favour with eight black jurors. These constructions tell us much about the public manipulation of fear. The general public has been held captive to sanitized media sensationalism. Power crimes are played down by the media, reported on occasion in the financial section of newspapers rather than as part of the regular news. Corporate crimes escape public condemnation because newspaper journalists and organizations fail to provide frequent, prominent and criminally oriented coverage of episodes of corporate crime" (Evans and Lundman, 1983: 529). As Conklin (1977) adds, corporate control of the media ensures diversion of public attention. The media treat these crimes as less serious than street crimes. Public attention and resources have been diverted from corporate crimes to street or public order crimes. Public outrage is not allowed to flourish. The following represents a typical newspaper account of a death in the workplace:

> One man was killed and two others were seriously injured when they were hit by a 2 1/2 ton fall of rock at the eighth level at Lake Nordic Mine, Tuesday night. Dead is former Sudbury man, Frank Damiani, 22, of 204 Larch Street, Sudbury. He is believed to have died instantly ... *Mine authorities said the three-men crew had just started drilling when the accident happened* ... (*Sudbury Star*, April 9, 1958: 1, emphasis added)

This report does not mention that twenty-nine miners who died accidentally the previous year nor the eleven up to that date of April, 1958 in the same basin. The definition of an accident in most dictionaries and in common usage relates to an unexpected, unforseen course of events, unintentional act, irregularity, occurring by chance. But in the mining industry there are trends and patterns that could be easily forecasted and prevented by their armies of geologists and engineers as with the Westray horror.

To simply dismiss as unscientific, anecdotal or even rhetorical the finding that racism pervades the criminal justice system leads one to question ethically the propriety of certain epistemological foundations of current policy decisions and highlight the limitations within traditional government texts in advancing any social justice issues. As Banton (1988: 9) has argued repeatedly, notions of objective, scientific and culture-free designations are fallacious, if not fictive. Social reform remains impeded with this twisted logic that denies glaring atrocities such as the Marshall, Peltier, Osborne, and Harper cases. These cases illustrate clearly how racism is supported by a conspiracy of community silence, legitimated by law and protected by the corrupt practices of state officials.

Donald Marshall: more than just a case of "the wrongfully convicted"

On March 29, 1982, Donald Marshall Jr., a Mi'kmaq from the Membertou Reserve, was released from prison after serving eleven years for the 1971 murder of Sandy Seale, a seventeen-year-old black youth. The Royal Commission on the Donald Marshall Jr. Prosecution (1989), appointed by the Nova Scotia government in October 1986, concluded after recording 16,390 pages of transcript evidence given by 112 witnesses during 93 days of public hearings that a miscarriage of justice occurred. The seven-volume report, released in January 1990 by the Commission of Inquiry, found that institutional and structural racism played a part in Marshall's wrongful conviction and imprisonment. An all-white jury, judge, prosecuting attorney and defence counsel failed to act professionally. The Sydney police officers who responded to the fatal stabbing of Seale acted incompetently, failing to question witnesses, search the area or even protect the crime scene. The investigating officer, Sergeant of Detectives John McIntyre, concluded on the basis of no legal evidence that Marshall stabbed Seale (Harris, 1986: 71). The police perspective was framed by cultural stereotypes which viewed Natives as troublesome. Witnesses were threatened and official accounts fabricated. Both the prosecuting attorney and defence counsel failed to discharge their duties. The prosecutor, Donald MacNeil, failed to interview key witnesses while the defence counsel failed to seek disclosure of the Crown's case and failed to put arguments before the Court of Appeal regarding fundamental errors of law during the trial. The trial judge, Mr. Justice Dubinsky, misinterpreted the Canada Evidence Act and made errors in law. Just ten days after the Marshall conviction, a witness reported to the police that another person had stabbed Seale. New evidence consistently emerged throughout the 1970s. Finally in 1982, the Marshall case was reopened, assigned to the RCMP and the then Minister of Justice Jean Chretien referred the case to the Nova Scotia Court of Appeal. In the subsequent reference, the Court of Appeal quashed the conviction and entered a verdict of acquittal. This body, however, still chose to blame Marshall for his wrongful conviction, suggesting that his "untruthfulness through this whole affair contributed in large measure to his conviction." Rather than focus attention on the errors in law and the falsification of police evidence, the Court of Appeal blamed Marshall saying that he had committed perjury. Ironically, throughout his trial and incarceration Marshall maintained his innocence. Equally interesting, Mr. Justice Leonard Pace, a member of this appellate panel, was the Attorney-General of Nova Scotia at the time of the original trial and appeal—a person to whom court officials were accountable. Despite the clear evidence of the injustices suffered by "Junior" Marshall, the government of Nova Scotia had been slow in compensating him; it had refused to acknowledge the criminal behaviour of the police and the court system (Head, 1991: 130). How did this happen?

What happens to the innocent victim serving a sentence of life imprisonment for a crime that he not only did not commit but for the incompetence, deception and corruption of authorities in the criminal justice system?

As james youngblood "sakej" henderson (1992: 39) concluded:

> Being an *Indian* is to accept the European colonial view of your racial inferiority.... In cruder terms, no one in the justice system was willing to put their "balls in a vice over an Indian", a member of a powerless, isolated race. It was not politically or socially wise for an attorney's career for him or her to challenge local or provincial authorities to protect this inferior human.

Leonard Peltier: punishing dissent

In February 1976, the murdered body of Anna Mae Aquash, a thirty-one-year-old Micmac from Nova Scotia, was found on the Pine Ridge Indian Reservation in South Dakota, the same reservation that seven months earlier spawned the murder charges against Peltier. According to the facts of the case, on June 27, 1975 two FBI agents came the Pine Ridge Reservation allegedly looking for stolen property. When they tried to enter a ranch without a search warrant, shots were fired and soon a large contingent of FBI agents flooded the reservation resulting in a full-scale shootout. Two FBI agents and one Native were killed. Peltier and two other Sioux Natives were charged with murdering the FBI agents. The two Sioux Natives were captured, but Peltier fled to Canada and was arrested in Alberta in 1976. His extradition hearings ended in December, 1976 and he was returned to the USA for trial. The principal evidence at Peltier's extradition was an affidavit signed by Myrtle Poor Bear, who stated that she was a friend of Peltier and was present at the shootings. Later it was discovered that she was not a friend of Peltier and was nowhere near the incident at the time of the shootings. There was evidence that she was coerced to sign the affidavit by the FBI. Following his conviction on two murder charges, it was discovered that, of the three male witnesses against Peltier, two had their charges dropped and later reported that they too were coerced. The evidence against Peltier has long since been discounted.

There was no serious effort to investigate the murder of the Indian woman killed at Pine Ridge in the same incident. The death of Anna Mae Aquash was ignored. Her body was found along a roadside (Allmand, 1993: A13). The medical examiner reported that she died of exposure; he also severed both her hands at the wrist and sent them to the FBI in a jar. Her body was buried in an unmarked grave without a death or burial certificate. Later it was revealed that this woman was a well-known activist in American Indian Movement (AIM), a fugitive and a close friend of Peltier. A subsequent autopsy discovered, however, that she died as result of .32-calibre bullet, at close range in the back of her head (ibid.). Both incidents raised concerns about the role of the FBI in crushing the American Indian Movement. As former Canadian Solicitor General Warren Allmand (1993, A13) wrote:

> They raise ... major questions regarding the Canadian criminal justice system and its relationship with the FBI in these cases. During the past year, substantial information has been released to the public with respect to the FBI's deliberate use of fraud in the conviction of Peltier.

There was an appeal in the US Federal Court at St. Paul, Minnesota in November, 1992 at which fifty-five Canadian Members of Parliament presented an amicus brief affirming that the affidavit submitted to the Canadian court in 1976 for the extradition of Peltier was fraudulent and should be declared void. Worldwide support continues as evident in petitions signed by sixty Italian MPs, forty-eight Dutch MPs, fifty-five members of Congress, etc. Peltier remains a political prisoner. His case had the effect of smashing the American Indian Movement (AIM) and demonstrates the depth of American hostility towards Native peoples. In 1993, during the third appeal attempt, the American 8th Court of Appeal heard from the FBI who admitted that they did not know who killed the agents. Peltier was being kept on the charge that he probably aided and abetted the criminal who killed the agents. Given that no other options are available Peltier, who is serving two life sentences, has finally appealed to President Clinton by applying for executive clemency.

Helen Betty Osborne and John Joseph Harper: the conspiracy of community complacency

In Manitoba a public inquiry was launched into miscarriages of justice. The Manitoba's Aboriginal Justice Inquiry (1991), headed by two commissioners, Mr. Justice Alvin Hamilton of the Court of Queen's Bench and Provincial Court Associate Chief Justice Murray Sinclair, was established in 1988 and completed in 1991 at a cost of three million dollars. The Inquiry investigated the deaths of Helen Betty Osborne and John Joseph Harper. As Priest (1989: 211) noted: "The timing of this inquiry was remarkable, coming in the middle of an election campaign and considering that the NDP were failing miserably in the polls."

In November 1971, several white youths abducted, gang raped and murdered nineteen-year-old Helen Betty Osborne, a Cree Native in Manitoba. Disguised by a veil of racism and conspiracy, the brutal slaying of Osborne went unsolved for nearly sixteen years. The murder of Betty Osborne was motivated by racism. The discriminatory attitudes of the RCMP investigators, the sixteen-year delay in laying charges against offenders whose identities were well-known. In 1972, the RCMP knew that four young men were with Osborne at the time of her death and that the community knew what had happened but failed to come forward to the RCMP for a variety of reasons. The inquiry cited dozens of instances of racism. For example, the police did not bother to obtain consent of parents of a Native student who was taken away for questioning. And yet, the same officers were courteous to the families of the white suspects. Ultimately, one man was convicted, another acquitted and two suspects never went to trial. According to the inquiry, it was clear that Osborne would not have been killed were she not simply dismissed as an Aboriginal. The commissioners condemned the collective silence of the northern Manitoba town of Le Pas, which at the time of the murder enjoyed segregated schools, bars, movie theatres and lunch rooms. As Priest summarized: "Justice failed Betty Osborne; four white boys and a silent town conspired against her. A foreign world stole her dignity little by little, until it finally killed her. Then it tried to ignore her murder."

On March 8, 1988, a Winnipeg police officer fatally shot, in a case of mistaken identity, John Joseph Harper, a thirty-seven-year-old executive director of the Island Lake Tribal Council. This officer, who often joked about Natives, was exonerated by the police chief within thirty-six hours of the shooting. According to the inquiry, much more attention was given to protecting the officer than devoted to uncovering the facts of the case (Roberts and York, 1991: 4). The report of the Aboriginal Justice Inquiry noted: "It is our conclusion that the City of Winnipeg Police Department did not search actively or aggressively for the truth about the death of J. J. Harper. Their investigation was, at best, inadequate" (ibid.). Likewise, this inquiry condemned the chief of police for ignoring racism on the force and for allowing officers to give false testimony. The inquiry commissioners wrote:

> We believe that [Cross] decided to stop and question Harper
> simply because he was a male Aboriginal person in his path....
> The Winnipeg Police Department was guided more by self-
> interest in the Harper investigation than by public interest.
> (Gillmor, 1992: 54)

In commenting on Aboriginal justice in Manitoba, the inquiry (1991) found
that Natives make up 12% of the province and 40% of the prison population.
Moreover, it discovered that there clearly exists a separate justice system
for Aboriginal people. The laws which courts apply are alien to Natives,
and the adversarial system does not reflect Aboriginal values. In brief, the
Aboriginal Justice Inquiry described Canada's treatment of its first citizen's
as an "international disgrace" (Roberts and York, 1991: 1). Commissioners
Hamilton and Sinclair wrote courageously:

> In almost every aspect of our legal system, the treatment of
> aboriginal people is tragic. We marvel at the degree to which
> aboriginal people have endured, and continue to endure,
> what the justice system is doing to them. They have paid the
> price of high rates of alcoholism, crime and family abuse.
> (Roberts and York, 1991: 1)

Poverty, social inequality and a pervasive misunderstanding of Native culture
by a dominant white society lie at the heart of a justice system which
impoverishes Aboriginal people and consigns them to the margins (ibid.).
The report recommended universal self-government for Natives followed
by a parallel but separate justice system. On subsequent radio call-in shows,
Manitoba's justice minister, quelling the anxieties of many Manitobans who
disliked the conclusions and recommendations of the inquiry, indicated
that the final report is merely the opinion of "two individuals—the two
judges who headed the inquiry ... governments aren't going to accept
everything in the report" (York, 1991: 5). Likewise, the federal Conservative
minister of justice adopted a cautious tone regarding the report. The mayor
of Winnipeg, however, added: "I think the police chief has been a very
good chief.... I think probably what happened is that time passed the
department by. It didn't keep up with changes in the community" (Gillmor,
1992: 76). The Winnipeg Police Association ridiculed the inquiry for
suggesting that an affirmative action plan should be adopted to bring in
133 Aboriginal people to the Winnipeg Police Department (ibid.).

Obviously, Native people will be treated fairly only if they were to have their own justice system. Tinkering is no alternative. The creation of Aboriginal policing, probation offices, alternatives to incarceration, especially for nonpayment of fines, cross-cultural and anti-racist training for all agents in the criminal justice system even as piecemeal steps is long overdue. But, a comprehensive justice delivery system requires a genuinely separate system. Less than one day after Manitoba rejected the idea of a separate Native justice system, Saskatchewan offered unconditional support. In response to the many recommendations and suggestions of the Manitoba Aboriginal Justice Inquiry, in 1992 Saskatchewan was taking steps towards the development of a separate justice system beginning with a Native justice of the peace program on the reserves. Native magistrates will deal with offences ranging from hunting and fishing violations to relatively minor Criminal Code infractions. As Dan Bellegarde, vice-chief of the Saskatchewan Federation of Indian Nations, remarked:

> We came to this review process not as supplicants but as full partners.... We see it as a very positive step towards not only dealing with people in conflict with the law, but also in the ongoing process of dialogue between governments.... It's part of a larger drive toward self-government [and] under self-government, our own justice system is inevitable and will occur in the near future under a controlled and developmental process. (*Globe and Mail*, 1, 02, 1992: A4)

A social lesson: transforming the collective conscience

How then is it possible to transcend these cultural impositions? What facilitates the articulation of a critical consciousness, a movement beyond the servitude of ideology, seductive illusions or self paralysis? Paradoxically, it seems that cultural enslavement is a condition of social freedom. Social beings are constituted in the context of cultural control. An awareness of one's own interpretive framework as part of a hegemonic force will lead to higher levels of self-consciousness. For Gramsci there is no abstract human nature, fixed and immutable, but instead there exists human nature as the totality of historically determined social relations (1971, 1985, 1988).

For Gramsci, a program of mass education based on the aspirations, rights and duties of the subordinated group that are not tied to the monopoly of the bourgeoisie is imperative. Gramsci was concerned with producing a world view, a philosophical and moral outlook, which necessitated the creation of new alliances. A renewed emphasis on humanism encourages the development of a new consciousness. The masses had to educate themselves and gain independence from the bias of those who own the organs of public opinion in order to transform lived realities. Education as acculturation enhances an awareness of objective conditions that need to be mastered (Gramsci, 1971: 34). An emphasis on good sense replaces common sense (ibid., 328). Critical self-consciousness signifies the creation of intellectual cadres. Intellectuals provide a political approach that is liberating and not accommodating to the dominant culture, that is, these change agents are transformative. The development of a new consciousness that highlights the role of ideas in changing cultural phenomena in keeping with proletarian ideals is consistent with the reflective capacity of historical subjects.

Intellectuals and praxis

Lamentably, traditional intellectuals have given expression to the legitimacy of the status quo. They advance knowledge that serves the capitalist mode of production. Their ideas remain far removed from the people they encounter, especially as they continue to sell a certain culture. Intellectuals, like all other people, are rooted in particular locations in the social structure. Such locations are used in shaping the meaning of one's work. Gramsci located the ideational control of intellectuals on vertical and horizontal axes. On the horizontal axis, there are traditional intellectuals, the learned members—artists, philosophers, writers—who characterize the historical continuity in their work as incremental knowledge. On the other extreme, there are organic intellectuals, who are directly related to the economic structures and perform economic tasks, control and adopt technology. Organic intellectuals are also scattered vertically ranging from co-opted technicians at the bottom to those at the top—the elite who amass fortune and dominate all others. Traditional intellectuals are the defenders of the status quo, representing and propagating the views of the dominant order.

In North America, oppositional cultural politics among academics is sporadic, if not negligible. The orthodoxies of conventional texts, the rigidity of disciplinary boundaries, careerism, the dysfunctional nature of bureaucratic learning centres, absence of financial incentives as well as the constant backdrop of state repression tend to dismiss, trivialize and punish prospective contestants who have developed an appreciation of the importance of an oppositional pedagogy. Conventional texts resist (Kumar, 1990) any commitment to the concrete world that articulates a need for social change. A philosophy of praxis, however, establishes a new language and sense of community. Constitutive unities are, in themselves, a product and process of politics (Golding, 1992: 45). Intellectual activity is related to moral reform. Although intellectuals are neither priests nor prophets, the challenge, however, for the intellectual is to encourage the best for the disadvantaged, such as the working class, by transforming the dominant cultural hegemony and creating a political consciousness. This class action will inevitably turn hegemony against itself. The strength of an intellectual group lies in its ability to transform the dominant cultural hegemony through the propagation of a new world view. Consciousness of hegemonic transformation harnesses the intellectual group's energies in the service of the proletariat. Consciousness gives birth to the authentic experiences and expressions of inequalities. The intellectual is a key figure in transforming cultural hegemony by relating with the worker interactively. This relationship frees the intellectual capacity negated by capitalism. The dissemination of these ideas is an important role for the intellectual, given his or her skills to articulate.

Intellectual and moral reforms, for Gramsci, were linked to a program of economic reform. Indeed, he added, "the programme of economic reform is precisely the concrete form in which every intellectual and moral reform presents itself" (Gramsci, 1971: X). In other words, Gramsci argued:

> The demagogy, the trickery, the untruth, the corruption of capitalist society are not accidental 'by-products of its structure; they are inherent in the disorder, in the unleashing of brutal passions, in the ferocious competition in which and by which capitalist society lives.... Capitalist private property dissolves every relation of common interest, binds and confuses conscience ... the gains of civilization, the present, the future are in perpetual danger. (Gramsci, 1971: 31)

The untainted or organic intellectual strives to redirect energy and with an authentic eye sees beyond the images, the saturation of false pictures of democracy. Self-objectification is achieved by positioning the self with the other.

Modern ideologies may be confronted by creating a new core of intellectuals and by educating the masses of people. Marxism, for Gramsci, is a practical tool in stimulating and motivating people. The need to build a new intellectual and moral order arises concretely. Gramsci recovered the subjectivity revealed in Marx's early writings, especially in reference to education and praxis. Cultural praxis is a mode of resistance that transcends the reality of domination. Under certain circumstances people collectively transform conditions and undermine the constraints that prevent the full realization of their individual and collective potential. Ethical priority assigns significance of praxis over theory and action over principle. A moral epistemology is of great utility in fostering intellectual and moral reform (Carceres, 1988).

Critical pedagogy and praxis are transformative, abandoning the meta-narrative in favour of a will to power. The professorate, for instance, is urged to become activist in avoiding assimilation, conquest and the service of the elites (Ginsburg, 1987). Intellectuals who engage with the masses formulate a world view that reflects the experience of the disadvantage and not merely the perpetuation of the status quo. But for Gramsci, all humans are intellectuals. Traditionally, intellectuals have been socialized within the dominant classes and therefore have served the interests of the powerful. Organic intellectuals are those generated from the working class and represent a danger to the powerful. They are dangerous because they act and think critically (Bodenheimer, 1976). The organic intellectual speaks with a political agenda, vision and commitment to change. The development of a counter hegemony, that is, the hegemony of the proletariat, forges an alliance of different social groups. Mass energies need to be enlisted in the struggle for ideological hegemony and in the construction of a progressive popular community out of the cleavages of the old society. Neither a leaderless mass movement nor the elite-run party can successfully forge a socialist identity that universalizes different struggles for narrow interests. During the initial period of a struggle a war of position will occur whereby the party will lead the cultural-ideological battle for moral-intellectual development. During military confrontations, the centralized combat party of professional revolutionaries assume primary importance in the war of movement (Boggs, 1972). Revolution, as a war of position, is extremely relevant because it conceives change not as mere seizure of power but as the building of a new culture of counter hegemony into a historical bloc that over time becomes the state (Adamson, 1987). A war of position (led by the party) and of manoeuvre (Hall, 1986) by the hegemonic party, as conceived in the works of Gramsci, must lead the nation as a whole and may have to sacrifice the short-term interests of its own social class in order to attain its broader goals (Garner and Garner, 1981). Both a war of movement (a direct assault on the state) and a war of position (hegemonic) are required to confront the two powerful aspects of the state that include the means of coercion (police and army) and hegemonic leadership in civil society (education, media). These are forms of attack against the state and social order. The war of manoeuvre consists of insurgency or violence, demanding that the revolutionary act as a military tactician working within armies.

Control for Gramsci does not rest solely with the repressive forces of the state, but rather on the ability of the dominant cultural hegemony to secure adherence by all members. An absence of class consciousness or even moral values aids in this control. Gramsci was concerned with creating a new being and not with simply bettering one's material lot, that is, a new way of perceiving the universe and one's position to it (ibid., 71) in order to transform bourgeois cultural hegemony.

From the previous chapter we learned to move beyond simple and banal reassertions that power is conditioned by diverse forms of property ownership. Rather, opportunities exist and await a critical recognition and interrogation of the modalities of power. The incremental transformation of radical research and the concretization of complex issues certainly inspire an authentic commitment to social theory. From Marx, we learn that we are equipped to grapple with the problems inherent in uniting theory and practice. Knowledge of current trends in theorizing and research is gradually becoming more susceptible to wider dissemination and not strictly limited to academic activities. By removing certain institutional blinders that hinder social inquiry, we are witnessing the embrace of a critical imagination. Subsequently, this exercise includes the more innovative elaboration of conventional sets of instruments, techniques of analysis and levels of empirical applications. Crime theory and research, for example, are social enterprises that are historically grounded and environmentally influenced. Observing the social aspects of crime research, one is puzzled by the relative dearth of historiography. An understanding of the concrete context of social inquiry has not been consistently nor ardently pursued in terms of the obvious links between sociology and history.

Crudely stated, the task of theorizing is to avoid exclusivity and to encourage the synthetic links between structural, dynamic and substantive categories—relations, process and the actor, setting or product, respectively. For instance, thought, class and political economy involve interrelated operationalized concomitants. The study of crime with its sole emphasis on the imputations of meanings risks the danger of becoming a barren and prosaic chronicle of exotic or even erotic inventories. It must be conceded that the central theme in crime is not the idea of designation but instead the combination of subjective activities, accomplishments and the processes that have stimulated the meanings of these products. Admittedly, the centre of activities is located in the theorist-researcher who must be recognized as mediating a collective historical existence. That is, in constructing theories, this actor is a driving force that articulates applications or empirically demonstrates conditions and contradictions in social relations. The product of this labour is a unification of existence and being. As empirical observers, we are equipped with an instructive dialectical methodology for unravelling the interrelatedness of concepts, techniques and applications. This presupposes not only an attitude of contemplation alone but also discovery, presentation and praxis. Far too often, we routinely extrapolate or factor single variables as predominant according to a programmatic teleology and underscore the immense signification of conscience, action and the intricacies of our own contingencies. The dynamics of change, for example, require the testing of hypotheses in practice.

A theory of crime derives a sense of conviction if grounded historically and politically. This approach to crime is unavoidably sensitized by notions of struggle. As Liazos (1973: 119) advises, crime cannot neglect "conditions of inequality." The centrality of inequality suggests that despite rhetorical claims of the state's unyielding neutrality, crime is a negotiable commodity politicized and de-politicized by state officials. Likewise, although crime is remotely related to the economic order, the economic order figures prominently in the options available to the subjected and in the lingering concerns of those subjecting.

Attempts to reconstruct a humanist-liberationist philosophy of crime research warrant a compelling integration of real conditions and possibilities, those productive forces and relations that structure class, control and conflict. Research is not a closed process, rectilinear or dialectical, but rather an open ongoing negotiation that cannot be separated easily from powerful influences. Besides acknowledging historical socio-political links, the emergence of a social theory invites a commitment to advocacy, education, reform and coalition-building. Although the separation of research and praxis is a theoretical abstraction, this division is not without consequences. Despite its pejorative or deviant designation, "praxis" gives impetus to intellectual confrontations, reduces uncertainty and highlights contradictions. Research is a social undertaking that assists in the development of consciousness of one's interactions and labour. A vital strength of this type of activity is the creation and use of information. The tendency to pay lip-service and emasculate a praxis model reduces research as a means to an end and becomes derivative of yet another ideological reproduction and legitimation. Despite the invisible controls of funding sources, crime research can construct some noteworthy inquiries about and excursions into social reform. A radical analysis suggests that the problematic of linkage cannot be resolved without examining the fundamental distribution of resources in our society. The analyst interrogates the role of the state and how it serves to enrich certain interests by bestowing disproportionate benefits upon them or helping to preserve the structure of class inequality. A critical approach is sensitive to what state agencies profess to be doing, exposing contradictions and recommending remedies. Ultimately, the social responsibility of the theorist is to probe into fundamental social values upon which law and the state depend. By developing a method of thinking, a perspective that strives to clarify the mythologies and ambiguities, crime research calls for a review of these ideals.

Lamentably, a further limitation which impacts on the pursuit of viable social directions is the moral posturing within the intellectual community. At one end, radical scholars are maligned and readily dismissed for using crime as a political platform. At the other end of the spectrum, indictments flourish against researchers who reinforce extant control practices and perpetuate the existing order. In any event, this divisive morality play trivializes actual and potential contributions. Simply, there are those intellectuals who function organically within economic tasks in exercising technical capacities. There are also those intellectuals for whom historical continuity is expressed in their work as cumulative knowledge (Cammett, 1967: 20).

Transformation is required not only in the direction of crime research but also in the attitudes towards this research. Upon further reflection, we must move beyond the convenience of traditional texts and clarify the significance of culture, political economy and the state to crime theories and methods. Our analysis of culture demonstrates the primacy of lived experience that is often overlooked. The lived experience is marked by inequalities throughout the social landscape. Traditional approaches reduce crime to a language that echoes prevailing ideologies thereby reducing crime to what Foucault describes as the chatter of criminology. Crime is about inequality and the attendant social relations in local sites that are culturally contextualized. Identity, as a constituted subject, is the negotiated outcome of is the process.

Culture, change and identity

Within the dominant culture, crime exists as an ideology, an immutable and objective reality independent of processes of social definition. This chapter, however, suggests that rules designating crime are created, injected with meaningfulness and dependent upon interpretations. Rules are constituted by social actors, internalized, applied and accepted as legitimate. The leading or dominant ideologies, as accounting processes of crime and control, are emergent articulations of moral justifications. Deviant identities or even truths about crime are advanced as total, exhaustive catch-all clauses, rather than as cultural indicators that situate ideology. Ideology is an interpretive scheme for making sense of phenomena, a methodology for classifying the social world. The available arsenal of moral rhetoric, language and symbols facilitates the phenomenal reduction of consciousness and intention. Juxtaposed against powerful ideological antidotes, there is the problem of discovering material conditions and developing an emancipatory consciousness. Emancipation requires a struggle for equal rights and duties, the abolition of class rule supported by the privileged, white, heterosexual male culture that shapes relations.

Traditional texts reduced crime to monolithic, totalized and essentialist conceptions within a narrow theoretical vision and an overarching conceptual closure. As Miles (1982: 3) noted, we should question "the way in which common sense discourse has come to structure and determine academic discourses...." Crime, as everyday practices and policies articulating hegemonic processes, is both contradictory and complementary—crime resists as well as accommodates. But, how are these antagonistic positions made possible? The situated reality of crime or conformity and the wider political economy is mediated by culture. Cultural reproduction mediates forms and processes.

Crime is constituted by different, even conflicting, discourses. Although as Laclau and Mouffe (1985) argue, the social is never totalized or complete, the social is mystified. The social aspects of crime are constituted within hegemonic processes that become concretized at local, cultural and political levels. What therefore passes typically as a subject of crime is so well filtered as to ignore fully racism, sexism and class inequalities. Accordingly, students of the sociology of crime are obliged to move beyond the text and interrogate the subtext of their own credulity and appreciate the fragmented nature of their own subjectivity. It is certainly an onerous task to move beyond cultural roles and expectations incubated within resources like law, bureaucratic rationality, media, manufactured common sense, education, employment etc. Such fundamental issues of race, gender and class continue to escape scrutiny. Not only are we compelled to look into this battleground but also to focus on the cultural reworking of larger discourses that deviantize non-whites, women and the poor. Avoiding the reductivist tendencies inherent in the dominant culture, we argue that race, gender and class are interconnected and should be analyzed as social constructions within the context of reproducing oppression. From Antonio Gramsci we learn about the social contexts within which people develop ideological commitments. In other words, we learn, for example, that human subjectivity is both constituted and constitutive. Classes are constituted by the dominant modes of production, and groups other than classes become potential agents of social change that aim to constitute their economic and political worlds. Human subjectivity is constituted; external structures (language, political institutions, economic forces) constitute subjectivity. Equally, consciousness chooses to constitute the world unencumbered by external forces. A coherent viewpoint aids in grasping what is really going on in the world (Bocock, 1986: 17).

Ideology is a superstructure understood in a specific historical context through concepts of hegemony, civil society, the state, the party and intellectuals (Hall, Lumley and McLennan, 1977). Gramsci's wider vision of the state incorporates coercion and hegemony. With the latter, the state can achieve consensus even among workers through ideological means, of which the most important is nationalism or patriotism. Likewise, welfare measures have been valuable in controlling the working class (Cueva and Martinez-Baracs, 1980). Cultural contradictions exist in the juxtapositions of freedom, liberty and equality. A culture industry has constructed crime as an attribute of individualism. Consequently, the individual or group of individuals who challenge are immediately rendered insignificant. As a text, culture is an expression of ideology that should be examined as to its production and consumption; its practices of encoding and decoding. A method to clarify the coding processes is available in a critical cultural theory, a long overdue perspective in the study of crime let alone criminology.

Critical cultural approaches provide an alternate framework for appreciating the form and content of crime. Implicitly, this social theory captures the historical development of ideologies, the nature of the hegemonic subject, the role of popular culture and the communication of privilege. Awareness is culturally mediated and linguistically conditioned. According to a "critical consciousness" (Said, 1983: 241), how can we deconstruct codes of thinking and critically elaborate on the conditions and consequences of crime? The answer rests with consciousness, knowing ourselves and our location (Gramsci, 1971; Jouve 1991: 8). Is self-knowledge an illusion? Is it not created in social relationships that link the conveniently bifurcated private and public worlds? Crime has become a discursively constituted institution that patterns and reproduces agency. Unfortunately, crime is seldom explicated or understood in relation to a cultural debate, moulded by illusions. Instead, conformity is invested with the attribution of the real, the functional and stable. The awareness of being different and seeing differences inspires manoeuvres that banish or correct the crises of challenges to the texts. Differences are fundamentally linked to individual identities that are reproduced as showpieces, as escapes or imported foreign values.

Culture privileges rich, white, able, and heterosexual males. The disadvantaged are always pacified and transformed as objects of exchange that become constituted as convenient commodities. Race, gender and class are foundational cultural forms that are historically grounded and culturally expressed in everyday hegemonic categories. Human subjects, from the deviant subject to the subjected reader, are controlled by the censorial gaze of institutions. Culture mediates, provides rationality and articulates a language that magically defines conformity by imposing a familiar context and generates universal commitment. Those individuals who do not belong are out of place according to the strictures of criminological culture. As Wiseman (1989: 42) suggested, the "suspicion is that culture and tradition have transmuted the institutionally chosen into the naturally given." This emphasis on cultural and social, however, does not deny the equally significant forces of economic and political structures. Crime is ideologically situated within institutions that shape self-identity. These protective cocoons filter trouble, funnel interpretations and marginalize differences according to universalized framed experiences and inoculated reflexivities (Giddens, 1992: 3). A priori conditioning incites intolerance. Crime is represented as a risk.

In this chapter the common sense, knowledge and beliefs about conformity are problematized. Additionally, crime is presented as a convenient intrusion into the lives of others. The response to crime is a staged performance. Culture manipulates sanctions by defining disturbances as local accommodations to contests or as totalizing narratives of trouble that warrant closure, containment and coercion.

The impoverished culture

The relationship between crime and culture is characterized by issues of inequality. Inequality is ubiquitous in Canadian society. Moreover, the dominant culture, supported by agencies of control, rewards the privileged while pathologizing the poor. Not only do we marginalize the poor but as a society we condemn them to a life of misery, to a life that is constantly at risk—far more susceptible to physical, emotional and mental illnesses, the dangers of survival, shorter life expectancies, more stressful family relationships, guaranteed illiteracy, etc. As a result, a large number of Canadians cannot enjoy their full rights of citizenship.

How then can the poor feel anything but removed, isolated and deviantized? Having been effectively silenced, who then speaks of, for and with the millions who are hungry, homeless, unemployed and even underemployed? In the USA, one of the world's richest countries, we notice the following striking features:

Poverty in the USA

- the US poverty rate is three times that of major European countries, ten times higher than Sweden;
- the USA has a much worse record of infant mortality than major European countries; it ranks twenty-second in the world!
- the USA ranks nineteenth in the world in the ratio of children to teachers in its schools, falling behind Lebanon and Libya.
- the USA and South Africa do not provide medical care and financial assistance to all pregnant women. The USA does not even provide unpaid maternity leave.
- in 1992 more than 38.9 million Americans had no health insurance coverage and another 40 million had such inadequate coverage that serious illness would lead to financial ruin.
- Black men in Harlem are less likely to reach the age of sixty-five than men in Bangladesh (one of the poorest countries in the world).
- the USA offers virtually no public day care
- the USA poverty rate is 18.1%, roughly double the rates of most European countries; Germany, 6.8%; France, 9.9%; Sweden, 8.6%; poverty among most vulnerable sectors is horrifying such as with single mothers. Astoundingly, 53.3% of single mothers in the USA live in poverty compared to 25.5% in Germany,

> 15.8% in France and 5.5% in Sweden (McQuaig, 1992b: B7;
> Time, 27, 12, 1994: 12)
> * the ranks of the poor in the USA have increased to 36.9 million
>   people in 1992; those living in poverty made up 14.5% of the
>   total population (*Toronto Star*, 5, 10, 1993: A20).
> * the USA official unemployment rate throughout 1992 was 7.5%
>   compared to Canada's 11.6%
> * there are approximately 10 million working Americans who
>   fail to clear the poverty line
>
> (Visano, 1993).

Americans and Canadians have not only become de-sensitized to poverty but have become all too accepting of the pathologizing liberal-conservative rhetoric of their respective governments. Poverty is still viewed as a behavioural problem. By attributing poverty to a lack of discipline or laziness, politicians and corporate interests divert attention away from the real underlying causes of injustice, notably economic inequalities, racism and misogyny. Canadian corporations, battered by a recession and pressured by foreign competition, have decided to make profits not poverty a priority. The net earnings in 1997 for major banks in Canada were as follows: Bank of Montreal, $1.3 billion; Toronto Dominion, $1.1 billion; Bank of Nova Scotia, $1.5 billion; National Bank, $342 million; Canadian Imperial Bank of Commerce, $ 1.6 billion; the Royal Bank, $1.7 billion—together the big banks rang up a record of $7.5 billion in profits in 1997 (*Toronto Star*, December 6, 1997: C1). The painful reality, however, lingers—hundreds of thousands of Canadians are forced to rely on food banks, food depots and soup kitchens. Food banks have become a necessity in Canada. In fact, there are more food banks in Toronto than MacDonald's outlets (Yalnizyan, 1990: 9). Canada's child poverty rate is 20.5%, and the 1997 youth unemployment was 16.7% compared to 14.2% in 1990 (*Toronto Star*, Sept 30, 1997: A18).

The state functions to provide a climate that enables the manipulations of power by corporations as well as one that legitimates profit accumulation. This commitment to free enterprise and private property was never a benign oversight. By denying the rights of the disadvantaged—consumers, workers, and the poor to participate, to know, to protect themselves—the powerful act with impunity. It is as Mills (1956: 95) observes, " better ... to take one dime from each of ten million people at the point of a corporation than $10,000 from each of ten banks at the point of a gun." Compliance with government inspection, review and scrutiny pose no great danger to business. Corporations also realize that some enforcement is necessary to prevent public disenchantment and to protect the capitalist system.

Institutional changes in the law and culture of business are also warranted. Corporate crime laws tend to be far too flexible. Business and law schools too have largely remained silent about ethics, human values and corporate social responsibility. Public accountability is enhanced by well-trained investigators. Regulatory agencies are ineffective because they assume a non-punitive educational role in dealing with corporations. Current approaches constitute reactive frames, emphasizing local control efforts to contain the power of multinational corporations. The costs of these crimes are seldom discussed.

On a more global level, we notice similar contradictions. Although capital generally owes no loyalty to any country, less-developed countries suffer disproportionate hardships. Crimes of capital are without boundaries and remain well prepared to exploit the very weak. Banks typically reap enormous benefits from doing business in developing countries. For example, debt is converted into equity—a method by which the lending bank takes ownership share in the country's developing industry instead of repayment. Also, they can sell their debt at a discount to others for investment in that debtor country. The developing nations have a $1.2 trillion debt. Third World countries pay $21 billion every year in a net transfer of resources to the industrialized nations. Debt payments to the International Monetary Fund alone accounts for $6.3 billion annually (Waters, 1992: v).

Globally, the tragedy of global impoverishment for greed has not abated and has had drastic consequences. Approximately 250,000 children under the age of five die every week from diseases of poverty, that is, one every seven seconds. As reported by the United Nation's annual report, *The State of the World's Children*, 40,000 children die every day unnecessarily— fourteen million a year from common preventable illnesses such as poor nutrition and other diseases of poverty (*Toronto Star*, 20, 12, 1988: A18 and 27, 12, 1987: B3). Everyday 10,000 people starve to death. The World Bank estimates that one billion of the word's 5. 5 billion people live on less than one dollar a day (*Toronto Star*, 18, 07, 1992: D6). According to UNICEF, 40 million children live on the street, 12 million die before their fifth birthday from preventable diseases; 140 million children still do not attend school;

every day 1,000 children in developing countries die of AIDS (*Toronto Star*, Sept 30, 1997: A18). In his address to the UN Conference on Environment and Development, Fidel Castro (1992: 2) noted:

> In the Third World ... infant mortality reaches levels of 115 deaths for every 1000 live births, where every year 14 million children die before they reach the age of five, where more than a billion people do not have access to the most elementary health services, where life expectancy is less than 63 years, and in the poorest countries less than 52, where more than 300 million children are deprived of their right to schooling, where almost a billion adults are illiterate, where more than 500 million people suffered from hunger in 1990, and where some 180 million children under the age of five suffer from malnutrition.

In Somalia alone, 300,000 children die annually while another 1.5 million are threatened with starvation (*Toronto Star*, 22, 08, 1993: A15). Forty thousand children die daily worldwide; one-third of them in Africa, a continent with only 10% of the world's population (*Toronto Star*, 18, 04, 1993: F3). By the end of the century, thirty-seven countries, most of them in Africa, will be unable to feed themselves with their own resources (*Toronto Star*, 27, 08, 1993: A12). Elsewhere, there are 50,000 child prostitutes in Brazil (*Toronto Star*, 25, 07, 1993: F3). Equally significant, there are 12 million South Africans who are caught up in desperate poverty (*Toronto Star*, 25, 07, 1993: F3). The eradication of poverty and underdevelopment is not an overriding concern to the industrialized countries (George, 1985: 7). According to the conservative World Bank, more than 10 million babies around the world die annually from preventable diseases. That is, 12.4 million children under the age of five died in 1990 in developing societies. The *meninos de rua* or impoverished street kids, are often blamed for the high crime rates in Brazil. They have become easy prey; on average four are killed daily. In July, 1993 in Rio de Janeiro, five men opened fire on a group of fifty sleeping children, killing eight. Although three military police officers were arrested for the shootings, international human rights groups have denounced the military police force as one of the most brutal. In greater Sao Paulo, for instance, the police killed 1470 people in 1992. In nearly every case the military tribunals that tried the police absolved them of wrongdoing (*Time*, 9, 08, 1993: 26-27). Of Brazil's 152 million people, there are 32 million children living in families earning less than $30 per person a month in one of the wealthiest economies in Latin America. The top 20% of Brazil's population earns twenty-six times as much as the bottom 20% (ibid.).

Canada's response to these crises remains shameful. Canada's foreign aid has dropped to .36% of the gross domestic product in 1997 compared to .45% in 1990 (*Toronto Star,* Sept 30, 1997: A18). Instead, the Canadian government is actively pursuing the Multilateral Agreement on Investment. Accordingly, Canada is to treat foreign investors the same as local companies. This investment accord with the world's twenty-eight richest countries is designed to enhance investment abroad to an unprecedented $171 billion while foreign investments in Canada will attain $180 billion (*Toronto Star,* Feb 18, 1998: A18).

Given the above backdrop of class injuries, it is now appropriate to examine the business of crime. In this section it is argued that traditional criteria and legal categories within orthodox criminological texts are insufficient both conceptually and substantively for understanding the crimes of privilege. It is not surprising that there is relatively little agreement and much equivocation as to the definition of corporate crime, white-collar crime, suite crime, professional crime (Friedrichs, 1992: 16; Snider, 1993). The study of crime has been too limited in scope—concentrating far too much attention on the crimes of the powerless. Stereotypes are created that celebrate the remarkable acumen and achievements of well-disguised thieves in the business suits of powerful suites. Class bias is evident in the cultural portrayal of these criminals.

The liberal institution of privacy or private peace are permissive contexts. Crimes are related to wider opportunities in the economic order, stages of capital development, the scale and complexity of opportunities, the nature of banking and commerce-funding. That is, the scope of business and the limitations of sanctions are extremely complicated, requiring sophisticated techniques. Traditional training, schooling and commonsensical interpretations legitimate these practices. Unsurprisingly, law enforcement efforts are ill prepared to combat apparently non-violent acts of fraud, guile and moral irresponsibility.

Constitution of costs: liabilities of law

It was abundantly clear that the Conservative governments of the 1980s and early 1990s were quite concerned about military spending. The highest single category in the federal budget, next to debt carrying charges, is defence. Former Prime Minister Campbell announced in 1992 expenditures of $4. 4 billion to buy fifty British high-tech helicopters (*Toronto Star*, 25, 07, 1992: B1). Canada spent $690 million on the Gulf War without any public debate (Smith, 1992: 36). The USA spent 1.3 trillion dollars in five years on militaristic build-up, much of it in preparation for armed intervention in Central America and Africa (Toronto Disarmament Network, 1992). According to early Pentagon estimates, the gross cost of Operation Desert Shield, including the deployment of troops, weapons maintenance, aircraft leasing and fuel, was $17.5 billion. A number of countries pledged to help: Saudi Arabia, Kuwait and United Arab Emirates offered $12 billion; Japan, $4 billion; Europeans, $2 billion; Germany, a billion (*Time*, 24, 09, 1990: 18). By March 1991, these estimates had changed remarkably: the projected US cost was $36.4 billion, Allied pledges were $43.8 billion (*Time*, 11, 03, 1991: 36). The estimated long-term costs to rebuild Kuwait are in excess of $100 billion (Colombo, 1992: 40). In the next five years the US Defense Department's budget will reach $1.5 trillion. Military spending budgetted for this year is $274 billion (Greider, 1993: 35). In 1993 the budget for the USA intelligence community, which is approved by Congress, is estimated at $28.5 billion. Spy satellites are estimated to be worth at least a billion dollars (*Toronto Star*, 27, 03, 1993: D7). In the past two decades the world has squandered 13 trillion dollars in military spending. In 1991, despite the end of the cold war, military spending approached a trillion dollars (Castro, 1992: 8). Despite massive cuts in military spending, the world still spends $800 billion dollars on armaments annually (ibid., 3). These amounts of money can easily provide adequate food, clean water, basic health and primary education to every adult and child on the planet (Prieur and Rowles, 1992: 18).

Within the last decade, consecutive Canadian governments have stripped away protections long enjoyed by Canadians. Additionally, the Canadian government introduced costly initiatives ranging from the Goods and Services Tax (GST) to the North America Free Trade Agreement (NAFTA). Misleading policies have been destructive; the rhetoric of redirecting scarce resources to the poor through such programs as the free market model is guiding government inaction in social programs. The 1990s have witnessed a push to roll back the few gains achieved over the decades. In reference to the so-called sacred universal programs, Canadians have been subjected to lofty promises and vague assurances couched within meaningless politically correct gestures. For instance, former Prime Minister

Mulroney was the co-chair of the World Summit for Children in 1990 and yet he did very little except cap annual increases in social spending. Despite shallow public talk, especially at an individual level, a shift is warranted that examines systemic deprivations.

Law enshrines individualism through such powerful notions of peace (private), property (personal) and freedom (individual). Individualism is a sacred institution enabling the accumulation of profit, as White (1986: 40) elaborates,

> The accommodation of the state and the legal system to the demands of the powerless takes different forms depending upon the particular circumstance. Aside from the direct use of coercive force, the usual route taken in advanced capitalist societies is through modification of specific legislation and/ or containment of immediate or potential conflict through administrative law.

The individualization of social problems is a liberal approach to seeing people in classless, ahistorical terms (ibid., 52). Strategies that promote effective and comprehensive intervention that truly aid the disadvantaged are missing. There does not appear to be a commitment to eliminate unemployment. A full employment strategy should never be abandoned despite the lack of political commitment to reducing unemployment. The answer to unemployment is jobs. Federal policies are influenced by the supply side and monetarist economic theories which maintain that the problems of low/poor investments and inflation are related to excessive government spending, heavy taxes and a large debt. According to this logic, to reduce the debt governments must reduce spending and reduce taxes. This restraint is primarily felt by the poor and low-income communities. Some key structural changes are required; they include the re-alignment of capital ownership, more legitimate access to surplus values and profit that is accountable, i.e., a realignment of control entails a restructuring of traditional power relations. Industrial citizenship, increased corporate responsibility and workers' control over their working lives are needed. The struggle for rights is basically a battle over economic rights. Economic insecurity constitutes an injustice as evident in mass lay-offs and plant closures which are at an all time high. Labour market policies in the areas of unemployment insurance, skills retraining, elimination of discriminatory practices must be implemented.

Culture frames experiences and encodes discourses. In so doing, culture distorts communication and legitimates inequalities. The dominant culture, especially in reference to welfare policies, sets socio-legal constraints. In turn, law conditions social justice. Examine, for example, the series of constitutional debates and accords regarding employment, social assistance, regional development, social covenants, etc. Enshrining property rights in to the constitution has been a keen interest of the federal government. The Constitutional Accord of July, 1992, as presented in the multilateral meetings, were to incorporate elements of a social charter. New non-justifiable provisions were to be added to Section 36 (1) of the Constitution Act of 1982, describing the commitment of the governments to the following:

- a health-care system that is comprehensive, universal, portable, publicly administered and accessible;
- adequate social services and benefits to ensure that all individuals have reasonable access to housing, food and other basic necessities;
- a high quality of primary and secondary education and ensuring reasonable access to post-secondary education;
- protecting the rights of workers to organize and bargain collectively;
- preserving and protecting the environment.

Moreover the following are also required:

- a universal social welfare system;
- re-establish and strengthen universal family benefits;
- protect the universality of health, social and education services;
- universal day care;
- full unemployment;
- more effective social programs;
- a fair tax system;
- reasonable standard of living for all.

But these guarantees were simply expressed as goals and had no legal standing. Governments, therefore, had no legal obligation to fulfil these lofty promises. The federal government as an ardent supporter of the UN frequently ignores the United Nations Universal Declaration of Human Rights, to which it had been signatory, which states:

> All human beings are born free and *equal in dignity and rights*.... Everyone is entitled to all the rights and freedoms

set forth in this Declaration, without distinction of any kind,
such as race, colour, sex, language, religion, political or other
opinion, national or social origin, birth or other status. (Hill,
1979: 2, emphasis added)

Conclusion: the inequalities of crime and culture

This chapter introduced a reworking of traditional texts by highlighting
the intellectual imperialism and the authoritarian nature of normative forms
and processes of cultural reproductions. Culture is a barrier to communication
that has become institutionalized within an absolutist and corporate
interpretive frameworks. Culture is ideologically constituted in the interests
of state and corporate capital. Culture is the fabric that clothes and protects
the body of privilege. Accordingly, crime demands denial by the authoritative
other; this other defines difference as inherently dangerous and therefore
deserving of discipline. This crime calculus is defended dogmatically
according to prevailing cultural codes. Common culture is a myth. The
commitment to many cultures disguises the subversion of racism, sexism
and class elitism. The text of a collective conscience, a moral binding force
or the cement of a nation articulates support for differences or pluralism
within a common culture. As Homi Bhabha notes:

> The dangers inherent in the concept of a contemporaneous
> "common" culture are not limited to politically conservative
> discourses. There is a pervasive, even persuasive, presence
> of such a paradigm in the popular rhetoric of multiculturalism
> .... lip service is paid to the representation of the marginalized.
> A traditional rhetoric of cultural authenticity is produced on
> behalf of the "common culture" from the very mouths of the
> minorities. (1992: 235)

In addition, Bhabha added: "The common culture promises individual
emancipation.... The common culture is the ideological purveyor of this
'impersonal' order of things" (1992: 242). Culture historicizes selectively
the experiences of exclusion suffered by women, people of colour and
the poor.

Any project committed to cultural analysis interrogates the character
of social order, locates this interrogation inside and outside the bounds of
conventional rules, steps back and looks into dominant institutional forms
that marginalize those deemed to be the other—the criminal, the deviant.
Culture, it is argued, normalizes exercises of power by constructing binary

oppositions. Accordingly, this cultural approach which relocates that which has occupied the margins to the centre, decentres and de-essentializes the subject by highlighting how the subject is constructed in contradictions (McMahon, 1998). The deference to essential elements of criminality are re-positioned and negotiable—always involving an open process of transformation.

Conclusions:
Crime, Culture
and Criticality

Introduction: resentment, resistance and risk

Cultural analysis of crime provides a refreshing approach to deconstructing notions of consent and common sense. Admittedly, culture mediates agency (interpretive approaches) and structure (deterministic approaches). Culture, like matters of faith, demands deference and participation. Criminology is informed by cultural studies. Crime and culture enjoy a symbiotic relationship, that is, the nature of crime shapes and is shaped by the quality of culture. This book argues for the necessity of reconceptualizing crime in terms of cultural discourses which enable an understanding of the political economy. To learn about crime is to question problematic positions of privilege which have not assumed much currency in everyday crime talk. If we are to do justice to crime we must move beyond the canons and confront the lived experiences.

Groves and Lynch (1990: 367) write:

> Experience exists. Hopes, fears, and memories exist. Pain
> and suffering exist, as do happiness and jubilation. If these
> feelings and experiences are beyond the grasp of some
> particularistic vision of criminology, so much the worse for
> criminology.

What then is the relationship between culture and discourse? For Foucault, discourse refers not only to speech acts but to a body of interlinked "statements" bound regularities, that both constructs and is reflexively constructed by social and personal reality (1979: 199-200). As Foucault states: "discursive practices *are* not purely and simply ways of producing discourse. They are embodied in technical processes, in institutions, in patterns of general behaviour, in forms for transmission and diffusion, and in pedagogical forms which, at once, impose and maintain them" (ibid., 200). Accordingly, relations of power are important. Crime acquires meaning definition in certain discourses, for discourses transfer ways of speaking into action, a process in which power is implicated. Particular discourses define reality and construct, as well as constrain, interpretations. Discourses are neither incorrigible nor fixed. Rather, discourses are related to various permutations of power, which, following Foucault, are shifting and fragmentary. This book argues that culture participates in this process of transformation despite the powerful discourses of crime that continually position them in particular ways. That is, these discourses have concealed the fact that crime is a remarkably elastic concept that is made coherent by deferring to diverse hegemonic projects. What remains a significant concern in this chapter is the realization of the limitations of traditional approaches to crime, narratives that support particularistic truth claims rather than more humane and rational methods. In fact traditions in criminology subjugate and inhibit resistance. Foucault writes, "Why do we say, with so much passion and so much resentment against our most recent past, against our present, and against ourselves, that we are repressed?" (1965: 288). It is the same in *Discipline and Punish* when Foucault responds to an imaginary reader who wonders why he spends so much time wandering among obsolete systems of justice and the obscure ruins of the torture chamber. "Why?" he replies. "Simply because I am interested in the past? No, if one means by that writing a history of the past in terms of the present. Yes, if one means writing a history of the present" (1979: 31). Following Foucault's preoccupation with power as the dominant social bond, this book locates freedom in resistance. Criminological theory enters into the difficult terrain of socio-political analysis. It is undoubtedly the case that researchers need to be more attentive to their positionality and privilege. Resistance is required at all levels of engagement—ideological, intellectual and methodological. As noted in the previous chapter, Gramsci used the term hegemony to denote the predominance of one social class over others. This represents not only political and economic control but also the ability of the dominant class to project its own way of seeing the world so that those who are subordinated by it accept it as common sense and natural. Commentators stress that this involves willing and active consent. Common sense is the manner in which the oppressed experience everyday struggles. The contradictions inherent in hegemony warrant attention: there are ongoing contradictions between ideology and everyday (lived) experiences attributable to powerful cultural agencies like the media.

Crime is always relegated to the margins, a threat to the homogeneity of cultural identity. The criminal is depicted as a foreigner, a symptom signifying trouble. For Kristeva (1991) the figure of the foreigner opens a space where politics is entwined with ethics. Regarding the "rejection of the other, " Kristeva argues that there is a non-integration of alterity within the common social body. Crime is not only a site but a process of incrementalization of ideas that stabilize over time to produce fixed consequences that affect interpretations. In fact, notions of crime account for our cultural identities. These normative practices inscribe homogeneity of common sense. Resistance to foreclosure invites subversive action, subversive relationships with the hegemonizing traditions are no facile task given the complications (omni-penetrations of culture) of essentializing cultures. Typically, culture, as a heterogeneous and transgressive domain, institutionalizes discourses, replete with images of crime. A critical perspective, however, interrogates the foundationalist notions by encouraging a more circumspect appreciation of the negotiative contexts of forms and practices as articulated in the manufacture of ideas and expressed in lived experiences. Binary modes of imaging and imagining reality are suspended in favour of emergent processes and interactions of power. Crime is a social accomplishment situated within the reproduction of particular orders. Cultural analysis focuses on the lived experiences, the intersections of political economy and history that are interwoven in the practices of everyday life. Thus, cultural analysis challenges all forms of power especially by incorporating the voices of the marginalized. In this regard, postmodernism provides interesting theoretic tools in highlighting the importance of provisional and relational understanding of crime. The great thinker Friedrich Nietzsche (1844-1900), the original postmodernist theorist, argued for severing ties with traditional reason and rationality imposed by the discourse of the master. In reference to criminology, much of this transformation relates to our embracing alternative conceptions of: society's social structure, role formation, human agency, discourse construction, knowledge or sense-making. Therefore, social change and social justice require a responsible and active debunking (deconstruction) by crimino-legal scholars and practitioners, addressing the politically constructed, ideologically articulated and media-driven dimensions of social problems (Arrigo, 1994; 1995).

Research as emancipatory: privilege, authenticity and action

The social organization of any research act consists of a wide spectrum of differentially constituted activities. Generally, researching crime invites many decisions that are oriented towards the generation of some knowledge. Knowledge, however, as the previous chapters highlighted, is not only ideologically situated but is also articulated as a legitimate consequence of research. But criminological research is a complex process that defies simplistic steps catalogued clearly and packaged uniformly as inventories of routines. Regrettably, the orthodoxy of crime research is deplete of methodological accounts. Instead, extant published studies relegate methodological concerns to a few ritualistic fleeting paragraphs homogenized within a dubious celebration of facile compliance that is presumed to be well understood by all readers. The difficulties, if not the pain of doing research, are glibly dismissed or at best blithely glossed over as irrelevant. Any commitment to research must assign priority to the dynamic interplay of theory, methods and ethics.

This discussion seeks to clarify the processes by which researchers may examine crime and culture by confronting the concomitant paradoxes inherent in doing ethnographies, we highlight specifically the role of the researcher and ethical (moral) considerations. In essence, the morality of the research enterprise is as much an object of investigation as the substantive focus on inquiry. Clearly, values affect the message by shaping the contours of the emergent knowledge of events.

Theories are as adequate as the methods used to advance them. Ethnographic research methods cannot be simply reduced to a finely scripted, a preconceived and programmatic narrative that defies flexibility and accommodation. The collection and analysis of data invite a commitment to knowledge generated from experiences with natural phenomenon. The processes of discovery, presentation and analyses of findings are essentially integrated. Social action becomes a negotiated and emergent production (Denzin, 1978: 1). It is this interactional context which shapes the structure of activities, relations and identities. Naturalistic field studies or ethnographies offer much promise in eliciting information that is clearly more sensitive to the situation and better captures the meaningfulness of events for the studied populations. Even with these approaches, it is imperative to move beyond the banal liberal rhetoric of simply appreciating individuals towards a more comprehensive analysis of culture and structure. Clearly, the people studied expect more than a trite appreciation; they expect more than a prurient interest that evaporates once the researcher leaves the site or once one has attained careerist aspirations.

An ethnography essentially encourages the researcher to grasp a first-hand knowledge about the social world in question, to experience the actors' experiences in their everyday worlds. As a general methodology, an ethnography displays an omnibus quality by incorporating an array of well-reasoned exercises that includes informal observations, direct observation and participation, conversational or informal interviewing, and formal unfocused interviews, as well as more egocentric inquiries, reflexivity and self-debates. Flexibility invites researchers to be more responsive to changing situations and more open to pursuing issues and leads to greater detail. An immersion in the everyday life of actors reflects a respect or an appreciation. Only by getting close to these "hosts" (Wax, 1980: 272) and spending time on their "turf" can the investigator discover the social construction of action. An appreciative stance demands a superior standard of sensitivity and an immediate willingness to explore matters which are meaningful to others.

An ethnography is extremely appropriate in researching that which remains hidden from official content analyses, notably the lives of populations designated as criminal. People in their natural turf tend to share information more readily with those who participate in their life or with others who indicate a more sensitive appreciation of their setting and activities. Ethnographies usually commence with only a few general concepts or hunches regarding the nature of social organizations. Under the general guidance of orienting concepts, data are collected on how actors organize their worlds or make sense of their social order. Gradually, the investigator organizes the data by sorting out similar and different contents into tentative formulations of categories. A number of constructs emerge as a result of these theoretical interpretations of empirical incidents. An ethnography facilitates the development of a moral insights.

An ethnography makes effective use of the relationships that researchers establish with their studied populations (subjects) in the field. The rapport and subsequent information collected are conditioned by the context in which researchers are placed; relations are typically constructed within processes of reciprocity. To ensure a naturalistic description, a role is required that is comfortable enough for the studied populations to accept and comfortable enough for the researcher to assume. This role includes movements back and forth between the world of one's hosts and one's own sociological discipline. Responsibility requires abilities to respond.

Roles range from complete participation to complete observation. There are benefits and dangers inherent in both extremes. With the latter, there is a tendency to remain too removed or too distant from events. With the former approach researchers "go native," over-identify and become that which they study. The roles researchers adopt and the roles assigned to them place them in the margins: they are in but not of the world of the observed. A marginal role does not prevent researchers from gaining intimate contact with the phenomenon as long as they are not complete strangers. It is essential that researchers follow through on commitments. Studied populations allow researchers to "hang out" with them and would often expect intensive involvements. The process of accompanying these field hosts throughout their full round of activities is extremely effective in securing and maintaining acceptance. But, even after being accepted, researchers are still considered outsiders since they are required to leave the field to write up the study.

Marginality, nonetheless, demands subservience. In essence, dependency characterizes all the relationships researchers develop. Research is a challenging enterprise that generates moral questions. As sociologists, however, we are required to confront a number of problems regarding ethics. On the one hand, the ethics of scientific inquiry demands uncompromising honesty and objectivity. It is unethical, for example, for researchers to encumber future investigators by making it impossible for others to conduct similar inquiries. There is also the often ignored ethics to society—the demand to ameliorate social conditions (Plummer, 1983). On the other hand, researchers must act responsibly towards their observed. We ought to avoid injury to their reputations caused by divulging confidential information. Researching violence, for example, by doing more violence to disadvantaged groups by privileged investigators is grossly unethical.

Every imaginable sociological enterprise raises ethical considerations. Likewise, entrance, presence and departure are unethical if they disrupt the long-term functioning of the social group, especially if findings are used for immoral ends, for increased crackdowns on certain populations by the police and for frothing up public hysteria about specific researched activities. To reduce any possible harm, representatives of the researched populations should be encouraged to read the manuscript individually and collectively. That is, the fertile grounds from which much information is mined runs the risk of being exploited and then abandoned. The issue of ethics is related to the respect for the empowerment not solely of the researcher but of the pre-existing culture and community that will suffer the consequences of the arrogance of researchers who quickly escape to publish their results.

While social scientists have an obligation to contribute to knowledge, they also have a duty to protect participants in the research. Confidentiality is the most familiar ethical question facing social scientists. The promise of confidentiality remains an inducement to subjects for their cooperation and, therefore, ethically binds the researcher to honour that commitment. This obligation to protect the identity of subjects becomes heightened especially with research subjects who are deviantized by the larger society.

Inseparable from this promise of confidentiality is the equally important issue of trust. To ensure trust, researchers ought not to detach themselves from the consequences of·their work. It behoves us not only to study significant problems and report the findings but also to be sensitive to the way findings can be subsequently used. In any research undertaking, trust needs to be developed and cannot be taken for granted. This becomes even more readily evident when dealing with a people who are street smart who have learned not to trust too many individuals inside and outside of their respective reference groups. Obviously, they had every reason to refuse participation given their fears of greater police involvement. Also related to trust and confidentiality is the issue of legality. This is not to suggest that there is no resistance. There is really no reason for the studied populations to believe that the research is innocuous and inconsequential.

Methodological flexibility and accommodating strategies are needed to negotiate the access to information. Personal disclosure on the part of the researcher is morally expected. Likewise, sociologists and criminologists can ill afford to ignore professional guidelines established by institutional sponsors and funding agencies. Openness is imperative; feedback and on-going input beyond the reciprocity of specific research roles enhance trust. According to Erikson (1965): "it is unethical for a sociologist to deliberately misrepresent his identity for the purpose of entering a private domain ... to deliberately misrepresent the character of the research." Moral distancing is highly problematic. Obviously, the following suggestions are helpful: first, the researcher must ensure that the studied populations enjoy the right to be fully informed about the precise nature and purposes of the research; second, consent must be freely given; third, assurances of confidentiality must be extended at all stages; and fourth, the rights of the studied groups to expect accurate (valid) portrayals. Thus, ethics and not convenience ought to triumph.

Validity and reliability are never equally maximized within any single methodology. In general, validity refers to the accuracy of data, that is, the accuracy of the picture one reports about the empirical world. Validity rests on how well the sociologist understands the actors' subjective categories for ordering their experiences. Reliability, however, refers to the consistency, uniformity or universality of findings over time and space. An obsession with reliability often results in operationally defining away the concerns for validity. The effects of intrusions are frequently dismissed in glossy and superficial justifications that fail to incorporate the accounts and anxieties of the hosts. Researchers are not always mindful of their situational roles as field guests.

Ethnographies defy conceptual closure; they are pliant and accommodating to the interests of the researched populations. Additionally, the primacy of the human agent (Katovich, 1987) and the emphasis on the experienced natural world implicate the often problematic issues of cultural reproduction, political economy and the state. For example, such concepts as crime, conflict, sexism, racism, homophobia, materialism, etc. are reflective of dominant cultural values (Murray, 1984; West, 1984; Wolf, 1991; Loseke, 1987; Denzin, 1987). Only by taking stock of the array of methodological procedures and their attendant strengths, does one acquire a critical appreciation of the permeability of ethnographies.

Likewise, ethical reviews need to be flexible in dealing with vulnerable populations. Traditional criteria are not just relaxed but recast as more sensitive. The dominant natural science models demand an elaboration of a programmatic inventory of stages and normative rules. Accordingly, scientific inquiry becomes counter-productive in the generation of knowledge. Conventional designs more is concealed than revealed. A priori justifications based on literature reviews, pilot projects or preliminary investigations tend to codify and ossify that which will be investigated. By standardizing too much to satisfy institutional monitors and funding sources, a version of the truth remains compromised if not lost altogether. By calculating procedures and timetables in advance, an artificial agenda is secured. Researchers mobilize their interpretations claiming a sense of objective reality.

Far too often it is argued that research that goes beyond the text by challenging deeply held traditions of research protocols is too threatening politically and conceptually too innovative. Research supported by state sponsored funding sources is too circumscribed politically and ensures the continued suspicion of less privileged researched populations. *Crime and Culture* is part of a larger project an inquiry into mechanisms of social change. As Dorothy Smith advocates, a shift is required whereby the researcher attempts to understand the world from inside; the social organization of the actors studied (Smith, 1987). We cannot deny their historical realities however unpleasant and critical. Mainstream research reflects mainstream values that exclude the voices of women and men of colour, of Aboriginal peoples, lesbians and gays, the poor, etc. (ibid., 107). Finally, within the last two decades there has been a keen interest in research that undermines the prevailing conventional insensitivities and refuses to maintain current inequalities. This critical research interrogates the subversive nature of conventional methodologies. To elucidate, critical ethnographies are liberative, moving beyond the contrived commandments of clip-board recipes towards embracing mechanisms for grounding more reflexively and subjectively the experiences of others. Critical ethnographies fully appreciate the limitations of conventional approaches by exploring the generic features, extra-local, historical, political interconnections of institutional orders. Engaging actively in the everyday events, this commitment situates the research by understanding the details of the lives of the disadvantaged. In addition, critical ethnographies examine how different cultures confine as well as liberate, and how culture mediates prevailing ideologies and the influences of the political economy. One's informants are not simply objects of inquiry but also change agents who have voices that articulate integrity and move well beyond the narrow interests of the researcher.

All research is obtrusive. Attempts, however, are warranted to minimize the dangers of field work. The use of multiple strategies and different vantage points succeeds in maximizing the accuracy of the events and experiences. For instance, historical sociology also provides a map for visualizing the relative locations of the research. E. P. Thompson (1963) advocated that researchers reveal their own perspectives on the research question. Individuals have agency while taking structure into account. Historical moments are central in explicating how structure and agency form moral careers and how social processes mediate structure and agency. Individual and cultural trajectories will easily identify social formations and the reproduction of control as outcomes of historically formed configurations. History thus serves to identify and inform the content of oppressive conditions.

Research as privilege: locating the authentic

Conventional research glosses over privilege. Privilege is differentially distributed according to race, gender and class. As Maguire (1987: 199) argues: "The challenge is to celebrate our collective accomplishments, however small, and nurture ourselves as we move slowly and imperceptibly, in the direction of change for social justice." Privilege, especially that of a white male (usually Anglo-American) heterosexist researcher, is not only normalized, but this supremacy is taken for granted in the discipline. How researchers experience the world influences their decisions to study the world. A shift is required that includes differences. A shift is only possible if researchers come to terms with their respective privileges. They must come to terms with their privilege by "undoing" themselves and not neglecting the sources of their own ignorance and arrogance. They render more knowable, more visible and more public the advantages that they have enjoyed (the secret paths), the ease and convenience with which they work (the networks of affiliation) and the structured benefits (power). The privileged need to listen both to themselves and to others. Traditional research suffers from selective amnesia and listens only to discriminating soft sounds, and adopts a stir and mix approach to inequalities. Privileged researchers must learn to move over, otherwise the laurels that they have selfishly created for themselves will inevitably become their wreaths. It is about time that these researchers acknowledge their indifference to differences, redefine their centres and connect with other forms of consciousness.

Tough choices are required in order to understand inequality. Sources of identification and positions of authority are sites of struggle. Critical ethnographies are premised on processes of learning and not simply crass cultural appropriation disguised as scholarship. This responsibility, if shouldered effectively, avoids the arrogance of the monolithic text and moves towards an attenuation of colonial discourses. Privilege is an abusive site that refuses to address its own limitations and recognize the authenticity of other experiences. Routinely learned principles embedded in well-revered texts contradict lived experiences. Privileged texts are based on biases that recognize as superior only those insights that are generated within well-protected corporate structures. The knowledge of the privileged sustains its own subjectivity and engineers its own research agenda.

Authenticity is a commitment to resistance, and as Trotman (1993) clarifies, authenticity moves beyond Western thinking to begin the work of constructing alternate social realities. The authentic social construction of a different reality (James, 1963b) requires the creation and transformation of hegemonic dominance. Authentic voices are seldom heard, voices which move people to social action. This search for the conscious voice will be determined by the social conditions in which it is generated (James, 1963b; Trotman 1993). An emphasis on the authentic voice furnishes us with occasions that enable us to be aware of the external world that corresponds with our ideas. Human beings are at the centre of their experiences, subjects in their world. But the world has the other, the dominant other, whose yardstick privileges a few and punishes many others.

Authenticity encourages an awareness of the self in the other and the other in the self. The authentic identity speaks with a clear voice that has come to terms with many struggles. There is a connection between the self as subject and the other; the location of the self in society. Authenticity considers the self as a knowing being, a powerful self that possesses a clear understanding of one's place in the world (ibid.).

As discussed in the previous chapter, research is an intellectual act that confronts privilege and takes responsibility for the plight of the disadvantaged classes. The inauthentic intellectual (Trotman, 1993: 28) is created within the dominant cultural hegemony; born of the same hegemonic dominance to be challenged. The authentic researcher is creative, developing new ways of relating to their world. This authentic agent breaks with hegemony and assumes a new sense of liberating responsibility that struggles to transcend the given. Knowing is the complexity of being human in the world in which subjects find themselves rooted (Trotman, 1993: 26). The knowing subject creates a different environment, new and liberated. In constructing an alternate cultural hegemony, the self validates the subject and transplants a way of seeing (ibid., 47) that juxtaposes the contradictions of the dominant hegemony with the realities of colonial societies.

In order to understand criminological texts, researchers need to articulate methodological problems inherent with both conventional and emerging strategies. The researcher as a cultural worker is oriented towards creative experiences, the unity of mind and body within a liberating consciousness and the pursuit of praxis.

Praxis: advocacy and "resistance research"

Where do we go from here? A commitment to social action concretizes a critical consciousness. A more omnibus approach to the study of crime seeks to understand structures of inequality, social trends, cultural contradictions and progressive transformations. Praxis, a theory-informed practical commitment to social change, unites ideas with and action. Praxis, as an ideologically progressive pedagogy, incorporates political confrontations and reflexivity. For far too long research has served as an ideological state apparatus and acted as an instrument of privilege. State funded research centres, state sponsored grants and private corporate funding have ensured the complicity of intellectuals in mystifying socially ratified discourses. Not only are these studies ideologically static, they are conducted by individuals and groups who profit from public funding by legitimating extant policies. Criminological research projects have traditionally made vulgar claims about objectivity, science and value-free logic. This emphasis on natural science criteria pacifies and depoliticizes. The 1990s have witnessed a paradigmatic shift in research styles. Critical engagement based on traditions of praxis is grounded in the everyday experiences of the studied populations. These experiences are expressions of underlying social structural inequalities, wider cultural contexts, the constraining effects of the dominant ideology on perceptions, the silencing of oppositional perspectives and the exploitation of crime as a commodity. Action research, allied with the struggles of diverse empowerment movements, is a call for resistance.

Of what benefit is research to the people studied? To what extent is the researcher prepared to learn? A critical ethnography maintains that the researched populations are able to make decisions even though their options are often limited. Participatory research is proactive and articulates, according to Maguire (1987) in *Doing Participatory Research: A Feminist Approach*, a commitment to the improvement of the lives of research participants. In fact, emancipatory research is oriented towards the "mobilization of human resources for the solution of social problems" (Hall, 1982: 23). This action-oriented philosophy encourages research with and not on people. A recognition that the researched populations have the capacity to change is less alienating, less elitist and more validating of their authentic experiences and capacities to act and change. Active and emotionally charged involvements open dialogue with all the participants—researchers and informants. Feedback, ongoing input and follow-ups involve continued collaboration with all relevant stakeholders.

Community (in) action

An agenda that invites the meaningful participation of the most affected incorporates genuine community-based community participation as a viable resource. Participation occurs within wider interactive contexts and articulates discourses of power and privilege. But, the appropriation of community resources by the state to legitimate programs, to re-socialize volunteers and to discredit discordance subverts any meaningful dialogue. The state seeks a banal accommodation to bureaucratic propaganda—image building rather than the capacity of the community to advise. Remedial palliatives like community watch, block parenting, crime stoppers, etc. are shallow gestures and bankrupt slogans that fail to confront structural deficiencies oriented instead towards the maintenance of dependency relations. Organizational analyses clearly suggest that bureaucracies are designed to maintain stability while concurrently generating limited outside input. Centralization protects the distribution of power. Controls in decision-making and policy formulations are deliberately complex and blurred, thereby defying facile access to and understanding of the vagaries of administrative privileges.

A characteristic feature of the criminal justice system is to shift from goal-oriented mission statements to procedural priorities. Thus, professionalism not voluntarism overwhelms. In unmasking authority structures it is evident that work in the crime industry is clouded in secrecy. Decisions, policies and strategies are effectively insulated and immune from general inspection. Secrecy is rationalized, in turn, as organizational imperatives. The norm of secrecy or the cowardice of anonymous committees is a valuable tool in controlling information and avoiding accountability. Secrecy is a screen behind which incompetence is protected. Keeping secret its expertise and motives, organizations treat knowledge as a powerful commodity, which is differentially distributed even within the bureaucracy. Experts are assigned exclusive tasks. Mysteries are perpetuated. Specialization dislocates and subordinates public input. Once the public has succeeded in participating in formal discussions, a further institutional layer surfaces—informal occupational cultures that do not necessarily share the political enthusiasm of community involvement. Within corrections, for example, the rank and file seek to protect their own control, self-interests and immunities from the encumbrances of management. The occupational culture arguably has reasons to suspect management-driven initiatives such as citizens advisory committees. Labour is seldom consulted in the wholesale array of impression management schemes that promote the progress and success of administrative plans. Alternatives that depart from co-optation are needed despite the resistance from bureaucrats who continue to act with impunity in disregarding the interests of constituencies in favour of their own organizational and political exigencies. As Doob

(1990: 420) admonishes: " we often do little to ensure that alternatives work as alternatives rather than as mere supplements to imprisonment." Likewise, Cohen (1985: 44) suggests: "community control has supplemented rather than replaced traditional methods."

An examination of advocacy and community-based empowerment provides a conceptually more comprehensive appreciation of community action in criminological research. From a public policy perspective, however, a focus on communities-in-action is threatening. This commitment to meaningful action does not suffer from the vagueness and vulnerability of state-sponsored community constructions. Changes in legislation, administrative rules and regulations that protect independent community input are long overdue. Moreover, vigilance on the part of community groups is needed in reclaiming that which more appropriately belongs to them. Community-based initiatives repeatedly confront numerous barriers that include, for example, the denial of a problem, the refusal to recognize the significance of community input, a self-arrogated sense of professionalism that fears change and remains suspicious of critical inquiry, a lack of commitment to change, a dysfunctional public accountability or a displacement of responsibility to name only a few. The following changes could easily be implemented: the researcher, for instance, needs to develop an understanding of community interests that moves beyond trite public statements; increase the flow of information; field questions from all community groups; encourage proactive consultation; utilize community resources; invite participation in the program planning and development stages; or select informants from a cross-section of the community who will articulate issues of inequality rampant in the criminal justice system such as the treatment of the First Nation communities.

Concrete steps in eradicating barriers are now necessary to move from a posture of reflection to one of action. During the initial stages of involving community groups, researchers would be well advised to: provide information to prospective informants; develop a brokerage role that would reach out to identify and encourage community or neighbourhood-based organizations; develop a capacity for inter-organizational collaboration; organize resources so that they could have a maximum impact; develop and implement explicit policies to improve community participation with appropriate protections against arbitrary decisions; co-ordinate community events and workshops; and collaborate with service providers and advocacy groups that work with the socially disadvantaged. According to Warren (1977: 251), even when organizations are transformed into something closer to their heart's desire, they may still remain as islands in a very hostile sea. The need for change directed at the societal level is crucial. As Galper (1975: 46) argues in reference to reform:

> They express concern for individual and social welfare, but they do so in a form shaped to limited and distorted values and structures and, thus ultimately undermine the pursuit of human welfare. They are established within a political and economic context. This context, we believe, acts to subvert.

Access is a central dynamic that influences interplay between the community and research. Access is not limited only to participation at the local level of community relations, but, more significantly, access refers to the level of involvement in policy formulation, advising senior bureaucrats, setting directions for change, funding criteria and ongoing consultations with community leaders. Access is not just the enjoyment of a few opportunities made available by university research protocols; access refers to the ownership of the agenda that to date has been exclusively controlled by the outsiders.

The struggle for change is a challenge, a political process that cannot be left to the benevolent gestures of researchers acting as authority agents. Briefly, problem solving is a collective accomplishment despite the rancorous cacophony of authorities denouncing the involvement of biased subjects. Structural barriers such as the rigid bureaucratic framework, inadequate legislation, systemic bias against any challenge to authority and ineffective accountability prevail. Mobilization of outside support, therefore, is justified. But, efforts to mobilize a large number of people to bring about change (Clarke et al, 1975: 1; Stone, 1990) are determined by several contingencies.

Mobilization, "the activation of human resources for collective participation" (ibid., 12) is shaped by the following factors: ideology, an able leadership and channels of communication or networks of cooperative relationships. Ideology sustains participation by providing a litany of invaluable rationalizations. This set of inter-related values re-socializes volunteers or activists to become receptive to new competing definitions. Additionally, ideology is a reflexive process that is directed at the self and recasts present troubles through past experiences. Ideological challenges invite, as Lofland (1985) suggests, ongoing conversions in social and personal identities. A change in consciousness emerges as long as alternative visions are explored and a distance from official accounts is maintained. Logically, this quasi-resistance is, in effect, an expression of agency, autonomy and accountability. Gradually, the self becomes oriented towards un-learning the conventions of corrections and increasingly familiar with more compelling, albeit more unorthodox explanations of power and the consequences of non-compliance. By moving beyond convenience and self-serving rationales, community representatives ideologically situate themselves as committed participants.

Ideology does not alone ensure a successful protest. The potential for mobilization is determined by the cohesiveness of the group, strengths of opposing control agents and the resources available. For Tilly (1978), mobilization is the process of creating commitments that generate a willingness to contribute resources. Group cohesiveness, with its attendant collaborative orientations towards advocacy, constitutes a pressure to change the state's approach to community interests. This emphasis on cojoint activities will undoubtedly empower any community organization to demand access. Also, coalition building with the socially disadvantaged, economically deprived, community-based organizations, feminist, anti-racist action groups, labour, Aboriginal associations, open and well-established communication networks with the media, opposition party members of the legislatures and civil liberties are formidable forces. Attempts by the state to promote inter- and intra-group conflicts in an effort to construct the community in its own image and likeness will falter.

The community is an elusive concept that has been too easily appropriated by the state to engineer support for limited initiatives that fail to grapple with fundamental inequalities in corrections. This term is contextually determined and discursively constructed to satisfy organizational interests. Without reference to the context of power, the community concept has become a pretext for intervention and exclusion. A commitment to local contests, for example, is perceived as counter hegemonic and subject to coercive measures. This sponge-like term enables the state to celebrate and parade research that it has effectively screened—to appoint those individuals and organizations who subscribe deferentially to authority and subject relations and enjoy the benefits of such complicity and deception that something is being done for the community.

The normative notion of the community is related to the concept of hegemony, leadership based on the consent of the ruled, consent secured by the diffusion and popularization of ruling class views. Consent of the ruled to their ongoing exploitation flows from the capitalists' hegemonic practices in all institutions of the state and civil society. Hegemony, achieved through institutions of civil society, is the predominance of one class over other classes through consent rather than force. This consent is manifested through a generic loyalty to the ruling class by virtue of their position in society. This position also entails that the ruling class uphold the prevailing traditions and mores of the period. The ruling class developed this hegemony through a level of homogeneity, self-consciousness and organization. Thus, hegemony is based on economic, ethical, social, philosophic and political interests. Hegemony means the permeation throughout society of an entire system of values, attitudes, morality or beliefs that are supportive of controlling class interests. This prevailing consciousness is internalized and becomes part of a common sense. The ideology of a community, as a system of ideas manifested in all aspects of social life, performs powerful policing functions. As a cultural form, this ideology legitimates social control by directing cognition, evaluations and ideals. With its links to political economy and the state, ideology encapsulates by distorting material conditions and privileges. For example, the dominant cultural ideologies incorporate features from other ideologies. For instance, legal myths about liberty and freedom have also become powerful instruments of domination. The talk of freedom has been appropriated conveniently by the community to justify and excuse inequalities in the name of community safety. Resistance, therefore, remains limited as long as we are fed, in Emperor Nero's words, some bread and circus. The ideological hegemony of the ruling classes is received by the masses as common sense, which blinds them to their own experiences and manufactured local and global community bonds. From neighbourhood watch to patriotism, the belief in the community is intellectualized as an ideology that functions cognitively as a mode of self-interpretation and social persuasion.

Overworked and hackneyed practices of voluntarism continue to evoke a degree of unreasonable optimism. Community initiatives are of dubious value when unaccompanied by meaningful programs that embrace universal entitlements. Historically, state sponsored community-based activities have been characterized by attractive legal palliatives replete with convenient mythologies. But more recently, the nature of the community has been subjected to considerable scrutiny. Clearly, the ramifications of community activism affect all sectors of the Canadian social landscape. Regrettably, however, well-informed community activists and committed representatives are eclipsed by distant gatekeepers—bureaucrats, politicians, consultants, business or commercial interests and countless other mercenaries who claim exclusive ownership of the community as a commodity. We need to journey beyond a reflexive celebration of a liberal rhetoric towards a more critical appraisal of the general implications of community activism. A prudent response to this pressing agenda warrants a detailed audit of accountability, independence and control.

A community is embedded within many contexts—social, political, economic and legal. Despite its hyperbolic niceties, the frequently invoked local context conceals as much as it reveals. A circumspect appreciation of current community initiatives demonstrates the inadequacies of prevailing traditional models. In brief, the community as envisaged in Canadian society is a product of orthodox liberalism and the ethos of convenient accommodation. This common belief in the sanctity of the community is enshrined in lofty, nostalgic and tantalizing mythologies. But, what community and whose community standards are we discussing? What are the inherent dangers of operationalizing the community according to stereotypic spatial criteria? How do state-contrived communities respond to the challenges of social justice? Foucault admonished: one should start with popular justice, with acts of justice by the people, and go on to ask what place a court could have within this (1980: 1). Does the community, therefore, appropriately reflect the dynamics, dialectics and diversity of Canadian society? Community participation as currently manifested does not alone facilitate the resolution of social disputes.

Admittedly, the above discussion suffers from anecdotal oversimplification and remains suspiciously idiosyncratic. Nevertheless, there are generic principles that are readily applicable to other research sites that demand a more rigorous investigation. This brief discussion urges students of criminology to juxtapose the rhetoric inviting community input with actual content and structure of community involvement, the imposed limitations that silence the voices of the concerned. Given the proliferation of chatter about increased community participation, students are further asked to problematize the relationship between the state and democratic accountability. Instead, community inaction is rewarded by the exaggerated privilege of being permitted to sit on committees struck by state functionaries. Communities-in-action, however, mobilize, advocate and articulate an agenda that provides an ongoing critique of power. Inequalities in corrections are ubiquitous. Victims feel ignored by an alienating system of justice; inmates, parolees and their families suffer deprivation; correctional officers complain about the insensitivities of management, stress and poor working conditions; and the general public remains ignorant and fearful of "alarming" crime rates, statistics that are often advanced to secure support for state practices.

Visioning in research: the community concept revisited

Community development is a catalyst for change. Both the researcher and the researched would benefit from organizational review of research, that is, a visioning of research objectives. This forecasting and stocktaking exercise includes:

i) the clarification of the history and mandate of specific research objectives;
ii) a process of connecting the purposes and goals to wider programs and activities;
iii) identification of financial costs in carrying out the research;
iv) the development of alternatives and options;
v) a review of the nature of community interests and an assessment of the benefits to be derived from the research to the membership;
vi) the establishment of procedures to enhance accountability and visibility of research by: developing partnerships and alliances; advisory assistance; public education strategies; ongoing consultation with the community regarding data collection; review structure of the research team to reflect more accurately the respondents; establish a working advisory group consisting of resources in the community; conduct effective and efficient information sharing; advisory and educative roles (newsletter, events: social and cultural outreach); facilitation sessions to determine the following: What connects the researcher to the project? What does the researcher want from the community? What kind of changes does the researcher want? The purpose of a praxis project is to generate strategies that provide for an equitable, sensitive and coherent set of immediate and long-term responses that enhance social justice.

Researched populations and researchers are mutually dependent brokers who ought to be involved in all aspects of the research design and implementation. Hence, representation from these diverse groups will be maintained. Ongoing evaluation is an integral part of all phases of the project. It is also anticipated that the research results will be useful and, in particular, the information will be shared with the participants. The intent is to return to local communities or neighbourhoods that which authentically belongs to them—their accounts. Traditional researchers typically appropriate and re-package their stories to fit foreign criteria. Why should this type of research be welcomed by local community interests? Regardless of the criminological site, we have yet to police the research according to social justice criteria. Aside from claims of anonymity and confidentiality, what have traditional researchers left behind in terms of assisting local initiatives?

Research is a moral drama in which researchers are required to make judgments about their methods, the data collected and the theoretical frames selected. Invariably, researchers have been reluctant to pursue a sociological imagination. They deny themselves the capacity to shift from one perspective to another; a capacity that intersects biography and history. Writing over three decades ago, C. W. Mills admonished in *The Sociological Imagination* ([1959], 1978) that a form of consciousness is required, a consciousness that links the personal troubles of milieu and public issues of social structure. It is a quality of mind that seems most dramatically to promise an understanding of the intimate realities of ourselves in connection with larger social realities. New rules of research within a culture of accountability are needed. To assist in this revolt against authority, we now refer briefly to the insights of anarchists. Regrettably, anarchism is poorly understood in traditional teachings in criminology.

According to the philosophy of anarchism, three qualities are salient: an emphasis on individual responses to the politics of truth; a rejection of professionalism and departmental academicism; and a belief in the sanctity of private life (Horowitz, 1964: 19-23). Action or propaganda by deed and not the illusory words on research protocols will better civilization. Much research is egoistic, an expression of the dominant culture which, in turn, is root of the problem (ibid., 23; Malatesta, [1907] 1949: 38). The writings of Bakunin, an activist who spent eight years in prison in the dungeons of Tsarist Russia, pervade the contributions of Fanon, Debray, Cleaver, Marcuse, etc. Fanon, like Bakunin, pinned his hopes not on the more advanced workers corrupted by middle-class values (the intellectuals) but on the unprivileged and un-Europeanized village labourers. For Fanon, the more primitive the person, the purer the revolutionary spirit (Avrich, 1988: 9). The anarchist belief in the evil powers of state authority has received considerable support in the knowledge that state bureaucracy often turns out to be dysfunctional in operation and disgusting in its repressiveness. The anarchist insistence on the values of mutual aid has been transformed into a celebration of the worth of voluntary organizations (Horowitz, 1964:

598). Nicola Sacco (1891-1927) and Bartolomeo Vanzetti (1888-1927), arrested on charges of murdering a shoe factory paymaster and guard at South Braintree, Massachusetts, were tried and convicted in an atmosphere of antiradical hysteria. The trial ended July 4, 1921, and they were electrocuted on August 23, 1927. Sacco worked as a nightwatchman in a shoe factory and Vanzetti sold fish. Both immigrants were social militants who advocated relentless warfare against government and capital. They preached insurrectionary violence and armed retaliation against the monstrous violence of the state (Avrich 1988: 174-175); they rejected any docile submission to the state. Liberty, they maintained, demanded an unrelenting struggle. As Vanzetti declared:

> Both Nick and I are anarchists ... the radical of the radical—
> the black cats, the terrors of many, of all the bigots, exploiters,
> charlatans, fakers, and oppressors.... I am and will be until
> the last instant an anarchist communist. (Avrich, 1988: 164)

Vanzetti further articulated: "Yes they can crucify our bodies today as they are doing, but they cannot destroy our ideas ... we were for the poor and against exploitation and oppression" (Horowitz, 1964: 288-290). During their incarceration, widespread doubt reached worldwide proportions and resulted in international protest movements. Likewise, the brilliant contributions of Emma Goldman (1869-1940) encouraged a healthy distrust of the state and its cultural agencies. In "Marriage and Love," she writes about the consequences of state intrusions:

> The institution of marriage makes a parasite of woman, an
> absolute dependent. It incapacitates her for life's struggle,
> annihilates her social consciousness, paralyzes her
> imagination, and then imposes its gracious protection, which
> is in reality a snare, a travesty on human character. (Horowitz,
> 1964: 280)

Conclusion: teaching as trouble and the controversy of crime

Sociologists are particularly prone to controversial encounters in the classroom. In order to most effectively manage classroom dynamics, they must anticipate what types of subject matter can be potentially troubling, contentious or controversial. From the standpoint of personal experience, one might begin to classify the controversial as that which generates arguments or opposing viewpoints. Or, the controversial might be the topic we are uncomfortable discussing. With this in mind, it is important to choose to explore, via a blending of theoretical and methodological considerations, how to teach controversial issues in the classroom. From the outset, it is asserted that pedagogical methods cannot be relegated to a strict inventory of rules, roles and recipes. With this in mind, the goal of effective teaching requires an outline of guiding principles for addressing controversy, and to contemplate how those guiding principles relate to particular concrete examples. Substantively focusing on issues related to social justice, an effective teacher provides a critical pedagogical alternative for instructors seeking ways to both: 1) address controversial topics; and 2) positively confront resistance to learning that is often generated by the inclusion of controversial course content. From an experiential standpoint, reflecting on respective controversial encounters in the classroom, it seems quite essential that these experiences serve as the inspiration for teaching projects (Jakubowski and Visano, forthcoming). When thinking about teaching controversy, endless ideas come to mind. What issues are considered to be controversial issues? How should one approach controversial topics in the classroom? What kinds of risks does one take in dealing with themes and ideas that generate controversy? How does one accommodate or negotiate resistance that arises from different constituencies in the face of controversy, dispute and challenge? In relation to these questions we remind ourselves that we must always remain cognizant of our responsibilities to those who are affected by what we teach and how we teach it. Teaching about controversy demands trust, friendship and accountability—to both our students in the classroom and the affected communities outside of the classroom. With this in mind, students and instructors must learn to define the controversial and develop the response or "inability" to respond to the problem on the part of students and instructors. Stemming from the introductory reflections, Jakubowski and Visano ask: 1) When dealing with controversy, why do instructors encounter problems in the classroom? And, 2) How must the process of teaching and learning change in order to overcome these in-class obstacles? Towards addressing these questions, they incorporate theoretical and methodological considerations: classroom inaction—traditional practices—and inaction in the classroom—critical alternatives. The former approach critically discusses some of the characteristics associated with traditional, "banking" (Freire 1970) methods of instruction, highlighting why these methods are inadequate for teaching controversy. The latter suggests principles to facilitate the search for critical alternatives in teaching and learning. To properly lay the foundations of these activities, it is essential to discuss more generally the notion of critical thinking—its essential components, various critical pedagogical ideals—an education that is interactive, experientially based, consciousness-raising, empowering and transformative, and introduce concepts that might be useful in journeying towards this ideal: 1) the Gramscian (1971) notion of the intellectual; 2) intersubjectivity; and 3) the dialectic. These philosophical notions ultimately become the basis upon which to build a critical learning process that, we argue, unfolds through four phases: 1) the articulation of social experience; 2) codification; 3) decodification; and 4) empowerment. Consistent with this assertion that there can be no strict inventory of critical pedagogical methods. For example, personal, self-reflective research in the form of student journals; problem-based and collaborative learning; the social distance assignment; field trips; community service learning and the pink triangle exercise. Finally, regardless of the content, there will always be a struggle whenever there is compatibility or affinity between teaching and learning and social justice work in utilizing methods, exercises and activities that reflect the pedagogical ideals and complement the critical pedagogical framework.

Specifically, a learning process invites alternatives such as hearing traditionally marginalized voices, the voices that are regularly silenced, to speak. This collaborative process encourages continuous questioning of the world around us and taking action on behalf of social justice—action towards change where change seems to be necessary. In essence, it is imperative to challenge people to contemplate the possibilities of people coming together and collectively participating in social analysis and the search for "collective solutions" (Czerny et al., 1994: 201; Jakubowski and Visano, forthcoming).

The divisive logic of traditional criminological text prioritizes one oppression over the other, there is no one oppression that is more important than the other. Individually and collectively, race, gender, class, ableism, ageism and heterosexism enable an interrogation of power and the unquestioned privilege. It is therefore critical and incumbent upon all of us to make the connections with historical trends, ideological closures, the political economy of inequality, etc., issues that have shaped and continue to shape liberal democratic states. Ideology generated by the state reproduces the order of the day by a mass media. This powerful force engineers social panics, ignores crimes of the powerful, conceals illusions, mystifies and defines crime as entertainment. Ideology, infused at all levels, colonizes, internalizes and engraves oppressive images. Mindful of Marx's dictum that a society's superstructure (its political and juridical ideas and systems) is not independent of but arises from its economic or material base, one may safely assert that self-consciousness is manipulated to such an extent that the psyche invests in perpetrating further enslavement. But like Marx, Gramsci asks repeatedly why individuals participate in reproducing the dominant order. While Gramsci did not fully solve this dilemma, his contribution was to suggest the salience of cultural factors in everyday struggle.

In the contemporary Western world there is a tendency to take for granted the relationship which exists between writing, knowledge and textual organization, between the words in the text and the form or structure in which they are presented or treated. The relationship between knowledge and traditional criminological texts, for example, is therefore indispensable to a particular cultural codes.

Crime as a text defines knowledge narrowly. In so doing, crime is objectified according to a limited range of self-serving organizational criteria. The range of discourses used to construct the delinquency consists of ideological practices. What is articulated as knowledge of crime is problematic given official and media formations of truth. Both law talk and media images exclude the authentic representation of crime, the diverse experiences and political struggles. This argument is based on the conceptualization of crime as inseparable from the structural components of culture. A more coherent framework is warranted in approaching crime as a consequence of power imbalances. When studying delinquency it is imperative to shift one's own deeply entrenched beliefs and engage in intellectual cynicism regarding organizational practices that constitute the text. Only by going behind and beyond that which is uniformly masqueraded as truths, only by going beyond what Marx referred to as "fetishism of the commodity," and only by going behind the illusions of the media and the narcissism of the familiar codes of crime can we hope to grapple with what we really know. In response to the question, "What do we know?", the following is asked: What do we want to know? Why do we want to know? These answers are located in respective subtexts of ignorance and arrogance.

The war on crime, for example, is an ideologically and linguistically mediated expression of punishment. With the backdrop of law, policing and the military, discourses assume a degree of objectifying facticity. Ideologically, criminals are interpolated as subjects to be disciplined. Crime is reconstructed as a juridic text to be read in terms of socio-legal narratives outside the world of situated meanings. Within popular texts, the mythologies of danger conceal the subtexts of vulgar politics. A plethora of images that exaggerate the nature of war shapes attitudes and world views as well as social relations that further produce collective expressions and complimentary texts of exclusion. This mastery of illusions, the intersection of crime talk and texts of profit, the mechanical and historical exploitation of the other and the referential targets of race succeed in fine-tuning an immediate attack mode. By constructing the enemy in terms of identifiable communities, the war on crime conveniently diverts attention away from an inquiry into the nature of a capitalist society, the culture inequality and the complicity of politics. On the other hand, the prospects of peacekeeping (structural, institutional and interactional) considers how cultural, political and social forms inform identities in relation to conflicting social narratives of the self and subjectivity. Therein lies the transformative possibilities of justice: the subject is fractured and complexly articulated within a plurality of discourses that are never stable, static or fixed. A criminal is not an objectified and foundational category. Instead, this category is constructed through historical and cultural practices at the everyday level. Unlike traditional interventive strategies, peacekeeping confronts privilege directly. Ongoing transformation constitutes the preferred meaning of recovery.

Current punitive orientations destroy the dignity of those individuals, organizations and communities defined as others. Moreover, punishment is constructed within a framework of sophisticated surveillance, characteristic of industrial and post-industrial societies. This ubiquitous regulation is legitimated by institutions that promote a particular peace that protects privacy and property. Typically in our society, privacy and property are articulated within a well-respected utilitarian framework of possessive individualism. In Canada and the USA, the politics of profit and the protection of privacy are interconnected conceptual projects that define basic social relations. The fabric of order as envisioned by liberalism is woven together by a wide assortment of different fibres constituting a stratified quilt. Crime talk generates widespread inequalities. Some individuals, groups and communities are treated as commodities to be rented, sold and discarded. In brief, our criminalized culture reflects a pathology of privilege.

Crime and Culture alerts us to the rhetorical shrill of sanctimonious zealots who bristle and swarm around prophets of profit who espouse the virtues of possessive individualism, consumerism and materialism. From the air brushed images of impossible perfection, as the baseline against which we judge human worth, to the mindless compliance with whatever world corporatism and market capitalism have to offer, an analysis of contemporary culture discourages the tunnel vision characteristic of certain criminological canons. *Crime and Culture* seeks to stimulate the imagination into action, connect knowledge with passion and develop strengths in interpreting notions of our jealously protected common sense. For example, throughout 1998 the general public has been sprayed with the malodorous climate in the White House as a result of the alleged misconduct of Bill Clinton. Ken Starr, the special prosecutor who has spent over $30 million in public money trying to nail Clinton, is bent on peddling political porn in a tribute to media barbarism and the flatulent meanderings of opportunism. In this regard, Gloria Steinem's admonition is quite appropriate: "I'd rather have a president who has orgasms from sex than from dropping bombs on Iraq" (Landsberg, 1998: A2). Implicit in this statement is a plea to go beyond the media, to interrogate the culture and develop a capacity to understand crime.

Criminology cannot hope to appreciate its traditions without the help of cultural studies. A cultural critique enables a degree of introspection. By looking deeply into the traditions of criminology, we gain an awareness that enables the discovery of foundational principles (core issues) that shape the identity of contemporary criminology. By deconstructing that which has been assigned considerable theoretical primacy, we inspire rich analyses that interrogate the hegemonic traditions in order to refine truth claims in light of lived experiences. This probative exercise liberates the imagination from contemporary canons as well. Gaining direct awareness of the nature of crime is by no means a facile task. But, a critical imagination is a tool that goes a long way in inspiring a re-thinking of the taken for granted (common sense) that is invariably implicated with the dominant culture. This conclusion is indeed a moment of embarking; a preparation to start anew and to self-cultivate. Admittedly, this discussion involves risks, that is, decisions that go beyond, behind and between the texts, subtexts and intertexts. There are no absolute truths about crime, only degrees of distortion. *Crime and Culture* is about cultivating a compassionate consciousness that confronts culture. Without such a commitment, cowardice continues. Whatever path is pursued, there is an awareness of the connectedness within the totality of relations, the absence of which is criminal.

Bibliography and Suggested Readings

A

Abadinsky, H. 1981. *Organized Crime*. Boston: Allyn and Bacon.

Abella, I. 1992. "Shalom." *Toronto Star* (December 3): H1-H4.

Abella, I. and H. Troper. 1983. *None is Too Many*. Toronto: Lester and Orpen Dennys.

Abraham, D. 1990. "Treat Women as Equals." *Sunday Sun* (Mar 4): C15.

Adachi, K. 1976. *The Enemy That Never Was: A History of the Japanese Canadians*. Toronto: McClelland Stewart.

Adams, H. 1975. *Prison of Grass*. Toronto: General Press.

Adamson, W. 1987. "Gramsci and the Politics of Civil Society." *Praxis-International* 7 (Oct-Jan): 3-4: 320-339.

Adler, F. 1975. *Sisters in Crime*. New York: McGraw-Hill.

Adler, F. and W. Laufer. 1993. *New Directions in Criminological Theory, Advances in Criminological Theory*. New Brunswick, NJ: Transaction.

Adler, F. Mueller, G. and W. Laufer. 1991. *Criminology*. New York: McGraw-Hill.

Adler, P. and P. Adler. 1980. "Symbolic Interactionism." In J. Douglas et al. (eds.), *Introduction to Sociology of Everyday Life*. Boston: Allyn and Bacon.

Adorno, T. 1964. *Prismen, Kulturkritik and Gesellschaft*. Frankfurt: Suhrkamp.

Adorno, T. and M. Horkheimer. 1989. Selections from "The Culture Industry: Enlightenment as Mass Deception." In R.Gottlieb (ed.), *An Anthology of Western Marxism*. New York: Oxford University Press.

Agnew, R. 1985. "A Revised Strain Theory of Delinquency." *Social Forces* 64 (September): 151-167.

Akers, R. 1968. "Problems in the Sociology of Deviance." *Social Forces* 46 (June): 455-465.

Akers, R. 1980. "Further Critical Thoughts on Marxist Criminology: Comments on Turk, Toby and Klockars." In J. Inciardi (ed.), *Radical Criminology*. Beverly Hills: Sage.

Akers, R. 1985. *Deviant Behaviour: A Social Learning Approach*. Belmont, California, Wadsworth.

Akers, R. 1994. *Criminological Theories*. Los Angeles: Roxbury.

Akers, R., H. Krohn, L.Lanza-Kaduce and M.Radosevich. 1979. "Social Learning and Deviant Behavior: A Specific Test of a General Theory." *American Sociological Review* 44: 636-655.

Alba, R. 1980. *Italian American*. Englewood Cliffs: Prentice-Hall.

Albanese, J. 1983. "God and The Mafia Revisited: From Valachi to Fratianno." In G. Waldo (ed.), *Career Criminals*. Beverly Hills: Sage.

Albanese, J. 1985. *Organized Crime in North America: Politics, Paradism and Prosecution*. Cincinnati: Pilgrimage.

Albini, J. 1971. *The American Mafia*. New York: Meredith.

Allahar, A. 1986. "Ideology, Social Order and Social Change." In L. Tepperman and J. Richardson (eds.), *The Social World: An Introduction to Sociology*. Toronto: McGraw-Hill Ryerson.

Allahar, A. 1993. "When Black First Became Worthless." *International Journal of Comparative Sociology* xxxiv, 1-2.

Allen, J. 1988. "The Masculinity of Criminality and Criminology: Interrogating Some Impasses." In M. Findlay and R. Hogg (eds.), *Understanding Crime and Criminal Justice*. Sydney Law Book Co.

Allmand, W. 1993. "15 Years Later, Few Answers About Murder of Anna Mae Aquash." Insight *Toronto Star* (August 31): A13.

Altheide, D. 1976. *Creating Reality*. Bevery Hills: Sage.

Althusser, L. 1971a. *Lenin and Philosophy*. New York: Monthly Review Press.

Althusser, L. 1971b. "Ideology and Ideological State Apparatuses." *Lenin and Philosophy and other Essays*. London: New Left Books.

Amiel, B. 1985. "Straight Talk on Blacks." *Toronto Sun* (Oct 1).

Amiel, B. 1992. "Racism: An Excuse for Riots and Theft." *Maclean's* (May 18): 15.

Amos, V. and P. Parmar. 1984 "Challenging Imperial Feminism." *Feminist Review*. 17 (July): 3-15.

Anderson, A. and J. Frideres 1981. *Ethnicity in Canada: Theoretical Perspectives*. Toronto: Butterworth.

Anderson, D. 1988a. "Fight Against Porn Bill Misses Point." *Toronto Star* (February 27): J1.

Anderson, D. 1988b. "Women Around the World Winning, Losing." *Toronto Star* (April 30): F1.

Anderson, J. 1972. *A Philip Randolph: A Biographical Portrait*. New York: Harvest.

Anderson, N. 1923. *The Hobo*. Chicago: University of Chicago Press.

Andrews, A. G. 1992. *Report*. Review of Race Relations Practices of Metro Toronto Police Metropolitan Toronto Council.

Annual Report, 1990. *Judiciary Equal Opportunity Program*. Bureau of Justice Statistics, US Department of Justice, Washington, D.C.

Annual Report, 1993. The Canadian Centre for Police Race Relations, Ottawa.

Anti-Defamation League. 1993. *Audit of AntiSemitic Incidents*, 1992.

Arato, A. and E. Gebbhardt. 1997. *The Essential Frankfurt Reader*. New York: Continuum.

Archard, P. 1979. *Vagrancy, Alcoholism, and Social Control*. Thetford, Norfolk: Macmillan.

Arendt, Hannah. 1994. "Some Questions of Moral Philosophy." *Social Research* 1994, 61, 4, winter, 739-764.

Arms, S. 1975. *Immaculate Deception*. Boston: Houghton Mifflin.

Armstrong, E.G. 1976. "On Phenomenology and Sociological Theory." *British Journal of Sociology* 27 (2): 251-253.

Armstrong, G. and M. Wilson. 1973. "City Politics and Deviancy Amplification." In I. Taylor and L. Taylor (eds.), *Politics and Deviance*. Harmondsworth: Penguin.

Armstrong, P. 1984. *Labour Pains: Women's Work in Crisis.* Toronto: Women's Press.

Armstrong, P. and H. Armstrong. 1983a. "Beyond Sexless Class and Classless Sex: Towards Feminist Marxism." *Studies in Political Economy* 10 (Winter): 7-43.

Armstrong, P. and H. Armstrong. 1983b. *The Double Ghetto.* Toronto: McClelland and Steward.

Arnold, D. 1970. *Subcultures.* Berkeley: Glendessary.

Arrigo, B. 1994 "Legal Discourse and the Disordered Criminal Defendant: Contributions from Psychoanalytic Semiotics and Chaos Theory." *Legal Studies Forum* 18 (1): 93-112.

Arrigo, B. 1995. *The Contours of Psychiatric Justice: A Postmodern Critique of Mental Illness, Criminal Insanity and the Law.* New York: Garland.

Avrich, P.1988. *Anarchist Portraits.* Princeton: Princeton University Press.

B

Backhouse, C. and L. Cohen 1981. *Sexual Harassment on the Job.* Englewood Cliffs: Prentice-Hall.

Backhouse, C. and L. Cohen. 1978 *The Secret Oppression: Sexual Harassment of Working Women.* Toronto: Macmillan.

Baer, J. 1991. *Women in American Law.* New York: Holmes & Meier.

Bain, G. 1991. "An Orgy Over Whether All Men Are Vile." *MacLeans* (Dec 23): 48.

Baker, D. 1992. *Power Quotes.* Detroit: Visible Ink.

Baker, T. and A. Mitchell. 1992. "Real and Hidden Unemployment, Updated." *Social Infopac,* 11 (February) 1: 1-8.

Baldwin, J. and A. Bottoms. 1976. *The Urban Criminal.* London: Tavistock.

Balbus, I. 1973. *The Dialectics of Legal Repression: Black Rebels Before the American Criminal Courts.* New York: Russell Sage.

Baldus, D.C., G. Woodworth and C. Pulaski, 1985 "Monitoring and Evaluating Contemporary Death Sentencing Systems: Lessons From Georgia." *University of California-Davis Law Review* 33: 1-74.

Ball, R. 1966. "An Empirical Exploration of Neutralization Theory." *Criminologica* 4: 22-32.

Banfield, E. 1970. *The Unheavenly City.* Boston: Little, Brown.

Banfield, E. 1974. *The Unheavenly City Revisited.* Boston: Little, Brown.

Bannerji, H. 1993. *The Writing On The Wall: Essays on Culture and Politics.* Toronto: TSAR.

Banton, M. 1988. *Racial Consciousness.* London: Longman.

Barak, G. 1980. *In Defense of Whom? A Critique of Criminal Justice Reform.* Cincinnati: Anderson.

Bardsley, B. 1987. *Flowers in Hell: An Investigation into Women and Crime.* London: Routledge and Kegan Paul.

Barnes, J. 1954. "Class and Communities in a Norwegian Island Parish." *Human Relations* 7: 39-58.

Barnet, R. and R. Muller. 1974. *Global Reach: The Power of the Multinational Corporations.* New York: Simon and Schuster.

Barnett, H. 1979. "Wealth, Crime and Capital Accumulation." *Contemporary Crises* 3 (April) 2: 171-186.

Barrett, M. 1980. *Women's Oppression Today: The Marxist/Feminist Encounter.* New York: Verso.

Barrett, S. 1987. *Is God A Racist? The Right Wing In Canada.* Toronto: U of T Press.

Barrett, S. and W.L. Marshall. 1990. "Shattering Myths." *Saturday Night* (June).

Bar-Tal, D. and L. Saxe. 1976. "Physical Attractiveness and its Relationship to Sex-Role Stereotyping." *Sex Roles* 2, 123-133.

Barthel, D. 1988. *Putting on Appearances: Gender and Advertising.* Philadelphia: Temple University Press.

Barthes, R. 1972, 1973. *Mythologies.* London: Cape.

Barthes, R. 1975. *Le Plaisir du Texte (The Pleasure of the Text.* translated by R. Miller.) New York: Hill and Wang.

Barthes, R. 1988. "Photography and Electoral Appeal." *Mythologies.* London: Collins.

Barthes, Roland. 1988b. *The Semiotic Challenge.* New York: Hill and Wang.

Baudrillard, Jean. 1993. *The Transparency of Evil.* Trans. James Benedict. Paris: Verso.

Bartky, S. 1990. *Femininity and Domination.* New York: Routledge.

Barzini, L. 1965. *The Italians.* New York: Bantom.

Bates, T. 1975. "Gramsci and the Theory of Hegemony." *Journal of the History of Ideas* 26 (April-June): 351-365.

Battaile, G. and C. Silet (eds.). 1980. *The Pretend Indians: Images of Native Americans in the Movies.* Dubuque: Iowa State U. Press.

Beaty, J. and S.C. Gwynne. 1991. "The Dirtiest Bank of All." *Time* (July 29).

Bearden, J. and L. Butler. 1977. *Shadd: The Life and Times of Mary Shadd Cary.* Toronto: N.C. Press.

Bechhoffer, L. and A. Parrot. 1991. "What is Acqaintance Rape?" In A Parrot and L. Bechhofer (eds.), *Acquaintance Rape.* Toronto: J. Wiley.

Becker, H. 1960. "Notes on the Concept of Commitment." *American Journal of Sociology* 66 (July): 32-40.

Becker, H. [1963], 1964. *Outsiders: Studies in the Sociology of Deviance.* New York: Free Press.

Becker, H. (ed.). 1968. *The Other Side: Perspectives on Deviance.* New York: Free Press.

Becker, H. 1970. "Problems of Inference and Proof in Participant Observation." In W. Filstead (ed.), *Qualitative Methodology.* Chicago: Rand McNally.

Becker, H. 1974. "Labelling Theory Reconsidered." In P. Rock and M. McIntosh (eds.), *Deviance and Social Control.* London: Tavistock, 41-66.

Becker, H. and B. Geer and E. Hugher and A. Strauss. 1961. *Boys in White.* Chicago: University of Chicago.

Becker, H. and B. Geer. 1970. "Participant Observation and Interviewing: A Comparison." In W. Filstead (ed.), *Qualitative Methodology.* Chicago: Rand McNally.

Beckford, G. and M. Witter. 1980. *Small Garden.Bitter Weed.* London: Zed Press.

Beechey, V. 1967. "Whose Side Are We On?" *Social Problems* 14: 239-247.

Beechey, V. 1978. "Women and Production: A Critical Analysis of Some Sociological Theories of Women's Work." In A. Kuhn and A.M. Wolpe (eds.), *Feminism and Materialism: Women and Modes of Production.* London: Routledge and Kegan Paul.

Beirne, P. and J. Messerschmidt. 1991. *Criminology.* New York: Harcourt, Brace and Jovanovich.

Bell, D. 1962. *The End of Ideology*. New York: Free Press.

Bell, D. 1984. "The Police Response To Domestic Violence: A Replication Study." *Police Studies* 7 (Fall) 3: 136-144.

Bell, D.J. 1982. "Policewomen: Myths and Reality." *Journal of Police Science and Administration* 10: 112-120.

Bell, D. and K. Lang. 1985. "The Intake Dispositions of of Juvenile Offenedrs." *Journal of Research in Crime and Delinquency* 22 (4): 309-328.

Bern, S.L. 1993. *The Lenses of Gender*. New Haven, Yale U. Press.

Ben-Ari, E. 1987. "Pygmies and Villages, Ritual or Play? On the Place of Contrasting Modes of metacommunication in Social System." *Symbolic Interaction* 10 (Fall)2: 187-208.

Benjamin, W. [1968] 1970. "Theses on the Philosophy of History." *Illuminations*, tr. Harry Zohn, London: Jonathan Cape.

Bennett, G. 1987. *Crimewarps.* New York:.

Bennett, J. 1981. *Oral History and Delinquency: The Rhetoric of Criminology*. Chicago: University of Chicago Press.

Benney, M. 1983. "Gramsci on Law, Morality and Power." *International Journal of the Sociology of Law* 11 (May) 2: 191-208.

Bennett, R. and J. Flavin 1994. "Determinants of Fear of Crime: the Effect of Cultural Setting." *Justice Quarterly* 11 (Sept)3: 358-381.

Benson, M. and F. Cullen. 1988. "The Special Sensitivity of White Collar Offenders to Prison: A Critique and Research Agenda." *Journal of Criminal Justice* 16: 207-215.

Benson, M., Cullen, F. and W. Maakestad. 1990. "Local Prosecutors and Corporate Crime." *Crime and Delinquency* 36 (July)3: 356-372.

Bequai, A. 1978. *Computer Crime*. Toronto: D.C. Heath.

Bequai, A. 1978. *White Collar Crime: A Twentieth Century Crime*. Lexington, Mass.: Heath Lexington Books.

Bequai, A. 1987. *Technocrimes*. Lexington, Mass.: Lexington Books.

Berg, L. and K.J. Budnick. 1986. "Defeminization of Women in Law Enforcement: A New Twist is the Traditional Police Personality." *Journal of Police Science and Administration* 14: 314-319.

Berger, D. (ed.). 1986. *History and Hate*. New York: Jewish Publications Society.

Berger, J. [1972] 1988. *Ways of Seeing*. London: B.B.C.

Berger, P. 1963. *Invitation to Sociology*. New York: Doubleday.

Berger, P. and T. Luckmann. 1967. *The Social Construction of Reality*. Garden City: Anchor.

Bergman, B. 1991. "Women in Fear." *Macleans* (November 11): 26-30.

Berlin, L. 1963. *Karl Marx: His Life and Environment*. London: Oxford University Press.

Bernard, J. 1973a. *The Sociology of Community*. Glencoe, Illinois: Scott, Foresman and Co.

Bernard, J. 1973b. "My Four Revolutions: An Autobiographical History of the ASA." In J. Huber (ed.), *Changing Women in a Changing Society*. Chicago: University of Chicago Press.

Berrigan, P. 1970. *Prison Journal of a Priest Revolutionary*. New York: Ballantine.

Berry, B. and J. Kasarda. 1977. *Contemporary Urban Ecology*. New York: MacMillan.

Birtle, L. 1977. *Canada and its People of African Descent.* Ottawa: Information Canada, #38.

Bertrand, M. A. 1994. "From La Donna Delinquente to a Postmodern Deconstruction of the "Woma Question." In *Social Control Theory Journal of Human Justice* 5, 2: 43-57.

Bhabha, H. 1990. "DissemiNation: Time, Narrative, and the Margins of the Modern Nation." In Homi K. Bhabha (ed.), *Nation and Narration.* London: Routledge.

Bhabha, H. 1992. "A Good Judge of Character: Men, Metaphors and The Common Culture." In T. Morrison (ed.), *Race-ing Justice, En-gendering Power.* New York: Pantheon.

Bianco, A. 1986. "Wall Street's Frantic Push to Clean Up Its Act." *Business Week* (June 9).

Bienvenue, R. and J. Goldstein. 1985. *Ethnicity and Ethnic Relations in Canada.* Toronto: Butterworth.

Bigus, O.E. and Hadden and Glase. 1982. "Basic Social Processes." In R.B. Smith and P. Manning (eds.), *Qualitative Methods VII Handbook of Social Science Methods.* Cambridge: Ballinger.

Billingsley, B. and L. Muzynaki. 1985. *No Discrimination Here.* Toronto: Urban Alliance on Race Relations and Social Planning Council of Metropolitan Toronto.

Birnie, L. 1990. *A Rock and A Hard Place: Inside Canada's Parole Board.* Toronto: Macmillan.

Bishop, A. 1994. *Becoming An Ally: Breaking the Silence of Oppression.* Halifax: Fernwood.

Bishop, D. and C. Frazier. 1988. "The Influence of Race in Juvenile Justice Processing." *Journal of Research in Crime and Delinquency* 25 (3): 242-263.

Black, D. 1976. *The Behaviour of Law.* New York: Academic.

Block, R. 1979. "Community Environment and Violent Crime." *Criminology* 17: 46-57.

Bloom, A. 1993. *Love and Friendship.* New York: General.

Bloom, A. 1987. *The Closing of the American Mind.* New York: Simon & Schuster.

Blum, A. 1970. "The Sociology of Mental Illness." In J. Douglas (ed.), *Deviance and Respectability.* New York: Basic.

Blumer, H. 1962. "Society as Symbolic Interactionism." In A.M. Rose (ed.), *Human Behaviour and Social Processes.* New York: Houghton-Mifflin.

Blumer, H. 1964. "What is Wrong With Social Theory." *American Sociological Review* 19 (February): 3-10.

Blumer, H. 1967. "Sociological Analysis and the Variable." In J. Manis and B. Meltzer (eds.), *Symbolic Interactionism.* Boston: Allyn and Bacon.

Blumer, H. 1969. *Symbolic Interactionism.* Englewood Cliffs: Prentice-Hall.

Blumer, H. 1979. "Introduction." In J. Wiseman *Stations of the Lost.* Chicago: University of Chicago Press.

Bocock, R. 1986. *Hegemony.* London: Tavistock.

Bode, J. 1978. *Fighting Back: How To Cope With the Medical, Emotional and Legal Consequences of Rape.* New York: MacMillan.

Bodemann, M. 1978. "A Problem of Sociological Praxis: The Case for Interventive Observation in Fieldwork." *Theoretical Sociology* 5: 387-420.

Bodenheimer, T. 1976. "The Role of Intellectuals in Class Struggle." *Synthesis* 1 (Summer): 20-27.

Bodley, J. 1990. *Victims of Progress.* Mountain View, Cal.: Mayfield.

Bogdan, R. 1976. "Youth Clubs in a West African City." In P. Meadows and E. Mizruchi (eds.), *Urbanism, Urbanization and Change Reading.* New York: Addison-Wesley.

Boggs, C. 1972. "Gramsci's Prison Notebooks: Part 2." *Socialist Revolution* 2 (Nov.-Dec) 6: 29-56.

Bohmer, C. 1973. "Judicial Attitudes Toward Rape Victims." *Judicature* 57 (February): 303-307.

Bohn, R. 1981. "Reflexivity and Critical Criminology." In G. Jensen (ed.), *Sociology of Delinquency: Current Issues.* Beverly Hills: Sage.

Boissevain, J. 1974. *Friends of Friends.* Oxford: Basil Blackwell.

Bolaria, B. Singh and P. Li. 1988. *Racial Oppression in Canada.* Toronto: Garamond.

Bonacich, E. 1972. "A Theory of Ethnic Antagonism: The Split Labour Market." *American Sociological Review* 37 (October): 547-559.

Bonacich, E. 1976. "Advanced Capitalism and Black/White Race Relations in the United States: A Split Labour Market Interpretation." *American Sociological Review* 41 (February): 34-51.

Bonger, W. 1969. *Criminality and Economic Conditions.* Bloomington: Indiana University Press.

Boorstin, D. 1971. "The Perils of Indwelling Law." In R. Wolff (ed.), *The Rule of Law.* New York: Simon and Shuster.

Boostrom, R. and J. Henderson.1983. "Community Action and Crime Prevention: Some Unresolved Issues." *Crime and Social Justice* 19 (Summer): 24-30.

Booth, C. et al. 1991. "Police Brutality." *Time* (March 25).

Bordua, D. 1959. "Juvenile Delinquency and Anomie: An Attempt at Replication." *Social Problem* 6: 230-238.

Borman, K. et al. 1984. *Women in the Workplace: Effects on Family.* Norwood, N.J.: Ablex.

Bott, E. 1971. *Family and Social Network.* London: Tavistock.

Bottomore, A. 1964. *Elites and Society.* New York: Basic.

Bourgeault, R. 1988. "Race and Class Under Mercantilism: Indigenous People in Nineteenth Century Canada." In Singh Bolaria and P. Li (eds.), *Racial Oppression in Canada.* Toronto: Garamond.

Bowsfield, H. 1988. *Louis Riel: Selected Readings.* Toronto: Copp Clark Pitman.

Boyd, N. 1988. *The Last Dance: Murder in Canada.* Scarborough: Prentice-Hall.

Boyd, S.B. and E.A Sheehy, 1986. "Feminist Perspectives on Law: Canadian Theory and Practice." *Canadian Journal of Women and the Law* 2 (1).

Bradley, H. 1989. *Men's Work, Women's Work.* Minneapolis, University of Minneapolis Press.

Brady, D. and A. Gregor. 1991. "L.A.P.D." *Time* (April 1).

Braithwaite, J. 1981."The Myth of Social Class and Criminality Reconsidered." *American Sociological Review* 46: 36-59.

Braithwaite, J. 1989. *Crime, Shame and Reintegration.* New York: Cambridge University Press.

Brake, M. 1980. *The Sociology of Youth Culture and Youth Subcultures.* London: Routledge and Kegan Paul.

Brake, M. 1985. *Comparative Youth Culture.* New York: Routledge and Kegan Paul.

Bray, R. 1980. *Sexual Assault in Canada.* Toronto: Faculty of Education, Guidance Centre, University of Toronto.

Brazao, D. 1994. "Throwing a lifeline to a northern hell." *Toronto Star* (March 13): A1, A6.

Breines, G. 1983. "The New Scholarship on Family Violence." *Journal of Women and Culture Society* 8: 1-13.

Breitman, G. 1990. *Malcolm X Speaks.* New York: Grove Weidenfeld.

Bretl, D. and J. Cantor. 1988. The Portrayal of Men and Women in US Television Commercials: A recent content analysis and trends over 15 years." *Sex Roles* 18: 595-609.

Briar, S. and I. Piliavin. 1965. "Delinquency, Situational Inducements and Commitment to Conformity." *Social Problems* 13: 35-45.

Brickey, S. and E. Comack (eds.). 1986. *The Social Basis of Law.* Toronto: Garamond.

Bridges, G, R. Crutchfield, and E. Simpson. 1987. "Crime, Social Structure and Criminal Punishment: White and Nonwhite Rates of Imprisonment." *Social Problems* 34: 345-357.

Bridges, G. et al. 1988. "Law, Social Standing and Racial Disparities in Imprisonment." *Social Forces* 66 (March) 3: 699-720.

Brinkerhoff, M. and E. Lurpi. 1988. "Interspousal Violence." *Canadian Journal of Sociology* 13 (4): 407-433.

Brodsky, C. 1976. *The Harassed Worker.* Lexington, Mass.: D.C. Heath.

Brooks, D and R. Althouse, 1993: 19 *Racism in College Athletes.* Morgantown: Fitness Information Technology.

Brown, J. and G. Howes. 1975. *The Police and the Community.* Lexington: D.C. Heath.

Brown, L. 1994. "Taming the TV Monster." *Starweek Magazine* (October).

Brown, R. 1979. "The Blacks of British Columbia." *Rikka* (Spring): 17-20.

Brown, R. 1985 "Social Reality as Narrative Text: Interactions, Institutions, and Polities as Language." *Current Perspectives in Social Theory.* 1985, 6, 17-37.

Browning, S. and L. Cao. 1992. "The Impact of Race on Criminal Justice Ideology." *Justice Quarterly* 9 (December)4: 685-702.

Brownmiller, S. 1975. *Against Our Will: Men, Women and Rape.* New York: Simon and Shuster.

Bruning. F. 1994. "Wife Beating—A Nation's Obsession." *Maclean's* (July 25)11.

Buckner, H.T. 1987. "Attitudes Toward Minorities: Four Year Results and Analysis." *The Review of Anti-Semitism.* League for Human Rights of B'Nai Brith of Canada.

Bunch, C. 1986. "Lesbians in Revolt." In M. Pearsall (ed.), *Women and Values.* Belmont: Wadsworth.

Bureau of Justice Statistics. 1990. "State and Local Police Departments." US Department of Justice, Washington, D.C. NCJ-133283/4.

Bureau of Justice Statistics. 1990a. "Justice Expenditures and Employment." Justice Statistics Clearinghouse Rockville Md US Department of Justice, Washington, D.C (Sept 1992).

Bureau of Justice Statistics. 1991. "Women in Prison." US Department of Justice, Office of Justice Programs, Washington, D.C.

Bureau of Justice Statistics. 1991b. *National Update* 1 (July)1: 1-10.

Bureau of Justice Statistics. 1991c. "Handgun Crime Victims." NCJ-123559, US Department of Justice, Washington, D.C.

Bureau of Justice Statistics. 1992. "Jail Inmates 1991." US Department of Justice (June).

Bureau of Justice Statistics. 1993. "Prisoners at midyear 1993." Justice Department US Department of Justice, Washington, D..C (October 3).

Bureau of Justice Statistics. 1993b. "20 years of measuring crime shows fewer offenses overall, But increased violence against minorities and the young." Justice Department US Department of Justice, Washington, D.C. (November 21) 202-307-0784.

Bureau of Justice Statistics. 1994. "Guns and Crime: Handgun Crime Victimization, Firearm Self-Defense, and Firearm Theft." NCJ-147003 US Department of Justice, Washington, D.C.

Bureau of Justice Statistics. 1994a. "Record Number of Handgun Crimes—Nears One Million a Year." 202-307-0784 US Department of Justice, Washington, D.C. (May 15).

Bureau of Justice Statistics. 1994b "Violent Offenders Increasingly Likely To Be Armed." 202-307-0784 US Department of Justice, Washington, D.C. (February 26).

Bureau of Justice Statistics. 1994c. "Selected Highlights on Firearms and Crime of Violence: Selected Findings from National Statistical Series." NCJ-146844. US Department of Justice, Washington, D.C.

Bureau of Justice Statistics. 1994d. "Violence Against Women." National Crime Victimization Survey Report, (NCJ-145325), (Jan 30), 202-307-0784 US Department of Justice, Washington, D.C.

Burger, J. 1987. *Report from the Frontier*. London: Zed Books.

Burgess, A. 1985. *Rape and Sexual Assault*. New York: Garland.

Burgess, E. 1926. *Urban Community*. Chicago: University of Chicago.

Burgess, E. and D. Bogue. 1967. *Urban Sociology*. Chicago: U. of Chicago.

Burgess, R. and R. Akers. 1966. "Are Operant Principles Tautological?" *The Psychological Record* 16 (July).

Burgess, R. and R. Akers. 1968. "Differential Association-Reinforcement Theory of Criminal Behaviour." *Social Problems* 14 (Fall): 128-147.

Burris, C.A. and P. Jaffe. 1983. "Wife Abuse As A Crime: The Impact of Police Laying Charges." *Canadian Journal of Criminology* 25: 309-318.

Bursick, R. 1984. "Urban Dynamics and Ecological Studies of Delinquency." *Social Forces* 63 (2): 393-413.

Bursick, R. and J. Webb. 1982. "Community Change and Patterns of Delinquency." *American Journal of Sociology* 88: 24-42.

Burtch, B. 1986. "Communal Midwifery and State Measure: The New Midwifery in B.C." Paper presented at Annual Meeting of the Canadian Sociology and Anthropology Association (June 5).

Burtch, B. 1992. *The Sociology of Law: Critical Approaches to Social Control*. Toronto: Harcourt, Brace and Jovanovich.

Buzawa, E.S. and C. Buzawa. 1985. "Legislative Trends in the Criminal Justice Response to Domestic Violence." In A. Lincoln and M. Straus (eds.), *Crime and The Family*. Springfield: Charles C. Thomas.

Bynum, T. and R. Paternoster, 1984. "Discrimination Revisited: An Exploration of Frontstage and Backstage Criminal Justice Decision Making." *Sociology and Social Research* 1 (69): 90-108 (Oct).

C

Cable, C. 1994 "Immigration Under Fire." *Profiles* (October), York University.

Cain, M. 1990 "Towards Transgression: New Directions in Feminist Criminology." *International Journal of Sociology of Law* 18 (1): 1-18.

Calhoun, C. 1995. *Critical Social Theory*. Cambridge: Blackwell.

Cameron, M. 1964. *The Booster and the Snitch*. Glencoe: Illinois Free Press.

Cammett, J. 1967. *Antonio Gramsci and the Origins of Italian Communism*. Stanford: Stanford University.

Cammett, J. 1967. *Indians and the Law*. Ottawa: Canadian Corrections Association.

Campbell, C. 1984. "The Canadian Left and the Charter of Rights." *Socialist Studies*.

Campbell, M. 1983. *Halfbreed*. Halifax: Goodread Biographies, Formac Publishing.

Canadian Centre for Occupational Health. 1983. *Mosaic of Mosaics: A Report on Occupational Health and Safety*. Hamilton.

Canadian Child Welfare Association et al. 1989. *A Choice of Futures: Canada's Commitment to its Children*. Ottawa.

Canadian Centre for Justice Statistics. 1992. *Adult Correctional Services in Canada, 1990-1991 Statistics*. Ottawa.

Canadian Corrections Association. 1967. *Indians and the Law*. Ottawa: Canadian Corrections Association.

Canadian Criminal Justice Association. 1993. *Bulletin* (Jan 15, 1993), Ottawa.

Canadian Criminal Justice Association. 1994. *Bulletin* (September 15), Ottawa.

Capeci, J. 1992. "Why The Mob Loves Canada." *Financial Post Magazine* (February): 10-18.

Caputo, T. et al. (eds.). 1989. *Law and Society: A Critical Perspective*. Toronto: HBJ Holt.

Carceres, M. 1988. "Gramsci, Religion and Socio-economic Systems." *Social Compass* 35 (2-3): 279-296.

Cardinal, H. 1969. *Unjust Society*. Edmonton: M.G. Hurtig.

Carew-Hunt, R. 1950. *The Theory and Practice of Communism*. Middlesex: Penguin.

Carlen, P. 1985. *Criminal Women*. Cambridge: Polity.

Carlsnaes, W. 1981. *The Concept of Ideology and Political Analysis: A Critical Examination of its Usage by Marx, Lenin and Mannheim*. Connecticut: Greenwood Press.

Carmichael, S. and C. Hamilton. 1967. *Black Power: The Politics of Liberation in America*. New York.

Carp, S. and L. Schade. 1992. "Tailoring Facility Programming to Suit Female Offenders' Needs." *Corrections Today* 54 (August) 6: 152-186.

Carrington, B. 1983. "Sport as a Side-Track: An Analysis of West Indian Involvement in Extra-Curricular Sport." *Race, Class and Education*: 40-62.

Carrington, K. 1993. Essentialism and Feminist Criminologies: relevant to all-specific to none!" *Critical Criminologist* 5, 4 (1993) 5, 6, 14, 15, 19.

Carroll, J. 1982. *Controlling White Collar Crime;Design and Audit for Security Systems*. Boston: Butterworth.

Carroll, L. and M. Mondrick. 1976. "Racial Bias in The Decision To Grant Parole." *Law and Society Review* 2 (1) Fall: 93-109.

Carroll, W. K. 1986. *Corporate Power and Canadian Capitalism*.Vancouver: U. of British Columbia Press.

Carson, C. 1991. *Malcolm X: The FBI File*. New York: Carroll and Graf.

Carson, W.G. and P. Wiles (eds.). 1971. *Crime and Delinquency in Britain*. London: Martin Robertson.

Carter, G.E. 1979. *Report to the Civic Authorities of Metropolitan Toronto and its Citizens*. Toronto.

Carter, R.H. 1991. *The 16th Round*. New York: Penguin.

Carver, H. 1969. *Cities in the Suburbs*. Toronto: U of T Press.

Case, F. 1977. *Racism and National Consciousness*. Toronto: Ploughshare Press.

Cashmore, E. and E. McLaughlin (eds.). 1991. *Out of Order? Policing Black People*. London: Routledge.

Cassidy, F. and R. Bish. 1990. "Indian Government in a Federal System." *Report*, National Indian Government Conference, Osgoode Hall Law School, York University, (October 3-5).

Castells, M. 1976. *The Urban Question*. London: Edward Arnold.

Castells, M. 1978. *City, Class and Power*. London: MacMillan.

Castro, F. 1992. Address of Fidel Castro to the United Nations Conference on Environment and Development. Special Supplement of *Granma International*, (June 28).

Cernkovich, S. 1978. "Value Orientations and Delinquency Involvement." *Criminology* 15 (February): 443-458.

Cernkovich, S. and P. Giordano. 1992. "School Bonding, Race and Delinquency." *Criminology* 30, 2: 261-291.

Chafetz, J. 1988. *Feminist Sociology*. Ithaca: F.E. Peacock.

Chaiton, S. and T. Swinton. 1991. *Lazarus and the Hurricane*. New York: Penguin.

Chambliss, W. 1964. " A Sociological Analysis of the Law of Vagrancy." *Social Problems* 12 (Summer): 67-77.

Chambliss, W. 1969. *Crime and Legal Process*. New York: McGraw-Hill.

Chambliss, W. 1973. "The Saints and Roughnecks." *Society* VII (November-December) 11: 24-31.

Chambliss, W. 1975. "Towards a Political Economy of Crime." *Theory and Society* 2 (Summer): 149-170.

Chambliss, W. 1978. *On The Take*. Bloomington: Indiana University Press.

Chambliss, W. 1988. *Exploring Criminology*. Bloomington: Indiana University Press.

Chambliss, W. 1989. "State Organized Crime." *Criminology* 27 (2): 183-208.

Chambliss, W. and A. Bloch. 1981. *Organized Crime*. New York: Elsevier.

Chambliss, W. and M. Mankoff (eds.). 1976. *Whose Law, What Order: A Conflict Approach to Criminality*. New York: John Wiley and Sons.

Chambliss, W. and R. Seidman. 1971. *Law, Order and Power*. Reading Mass.: Addison-Wesley.

Chapeskie, W. 1992. "Canadian Gun Ban List." waynec@csr.UVic.CA (6 Aug) - 0700.

Chapkis, W. 1986. *Beauty Secrets*. Boston: South End.

Charon, J. 1979. *Symbolic Interactionism*. Englewood Cliffs: Prentice-Hall.

Check, J. and N. Malamuth. 1983. "Sex Role Stereotyping and Reactions to Depictions of Stranger versus Acquaintance Rape." *Journal of Personality and Social Psychology* 45 (2): 344-356.

Chen, M. and T. Regan. 1985. *Work in the Changing Canadian Society*. Toronto: Butterworth.

Cheney, P. 1994. "Canada. Canada." *Toronto Star* (July 24): F1, F4, F5, F6, F7).

Chesney-Lind, M. 1992. "Girls' Crime and Woman's Place: Toward a Feminist Model of Female Delinquency." In J.Sullivan and J.L. Victor (eds.), *Criminal Justice 92/93*. Gulford, Conn.: Dushkin.

Chesney-Lind, M. and R. Sheldon. 1992. *Girls, Delinquency and Juvenile Justice*. Belmont: Brooks/Cole.

Chilton, R. 1964. "Continuity in Delinquency Area Research: A Comparison of Studies for Baltimore, Detroit and Indianapolis." *American Sociological Review* 29 (February): 71-83.

Chimbos, P. 1971. "Some Aspects of Organized Crime in Canada: A Preliminary Review." In W. Mann (ed.), *Social Deviance in Canada*. Toronto: Copp Clark.

Chiricos, T. and G. Waldo. 1975. "Socio-Economic Status and Criminal Sentencing." *American Sociological Review* 40 (December): 752-772.

Chisholm, P. 1993. "The Fear Index." *Maclean's* (January 4): 24-25.

Chomsky, N. 1987. *Pirates and Emperors*. New York: Black Rose.

Chomsky, N. 1989. *Necessary Illusions*. Toronto: CBC Enterprises.

Chomsky, N. 1992. *What Uncle Sam Really Wants*. Berkeley: Odonian Press.

Churchill, L. 1971. "Ethnomethodology and Measurement." *Social Forces* 50 (December) 2: 182-191.

Cicourel, A. 1968. *The Social Organization of Juvenile Justice*. New York: Wiley.

Citron, A. 1972. *The Rightness of Whiteness*. Detroit: Wayne State University.

Clairmont, D. and D. Magill. 1983. "Africville: Transformation and the Emergence of a Deviance Service Centre." In T. Fleming and L. Visano (eds.), *Deviant Designations*. Toronto: Butterworth.

Clark, J. and E. Wenninger. 1962. "Socio-Economic Class and Area as Correlates of Illegal Behaviour Among Juveniles." *American Sociological Review* 27 (6): 826-834.

Clark, J. and E. Wenninger. 1963. "Goal Orientations and Illegal Behaviour Among Juveniles." *Social Forces* 42: 49-59.

Clark, K. 1965. *Dark Ghetto*. New York: Harper Row.

Clark, L. and D. Lewis. 1977. *Rape: The Price of Coercive Sexuality*. Toronto: Women's Press.

Clark, R. 1994. "Vaunted Three Strikes Law Locks up Little Fish for Life." *Toronto Star* (May 14): B4.

Clarke, D.G. and Blankenburg, W. 1973. "Advertising: It Loves Us But Is It Our Friend?" In D.G. Clark and W. Blankenburg (eds.), *You and The Media: Mass Communication and Society*. San Francisco: Canfoeld Press.

Clarke, H. et al. 1975. *Prophecy and Protest*. Toronto: Gage.

Clarke, M. J. 1978. "White Collar Crime, Occupational Crime, and Legitimacy." *International Journal of Criminology and Penology* 6 (May)2: 121-136.

Clark, R. 1986. *Corporate Law*. Boston: Little, Brown and Co.

Clement, W. 1975. *The Canadian Corporate Elite*. Toronto: McClelland and Stewart.

Clifford, D. 1991. "Cuts in Programs Cloud Future for Poor Children." *Globe and Mail* (December 28): A9.

Clinard, M. 1952. *The Black Market: A Study of White-Collar Crime*. New York: Rinehart.

Clinard, M. (ed.). 1964. *Anomie and Deviant Behaviour*. New York: Free Press.

Clinard, M. 1974. *Sociology of Deviant Behaviour*. New York: Holt, Rinehart and Winston.

Clinard, M. 1979. *Illegal Corporate Behaviour*. U.S. Department of Justice, Washington (October).

Clinard, M. 1983. *Corporate Ethics and Crime: The Role of Middle Management*. Beverly Hills: Sage.

Clinard, M. and P. Yeager. 1978. "Corporate Crime—Issues in Research." *Criminology* 16 (August)2: 255-272.

Clinard, M. and P. Yeager. 1980. *Corporate Crime*. New York: Free Press.

Clinard, M. and P.Yeager. 1980. "Corporate Organization and Criminal Behaviour." In M.D.Ermann and R.J. Lundan (eds.), *Corporate and Governmental Deviance*. New York: Oxford U. Press.

Cloward, R. and L. Ohlin. 1959. *Delinquency and Opportunity: A Theory of Delinquent Gangs*. Glencoe Illinois: Free Press.

Cloward, R. 1959. "Illegitimate Means, Anomie and Deviant Behaviour." *American Sociological Review* 24 (April): 164-176.

Coakley, J. 1986. *Sport in Society: Issues and Controversies*. St.Louis: C.V. Mosby.

Cockburn, A. 1993. "The Missile Attack was entirely lawless." *Globe and Mail* (July 5): A10.

Coelho, E. 1989. *Caribbean Students in Canadian Schools*. Toronto: Carib-Can Publishers.

Cohen, A. 1955. *Delinquent Boys: The Culture of the Gang*. New York: Free Press.

Cohen, A. 1966. *Deviance and Control*. Englewood Cliffs, N.J.: Prentice-Hall.

Cohen, C. and J. Sokolovsky. 1981. "A Re-Assessment of the Sociability of Long-Term Skid Row Residents: A Social Network Approach." *Social Networks* 3: 93-105.

Cohen, J. M. and M. J. 1980. *The Penguin Dictionary of Quotations*. New York: Penguin.

Cohen, S. [1972], 1990. *Folk Devils and Moral Panics*. Oxford: Basil Blackwell.

Cohen, S. 1979. "The Punitive City: Notes on the Dispersal of Social Control." *Contemporary Crises* 3: 339-363.

Cohen, S. 1973. *The Manufacture of News*. London: Anchor.

Cohen, S. 1985. *Visions of Social Control*. Cambridge: Polity.

Cohen, T. 1988. *Race Relations and the Law*. Toronto: Canadian Jewish Congress.

Cohn, E.S.and S. 0. White. 1992. *Legal Socialization: A Study of Norms and Rules*. New York: Springer-Verlag.

Colapinto, J. 1994. "A Boy and His Gun: An American Tragedy." *Rolling Stone* (October): 65.

Coleman, J. 1989. *The Criminal Elite*. New York: St.Martin's.

Colombo, J. R. 1992. *Canadian Global Almanac: A Book of Facts*. Toronto: Macmillan.

Collective Revolutionary Ant-Racist Action Communique. 1993. *Arm the Spirit*. Autonomous/*Anti-Imperialist Journal* (Fall) 16.

Collins, R. 1979. *The Credential Society.* New York: Academic.

Comeau, P. and A. Santin. 1990. *The First Canadians.* Toronto: Lorimer.

Cornish, S. 1993. *The Westray Tragedy: A Miner's Story.* Halifax: Fernwood.

Commission on Systemic Racism in the Ontario Criminal Justice System. 1994. *Racism Behind Bars, Interim Report.* Toronto: Queen's Printer.

Commissioner's Directive. 1987. "Citizens' Advisory Committee." #023, (January 01).

Conde, C. and K. Beveridge. 1986. *First Contract: Women and the Fight to Unionize.* Toronto: Between the Lines.

Conklin, J. 1977. *Illegal But not Criminal.* Englewood Cliffs: Prentice-Hall.

Contenta, S. 1993. "The Super Elite Can Often Find New Work." Insight *Toronto Star* (August 23): A11.

Contenta, S. 1994. "The Politics of Parole." *Toronto Star* 14, 05, B1, B4.

Cook, K. 1984. *Images of Indians Held by Non-Indians: A Review of Current Canadian Research.* Ottawa: INAC.

Cook, K. and R. Emerson. 1978. "Power, Equity and Commitment in Exchange Networks." *American Sociological Review* 43 (Oct): 721-739.

Cooley, C.H. [1902] 1956. *Human Nature and the Social Order.* New York: Charles Scribner's Sons.

Cooper, M. and G. Goldin. 1992. "Some People Don't Count." In D. Hazen (ed.), *Inside the L.A. Riots.* Los Angeles: Institute for Alternative Journalism.

Cooper, V. W. 1985. "Women in Popular Music: A Quantitative Analysis of Feminine Images Over Time." *Sex Roles* 13: 499-506.

Copeland, M. 1989. "Rushton's Scientificism." *Active Voice* 1 (April): 2.

Corbett, C. 1957. *Canada's Immigration Policy.* Toronto: U of T Press.

Corea, G. 1985. *The Mother Machine: Reproductive Technologies From Artificial Insemination To Artificial Wombs.* Toronto: Fitzhenry and Whiteside.

Corelli, R. 1994. "Murder Next door." *Maclean's* (April 18): 14-15).

Cornea, G. 1977. *The Hidden Malpractice: How American Medicine Treats Women As Patients and Professionals.* New York: William Morrow.

Cormier, J. 1991. "Toronto's Race Crisis." *Chatelaine* February.

Corradi, Consuelo. 1991. "Text, Context and Individual Meaning: Rethinking Life Stories in a Hermeneutic Framework." *Discourse and Society* 1991, 2, 1, Jan, 105-118.

Correctional Services Canada. 1991. *Basic Facts.* Ottawa.

Correctional Services of Canada. 1981. *Citizens' Advisory Committee: Aid to Corrections.*

Correctional Services of Canada. 1984. *Working Together: Citizens' Advisory.*

Correctional Services of Canada. 1991. *Basic Facts About Corrections in Canada 1991.* Ottawa: Minister of Supply and Services.

Corrigan, P. 1979. *Schooling the Smash Street Kids.* London: Macmillan.

Cose, E. 1994. "Color-Coordinated Truths." *Newsweek* (October 24).

Coser, L. 1956. *The Functions of Social Conflict.* London: Routledge and Kegan Paul.

Cott, N. *The Grounding of Modern Feminism.* New Haven: Yale University Press.

Couch, C. 1984. "Symbolic Interactionism and Generic Principles." *Symbolic Interactionism* 7: 1-14.

Council on Interracial Books for Children (1973) 4, No. 3-4: 72-73.

Counihan, C. 1986. "Antonio Gramsci and Social Science." *Dialectical Anthropology* 11 (1): 3-9.

Courtney, A. and T. Whipple. 1983. *Sex Stereotypes in Advertising*. Lexington, Mass.: Lexington Books.

Covington, J. and R.B. Taylor. 1991. "Fear of Crime in Urban Residential Neighbourhoods." *Sociological Quarterly* 32: 231-249.

Cox, A. 1988. *Native People, Native Lands*. Toronto: McClelland and Stewart.

Cox, K. 1973. *Conflict, Power and Politics in the City*. New York: McGraw-Hill.

Cox, K. 1992. "Study Links Poverty to Crimes by Women." *Globe and Mail*, April 11, 1992: A5.

Crane, D. 1989. "How We Rate on Social Spending." *Toronto Star* (April 24): A16.

Crane, D. 1993. "Corporate Giants, Not Governmnets Are Calling the Economic Shots, UN Report Says." *Toronto Star* (July 21): A19.

Craven, P. and B. Wellman. 1973. "The Network City." *Research Paper #59* Toronto: Centre for Urban and Community Studies, University of Toronto.

Cressey, D. 1969. *Theft of a Nation*. New York: Harper and Row.

Cressey, D. 1971. *Organized Crime*. London: W. Heffer and Sons.

Crew, K. 1991. "Sex Differences in Criminal Sentencing: Chivalry or Patriarchy?." *Justice Quarterly* 8 (March) 1: 60-83.

Crichlow, W. and L. Visano. 1994. "A Liberal Text of Equality and Subtexts of Oppression." Unpublished paper. OISE and York University.

Crites, L. and W. Hepperle (eds.). 1987. *Women, the Courts and Equality*. Newbury Park, Ca: Sage.

Croteau, M. and W. Worcester. 1993. *The Essential Researcher*. New York: Harper Perennial.

Cueva, A. and A. Martinez-Baracs. 1980. "An Interview with Christine Buci-Glucksman." *Revista Mexicana de Sociologia* 42 (Jan-Mar) 1: 289-301.

Currie, D. 1986. "Female Criminality: A Crisis in Feminist Theory." In B. Maclean (ed.), *Political Economy of Crime*. Scarborough: Prentice-Hall.

Currie, D. and M. Kline. 1991. Challenging Privilege: Women, Knowledge and Feminist Struggles." *Journal of Human Justice* 2 (Spring): pp. 2.

Currie, E. 1973. "A Dialogie with Anthony Platt." *Issues in Criminology* 8.

Currie, E. 1985. *Confronting Crime*. New York: Pantheon.

Cusson, M. 1983. *Why Delinquency?* Toronto: U of T Press.

Czerny, M., J. Swift and R. Clarke. 1994 *Getting Started on Social Analysis in Canada*, 3rd edition. Toronto: Between The Lines.

D

Dahrendorf, R. 1958a. "Toward a Theory of Social Conflict." *Journal of Conflict Resolution* 2: 170-183.

Dahrendorf, R. 1958b. "Out of Utopia: Toward a Reorientation of Sociological Analysis." *American Journal of Sociology* 64: 115-127.

Dahrendorf, R. 1959. *Class and Class Conflict in Industrial Society*. Stanford: Stanford University Press.

Daley, K. 1989. "Neither Conflict not Labelling not Paternalism Will Suffice: Intersections of Race. Ethnicity, Gender and Family." *Crime and Delinquency* 35 (January) 1: 136-168.

Dalglish, B. 1994. "Are They worth it?" *Maclean's* (May 9): 34.

Dalton, K. 1978. "Menstruation and Crime." In Savitz and Johnson (eds.), *Crime in Society* New York: John Wiley.

Daly, K. 1987. "Discrimination in the Criminal Courts: Family, Gender, and the Problem of Equal Treatment." *Social Forces* 66: 152-170.

Daly, M. 1973. *Beyond God the Father.* Boston: Beacon.

Daly, M. 1978. *Gyn/Ecology.* Boston: Beacon.

Daly, M. 1989. "Rethinking Judicial Paternalism: Gender, Work-Family Relations and Sentencing." *Gender and Society* 3: 9-36.

Dank, B. 1971. "Coming Out in the Gay World." *Psychiatry* 34 (May): 182.

Danner, M. 1991. "Socialist Feminism: A Brief Introduction." In B. Maclean and D. Milovanovic (eds.), *New Directions in Critical Criminology.* Vancouver: Collective Press.

Daubney, Report of the Standing Committee on Justice and Solicitor General on its review of the sentencing, correctional release and related aspects of corrections. 1988. *Taking Responsibility.* Ottawa: Supply and Services.

Davidson, B. 1992. "Columbus: The Bones and Blood of Racism." *Race and Class* 33 (January-March): 17-25.

Davidson, T. 1978. *Conjugal Crime: Understanding the Wife Beating Problem.* New York: Hawthorn.

Davies, I. 1995. *Cultural Studies and Beyond.* London: Routledge.

Davis, A. 1983. *Women, Race & Class.* New York: Vintage.

Davis, A. 1989. *Women, Culture, Politics.* New York: Vintage Books.

Davis A. et al. 1971. *If They Come In the Morning.* San Francisco: Signet.

Davis, M. 1992. *City of Quartz.* New York: Vintage.

Davis, N. 1975. *Sociological Construction of Deviance.* Dubuque: W.C. Brown.

Davis, N. and C. Stasz. 1990. *Social Control of Deviance.* New York: McGraw-Hill.

Davis, R. and M. Zannis. 1973. *The Genocide Machine in Canada.* Montreal: Black Rose.

Dawson, P. 1983. "Social and Cultural Reproduction and the School's Role in Social Mobility." In P. Li and B. Singh (eds) *Racial Minorities in Multicultural Canada.* Toronto: Garamond.

Dean, J. and W. Whyte. 1969. "How Do You Know If the Informant is Telling the Truth." In G. McCall and J. Simmons (eds.), *Issues in Participant Observation.* Reading: Addison.

de Beauvoir, S. 1960. *The Second Sex.* London: Four Square Books.

De Fleur, M. and R. Quinney. 1966. "A Reformulation of Sutherland's Differential Association Theory and Strategy of Empirical Verification." *Journal of Research in Crime and Delinquency* 3 (January) 1: 1-22.

De Franco, E. 1973. *Anatomy of a Scam.* Washington: U.S. Government Printing.

De Grazia, S. 1948. *The Political Community, A Study of Anomie.* Chicago: University of Chicago Press.

De Jong, K. 1985. "Charter of Rights and Freedoms." *The Study Day Papers.* Charter of Rights Educational Fund, Toronto.

DeKeseredy, W. and B. MacLean. 1993. "Critical Criminological Pedagogy in Canada: Strengths, Limitations, and Recommendations for Improvements." *Journal of Criminal Justice Education* 4 (Fall)2: 361-376.

DeKeseredy, W and M. Schwartz. 1996. *Contemporary Criminology*. New York: Wadsworth.

De la Motta, K. 1984. *Blacks in the Criminal Justice System*. Unpublished MSc thesis. University of Aston.

De Maris, O. 1986. *The Boardwalk Jungle*. Toronto: Bantam.

De Mont, J. 1991. "Putting Rage to Work." *MacLeans* (August 19).

Denney, D. 1992. *Racism and Anti-Racism in Probation*. London: Routledge.

Denisson, D. and L. Tobey. 1991. *The Advertising Handbook*. Bellington, Washington: International Self-Counsel Press, 1991.

Dentler, R. and K. Ericson. 1959. "Functions of Deviance in Groups." *Social Problems* 7: 99-107.

Denzin, N. 1970. "Rules of Conduct and the Study of Deviant Behaviour: Social Relationships." In J. Douglas (ed.), *Deviance and Respectability*. New York: Basic.

Denzin, N. 1970. "Symbolic Interactionism and Ethnomethodology." In J. Douglas (ed.), *Understanding Everyday Life*. Chicago: Aldine.

Denzin, N. 1970. *The Research Act*. Chicago: Aldine.

Denzin, N. 1978. *Sociological Methods: A Sourcebook*. New York: McGraw-Hill.

Denzin, N. 1984. *On Understanding Emotion*. San Francisco: Jossey-Bass.

Denzin, N. 1987. "On Semiotics and Symbolic Interactionism." *Symbolic Interactionism* 10 (1): 1-19.

Denzin, N. 1988. *Interpretive Interactionism*. Newbury Park, California: Sage.

Denzin N. 1989. *The Research Act: A Theoretical Introduction to Sociological Methods*, 3rd edition. Prentice-Hall, Englewood Cliffs, N.J.

Department of Justice. 1990. *After Sexual Assault. Your Guide to the Criminal Justice System*. Ottawa: Minister of Justice, Communications and Public Affairs.

Department of Justice. 1993. "Questions and Answers on Perceptions of Justice." Ottawa: Research and Statistics Sections, Department of Justice (March).

Department of Justice. 1993b. "Toward Safer Communities: Violent and Repeat Offending by Young People." Ottawa: Young Offenders Project, Department of Justice.

Department of Justice. 1994. Justice Information Backgrounder: Proposed Young Offender Act Amendments Communications and Consultation Branch (June).

Department of Justice. 1995. Justice Information Communications and Consultation Branch.

de Rooy, E. 1994. "Sexism in Television Commercials: A Comparative Content Analysis and probe into Subjects Perceptions." Graduate Programme, Psychology, doctoral dissertation, York University.

de Saussure, F. 1986. *Course in General Linguistics* (translation R. Harris). Illinois: Open Court.

Deutscher, L. 1970. "Words and Deeds: Social Science and Social Policy." In W. Filstead (ed.), *Qualitative Methodology*. Chicago: Rand McNally.

Dex, S. 1985. *The Social Division of Work: Conceptual Revolutions in the Social Sciences*. New York: Harvester Press.

Diebel, L. 1994. "Meet Mr Big." *Toronto Star* (July 17): F1-F7.

Di Leonardo, M. 1991. *Gender at the Crossroads of Knowledge*. Los Angeles: University of California Press.

Diop, C. 1974. *The African Origin of Civilization*. New York: L. Hill and Co.

Ditton, J. 1979. *Controlology-Beyond the New Criminology*. London: Macmillan.

Dobash, R.E. and R.P. Dobash. 1977. "Love, Honour and Obey: Institutional Ideologies and the Struggle for Battered Women." *Contemporary Crisis* 1: 403-415.

Dobash, R.E. and R.P. Dobash. 1979. *Violence Against Wives: A Case Against Patriarchy*. New York: Free Press.

Donovan, J. 1992. *Feminist Theory*. New York: Continuum.

Donzelot, J. 1979. *The Policing of Families*. New York: Pantheon.

Doob, A. 1990. "Community Sanctions and Imprisonment: Hoping for a Miracle but not Bothering Even to Pray for It." *Canadian Journal of Criminology* 32, 3: 415-428.

Doob, A. 1991. *Report* "Workshop on Collecting Race and Ethnicity Statistics in the Criminal Justice Sytem." (October) Centre of Criminology, University of Toronto.

Doob, A. and J. Roberts. 1988. "Public Punitiveness and Public Knowledge of the Facts: Some Canadian Surveys." In N. Walker and M. Hough (eds.), *Public Attitudes to Sentencing: Surveys From Five Counties*. Aldershot, U.K.: Gower.

Douglas, J. 1972. *Research on Deviance*. New York: Random House.

Douglas, J. 1978. *Crime at the Top*. New York: Lippincott.

Dowdesdell, J. 1986. *Women on Rape*. New York: Thompson Publishing Group.

Downes, D. and P. Rock. 1984. *Understanding Deviance*. New York: Oxford University Press.

Doyle, R. and A. Mitchell. 1989. "Lone Parent Families in Toronto." *Social Infopac* 7 (November) 4: 1-12.

Doyle, R. and L. Visano. 1986. "Increasing Accountability: A Look at the U.S. Committee for Responsive Philanthropy." *Philanthropist* vi, (Spring)1: 34-40.

Doyle, R. and L. Visano. 1987. "Access to Health and Social Services for Members of Diverse Cultural and Racial Groups in Metropolitan Toronto." Report I *A Time for Action* and Report II *A Programme for Action*. Toronto: Social Planning Council.

Doyle, R., L. Visano and J. Ward. 1989. *Opening The Umbrella*. Toronto: Japanese Canadian Family Services.

Drakich, J. 1986. "Generic Processes in the Development of Self Conception." *Ethnographic Research Conference*. University of Waterloo, (May 13-16).

Drainville, D. 1985. "Poverty in Canada." A Discussion Paper prepared for the Primate of the Anglican Church of Canada and the Board of Directors of Stop 33. (June).

Driedger, L. 1987. *Ethnic Canada: Identities and Inequalities*. Toronto: Copp Clark.

Duberman, M. 1989. *Paul Robeson*. New York: Ballantine.

Dubin, R. 1959. "Deviant Behaviour and Social Structure: Continuities in Social Theory." *American Sociological Review* 24 (August): pp. 147-164.

Dubro, J. 1985. *Mob Rule: Inside the Canadian Mafia*. Toronto: Macmillan.

Du Bois, W.E.B. 1977 [1935]. *Black Reconstruction in the United States, 1860-1880*. New York: Russell & Russell.

Du Charme, M. 1986. "The Coverage of Canadian Immigration Policy Globe and Mail, 1980-1985." *Currents* 3 (Spring): 3.

Duclos, N. 1987. "Breaking the Dependency Circle: The Family Law Act Reconsidered." *University of Toronto Faculty of Law Review* 45 (1).

Duclos, N. 1993. "Disappearing Women: Racial Minority Women in Human Rights Cases." *Canadian Journal of Women and the Law* 6: 25-51.

Duffy, A. 1988. "Struggling with Power: Feminist Critiques of Family Inequality." In N. Mandell and A. Duffy (eds.), *Reconstructing the Canadian Family: Feminist Perspectives* Toronto: Butterworth.

Duffy, A. and N. Pupo. 1992. *Part-time Paradox: Connecting Gender, Work and Family* Toronto: McClelland & Stewart.

Dunphy, C. 1993. "Why Do Indian Teens Kill Themselves." *Toronto Star* (March 2): A1, 10 and 11.

During, S. 1987. "Post-modernism or Post Colonialism Today." *Textual Practice* 1 (1): 32-47.

Durkheim, E. [1893] 1933. *Division of Labour in Society.* New York: Free Press and 1964 edition with Free Press (NY).

Durkheim, E. [1897] 1951. *Suicide.* Translated by G. Simpson. New York: Free Press.

Durkheim, E. [1895] 1965. *The Rules of the Sociological Method.* Translated by S. Solovay and J. Mueller, edited By G. Catlin. New York: Free Press; and 1938 edition with Chicago: University of Chicago Press.

Dworkin, A. 1981. *Pornography: Men Possessing Women.* New York: Putnam.

Dworkin, A. 1983. *Right-Wing Women.* New York: Wideview/Perigee.

E

Eaton, M. 1986. *Justice For Women? Family Court and Social Control.* Philadelphia: Open University Press.

Eberts, M. 1985. "Sex and Equality Rights." In A. Bayefsky and M. Eberts (eds.), *Equality Rights and the Canadian Charter of Rights and Freedoms.* Toronto: Carswell.

Economic Council of Canada. 1976. "People and Jobs: A Study of the Canadian Labour Market." Ottawa: Economic Council of Canada.

Economic Council of Canada. 1992. *A Lot To Learn.* Policy Paper. Ottawa.

Edelhertz, H. 1970. *The Nature, Impact and Prosecution of White Collar Crime.* Washington, D.C.: Nile and C.J.

Edwards, H. 1969. *Revolt of the Black Athlete.* New York: Free Press.

Edwards, H. 1973. *Sociology of Sport.* University of California: Dorsey Press.

Edwards, H. 1988. "The Single-Minded Pursuit of Sports, Fame and Fortune-An Institutionalized Triple Tragedy in Black Society." *Ebony* 8 (August): 139-140.

Edwards, M. 1992. "Towers and Tombstones: Construction Workers' Health & Safety." *Our Times* (September): 21-24.

Effrat, M. (ed.). 1974. *The Community: Approaches and Perspectives.* New York: Free Press.

Effron, E. 1971. *The News Twisters.* Los Angeles: Nash.

Ehrenreich, B. 1989. "Life Without: Reconsidering Socialist-Feminist Theory." In R. Gottlieb (ed.), *An Anthology of Western Marxism.* New York: Oxford University Press.

Eichler, M. 1985. "And the Work Never Ends: Feminist Contributions." *Canadian Review of Sociology and Anthropology* 22 (December): 619-644.

Eichler, M. 1988. *Families in Canada Today-Recent Changes and Their Policy Consequences.* Toronto: Gage Educational.

Eichler, M. 1990. "The Relationship Between Sexist, Non-Sexist, Woman-Centred and Feminist Research in the Social Sciences." In G. Hoffman Memiroff (ed.), *Women and Men.* Montreal: Fitzhenry and Whiteside.

Eisenstein, H. 1983. *Contemporary Feminist Thought*. Boston: GK Hall.

Eisentein, Z. (ed.). 1979. *Capitalist Patriarchy and the Case for Socialist Feminism*. New York: Monthly Review Press.

Eisentein, Z. 1988. *The Female Body and the Law*. Berkeley: University of California Press.

Ekland-Olson, S. l988. "Structured Discretion, Racial Bias and the Death Penalty: The First Decade After Furman in Texas." *Social Science Quarterly* 69: 853-73.

Elias, R. 1986. *The Politics of Victimization, Victims, Victimology and Human Rights*. New York: Oxford Press.

Elkins, R. 1977. " Corporations and the Criminal Law-An Uneasy Alliance." *Kentucky Law Journal* 65, 1: 73-129.

Elliot L. and R. Morris. 1987. "Behind Prison Doors." In E. Adelberg and C. Currie (eds.), *Too Few To Count: Canadian Women in Conflict with the Law*. Vancouver: Press Gang Publishers.

Elmer-Dewitt, P. 1992. "Rich vs. Poor." *Time* (June 1): 22.

Elliott, J. and A. Fleras. 1992. *Unequal Relations*. Scarborough: Prentice-Hall.

Elliott, M. et al. 1993. "Global Mafia: A Mewsweek Investigation." *Newsweek* (December 13, 1993): 22-30.

Ellis, J. l984. "Prosecutorial Discretion to Charge in Cases of Spousal Violence: A Dialogue." *Journal of Criminal Law and Criminality* 75: 56-102.

Ellis, M. 1988. *Surviving Procedures After a Sexual Assault*. Vancouver: Press Gang.

Ellul, J. 1967. *The Technological Society*. New York: Alfred A. Knopf.

Elmer-Dewitt, P. 1993. "The Amazing Video Game Boom." *Time* (September 27), 41.

Emerson, R. and S. Messinger. 1977. "The Micro-Politics of Trouble." *Social Problems* 25 (December) 2.

Empey, L. and M. Ericson. 1965. "Class Position, Peers and Delinquency." *Sociology and Social Research* 49: 268-282.

Emrich, R. 1966. "The Basis of Organized Crime in Western Civilization." Paper Submitted to the President's Commission on Law Enforcement and Administration of Justice (October 14).

Enchin, H. 1992. "Competitiveness not new to Canadians." *Globe and Mail* (May 7): B1.

Engels, F. [1920] 1971. "Crime and the Conditions of the Working Class." In W. G. Carson and P. Eiles (ed.), *Crime and Delinquency*. Britain: Martin Robertson.

Engels, F. [1845] 1975. "The Condition of the Working Class in England." In K. Marx and F. Engels *Collected Works V.4*. New York: International Publishing.

England, R. 1960. "A Theory of Middle-Class Juvenile Delinquency." *Journal of Criminal Law, Criminology and Police Science* 50: 535-540.

Engstad, P. 1975. "Environmental Opportunities and the Ecology of Crime." In R. Silverman and J. Teevan (eds.), *Crime in Canadian Society*. Scarborough: Butterworth.

Erez, E. 1989. "Gender Rehabilitation and Probation Decisions." *Criminology* 27 (2): 307-327.

Erickson, B. 1981. *Networks and Attitudes: Theoretical Implications of Different Network Structure Models for Attitude Similarity*. Toronto: Structural Analysis Programme, University of Toronto.

Erickson, M. and J. Gibbs 1979. "Community Tolerance and Measures of Delinquency." *Journal of Research in Crime and Delinquency* 17: 55-79.

Ericson, R. 1974. "Turning the Inside Out: On Limiting the Use of Imprisonment." Toronto JHS Education Series 1 (3).

Ericson, R. 1975. *Criminal Reactions: The Labelling Perspective*. West Mead: Saxon House.

Ericson, R. 1977. "Social Distance and Reaction to Criminality." *British Journal of Criminology* 17 (1): 16-29.

Ericson, R. 1981. *Making Crime: A Study of Detective Work*. Toronto: Butterworth.

Ericson, R. 1984. *The Constitution of Legal Inequality*. Ottawa: Carleton University.

Ericson, R., P. Baranek and J. Chan. 1992. "Representing Order." In H. Holmes and D. Taras (eds.), *Seeing Ourselves, Media Power and Policy in Canada*. Toronto: Harcourt, Brace, Jovanovich.

Ercison, R., Haggerty, K. and K. Carriere. 1993. "Community Policing as Communications Policing." In D. Dolling and T. Feltes (eds.), *Community Policing: Comparative Aspects of Community Oriented Police Work*. Holzkirchen: Felix-Verlag.

Erikson, K. 1962. "Notes on the Sociology of Deviance." *Social Problems* 9 (Spring), 308; also the 1964 edition in H. Becker (ed.), *The Other Side*. New York: Free Press.

Erikson, K. 1965. "A Comment on Disguised Observations in Sociology." *Social Problems* 12 (4): 366-373.

Erikson, K. [1964] 1966. *Wayward Puritans*. New York: Wiley and Sons.

Erlanger, H. 1975. "Is There a Subculture of Violence in the South?." *Journal of Criminal Law and Criminology* 66: pp. 483-490.

Ermann, M.D. and R. Lundman. 1978. *Corporate and Government Deviance*. New York: Oxford U. Press.

Ermann, M.D. and R. Lundman. 1982. *Corporate Deviance*. New York: C.B.S. Publ.

Este, C. and B. Edmonds. 1981. "Symbolic Interactionism and Social Policy Analysis." *Symbolic Interaction* 4: 75-86.

Evans, S. and R. Lundman. 1983. " Newspaper Coverageof Corporate Price-Fixing." *Criminology* 21, 4: 529-541.

F

Fabain, J. 1990. "Presence and Representation: The Other and Anthropological Writing." *Critical Inquiry* 16: 753-772.

Fagan, J., Piper, E. and M. Moore. 1986. "Violent Delinquents and Urban Youths." *Criminology* 24 (August) 3: 439-471.

Fairley, G. 1990. *Wife Beating and its Relationship to Control of Wives and Male Adherence to Patriarchal Ideology*. M.S.W. Dissertation, York University.

Faludi, S. 1991. *Backlash: The Undeclared War Against American Women*. New York: Doubleday.

Fanon, F. 1967 [1982]. *Black Skin, White Masks*. New York: Grove.

Fanon, F. 1968. *The Wretched of the Earth*. New York: Grove.

Faris, R.E. and H.W. Dunham. 1939. *Mental Illness in Urban Areas*. Chicago: University of Chicago Press.

Farrell, R. and V. Swiggert. 1985. "The Corporation in Criminology: New Directions for Research." *Journal of Research in Crime and Delinquency* 22 (February)1: 83-94.

Fava, S. 1968. *Urbanism in World Perspective.* New York: T. Crowell.

Feagin, J.R. 1973. "Community Disorganization: Some Critical Notes." *Sociological Inquiry* 43 (December): 123-146.

Fedarko, K. 1994. "Hot Town, Hard Times." *Time* (August 22): 16-23.

Feinman, C. 1979. "Sex Role Stereotypes and Justice for Women." *Crime and Delinquency* 25 (1): 87-94.

Feld, M. 1977. "Professionalism, Nationalism, and the Alienation of the Miltary." In M. Feld (ed.), *The Structure of Violence: Armed Forces As Social Systems* London: Sage.

Ferdinand, T. and E. Luchterhand. 1970. "Inner City, Youth, the Police, the Juvenile Court and Justice." *Social Problems* 17: 511-527.

Ferguson, J. 1992. "Committee to Report on Breast Implants." *Toronto Star* (February 18): A10.

Ferraro, K. J. Johnson. 1983. "How Women Experience Battering: The Process of Victimization." *Social Problems* 30 (February): 325-338.

Feuer, L. (ed.). 1959. *Basic Writings on Politics and Philosophy: Marx and Engels.* New York: Doubleday.

Field, S. and M. Straus. 1989. "Escalation and Resistance of Wife Assault in Marriage." *Criminology* 27 (1): 141-161.

Figgie Report on Fear of Crime. 1980. *America Afraid, Part One: The General Public.* Willoughby, Ohio: Research and Forecasts, Inc.

Filstead, W. 1970. *Qualitative Methodology.* Chicago: Rand McNally.

Filstead, W. (ed.). 1972. *An Introduction To Deviance.* Chicago: Markham.

Fine, G. "Small Groups and Culture Creation." *American Sociological Review* 44: 733-745.

Fine, G. and S. Kleinman 1979. "Rethinking Subculture: An Interactionist Analysis." *American Journal of Sociology* 85 (1): 1-20.   ·

Fine, R. 1977. "Labelling Theory: An Investigation into the Sociological Critique of Deviance." *Economy and Society* 6: 166-193.

Finn, G. and A. Miles (eds.) 1982. *Feminism in Canada.* Montreal: Black Rose.

Fiore, G. 1971. *Antonio Gramsci: Life of a Revolutionary.* New York: E. P. Dutton.

Fischer, C. 1976. *The Urban Experience.* New York: Harcourt, Brace and Jovanovich.

Fischer, C. et al. 1977. *Networks and Places.* New York: Free Press.

Fishburn, K. 1982. *Women in Popular Culture—A Reference Guide.* Connecticut.

Fishcoff, S. 1993. "Hate on Campus." *Reform Judaism* (Fall).

Fisher, R. 1988. *Out of the Backyard: Readings on Canadian Native History.* Toronto: Copp Clark.

Fitzpatrick, P. 1987. "Racism and the Innocence of Law." *Journal of Law and Society* 14: 119-131.

Fitzpatrick, P. 1990. "Racism and the Innocence of Law." In D. Goldberg (ed.), *Anatomy of Racism.* Minneapolis: University of Minnesota.

Fleischer, H. 1973. *Marxism and History.* Frankfurt: Suhrkamp.

Fleming, T. (ed.). 1985. *New Criminologies in Canada.* Toronto: Oxford University Press.

Fleming, T. and L. Visano (eds.). 1983. *Deviant Designations.* Toronto: Butterworth.

Flemming, R.B., P. F. Nardulli, and J. Eisenstein. 1992. *The Craft of Justice: Politics and Work in Criminal Court Communities.* Philadelphia: University of Pennsylvania Press.

Foster, D. 1993. "The Disease is Adolescence." *Rolling Stone* (December 9).

Foucault, M. 1965. *Madness and Civilization: A History of Insanity in the Age of Reason.* New York: Vintage.

Foucault, M. 1970. *The Order of Things.* New York: Vintage.

Foucault, M. 1979. *Discipline and Power.* New York: Pantheon.

Foucault, M. 1977b. "The Political Function of the Intellectual." *Radical Philosophy* 17: 12-4.

Foucault, M. 1980. *Power and Knowledge: Selected Interviews and Other Writings 1972-1977.* Edited by C. Gordon New York: Vintage.

Foucault, M. 1980b. *The History of Sexuality Vol I.* New York: Vintage.

Fox, J. and T. Hartnagel. 1979. "Changing Social Roles and Female Crime in Canada: A Time Series Analysis." *Canadian Review of Sociology and Anthropology* 16 (1).

Francis, D. 1992. *Controlling Interest: Who Owns Canada?* Toronto: Macmillan.

Francis, D. 1993. "The New Love Affair with Transnationals." *Maclean's* (Dec. 20): 9.

Frank, N. 1988. " Unintended Murder and Corporate Risk-Taking: Defining the Concept of Justifiability." *Journal of Criminal Violence* 16: 17-24.

Freeman, M. D. 1982. "Legal Ideologies, Patriarchal Ideologies and Domestic Violence: A Case Study of the English Legal System." In S. Spitzer and R. Simon (eds.), *Research in Law, Deviance and Social Control: A Research Annual.* London: J.A.I. Press.

Freire, P. 1974. *Pedagogy of the Oppressed.* New York: Seabury.

French, M. 1992. *The War Against Women.* New York: Ballantine.

Frideres, J. 1988. "Institutional Structures and Economic Deprivation: Native People in Canada." In B. Singh Bolaria and P. Li (eds.), *Racial Oppression in Canada.* Toronto: Garamond.

Friedrichs, D. 1992."White Collar Crime and the Definitional Quagmire: A Provisional Solution." *Journal of Human Justice* 3 (Spring)2: 5-21.

Friedenberg, E. 1971. "The Side Effects of the Legal Process." In R. Wolff (ed.), *The Rule of Law.* New York: Simon and Shuster.

Friedenberg, E. 1975. *The Disposal of Liberty and Other Industrial Wastes.* Garden City: Doubleday.

Friedenberg, E. 1980. *Deference To Authority: The Case of Canada.* New York: Sharpe.

Friedman, J. and R. Wulff. 1975. *The Urban Transition.* London: Edward Arnold.

Fromm, E. 1941. *Escape From Freedom.* New York: Holt, Rinehart and Winston.

Fromm, E. 1961. *Marx's Concept of Man.* New York: Fredrick Ungar.

Frum, D. 1992. "Saving for a Rainy Day." *Saturday Night* (February 18-25): 64-65.

Fukurai, H., Butler, E. and R. Krooth. 1994. "Where did Black Jurors Go? A Theoretical Synthesis of Racial Disenfranchisenment in the Jury System and Jury Selection." In D. Baker (ed.), *Reading Racism and the Criminal Justice System* Toronto: Canadian Scholars' Press.

G

Gabor, T. 1994. "The Suppression of Crime Statistics on Race and Ethnicity: The Price of Political Correctness." *Canadian Journal of Criminology* 36 (April) 2: 153-163.

Gallant, M. and S. Kleinman. 1985. "Making Sense of Interpretations: Response to Rawls on the Debate Between Symbolic Interactionism and Ethnomethodology." *Symbolic Interactionism* 8 (1): 141-145.

Galper, J. 1975. *The Politics of Social Services*. Englewood Cliffs, N.J.: Prentice-Hall.

Gannage, C. 1986. *Double Day, Double Bind: Women Garment Workers*. Toronto: Women's Press.

Gans, H. 1972. *People and Plans*. Harmondsworth: Penguin.

Garfinkel, H. 1949. "Research Note on Inter-and Intra-Racial Homicides." *Social Forces* 27, 369-381.

Garfinkel, H. 1967. *Studies in Ethnomethodology*. Englewood Cliffs: Prentice-Hall.

Garner, L. and R.Garner. 1981. "Problems of the Hegemonic Party: The PCI and the Structural Limits of Reform." *Science and Society* 45 (Fall) 3: 257-273.

Garofolo, J. and J. Laub. 1978. "The fear of Crime: Broadening Our Perspective." *Victimology: An International Journal* 3 (3-4): 242-253.

Garza, C. 1992. "Postmodern Paradigms and Chicana Feminist Thought: Creating 'Space and Language'." *Critical Criminologist* (Autumn/ Winter) 4, 3/4: 1.

Gates, L. H. Jr. 1990. "Critical Remarks." In D. Goldberg (ed.), *Anatomy of Racism*. Minneapolis: University of Minnesota.

Gates, L. H. Jr. 1993. "Introduction." In K. Whittemore and G. Marzorati (eds.), *Voices in Black and White*. New York: Franklin Square.

Gates, L. H. Jr. 1993. "Portraits In Black." In K. Whittemore and G. Marzorati (eds.), *Voices in Black and White*. New York: Franklin Square.

Gates, L.H. Jr. 1993b. "Black Intellectuals, Jewish Tensions: A Weaving of Identities." *New York Times* (April 14): A15.

Gates, H.L. Jr. 1994. "Why Now?" *The New Republic* (October 31).

Gavigan, S. 1986. "On Bringing on Menses: The Criminal Liability of Women and the Therapeutic Exception in Canadian Abortion Law." *Canadian Journal of Women and Law* 1: 279-312.

Gehrke, L. 1985. "The Charter and Publicly Assisted Housing." *Journal of Law and Social Policy* (Fall).

Geis, G., Jesilow, P., Pontell, H. and M. J. O'Brien. 1985. "Fraud and Abuse of Government Medical Benefit Programs by Psychiatrists."*American Journal of Psychiatry* 142, (February)2: 231-234.

Geis, G. and R. F. Meier. 1979. "White Collar Offender." In H.Toch (ed.), *Psychology of Crime and Criminal Justice*. New York: Holt, Rinehart and Winston.

Geis, G. and E. Stotland. 1980. *White Collar Crime* Beverly Hills: Sage.

Gellner, E. 1959. *Words and Things*. London: Routledge and Kegan.

Gelles, R. 1974. *The Violent Home*. Beverly Hills: Sage.

Gelles, R. 1980. "Violence in the Family: A Review of Research in the Seventies." *Journal of Marriage and the Family* 7: 873-885.

Gelles, R. and M. Straus. 1988. *Intimate Violence*. Toronto: Simon and Shuster.

Genos, G. 1977. "Situation versus Frame Analysis: The Interactionist and Structural Analysis of Everyday Life." *American Sociological Review* 42 (6).

George, S. 1985. *Feeding the Few: Corporate Control of Food.* Toronto: Institute for Policy Studies.

Gerbmer, G. 1978. "The Dynamics of Cultural Resistance." In G. Tuchman, A.K. Daniels and J. Benet. *Hearth and Home: Images of Women in the Mass Media.* New York: Oxford U. Press.

Gerth, H. and C. W. Mills. 1946. *Max: Essays in Sociology.* New York: Oxford University Press.

Gerth, H. and C. W. Mills. 1953. *Character and Social Structure.* New York: Harcourt, Brace and World.

Gibbons, D. 1979. *The Criminological Enterprise: Theories and Perspectives.* Englewood Cliffs: Prentice-Hall.

Gibbons, D. and J. Jones. 1971. "Some Critical Notes on Current Definitions of Deviance." *Pacific Sociological Review* 14: 20-37.

Gibbons, D. and J. Jones 1975. *The Study of Deviance.* Englewood Cliffs: Prentice-Hall.

Gibbs, J. 1966. "Conceptions of Deviant Behaviour-The Old and the New." *Pacific Sociological Review* 9 (Spring): 9-14.

Gibbs, J. 1967. *Urban Research Methods.* Princeton: Van Nostrand.

Gibbs, J. and K. Erickson. 1975. "Major Developments in the Sociological Study of Deviance." In A. Inkeles, J. Coleman and N. Smelser (eds.), *Annual Review of Sociology.*

Gibbs, N. 1990. "Homeless, U.S.A." *Time* (December 17): 14-19.

Gibbs, N. 1993. "Up In Arms." *Time* (December 20): 14-20.

Giddens, A. 1973. *The Class Structure of Advanced Societies.* New York: Harper Row.

Giddens, A. 1976. *New Rules of Sociological Methods.* New York: Basic.

Giddens, A. 1978. *Durkheim.* Glasgow: Fontana.

Giddens, A. 1981. *Contemporary Critique of Historical Materialism.* London: Macmillan.

Giddens, A. 1982. *Profiles and Critiques of Social Theory.* London: Macmillan.

Giddens, A. 1984. *The Constitution of Society: Outline of Theory of Structuration.* Cambridge: Polity Press.

Giddens, A. 1986. *Sociology: A Brief But Critical Introduction.* London: Macmillan.

Giddens, A. 1992. *Modernity and Self-Identity.* Stanford: Stanford University Press.

Gill, D., Mayor, B. and Blair, M. 1992. *Racism and Education: Structures and Strategies.* London: Sage.

Gillis, A. R. and J. Hagan. 1979. "Density, Delinquency and Design: Formal and Informal Control and the Built Environment." Research Paper # 109, Centre for Urban and Community Studies.

Gillmor, D. 1992a. "Chief Justice." *Saturday Night* (March): 59-60.

Gillmor, D. 1992. "Recoil." *Saturday Night* (May) 51-77.

Gilmore, Al-Tony. 1979. "Aint Dat Some Thin?" *Weekend Magazine* (August 25): 8-9.

Ginsburg, E. and F. Henry. 1985. *Who Gets Work.* Toronto: Urban Alliance and Social Planning Council.

Ginsburg, M. 1987. "Contardictions in the Role of Professor as Activist." *Sociological Focus* 20 (April) 2: 11-122.

Giordano, P. and S. Cernkovich. 1979. "On Implicating the Relationship Between Liberation and Delinquency." *Social Problems* 26 (4): 467-481.

Giordano, P. 1983. "Sanctioning the High-Status Deviant: An Attributional Analysis." *Social Psychology Quarterly* 46 (Dec): 329-342.

Giroux, H. 1983. *Theory and Resistance: A Pedagogy for the Opposition.* South Hadley, Ma.: Bergin and Garvey.

Gittens, M. and D. Cole. 1994. "Speaking Notes." *Release of the Commission's Interim Report, Racism Behind Bars.* Toronto: Commission on Systemic Racism (February 1).

Glasbeek, H. and M. Mandel. 1984. "The Legislation of Politics in Advanced Capitalism: The Canadian Charter of Rights and Freedoms." *Socialist Studies* 2.

Glaser, B. and A. Strauss. 1967. *The Discovery of Grounded Theory.* Chicago: Aldine.

Glaser, D. 1956. "Criminality Theories and Behaviourial Images." *American Journal of Sociology* 61 (March): 433-444.

Glendon, M.A. 1991. *Rights Talk: The Impoverishment of Political Discourse.* New York: The Free Press.

Glickman, Y. 1985. "Anti-Semitism and Jewish Social Cohesion." In R. Bienvenue and J. Goldstein (eds.), *Ethnicity and Ethnic Relations in Canada.* Toronto: Butterworth.

Glueck, S. 1956. "Theory and Fact in Criminality." *British Journal of Criminology* 7 (October): pp. 94.

Glueck, S. and E. Gleuck. 1950. *Unravelling Juvenile Delinquency.* New York: Commonwealth Fund.

Goddard, J. 1991. "A Helping Hand." *Saturday Night* (December): 35-36 and 67-70.

Goff, C. and C. Reasons. 1978. *Corporate Crime in Canada.* Scarborough: Prentice-Hall.

Goff, C. and C. Reasons. 1979. "Corporate Crime and Punishment." In E. Vaz and A.Lodhi (eds.), *Crime and Delinquency in Canada.* Scarborough: Prentice-Hall.

Goffman, E. 1959. *Presentation of Self in Everyday Life.* New York: Anchor.

Goffman, E. 1961. *Asylums.* New York: Doubleday.

Goffman, E. 1961b. *Encounters: Two Studies in the Sociology of Interaction.* Indianapolis: Bobs-Merrill.

Goffman, E. 1963a. *Stigma.* Englewood Cliffs: Prentice-Hall.

Goffman, E. 1963b. *Behaviour in Public Places.* Glencoe, Illinois: Free Press.

Goffman, E. 1967. *Interaction Ritual.* New York: Anchor.

Goffman, E. 1973. *Frame Analysis.* New York: Harper.

Goffman, E. 1979. *Gender Advertisements.* New York: Harper and Row.

Golding, S. 1992. *Gramsci's Democratic Theory: Contributions to Post-Liberal Democracy.* Toronto: University of Toronto Press.

Goldman, R. and A. Rajagopal. 1991. *Mapping Hegemony.* New York: Ablex.

Gomme, I. 1993. *The Shadow Line: Deviance and Crime in Canada.* Toronto: HBJ.

Gomme, I. 1985 "Predictors of Status and Criminal Offenses Among Male and Female Adolescents in an Ontario Community." *Canadian Journal of Criminology* 27: 147-159.

Gordon, D. 1973. "Capitalism, Class and Crime in America." *Crime and Delinquency* (April) 2: 163-186.

Gordon, M. 1988. "Technofacism and the Corporate Media Culture." *Lexicon* (January): 6.

Gorden, P. 1988. "Black People and the Criminal Law: Rhetoric and Reality." *International Journal of Sociology of Law.*

Gordon, R. A. 1967. "Issues in the Ecological Study of Delinquency." *American Sociological Review* December 32 (6): 927-944.

Gould, A. (ed.). 1991. *What Did They Think of the Jews?* Toronto: Stewart House.

Gouldner, A. 1960. "The Norm of Reciprocity." *American Journal Review* 25 (April): 161-178.

Gouldner, A. 1968. "The Sociology as Partisan: Sociology and the Welfare State." *American Sociologist* 3 (May): pp. 103-116.

Gouldner, A. 1970. *The Coming Crisis of Western Sociology.* New York: Basic.

Gove, W. 1980. *The Labelling of Deviance.* Beverly Hills: Sage.

Grahame, K. 1985. *No Safe Place.* Toronto: Women's Press.

Gramsci, A. 1957. *The Modern Prince and Other Writings.* Edited By L. Marks. New York: International.

Gramsci, A. 1971. *Prison Notebooks: Selections.* Translated by Q. Hoare and G. Smith. New York: International Publishers.

Gramsci, A. 1985. *Antonio Gramsci: Selections From Cultural Writings.* Edited by D. and G. Nowell-Smith. Translated by W. Melhower. Cambridge: Harvard University Press.

Gramsci, A. 1988. *Antonio Gramsci: Selected Writings 1916-1935.* Edited By D. Forgacs. New York: Schocker.

Grant, A. 1990. "The Administration of Justice." National Indian Government Conference. Osgoode Hall Law School, York University: (October 3-5).

Gray, J. and D. Smith. 1985. *Police and People in London: The PSI Report.* Aldershot: Gower.

Greenburg, D. 1975. "Problems in Community Corrections." *Issues in Criminology* 10 (Spring): 1.

Greenberg, D. (ed.) . 1981. *Crime and Capitalism.* Palo Alto, California: Mayfield.

Greenberg, J. 1990. "All About Crime." *New York* (Sept 3): 20-32.

Greenglass, E. 1982. *A World of Difference: Gender Roles in Perspective.* Toronto: J.Wiley and Sons.

Greenwood, F. J. 1980. *Report of the Task Force on the Use of Firearms by Police Officers.* Toronto: Ontario Ministry of the Solicitor General.

Greer, S. 1962. *The Emerging City.* New York: Free Press.

Greer, S. 1962b. *Governing the Metropolis.* New York: John Wiley and Sons.

Greer, S. 1972. *Urbane View.* London: Oxford University Press.

Gregory, J. 1986. "Sex, Class and Crime: Towards a Non-Sexist Criminology." In B. Maclean (ed.), *Political Economy of Crime.* Scarborough: Prentice-Hall.

Gregory, S. 1992. "The Hidden Hurdle." *Time* (March 16): 42-45.

Greider, W. 1993. "Guns or Budget? Clinton's Options." *Rolling Stone* (March 4): 35-37, 77.

Griffins, S. 1971. "Rape: The All American Crime." *Ramparts* 10: 26-35.

Grimes, R. and A. Turk. 1978. "Labelling in Context: Conflict, Power and Self Definition." In M. Krohn and R. Akers (eds.), *Crime, Law and Sanctions: Theoretical Perspectives.* Beverly Hills: Sage.

Grogono, B. 1985. "Even Laurier was Biased: Head Tax in the Face for New Canadians." *The Medical Post* 3 (February 5): 21.

Gross, B. 1967. "The City of Man: A Social System Reckoning." In W. E. Wald (ed.), *Environment for Man*. Bloomington: Indiana University Press.

Gross, E. 1978. "Organizational Crime—A theoretical perspective." In N. Denzin (ed.), *Studies in Symbolic Interaction*. Greenwich, Conn.: JAI Press.

Gross, S. and R. Mauro. 1988. *Death and Discrimination*. Boston: Northeastern University Press.

Grossberg, L. 1986. "Reply to the Critics." *Critical Studies in Mass Communication* 3: 86-95.

Grossberg, L., Nelson, C. and P. Treicher. 1992. *Cultural Studies*. London: Routledge.

Grouppi, L. 1977. *The Concept of Hegemony in Gramsci*. Athens: Themelio.

Grove, S. 1986. "The Glass Ceiling." *Toronto Star* (July 11): B1.

Groves, W. and M. Lynch. 1990. "Reconciling Structural and Subjective Approaches to the Study of Crime." *Journal of Research in Crime and Delinquency* 27, 4: 348-375.

Guberman, C. and M. Wolfe. 1985. *No Safe Place*. Toronto: Women's Press.

Gunderson, M. 1981. "Unemployment among Young People and Government Policy in Ontario." Toronto: Ontario Economic Council, Discussion Paper Series.

Gunn, R. and C. Minch. 1988. *Sexual Assault: The Dilemma of Disclosure, The Question of Conviction*. Winnipeg: University of Manitoba Press.

Gurwitsch, A. 1966. "The Last Word on Edmund Husserl." In Gurwitsch, A. (ed.), *Studies in Phenomenology and Psychology* Evanston, Ill.: Northwestern U. Press.

Gusfield, J. 1955. "Fieldwork and Reciprocities in Studying a Social Movement." *Human Organization* 14: 29-34.

Gusfield, J. 1963. *Symbolic Crusade*. Urbana: University of Illinois Press.

Gusfield, J. 1981. *The Culture of Public Problems*. Chicago: University of Chicago Press.

Gutek, B. 1985. *Sex and the Workplace*. San Francisco: Jossey-Bass.

Gwyn, R. 1993. "La Cosa Nostra Is Turning Out To Be Vulnerable." *Toronto Star* (May 23): F1 and F3.

H

Habermas, J. 1974. "Habermas Talking: An Interview With Boris Frankel." *Theory and Society* Vol. 1.

Habermas, J. 1974. *Theory and Practice*. London: Heinemann Educational Books.

Habermas, J. 1976. *Legitimation Crisis*. London: Heinemann Educational Books.

Habermas, J. 1983. "Modernity-An Incomplete Project." In I. Foster (ed.), *Anti-Aesthetic Essays on Post-modern Culture*. Seattle: Bay Press.

Habermas, J. 1984. *The Theory of Communication Action: Reason and Realization of Society*. Boston: Heinemann Educational Books.

Hackett, R R. Pinet and M. Ruggles. 1992. "From Audience-Commodity to Audience-Community: Mass Media in B.C." In H. Holmes and D. Taras (eds.), *Seeing Ourselves, Media Power and Policy in Canada*. Toronto: Harcourt, Brace, Jovanovich.

Hagan, J. 1974. "Extra-Legal Attributes and Criminal Sentencing: An Assessment of a Sociological Viewpoint." *Law and Society Review* 8 (3): pp. 357-383.

Hagan, J. 1977. "Criminal Justice in Rural and Urban Communities: A Study of Bureaucratization of Justice." *Social Forces* 55 (3): 597-612.

Hagan, J. 1980. "The Legislation of Crime and Delinquency: A Review of Theory, Method and Research." *Law and Society Review* 14 (3): 603-628.

Hagan, J. 1985. *Modern Criminology*. Toronto: McGraw-Hill.

Hagan, J. 1985. "Toward a Structural Theory of Crime, Race and Gender." *Crime and Delinquency* 31 (1).

Hagan, J. 1986. "Towards a Structural Theory of Crime, Race and Gender." In R. Silverman and Teevan (eds.), *Crime in Canadian Society*. Toronto: Butterworth.

Hagan, J. 1991. *Disreputable Pleasures*. Toronto: Mcgraw Hill.

Hagan, J., I.Nagel and C. Albonetti. 1980. "The Differential Sentencing of White Collar Offenders in Ten Federal District Courts." *American Sociological Review* 45 (October): 802-820.

Hagan, J. and A. Palloni. 1988. "Club Fed and the Sentencing of White Collar Offenders Before and After Watergate." *Criminology* 24 (4): 603-621.

Hagan, J. Silvia, E. and J. Simpson.1977. "Conflict and Consensus in the Designation of Deviance." *Social Forces* (5): 320-340.

Hagan, J. and J. Simpson.1977. "Ties That Bind: Conformity and the Social Control of Student Discontent." *Sociology and Social Research* 61: 520-538.

Hagan, J., Simpson, J. and A. R. Gillis. 1987. "Class in the Household: A Power-Control of Gender and Delinquency." *American Journal of Sociology* 92: 788-816.

Hazen, D. (ed.). 1992 *Inside The L.A. Riots*. Los Angeles: Institute for Alternative Journalism.

Hale, E.B. l974. *The Police are the Public and the Public are the Police*. Task Force Report on Policing in Ontario, Toronto: Ministry of the Solicitor General.

Haley, A. 1990. *The Autobiography of Malcolm X*. New York: Ballantine.

Haliechuk, R. 1994. "Biggest Cash Paid to Brokers, Distillers." *Toronto Star*, (June 19): D1.

Hall, B. 1982. "Breaking the Monopoly of Knowledge: Research Methods, Participation and Development." In B. Hall, A.Gillette and R. Tandon (eds.), *Creating Knowledge: A Monopoly?* New Delhi: Society for Participatory Research in Asia.

Hall, E. and A. Simkus. 1975. "Inequality in the Types of Sentences Received by Native Americans and Whites." *Criminology* 13: 199-222.

Hall, J. 1994. "Young, Black and Male: Myths Mar Jamiacan Success Story." *Toronto Star* (May 15): C9.

Hall, P. 1987. "Interactionism and the Study of Social Organization." *Sociological Quarterly* 28 (Spring) 1: 1-22.

Hall, S. 1981. "The Whites of their Eyes: Racist Ideologies and the Media." In G. Bridges and R. Brunt (eds.), *Silver Linings: Some Strategies for the Eighties*. London: Lawrence and Withart.

Hall, S., B. Lumley and G. McLennan. 1977. "Politics and Ideology: Gramsci." *Working Papers in Cultural Studies* 10: 45-76.

Hall, S., Critcher, C., Jefferson, T., Clark, J. and B. Roberts. 1978. *Policing the Crisis*. London: Macmillan.

Hall, S. 1986. "Gramsci's Relevance for the Study of Race and Ethnicity." *Journal of Communication Inquiry* 10 (Summer)2: 5-27.

Hall, S. 1988. "Toad in the Garden: Thatcherian Among the Theorist." In C. Nelson and L. Grossberg (eds.), *Marxism and the Interpretation of Culture*. Urbana: University of Illinois.

Hall, S. and T. Jefferson. 1975. *Resistance Through Ritual: Working Class Youth Subcultures in Post-War Britain*. London: Hutchinson.

Halliday, M.A.K. 1978. *Language as Social Semiotic: the Social Interpretation of Language and Meaning*. London: Arnold.

Halmi, K., J. Falk and E. Schwartz. 1981. "Binge-Eating and Vomiting: A Survey of College A Population." *Psychological Medicine* 11: 697-707.

Hamilton, R. 1979. *The Liberation of Women: A Study of Patriarchy and Capitalism*. London: George Allen and Unwin.

Handelman, S. 1994. "The State of Black America." *Toronto Star* (July 24) E1, E4.

Hans, V. and N. Vidmar. 1986. *Judging the Jury*. New York: Plenum.

Harcourt, M. 1984. "Vancouver, A Multicultural City That Works." National Symposium in Policing and Multicultural, Multiracial Urban Communities. Vancouver: (October 15).

Harding, J. 1971. "Canada's Indians: A Powerless Minority." In J. Sharp and J. Hoflry (eds.), *Poverty in Canada*. Scarborough: Prentice-Hall.

Harding, S. 1987. *Feminism and Methodology*. Bloomington: Indiana University Press.

Hariman, R. (ed.). 1990. *Popular Trials: Rhetoric, Mass Media, and The Law*. Tuscaloosa: The University of Alabama Press.

Harm, N. 1992. "Social Policy on Women Prisoners: A Historical Analysis." *Affilia Journal of Women and Work* 7 Spring 1: 90-107.

Harney, R. 1978. *Italphobia*. Toronto: Multicultural History Society of Ontario.

Harries, K. 1974. *The Geography of Crime and Justice*. New York: McGraw-Hill.

Harris, D. 1994. "Does Your Pay Measure Up." *Working Woman* (January): 26.

Harris, M. 1986. *Justice Denied*. Toronto: Macmillan.

Harris, O. 1981. "Households as Natural Units." In K. Young, C. Wolkowitz and R. McCullagh (eds.), *Of Marriage and the Market*. London: C. S. E. Books.

Harris, O. and K. Young. 1981. "Engendered Structures: Some Problems in the Analysis of Reproduction." In J. Kahn and J. Llobera (eds.), *The Anthropology of Pre-Capitalist Societies*. London: Macmillan.

Hartmann, H. 1979. "Capitalism, Patriarchy and Job Segregation by Sex." In Z. Eisenstein (ed.), *Capitalist Patriarchy and the Case for Socialist Feminism*. New York: Monthly Review Press.

Hartmann, H. 1989. "The Unhappy Marriage of Marxism and Feminism: Towards a More Progressive Union." In R. Gottlieb (ed.), *An Anthology of Western Marxism*. New York: Oxford University Press.

Hathaway, J. 1985. "Poverty, Law and Equality Rights: Preliminary Reflections." *Journal of Law and Social Policy* 1 (Fall).

Hatt, P. and A. Reiss (eds.). 1957. *Cities and Society*. New York: Free Press.

Havemann, P., Foster, L., Couse, K. and R. Mattonovich. 1984. "Law and Order for Canada's Indigenous People." Prairie Justice Research Consortium of Human Justice. University of Regina, No 1984-7.

Hawkins, D. 1969. "God and the Mafia." *Public Interest* 14: 24-51.

Hawthorn, H. 1967. *A Survey of Contemporary Indians in Canada*. Vol. II. Ottawa: Indian Affairs.

Hay, D. et al. 1975. *Albion's Fatal Tree*. London: Allen Lane / Penguin.

Head, W. 1975. *The Black Presence in the Canadian Mosaic*. Toronto: Human Rights Commission.

Head, W. 1976. "Perceptions of Police Attitudes and Practices Toward Blacks and Other Visible Minorities in Metro Toronto." In *Law Enforcement and Race Relations*. Social Planning Council.

Head, W. 1991. "The Donald Marshal Prosecution: A Case Study of Racism and the Criminal Justice System." *Currents* (April) Vol. 7 No. 1: 9-13.

Hebdige, D. 1979. *Subculture: The Meaning of Style*. New York: Methuen.

Hegel, G. 1967. *Colour Blind Justice*. Society of Black Lawyers, Unpublished paper.

Held, V. 1996. *How Not To Take It Personally* .New York: McGraw-Hill.

Hemeon, J. 1994. "Why Stock Fraud Artists Are Getting Away With It." Business, *Toronto Star* (June 6) B1.

Henderson, J. 1992. "The Marshall Inquiry: A View of the Legal Consciousness." In J. Mannette (ed.), *Elusive Justice*. Halifax: Fernwood.

Henham, R. 1988. "The Importance of Background Variables in Sentencing Behaviour." *Criminal Justice and Behaviour* 15: pp. 255-263.

Henry, F. 1973. *Forgotten Canadians: The Blacks of Nova Scotia*. Don Mills: Longman.

Hepburn, J. 1976. "Testing Alternative Models of Delinquency Causation." *Journal of Criminal Law and Criminology* 67 (December): 450-460.

Henry, K. 1981. *Black Politics in Toronto Since World War One*. Toronto: The Multicutural History Society of Ontario.

Hernandez, Pacinid. 1986. *Resource Development and Indigenous People*. Occasional Paper no.15, Cambridge, Ma.

Hewitt, P., G. Flett, W. Turnbull-Donovan and S.F. Mikail. 1991. "The Multidimensional Perfectionism Scale: Reliability, Validity and Psychometric Properties in Psychiatric Samples." *Psychological Assessment: A Journal of Consulting and Clinical Psychology* 3, 464-468.

Heyl, B. 1979. *The Madam As Entrepreneur*. New Brunswick: Transaction.

Hickling-Johnston Report. 1982. *Management Review of the Metropolitan Toronto Police Force*. Toronto: Metropolitan Toronto Police Force.

Hill, D. 1979. *Human Rights in Canada: A focus on Racism*. Canadian Labour Congress.

Hill, D. 1984. "Remarks." National Symposium on Policing in Multicultural and Multiracial Urban Communities. Vancouver: (October).

Hill, D. 1985. "Policing in a Multicultural Canada." *Currents* (Summer): 3-6.

Hillery, G. 1955. Definitions of Community: Areas of Agreement." *Rural Sociology* 20 (June): 111-123.

Hinch, R. 1989. "Its Marxism Not Conflict Theory." *Canadian Critical Criminology: A Newsletter* 2 (Fall): 3-4.

Hindelang, M. 1970. "The Commitment of Delinquents to Their Misdeeds: Do Delinquents Drift?" *Social Problems* 17: 502-509.

Hindelang, M. 1978. "Race and Involvement in Common Law Personal Crimes." *American Sociological Review* 43: 93-109.

Hirschi, T. 1969. *Causes of Delinquency*. Berkeley: University of California Press.

Hirschi, T. 1975. "Labelling Theory and Juvenile Delinquency: An Assessment of the Evidence." In W. Gove (ed.), *The Labelling of Deviance*. New York: Halstead.

Hirschi, T. 1987. "Review of Explaining Delinquency and Drug Use by Delbert S. Elliott, David Huizinga, and Suzanne Ageton." *Criminology* 25: 193-201.

Hirst, P. 1972. "Marx and Engels on Law, Crime and Morality." *Economy and Society* 1: 28-56.

Hirst, P. 1979. *Law and Ideology.* London: Macmillan.

Hobbes, T. 1946. *Leviathon.* Edited by M. Oakeshott. London: Oxford Blackwell.

Hobsbaum, E. 1965. *Primitive Rebels.* New York: Norton.

Hobsbaum, E. 1969. *Bandits.* London: Ebinizer, Baylis and Sons.

Holland, J. 1973. *Making Vocational Choices: A Theory of Careers.* Englewood Cliffs: Prentice-Hall.

Hollingshead, A.B. 1975. *Elmtown's Youth and Elmtown Revisited.* New York: John Wiley and Son.

Holloway, J. and S. Picciotto (eds.). 1978. *State and Capital.* London: Arnold.

Holmes H. and D. Taras (eds.). 1992. *Seeing Ourselves, Media Power and Policy in Canada.* Toronto: Harcourt, Brace, Jovanovich.

Holmstrom, L. and A. Burgess. 1975. "Rape: The Victim and the Criminal Justice System." *International Journal of Criminology and Penology.*

Holnzer, B. 1968. *Reality Construction in Society.* Cambridge: Schenknan.

Holstrom, L. 1978. *The Victim of Rape.* Toronto: Wiley-Interscience.

Home Office, 1986. *The Ethnic Origin of Prisoners: The Prison Population.* Statistical Bulletin No.17.

Homer, F. 1974. *Guns and Garlic: Myths and Realities of Organized Crime.* West Layfayette: Purdue Research Foundation.

hooks, b. 1981. *Aint I A Woman: Black Women and Feminism.* Boston: South End Press.

hooks, b. 1984. *Feminist Theory: From Margin to Center.* Boston: South End Press.

hooks, b. 1987. "Feminism: A Movement to End Sexist Oppression." In A. Phillips (ed.), *Feminism and Equality.* Oxford: Basil Blackwell.

hooks, b. 1990. *Yearning.* Toronto: Between the Lines.

hooks. b. 1990b. "Postmodern Blackness." *Postmodern Culture* 1 (Sept)1.

Hook, S. 1933. *Towards the Understanding of Karl Marx: A Revolutionary Interpretation.* Ann Arbor: University of Michigan.

Hoose, P. 1989. *Necessities.* New York: Random House.

Horii, G. 1992. "No Surrender." *Matriart: A Canadian Feminist Art Journal* 3, 1: 3.

Horkheimer, M. and T. Adorno. 1989. *Dialectic of Enlightenment.* New York: Herder and Herder.

Horkheimer, M. 1936. *Critical Theory: Selected Essays.* New York: Continuum.

Hornung, R. 1991. *One Nation Under the Gun: Inside the Mohawk Civil War.* New York: Stoddart.

Horowitz, I. 1964. "A Postscript to the Anarchists." *The Anarchists* New York: Dell.

Horowitz, I. and M. Liebowitz. 1968. "Social Deviance and Political Marginality." *Social Problems* 15 (Winter): 280-296.

Hudson, B. 1989. "Discrimination and disparity: the influence of race on sentencing." *New Community* 16 (1): 21-32.

Hughes, D. and E. Kallen. 1974. *The Anatomy of Racism: Canadian Dimensions.* Montreal: Harvest House.

Hughes, E. 1937. "Institutional Office and the Person." *American Journal of Sociology* 43 (November): 409-410.

Hughes, E. 1958. *Men and Their Work.* Glencoe: Free Press.

Hughes, E. 1971. *The Sociological Eye*. Chicago: Aldine.

Humana, C. 1992. *World Human Rights Guide*. New York: Oxford U. Press.

Humphreys, G. 1987. "Trends in Levels of Academic Achievement of Blacks and Other Minorities." *Intelligence* 11.

Humphreys, L. 1979. *Tearoom Trade*. New York: Aldine.

Hunt, A. 1993. *Explorations In Law and Society: Toward Constitutive Theory of Law*. New York: Routledge.

Hurst, L. 1992. "Shades of the 30's." *Toronto Star* (February 9): B1.

Hurst, L. 1992b. "Feminism's Fault Lines." *Toronto Star* (November 28): D1.

Husserl, E. *The Idea of Phenomenology*. Translated By W. Alston and G. Naknnikian. Hague: Martinus Nijhoff.

Hylton, J. 1981. "Community Corrections and Social Control: The Case of Saskatchewan Canada." *Contemporary Crises* 5: 193-215.

Hylton, J. 1986. "The Native Offender in Saskatchewan." *Canadian Journal of Criminology* 24 (2).

Hyman, R. 1993. *The Pan Dictionary of Famous Quotations*. London: Grange.

I

Iacovetta, F. 1985. "From Contadina to Worker: Southern Italian Working Women in Toronto." *Polypony*, 7 (Fall/Winter)2.

Iacovetta, F. 1993. "Murder or self-defence: The case of Angelina Napolitano." *the eyetalian* (Fall).

Ianni, F. 1974. *Black Mafia: Ethnic Succession in Organized Crime*. New York: Simon and Shuster.

Ianni, F. and E. Reuss-Ianni. 1973. *A Family Business*. New York: New American Library.

Inciardi, J. (ed.). 1980. *Radical Criminology*. Beverly Hills: Sage.

Inciardi, J. 1984. "Little Girls and Sex." *Deviant Behavior* 5: 71-78.

Ingstrup, O. 1987. *Mission Statement of the National Parole Board*. National Parole Board, Communications Division.

Institute of Race Relations. 1982. *Patterns of Racism Book II*. London: Institute of Race Relations.

Institute of Race Relations. 1987. *Policing Against Black People*. London: Institute of Race Relations.

Ireland, D. 1992. "The Verdict." In Hazen, D. (ed.),. *Inside The L.A. Riots*. Los Angeles: Institute for Alternative Journalism.

Irigaray, L. 1985. "The Power of Discourse." *This Sex Is Not One*. Ithaca: Cornell University Press.

Irvine, M. J. 1978. *The Native Inmate in Ontario*. Ministry of Correctional Services, Toronto: Support and Services Division.

Israel, J. 1971. *Alienation From Marx to Modern Sociology*. Boston: Allyn and Bacon.

Itwaru, A. 1987 "On the Reflexivity of Text and Power." Unpublished paper. York University (May).

Itwaru, A. 1989a. *Mass Deception*. Toronto: Terebi.

Itwaru, A. 1989b. *Critiques of Power*. Toronto: Terebi.

J

Jackson. T.J. 1985. "The Concept of Cutural Hegemony: Problems and Possibilities." *The American Historical Review* 90 (June).

Jacobs, D. 1978. "Inequality and the Legal Order: An Ecological Test of the Conflict Model." *Social Problems* 25 (June).

Jacobs, D. 1979. "Inequality and Police Strength: Conflict Theory and Coercive Control in Metropolitan Areas." *American Sociological Review* 44: 913-925.

Jacobs, D. and D. Britt. 1979. "Inequality and Police Use of Deadly Force: An Empirical Assessment of a Conflict Hypothesis." *Social Problems* 26 (4): 403-412.

Jacobs, J. 1961. *The Death and Life of Great American Cities.* New York: Vintage.

Jaffe, P., Wolfe, D., Telford, A. and G. Austin. 1986. "The Impact of Police Charges Incidents of Wife Abuse." *Journal of Family Violence* 1 (1).

Jaggar, A. and P. Rothenberg. 1984. *Feminist Frameworks.* New York: McGraw-Hill.

James, C.L.R. 1963a. *The Black Jacobins.* New York: Vintage.

James, C.L.R. 1963b. *Beyond A Boundary.* London: Hutchinson.

James, C.L.R. 1980. *Spheres of Influence.* London: Allison and Busby.

Jannigan, M. 1992. "Lonely Cries of Distrust." *Maclean's* (March 16): 22-24.

Jansen, C. 1994. "Want to Count Crimes by Race? Here are the Not-so-simple Ways." *Toronto Star,* (May 8: F4).

Jaywardene, C. 1979. "Policing the Indian." *Crime and Justice* 7/8 (1).

Jeffery, C.R. 1971. *Crime Prevention Through Environmental Design.* Beverly Hills: Sage.

Jenkins, F. 1973. *Like Nobody Else: The Fergie Jenkins Story.* Chicago: Henry Regnery.

Jennings, K. 1993. "Black Youth in Police Crosshairs." *Covert Action* 45 (Summer): 50.

Jensen, A.R. 1969. "How Much Can We Boost IQ and Scholastic Achievement?" *Harvard Educational Review* 33, 1-123.

Jensen, A.R. 1980. *Bias in Mental Testing.* New York: Free Press.

Jiryis, S. 1976. *The Arabs in Israel.* London: Monthly Review Press.

Johnson, D. 1989. "Native Rights as Collective Rights: A Question of Group Preservation." *Canadian Journal of Law and Jurisprudence* (11).

Johnson, E. 1957. "Selective Forces in Capital Punishment." *Social Forces* 36: 165-169.

Johnson, J. and J. Douglas. 1978. *Crime at the Top.* New York: Lippincott.

Johnson, K.A. 1986. "Federal Court Processing of Corporate, White Collar and Common Crime Economic Offenders Over the Past Three Decades." *Mid-American Review of Sociology* 11 (Spring)1: 25-44.

Johnston, J.P. 1994. "Academic Approaches to Race-crime Statistics do not Justify Their Collection." *Canadian Journal of Criminology* 36, 2, (April) 166-174.

Jolly, S. 1982. "Natives in Conflict with the Law." *Correctional Options* (Fall).

Jolly, S. 1982b. "Native People in Conflict with the Criminal Justice System: The Impact of the Ontario Native Criminal on Justice." Paper Presented at the American Society of Criminology 34th Annual Meeting (November 4).

Jolly, S. 1983. *Warehousing Indians: Fact Sheet on the Disproportionate Imprisonment of Native People in Ontario 1981-1982.* Toronto: Ontario Native Council.

Jolly, S. and A. Birkenmayer. 1981. *The Native Inmate in Ontario.* Toronto: Ontario Native Council and Correctional Services.

Joseph, G. and J. Lewis. 1981. *Common Differences, Conflictss in Black and White Feminist Perspectives.* Boston: South End.

Jouve, N.W. 1991. *White Woman Speaks With Forked Tongue: Criticism as Autobiography.* London: Routledge.

K

Kahn, A. 1973. *Social Policy and Social Services.* New York: Random House.

Kahne, M. and C. Schwartz. 1978. "Negotiating Trouble: The Social Construction and Management of Trouble in a College Psychiatric Context." *Social Problems* 25 (June): 5.

Kairys, D. 1982. "Legal Reasoning." In *The Politics of Law.* New York: Pantheon.

Kallen, E. 1982. *Ethnicity and Human Rights in Canada.* Toronto: Gage.

Kallen, E. 1989. *Label Me Human.* Toronto: U of T Press.

Kanter, R. 1977. *Men and Women of the Corporation.* New York: Basic.

Kapis, R. 1978. "Residential Succession and Delinquency: A Test of Shaw and McKay's Theory of Cultural Transmission." *Criminology* 15 (4): 459-486.

Karp, D., Store, G. and W. Yoels. 1977. *Being Urban.* New York: DC Heath.

Kashmeri, Z. 1984. "Organized Crime Takes in 20 Billion a Year Study Says." *Globe and Mail* (January 13): 1-3.

Kasper, A. 1986. "Consciousness Re-Evaluated: Interpretive Theory and Feminist Scholarship." *Sociological Inquiry* 56: 29-49.

Katovich, M. 1987. "Identity, Time, and Situated Activity: An Interactionist Analysis of Dyadic Transaction." *Symbolic Interaction* 10 (Fall) 2: 187-208.

Katz, F. 1966. "Social Participation and Social Structure." *Social Forces* 45 (December): 199-210.

Katz, J. 1972. "Deviance, Charisma and Rule-Defined Behaviour." *Social Problems* 20 (Fall) 2: 186-201.

Katz, J. 1978. *White Awareness.* Norman University of Oklahoma Press.

Katz, J. 1993. "Time Warner Runs Up the White Flag." *Rolling Stone* (March 4): 40-41.

Keil, T. and V. Gennaro. 1990. "Race and the Death Penalty in Kentucky Murder Trials: An Analysis of Post-Gregg Outcomes." *Justice Quarterly* 7 (March) 1.

Keil, T. and G. Vito. 1989. "Race Homicide Severity and Application of the Death Penalty: A Consideration of the Barnett Scale." *Criminology* 27 (3): 511-535.

Kempf, K. et al. 1986. "Older and More Recent Evidence on Racial Discrimination in Sentencing." *Journal of Qualitative Criminology* 2 (1): 29-47.

Kempton, M. 1992. "Another Case of Multiculturalism." *The New York Review* (April 9): 52.

Keohane, N. and B. Gelpi. 1982. "Foreword." In N. Keohane, M. Rosaldo and B. Gelpi (eds.), *Feminist Theory: A Critique of Ideology.* Chicago: University of Chicago.

Kessler, J. 1993. FYI France: Bib.de France, preservation, and Umberto Eco <kessler@well.sf.ca.us> PACS-L@UHUPVM1.BITNET (Feb) re. "No, Imaging Has Not Killed the Civilization of the Written Word: The Revenge of the Books." *Le Nouvel Observateur* no.1406, 17-23 Octobre, 1991.

Key, W.B. 1981. *Subliminal Seduction.* New York: Signet.

Kim, J. 1994. "Where Women Stand." *Working Woman* (January): 31.

King, Scott, C. 1993. *The Martin Luther King Jr. Companion.* New York: St. Martin's Press.

King, M.L. Jr. 1963. *The Strength to Love.* New York: Harper and Row.

King, M.L. Jr. 1964. *Why We Can't Wait.* New York: Harper and Row.

King, M.L. Jr. 1967a. *Where Do We Go From Here?* New York: Harper and Row.

King, M.L. Jr. 1967b. *The Trumpet of Conscience.* New York: Harper and Row.

Kinnon, D. 1981. *Report on Sexual Assault in Canada.*, Report to the Canadian Council on the Status of Women (December).

Kinsey, A. et al. 1948. *Sexual Behaviour in the Human Male.* Philadelphia: Saunders.

Kirby, C. and T. Renner. 1986. *Mafia Assassin.* Toronto: Methuen.

Kirkham, M. 1986. "A Feminist Perspective in Midwifery." In C. Webb (ed.), *Feminist Practice in Women's Health Care.* Chichester: J. Wileg and Sons.

Kirshenbaum, J. 1992. "Scorecard." *Sports Illustrated* 77 (23): 13-14.

Kitsuse, J. 1962. "Societal Reaction to Deviant Behaviour." *Social Problems* 9 (Winter): 247-256.

Kitsuse, J. 1964. "Societal Reaction to Deviant Behaviour: Problems of Theory and Method." In H. Becker (ed.), *The Other Side.* New York: Free Press.

Kitsuse, J. 1975. "New Conception of Deviance and its Critics." In W. Gove (ed.), *The Labelling of Deviance: Evaluating a Perspective.* New York: J. Wiley and Sons.

Kitsuse, J. and D. Detrick. 1959. "Delinquent Boys: A Critique." *American Sociological Review* 24: pp. 208-215.

Klein, D. 1973. "The Etiology of Female Crime: A Review of the Literature." *Issues in Criminology* 8: pp. 3-29.

Klein, M. 1979. "Deinstitutionalizationand Diversion of Juvenile Offenders: A Litany of Impediments." In N. Morris and M. Tonrey (eds.), *Crime and Justice.* Chicago: University of Chicago Press.

Klinck, C. and R. Watters. 1966. *Canadian Anthology.* Toronto: Gage.

Klockars, C. 1978. "The Contemporary Crises of Marxist Criminology." *Criminology* 16 (3): pp. 477-515.

Knudten, R.D. 1970. *Crime in a Complex Society.* Illinois: Dorsey.

Koch, G. and S. Clarke. 1976. "The Influence of Income and Other Factors on Whether Criminal Defendants Go to Prison." *Law and Society Review* 2 (1) Fall: 57-93.

Koenig, E. 1975. "Overview of Attitudes Towards Women in Law Enforcement." *Public Administration Review* (38).

Konopka, G. 1966. *The Adolescent Girl in Conflict.* Englewood Cliffs: Prentice-Hall.

Korbin, S. 1951. "The Conflict of Values in Delinquency Areas." *American Sociological Review* 16: pp. 653-661.

Koss, M. C. Giducz and N. Wisniewski. 1987. "The Scope of Rape: Incidence and Prevalence of Sexual Aggression and Victimizatiobn in a National Sample of Higher education Students." *Journal of Consulting and Clinical Psychology* 55: 162-170.

Koss, M. et al. 1988. "Stranger and Acquaintance Rape: Are There Differences in the Victim's Experiences?" *Psychology of Women Quarterly* 12: 1-24.

Koss, M.P. 1987. "The Scope of Rape: Incidence, Aggression and Victimization in a National Sample of Higher Education Students." *Journal of Consulting and Clinical Psychology* 3: 229-244.

Koulack, D. 1991. "New Rape Shield is a Transparent Curtain." *Globe and Mail* (September 6): A15.

Kramer, M. 1993. "Clinton's Drug Policy is a Bust." *Time* (December 20): 21.

Krauthammer, C. 1990. "Black Rejectionists." *Time* (July 23): 39.

Krebs, D. and A. Adinolfi. 1975. "Physical Attractiveness, Social Relations and Personal Style." *Journal of Personality and Social Psychology* 31, 245-253.

Krisberg, B. 1975. *Crime and Privilege: Toward a New Criminology.* Englewoods Cliffs: Prentice-Hall.

Krisberg, B. 1975. *The Gang and the Community.* Berkeley: University of California.

Kristeva, J. 1976. Signifying Practice and Mode of Production." *Edinburgh Magazine* (1).

Kristeva, J. 1991. *Strangers to Ourselves,* Translated by Leon S. Roudiez. New York: Columbia UP, 1991.

Kritzer, H. K. 1991. *Let's Make a Deal: Understanding the Nnegotiation in Ordinary Litigation.* Madison, WI: University of Wisconsin Press, 1991.

Krohn, M. et al. 1980. "Social Status and Deviance." *Criminology* 18: 303-317.

Krohn, M. and J. Massey. 1980. "Social Control and Delinquent Behaviour: An Examination of the Elements of the Social Bond." *Sociological Quarterly* 21 (Autumn): 529-544.

Kropatkin, P. and R. Kusserow. 1986. *Management Principles for Asset Protection.* New York: J. Wiley and Sons.

Kubat, D. 1979. *The Politics of Migration.* New York: Centre for Migration Studies.

Kulchyski, P. 1994. *Unjust Relations: Aboriginal Rights in Canadian Courts.* Toronto: Oxford University Press.

Kumar, A. 1990. "Towards Postmodern Marxist Theory: Ideology, State and the Politics of Critique." *Rethinking Marxism* 3 (Fall-Winter) 3-4: 149-155.

Kunjufu, J. 1984. *Developing Positive Self Images and Discipline in Black Children.* Chicago: African American Images.

Kurtz, H. 1981. "Corporate Criminals, Pros and Cons? An Exchange Theory Approach." *Sociological Spectrum* 1 (April-June) 2: 159-166.

L

Lacan, J. 1977. *Ecrits: A Selection.* (Sheridan translation). New York: Norton.

La Capra, D. 1972. *Emile Durkheim, Sociologist and Philosopher.* Ithaca: Cornell University Press.

Lacayo, R. 1994 "Stranger in the Shadows." *Time* (November 14).

Laclau, E. 1977. *Politics and Ideology in Marxist Theory.* London: New Left Books.

Laclau, E. and C. Mouffe. 1985. *Hegemony and Socialist Strategy: Towards a Radical Democratic.* New York: New Left Books.

La Grange, R. and H.R. White. 1985. "Age Differences in Delinquency: A Test of Theory." *Criminology* 23 (February): 19-45.

Lakoff, S. 1964. *Equality in Political Philosophy.* Boston: Beacon.

Lamothe, L. 1991. "Asian Crime Statistics Shock." *Toronto Sun* (July 25): 3.

Landau, W. and Nathan. 1983. "Selecting Delinquents for Cautioning in the London Metropolitan Area." *British Journal of Criminology* 23 (2).

Lander, B. 1954. *Towards an Understanding of Juvenile Delinquency*. New York: Columbia University Press.

Landis, J. and F. Scarpitti. 1965. "Perceptions Regarding Value Orientation and Legitimate Opportunity: Delinquents and Non-Delinquents." *Social Forces* 84: pp. 57-61.

Lansberg, M. 1998. "Lunatic US Right has Let Loose the Hounds." *Toronto Star* Feb 1: A2.

LaPrairie, C. 1982. "Native Juveniles in Court: Some Preliminary Observations." In T. Fleming and L.A. Visano (eds.), *Deviant Designations*. Toronto: Butterworth.

LaPrairie, C. 1984. "Selected Criminal Justice and Socio-Demographic Data on Native Women." *Canadian Journal of Criminology* 26: pp. 161-169.

LaPrairie, C. 1990. "The Role of Sentencing in the Over-representation of Aboriginal People in Correctional Institutions." *Canadian Journal of Criminology* (July): 429-440.

LaPrairie, C. 1994. *Seen But Not Heard: Native People in the Inner City*. Report #1, Department of Justice, Aboriginal Justice Directorate, Ottawa.

Laqueur, W. and B. Rubin. 1990. *The Human Rights Reader*. New York: Meridian.

La Roque, E. 1975. *Defeathering the Indian*. Agincourt: Canadian Book Society.

Lauderdale, P. 1976. "Deviance and Moral Boundaries." *American Sociological Review* 41: pp. 660-676.

Law, J. 1979. *The Second X: Sex Role and Social Role*. New York: Elsevier.

Law Reform Commission of Canada. 1986. *Workplace Pollution*. Working Paper 53, Ottawa.

Leab, D. 1976. *From Sambo to Superspade*. Boston: Houghton Mifflin.

League for Human Rights of B'nai Brith. 1993. *Audit of Anti-Semitic Incidents 1992*.

Leavitt, R. 1976. *Peacable Primates and Gentle People*. New York: Harper and Row.

Lee, B. 1980. "The Disappearance of Skid Row: Some Ecological Evidence." *Urban Affairs* 16 (September) 1.

Lee, J. and L.A. Visano. 1981. "Official Deviance in the Legal System." In H. Ross (ed.), *Law and Deviance*. Beverly Hills: Sage.

Lefcourt, R. 1971. *Law Against the People*. New York: Random House.

Lefebvre, H. 1969. *The Sociology of Karl Marx*. New York: Random House.

Lemert, E. [1951] 1952. *Social Pathology*. New York: McGraw-Hill.

Lemert, E. 1962. "Paranoia and the Dynamics of Exclusion." *Sociometry* 25: pp. 2-25.

Lemert, E. 1967. "The Concept of Secondary Deviation." *Human Deviance, Social Problems and Social Control*. Toronto: Prentice-Hall.

Lemert, E. 1971. *Human Deviance, Social Problems and Social Control*. Englewood Cliffs: Prentice-Hall.

Lemert, E. 1982. "Issues in the Study of Deviance." In M. Rosenberg, R. Stebbins and A. Turowetz (eds.), *The Sociology of Deviance*. New York: St. Martin's Press.

Lemke, J.L. 1988. "Text Structure and Text Semantics." In E. Steiner and R. Veltman (eds.), *Pragmatics, Discourse and Text*. London: Pinter.

Lerner, G. 1972. *Black Women in White America*. New York: Pantheon.

Letkemann, P. 1973. *Crime as Work*. Englewood Cliffs: Prentice-Hall.

Levens, B. and D. Dutton. 1980. *The Social Service Role of Police-Domestic Crisis Intervention*. Vancouver: Supply and Services.

Levi J. N.and A. Graffam Walker (eds.). 1990. *Language in the Judicial Process*. New York: Plenum Press.

Levin-Waldman, O. 1993. "Can Locke's Theory of Property Inform the Court on Fifth Amendment 'Takings' Law?" Prepared for the 1993 Annual Meeting of the American Political Science Association, Washington, D.C.

Levine.J.P. 1992. *Juries and Politics*. Pacific Grove, California: Brooks/Cole.

Levinger, G. 1966. "Sources of Marital Dissatisfaction Among Applicants for Divorce." *American Journal of Orthopsychiatry* 26 (October): 803-897.

Levitt, C. and W. Shaffir. 1987. *The Riot at Christie Pitts*. Toronto: Lester and Orpen Dennys.

Levy, H. 1994. "Punishing the Idea Behind the Crime." *Toronto Star* (July 5): A15.

Lewin, E. and A. Lewin. 1988. *The Random House Thesauraus of Slang*. New York: Random House.

Lewis, C. 1989. *Report*. Eighth Annual Report of Public Complaints Commission.

Lewis, S. 1992. *Report on Race Relations in Ontario* (June). Toronto: Queen's Park.

Lewis, D. 1991. *Speaking Notes, Solicitor General's Announcement on Regional Facilitates for Federally Sentenced Women*. Halifax: (July 31).

Lewis, N. 1964. *The Honoured Society*. New York: G.P. Putnam and Sons.

Leyton, E. 1979. *The Myth of Delinquency*. Toronto: McClelland and Stewart.

Leyton, E. 1986. *Hunting Humans*. Toronto: McLelland & Stewart.

Lezak, S. and M. Leonard. 1984. "The Prosecutor's Discretion: Out of the Closet-Not Out of Control." *Oregon Law Review* 63: 247-264.

Lazere, D. 1977. "Mass Culture, Political Consciousness, and English Studies: An Introduction." *College English* 38 (April)8: 751-767.

Li, P. 1988. *Ethnic Inequality in a Class Society*. Toronto: Wall and Thompson.

Li, P. 1990. *Race and Ethnic Relations in Canada*. Toronto: Oxford University Press.

Li, P. 1992. "Race and Gender as Bases of Class Fractions and Their Effects on Earnings." *Canadian Review of Sociology and Anthropology* 29 (4): 488-510.

Li, P. and B. Singh Bolaria. 1983. *Racial Minorities in Multicultural Canada*. Toronto: Garamond.

Liazos, A. 1973. "The Poverty of the Sociology of Deviance: Nuts, Sluts and Perverts." *Social Problems* 20 (Summer): 103-120.

Lichtman, R. 1970. "Symbolic Interactionism and Social Reality: Some Marxist Queries." *Berkeley Journal of Sociology* XV: 75-94.

Liddle, A.M. 1989. "Feminist Contributions to an Understanding of Violence Against Women-Three Steps Forward, Two Steps Back." *Canadian Review of Sociology and Anthropology* 26 (5): 759-775.

Lieber, M. 1994. "A Comparison of Juvenile Court Outcomes for Native Americans, African Americans, and Whites." *Justice Quarterly* 11 (June)2.

Liebow, E. 1967. *Tally's Corner*. Boston: Little, Brown.

Liebowitz, L. 1975. "Perspectives on the Evolution of Sex Differences." In R. Reiter (ed.), *Towards An Anthropology Of Women*. New York: Monthly Review Press.

Liepner, M. and B. Griffith 1990. *Applying the Law*. Toronto: McGraw-Hill Ryerson.

Light, A. 1992. "Ice-T: The Rolling Stone Interview." *Rolling Stone* (August 20): 29-32, 60.

Linden, M. 1982. *Immigrant Welfare: A Research Perspective*. Sydney: Social Welfare Research Centre of the University of New South Wales.

Linden, R. 1982. *Women in Policing*. Manitoba: University of Manitoba.

Linden, R. 1987. *Criminology: A Canadian Perspective*. Toronto: Holt, Rinehart and Winston.

Linden, R., Currie, R. and L. Driedger. 1985. "Interpersonal Ties and Alcohol Use Among Mennonites." *Canadian Review of Sociology and Anthropology* 22: 559-573.

Lines, R. 1992. "Dare to Struggle." In K. McCormick and L. A. Visano (eds.), *Canadian Penology*. Toronto: Canadian Scholars' Press.

Lines, R. 1992b. "On The Prowl." Graduate paper submitted for Sociology of Resistance, York University, North York.

Linton, M. 1988. "Are We Better Off." *Sunday Sun* (July 31): C 8-9.

Lippman, J. 1992. "How Television is Shaping World's Culture." *Toronto Star* (December 21): A21.

Lippman, W. 1992. *Public Opinion*. New York: Macmillan.

Lips, H. 1991. *Women, Men and Power*. California: Mayfield Publishing.

Liska, A. 1987. *Perspectives on Deviance*. Englewood Cliffs: Prentice-Hall.

Liska, A. and M. Reed 1985. "Ties to Conventional Institutions and Delinquency: Estimating Reciprocal Effects." *American Sociological Review* 50 (August): 547-560.

Lithwick, N. 1970. *Urban Canada: Problems and Prospects*. Ottawa: Central Housing and Mortgage Corporation.

Lizotte, A. 1978. "Extra-Legal Factors in Chicago's Criminal Courts: Testing the Conflict Model of Criminal Justice." *Social Problems* 25 (5): 564-580.

Lloyd, C. et al. 1979. *Women in the Labour Market*. New York: Columbia University Press.

Lloyd, D. 1974. *The Idea of Law*. London: Penguin.

Locke, A.L. 1992. *Race Contacts and Interracial Relations*. Edited by J. Stewart. Washington: Howard University Press.

Locke, J. 1988 *Two Treatises of Government*. Edited by Peter Laslett. Cambridge and New York: Cambridge University Press.

Lockwood, D. 1956. "Some Remarks on the Social System." *British Journal of Criminology* 7: 134-148.

Lofland, J. 1969. *Deviance and Identity*. Englewood Cliffs: Prentice-Hall.

Lofland, J. 1976. *Analyzing Social Settings*. Belmont: Wadsworth.

Lofland, J. 1985. *Protest*. New Brunswick, N.J.: Transaction.

Lofland, L. 1973. *A World of Strangers*. New York: Basic.

Lombroso, C. and W. Ferrero. [1893] 1958. *The Female Offender*. New York: Wisdom.

London, Borough of Newham. 1987. *The Newham Crime Survey*. London: Borough of Newham.

Long, L. 1985. "The Abortion Issue: An Overview." *Alberta Law Review* 23 (3): 453-478.

Long, W.O. 1991. "Gender Role Conditioning and Women's Self Concept." *Journal of Humanistic Education and Development* 30: 19-29.

Longino, H. 1980. "Pornography, Oppression and Freedom: A Closer Look." In L. Lederer (ed.), *Take Back the Night*. New York: William Morrow and Company.

Lont, C. M. 1990. The Roles Assigned to Females and Males in Non-music Radio Programming." *Sex Roles* 22: 661-668.

Lopiano, D. 1993. "Stop The Rhetoric: Daughters Deserve What the Law Requires." *USA Today* (July 2): C12.

Lord, L.K. 1986. "A Comparison of Male and Female Police Officer's Stereotypic Perceptions of Women and Women Peace Officers." *Journal of Police Science and Administration* 14: 83-97.

Lorde, A. 1984. *Sister Outsider*. Freedom, Ca.: The Crossing Press Freedom Series.

Loseke, D. 1987. "Lived Realities and the Construction of Social Problems: The Case of Wife Abuse." *Symbolic Interaction* 10 (2): 229-243.

Lovdal, L.T. 1989. "Sex Role Messages in Television Commercials: An Update." *Sex Roles* 21: 715-724.

Lowenberger, L., Wilke, C. and E. Abner. 1985. "Welfare: Women, Poverty and the Charter." *Journal of Law and Social Policy* 1 (Fall).

Luces, S. 1985. *Marxism and Morality*. Oxford: Clarendon.

Luciuk, L. 1994. *Righting An Injustice: The Debate over Redress for Canada's First National Internment Operations*. Toronto: Justinian Press.

Luksic, I. 1989. "The First Uses of the Concept of Hegemony in Gramsci." *Athropos* 20 (3-4): 348-354.

Lukes, S. 1975. *Emile Durkheim: His Life and Work*. Harmondsworth: Penguin.

Luxton, M. 1981. *More Than a Labour Law*. Toronto: Women's Press.

Lynch, M. 1989. *A Primer in Radical Criminology*. New York: Harrow and Heston Publishers.

Lyman, M. and M. Scott. 1970. *The Sociology of the Absurd*. New York: Appleton-Century-Crofts.

Lyman, M. and M. Scott. 1967. "Territoriality: A Neglected Sociological Dimension." *Social Problems* 15: 236-249.

Lyman, S. and M. Scott. 1970. *Revolt of the Students*. Columbus: Charles E. Merrill.

Lyman, S. 1984. "Interactionism and the Study of Race Relations at the Microsociological Level: The Contribution of Herbert Blumer." *Symbolic Interaction* 7: 107-120.

Lyons, O. 1990. "Spirituality, Equality and Natural Law." National Indian Government Conference. Osgoode Law School, York University: (October 3-5).

Lyotard, J.F. 1984. *The Post-modern Condition*. Translated by G. Bennington and B. Massumi. Minneapolis: University of Minnesota.

Lystad, M. 1986 *Violence in the Home: Interdisciplinary Perspectives*. New York: Brunner and Mazel.

M

MacGuigan, M. 1977. *Report: The Penitentiary System In Canada*. Ottawa: Supplies and Services.

Mackie, M. 1987. *Constructing Women and Men*. Toronto: Holt, Rinehart and Winston.

MacKinnon, C. 1979. *Sexual Harassment of Working Women*. New Haven: Yale University Press.

MacKinnon, C. 1982. "Feminism, Marxism, Method and the State: An Agenda for Theory." *Signs: Journal of Women in Culture and Society* 7 (3): 515-544.

MacKinnon, C. 1983. "Feminism, Marxism, Method and the State: Toward Feminist Jurisprudence." *Signs* (7): 635.

MacKinnon, C. 1987. *Feminism Unmodified*. Cambridge: Harvard University Press.

MacKinnon, C. 1989. *Toward a Feminist Theory of the State*. Cambridge: Harvard University Press.

MacLean, B. 1986. "Alienation, Reification and Beyond: The Political Economy of Crime." In B. MacLean, *Political Economy of Crime*. Scarborough: Prentice-Hall.

MacLean, B. 1989. "Editor's Introduction: Critical Justice Studies in Canada." *Journal of Human Justice* 1 (1).

MacLean, B. and D. Milovanovic. 1990. *Racism, Empiricism and Criminal Justice*. Vancouver: The Collective Press.

Maclean, B. and R. Ratner 1987. "An Historical Analysis of Bills C-67 and C-68: Implications for the Native Offender." *Native Studies Review* 3: 31-58.

Macleod, L. 1980. *Wife Battering in Canada: The Vicious Circle*. Ottawa: Supply and Services.

Macleod, L. 1987. *Battered But Not Beaten: Preventing Wife Battering in Canada*. Canadian Advisory Council on the Status of Women.

Macpherson, C.B. 1964. *The Political Theory of Possessive Individualism: Hobbes to Locke*. London: Oxford University Press.

Magee, J. 1993. "Managing with a Pathological Institution: Judicial Review in American Democracy." Annual Meeting of the American Political Science Association, September 2-5.

Maghan, J. 1992. "Black Police Officer, Recruits: Aspects of Becoming Blue." *Police Forum* (January): B 11.

Maguire, P. 1987. *Doing Participatory Research: A Feminist Approach*. Amherst, Massachusetts: The Center for International Education, University of Mass.

Mahoney, K. 1985. *Women, the Law and the Economy*. Toronto: Butterworth.

Mainardi, P. 1971. "The Politics of Housework." In R. Morgan (ed.), *Sisterhood is Powerful*. New York: Vintage.

Mair, G. 1986. "Ethnic Minorities, Probation and the Magistrate's Courts." *British Journal of Criminology* 26: 147-155.

Makihara, K. 1994. "Lawmakers, Beware." *Time* (March 21): 48.

Malatesta, E. 1907 (1949). *Anarchy*. London: Freedom Press.

Malcolm, X. 1970. *By Any Means Necessary*. Edited By G. Breitman. New York: Pathfinders.

Maloney, Arthur. 1975. *Report to the Metropolitan Toronto Board of Commissioners of Police*. Toronto: The Metropolitan Toronto Review of Citizen-Police Complaint Procedure.

Manitoba Indian Brotherhood. 1975. *The Shocking Truth About Indians in Text Books*. Winnipeg: Manitoba Indian Brotherhood.

Mankoff, M. 1970. "Power in Advanced Capitalist Society: A Review Essay on Recent Elitist and Marxist Criticisms of Pluralist Theory." *Social Problems* 17: 418-430.

Mankoff, M. 1972. *The Poverty of Progress*. New York: Holt, Rinehart and Winston.

Mankoff, M. 1978. "On the Responsibility of Marxist Criminologies: A Reply to Quinney." *Contemporary Crises* 2: 293-301.

Mann, C. 1984. *Female Crime and Delinquency*. Birmingham: University of Alabama.

Mann, C. R. 1993. *Unequal Justice: A Question of Colour*. Bloomington: Indiana University Press.

Mann, E. and J. Lee. 1979. *The RCMP vs. the People.* Don Mills: General.

Manning, P. 1972. "Observing the Police: Deviants, Respectables and the Law." In J. Douglas (ed.), *Research on Deviance.* New York: Random House.

Manning, P. 1991. "Strands in the Postmodern Rope: Ethnographic Themes." *Studies in Symbolic Interactionism* 12.

Marano, Estroff H. 1993. "Inside the Heart of Marital Violence." *Psychology Today* November/December 1993.

Marcuse, H. 1964. *One Dimensional Man.* Boston: Beacon.

Marcuse, H. 1968. *Negations: Essays in Critical Theory.* Boston: Beacon.

Maroney, H. and M. Luxton (eds.). 1987. *Feminism and Political Economy: Women's Work, Women's Struggles.* Toronto: Methuen.

Marshall, K. 1990. "Women in Professional Occupations: Progress in the 1980's." In C. McKiet and K. Thompson, *Canadian Social Trends.* Toronto: Thompson Educational Publishing.

Martin, D. 1981. *Battered Wives-Revisited, Updated*: Volcano, California: Volcano Press.

Martin, D. 1986. *Battered Wives.* San Francisco: Glide.

Martin, K. 1947. *The Press the Public Wants.* London: Hogarth.

Martin, R. 1984. "The Judges and the Charter." *Socialist Studies* (2).

Martin, S. 1980. *Breaking and Entering: Policewomen on Patrol.* Berkeley: University of California.

Martin, S. 1986. "Canada's Abortion Law and the Charter of Rights and Freedoms." *Canadian Journal of Women and the Law* (1): 339-384.

Martin, W. 1981. "Toward Specifying a Spectrum-Based Theory of Enterprise." *Criminal Justice Review* 6 (Spring): 54-57.

Marx, G. 1981. "Ironies of Social Control: Authorities as Contributors to Deviance Through Escalation, Non-Enforcement and Covert Facilitation." *Social Problems* 28 (February): 221-246.

Marx, K. 1930. *The Poverty of Philosophy.* New York: International.

Marx, K. 1956. *Selected Writings in Sociology and Social Philosophy.* Edited by T. Bottomore. London: Watts and Company.

Marx, K. [1848] 1965. *The Communist Manifesto.* Chicago: Gateway.

Marx, K. 1965. *Capital Volume 1: A Critical Analysis of Capitalist Production.* Moscow: Progress Publishing.

Marx, K. 1965. *Selected Correspondence.* Moscow: Progress Publishing.

Marx, K. 1969a. *Capital: Volumes I, II, III: A Critique of Political Economy.* Moscow: Progress Publishers.

Marx, K. 1969b. "The Eighteenth Brumaire of Louis Bonaparte." In K. Marx and F. Engels, *Selected Works*, Vol. I. Moscow: Progress Publishing.

Marx, K. 1969c. *The Productivity of Crime: Theories of Surplus Value*, Vol. I. Moscow: Foreign Languages Publishing.

Marx, K. [1848] 1958, 1969. *Selected Works*, Vol. I, ll. Moscow: Progress Publishing.

Marx, K. 1973. *Grundrisse: Foundations of the Critique of Political Economy.* London: Allen.

Marx, K. 1973. *Selected Writings in Sociology and Social Philosophy.* New York: Penguin.

Marx, K. 1976. *The Poverty of Philosophy.* Toronto: Norman Bethune Institute.

Marx, K. 1977. *The Economic and Philosophic Manuscripts of 1844.* Moscow: Progress Publishers.

Marx, K. 1978. *The Marx-Engels Reader.* Edited by R. Tucker. New York: W.W. Morton.

Marx, K. 1984. *Collected Works: Vol. 10, 11 and 19.* New York: International Publishers.

Marx, K. and F. Engels. [1947] 1960, 1973. *The German Ideology, Parts 1, 111.* New York: International.

Marx, K. and F. Engels. 1962. *Selected Works.* Moscow: Foreign Language Press.

Marx, K. and F. Engels. 1972. *Karl Marx and Frederick Engels On Colonialism.* New York: International.

Masotti, L.H. and D.R. Bowen. 1968. *Riots and Rebellion: Civil Violence in the Urban Community.* Beverley Hills: Sage.

Massey, D.S, and N.A. Denton. 1993. *American Apartheid: Segregation and the Making of the Underclass.* Cambridge: Harvard University Press.

Mathes, D. 1988. "Justice System Hurt Women By Issuing Weak Sentence." *Toronto Star* (September 26): A 21.

Matza, D. 1964. *Delinquency and Drift.* New York: J. Wiley.

Matza, D. 1969. *Becoming Deviant.* Englewood Cliffs: Prentice-Hall.

Matza, D. and G. Sykes. 1961. "Juvenile Delinquency and Subterranean Values." *American Sociological Review* 26 (October): 712-719.

Matza, D. and G. Sykes. 1970. "Techniques of Delinquency." In M. Wolfgang, M. Savitz and N. Johnston (eds.), *Sociology of Crime and Delinquency.* New York: J. Wiley.

McBarnet, D. 1992. "Legitimate Rackets: Tax Evasion, Tax Avoidance, and the Boundaries of Legality." *Journal of Human Justice* 3 (Spring) 2: 56-74.

McCall, G. and J. Simmons. 1969. "The Nature of Participant Observation." In G. McCall and J. Simmons (eds.), *Issues in Participant.* Reading: Addison-Wesley.

McCannel, C. 1986. *A Guide to Canada's Immigration Law.* Regina: Public Legal Education of Saskatchewan.

McClintock, F. and N. Avison. 1968. *Crime in England and Wales.* London: Heinman.

McCormick, K. and L. Visano. 1992. "Community (in)action and Corrections." In K. McCormick and L. Visano (eds.), *Canadian Penology.* Toronto: Canadian Scholars' Press.

McCormick, K. and L. Visano (eds.). 1992. *Understanding Policing.* Toronto: Canadian Scholars' Press.

McCormick, P. 1994. *Canada's Courts.* Toronto: James Lorimer & Co.

McDonald, L. l984. "The Supreme Court of Canada and the Equality Guarantee in the Charter," *Socialist Studies.*

McGowan, J. 1982. "How To Recruit More Black Police Officers: One Obvious Answer to Race Riots." *Police Journal* 55 (1): 39-41.

McIntosh, M. 1974. *Perspectives on Marginality.* Boston: Allyn and Bacon.

McIntosh, M. 1978. "The State and the Oppression of Women." In A. Kuhn and A. Wolpe (eds.), *Feminism and Materialism: Women and Modes of Production.* London: Routledge and Kegan Paul.

McLaren, P. l989. *Life in Schools.* Toronto: Irwin.

McMahon, M. 1992. *The Persistent Prison?* Toronto: U of T. Press.

McMahon, S. 1998. *Crime, Culture and Women.* Toronto: Centre for Police Studies at York University.

McMullan, J. 1987. "Epilogue: Law, Justice and the State." In R. Ratner and J. McMullan (eds.), *State Control*. Vancouver: University of British Columbia.

McMullan, J. 1992. *Beyond the Limits of the Law: Corporate Crime and Law and Order*. Halifax: Fernwood.

McMullan, J and R. Ratner. 1983. "State, Labour, Justice in British Columbia." In T. Fleming and L. Visano (eds.), *Deviant Designations*. Toronto: Butterworth.

McNulty, F. 1981. *The Burning Bed: A True Story of An Abused Wife*. New York: Bantam.

McPhail, T. 1981. *Electronic Colonialism*. Beverly Hills: Sage Library of Social Research.

McQuaig, L. 1991 *The Quick and the Dead, Brian Mulroney, Big Business and the Seduction of Canada*. Toronto: Viking.

McQuaig, L. 1993. *The Wealthy Banker's Wife: The Assault on Equality in Canada*. Toronto: Penguin.

McSheehy, W. 1979. *Skid Row*. Cambridge: Schenkman.

Mead, G. 1934. *Mind, Self and Society*. Chicago: University of Chicago Press.

Meadows, P. and E. Mizruchi (eds.). 1976. *Urbanism, Urbanization and Change: Comparative Perspectives Reading*. Mass: Addison-Wesley.

Melbin, M. 1978. "Night as a Frontier." *American Sociological Review* 43 (February): 1.

Mellor, J.R. 1977. *Urban Sociology in an Urbanized Society*. London: Routledge and Kegan Paul.

Melossi, D. 1985. "Overcoming the Crisis in Critical Criminology: Toward A Grounded Labelling Theory." *Criminology* 23: 193-208.

Memmi, Albert. 1965 *The Colonizer and the Colonized*. New York: Orion.

Menard, S. and D. Elliott. 1994. "Delinquent Bonding, Moral Beliefs, and Illegal Behaviour: A Three-Wave Panel Model." *Justice Quartely* 11 (June) 2: 173-188.

Menchu, R. 1989. *I Rigoberta Menchu: An Indian Woman in Guatemala*. New York: Verso.

Menzies, H. 1981. *Women and the Chip: Case Studies of the Effects of Information on Employment in Canada*. Montreal: Institute for Research on Public Policy.

Menzies, R. and D. Chunn. 1991. "Kicking Against the Pricks: The Dilemma of Feminist Teaching in Criminology." In B. MacLean and D. Milovanovic (eds.), *New Directions in Critical Criminology*. Vancouver: Collective Press.

Merger, M. 1985. *Race Awareness*. Toronto: Oxford University Press.

Merrignton, J. 1968. "Theory and Practice in Gramsci's Marxism." *Sociologist Register*. 145-176.

Merton, R.K. 1938. "Social Structure and Anomie." *American Sociological Review* 3 (October): 672-682.

Merton, R.K. 1957. *Social Theory and Social Structure*. New York: Free Press.

Merti, S and J. Ward. 1985. *Keegstra*. Saskatoon: Western Producer Prairie Books.

Messner, S. 1980. "Income Inequality and Murder Rates." *Social Research* 3: 185-198.

Metrac. 1987. *Meeting the Challenge*. Metro Action Committee on Public Violence Against Women and Children.

Meyrowitz, J. 1992. "Television: The Shared Arena." In H. Holmes and D. Taras (eds.), *Seeing Ourselves, Media Power and Policy in Canada*. Toronto: Harcourt, Brace, Jovanovich.

Michalowski, R. 1985. *Order, Law and Crime*. New York: Random House.

Michelson, W. 1976. *Man and His Environment: A Sociological Approved Reading.* Mass.: Addison-Wesley.

Mies, M. 1986. *Patriarchy and Accumulation on a World Scale.* London: Zed Books.

Miles, R. 1982. *Racism and Migrant Labour.* London: Routledge and Kegan Paul.

Miles, R. 1989. *Racism.* London: Routledge and Kegan Paul.

Milgram, S. 1970. "The Experience of Living in Cities." *Science* 167: 1461-1468.

Milgram, S. 1971. *Obedience to Authority.* New York: Harper and Row.

Miliband, R. 1969. *The State in Capitalist Society.* London: Quartet.

Miliband, R. 1977. *Marxism and Politics.* New York: Oxford Press.

Miller, D. and W. Form. 1951. *Industrial Sociology.* New York: Harper and Row.

Miller, G. 1983. "Holding Clients Responsible: The Micro-Politics of Trouble in a Work Incentive Program." *Social Problems* 31: 139-151.

Miller, S. and P. Roby. 1970. *The Future of Equality.* New York: Basic.

Miller, W. 1958. "Lower Class Culture as a Generating Milier of Gang Delinquency." *Journal of Social Issues* 14: 5-19.

Mills, C.W. 1940. "Situated Actions and Vocabulary of Motives." *American Sociological Review* (December): 904-913.

Mills, C.W. 1943. "The Professional Ideology of Social Pathologists." *American Journal of Sociology* 49: 165-180.

Mills, C.W. 1951. *White Collar.* New York: Oxford University Press.

Mills, C.W. 1956.*The Power Elite.* New York: Oxford University Press.

Mills, C.W. [1959] 1978. *The Sociological Imagination.* New York: Oxford University Press.

Mills, C.W. 1967. "The Cultural Apparatus." In I.L. Horowitz (ed.), *Power, Politics and People: The Collected Essays of C.W. Mills.* New York: Oxford University Press.

Milovanovic, D. 1990. "Radical Criminology: A Descriptive Topology." *Critical Criminologist* 2 (Autumn) 3.

Milovanovic, D. 1992. *Postmodern Law and Disorder: Psychoanalytic Semiotics and Juridic Exegesis.* Liverpool: Deborah Charles.

Minch, C., R. Linden and S. Johnson. 1987. "Attrition in the Processing of Rape Cases." *Canadian Journal of Criminology* 29 (October) 4: 389-404.

Minor, W. 1984. "Neutralization as a Hardening Process: Considerations in Re-Modelling of Change." *Social Forces* 62: 995-1019.

Mints, R. 1973. "Interview with Ian Taylor, Paul Walton and Jack Young." *Issues in Criminology* 9 (Spring) 1.

Mitchell, A. and G. Abbate. 1994. "Crime-Race Data Laden With Hazards." *Toronto Star* (June 11) A1, A6, A7.

Mitchell, A. and J. Patterson. 1990. "A Look at Poverty Lines." *Social Infopac.* Toronto: Social Planning Council of Metropolitan Toronto.

Mitchell, J. 1971. *Women's Estate.* New York: Random House.

Mitchell, J. 1989."Women's Estate." In R. Gottlieb (ed.), *An Anthology of Western Thought.* New York: Oxford University Press.

Mitchell, J.C. (ed.). 1969. *Social Networks in Urban Situations.* Manchester: University of Manchester Press.

Mitchell, R. 1984. "Alienation and Deviance Theory Reconsidered." *Sociological Inquiry* 54 (Summer): 330-345.

Mitchell, T. 1988. *Colonising Egypt.* Cambridge: University of Cambridge Press.

Mizruchi, E. 1938. "Alienation and Anomie: Theoretical and Empirical Perspectives." In I. Horowitz (ed.), *The New Sociology: Essays in Honour of C.W. Mills*. New York: Oxford University Press.

Mohr, J.H. 1973. "Facts, Figures, Perceptions and Myths-Ways of Describing and Understanding Crime." *Canadian Journal of Corrections and Criminology* 15: 39-49.

Mohr, R. 1990. "Sentencing as a Gendered Process: Results of a Consultation." *Canadian Journal of Criminology* (July): 479-485.

Mokhibar, R. 1988. *Corporate Crime and Violence: Big Business and the Abuse of the Public Trust*. San Francisco: Sierra Books.

Molnar, A. 1989. "Racism in America: A Continuing Dilemma." *Educational Leadership* (October): 71-72.

Moog, C. 1990. *Are They Selling' Her Lips: Advertising and Identity*. New York: William Morrow.

Moore, M. and R. Trojanowicz. 1988. "Policing and the Fear of Crime." *Perspectives on Policing* 3 (June).

Moore, T. and L. Cadeau. 1985. "The Representation of Women, the Elderly and Minorities in Canadian Television Commercials." *Canadian Journal of Behavioural Science* 17: 215-225.

Moorhouse, C. and B. Chan. 1986. *The Shaping of Ethnic Identities Among Chinese in Canada*. Draft Paper prepared for Qualitative Research Conference, University of Waterloo.

Morgen, S. and A. Bookman. 1988. "Rethinking Women and Politics: An Introductory Essay." In A. Bookman and S. Morgen (eds.), *Women and the Politics of Empowerment*. Philadelphia: Temple University Press.

Morgentaler, H. 1988. "Morgentaler vs. The Queen." 19556 *S.C.C. 1988* (June 28).

Morris, A. 1987. *Women, Crime and Criminal Justice*. Oxford: Basil Blackwell.

Morris, R. 1968. *Urban Sociology*. London: George Allen and Unwin.

Morris, R. and C. M. Lanphier 1977. *Three Scales of Inequality*. Don Mills: Academic.

Morris, T. 1958. *The Criminal Area*. London: Routledge and Kegan Paul.

Morris, T. 1976. *Deviance and Control: The Secular Heresy*. London: Hutchinson.

Morrison, K. 1987 "Stabilizing the Text: The Institutionalization of Knowledge in Historical and Philosophic Forms of Argument." *Canadian Journal of Sociology* 12 (3): 242-274.

Morrison, T. 1992. *Race-ing Justice, En-gendering Power*. New York: Pantheon.

Mosca, G. 1933. "Mafia." In *Encyclopedia of Social Sciences IV*. London: Macmillan.

Mouffe, C. 1988. "Hegemony and New Political Subjects: Toward a New Concept of Democracy." In C. Nelson and L. Grossberg (eds.), *Marxism and the Interpretation of Culture*. Urbana: University of Illinois.

Mourbese P. 1994. "Immigrant: A Label that Sticks for Life." *Toronto Star* (June 27) A17.

Moyer, I. 1992. *The Changing Roles of Women in the Criminal Justice System*. Prospect Heights, Ill.: Waveland Press.

Multiculturalism and Canadians: Attitude Study. 1991. National Survey Multiculturalism and Citizenship Canada Agnus Reid Group, August 1991.

Mulvey, L. 1988. *Visual and Other Pleasures*. Bloomington: Indiana University Press.

Muraskin, R. and T. Alleman 1993. *It's a Crime: Women and Justice.* Englewood Cliffs, NJ: Prentice Hall.

Murdock, G. 1973. "Culture and Classlessness-The Making and Unmaking of a Contemporary Myth." Symposium on Work and Leisure University of Salford.

Murray, N. 1992. "Columbus and the U.S.A.: From Mythology to Ideology." *Race and Class* 33 (January-March) 3: 49-65.

Murray, S. 1984. *Social Theory, Homosexual Realities.* New York: Gai Saber.

N

Nagel, I. and J. Hagan. 1983. "Genders and Crime: Offense Patterns and Criminal Court Sanctions." In M. Tonry and N. Morris (eds.), *Crime and Justice: An Annual Review of Research.* Vol. 4 Chicago: University of Chicago Press.

NAACP. 1993. "Beyond King: An NAACP Report on Police Conduct and Community Relations." *Report.* Baltimore: NAACP (April).

NRA. 1993. *The National Rifle Firearms Fact Card 1993.* Institute for Legislative Action, Washington.

National Institute of Justice. 1985. *Crime and Protection of America: A Study of Private Security and Law Enforcement Resources and Relationships.* Washington, D.C.: U.S. Department of Justice.

National Women's Political Caucus. 1993. Fact Sheet on Women's Political Progress. (June 7), Washington, D.C.

Needleman, M. and C. Needleman. 1979. "Organizational Crime: Two Models of Criminogenesis." *Sociological Quarterly* 20 (Autumn) 4: 517-528.

Nelkin, D. and M. Brown. 1984. *Workers at Risk: Voices from the Workplace.* Chicago: University of Chicago.

Nelli, H. 1981. *The Business of Crime.* Chicago: University of Chicago.

Nettler, G. 1974. *Explaining Crime.* New York: McGraw-Hill.

Neugebauer, R. 1992. "Misogyny, Law and the Police: Policing Violence Against Women." In K. McCormick and L. Visano (eds.), *Understanding Policing.* Toronto: Canadian Scholars' Press.

Newman, O. 1973. *Defensible Space-Crime Prevention Through Environmental Design.* New York: Macmillan.

Newman, P. 1991. *Merchant Princes.* Toronto: Penguin.

Newson, J. 1993. "Talking Back: The Politics of Language." *OCUFA Forum Special Supplement.* (December): 2.

Newsweek. 1992. "Women in Jail: Unequal Justice." In J.Sullivan and J. L. Victor, *Criminal Justice.* Gulford, Conn.: Dushkin.

Nielsen, J. 1990. *Sex and Gender in Society, Perspectives on Stratification.* Illinois: Waveland.

Nietzsche, F. 1977. *A Nietzsche Reader.* Translated by R. Hollingdale. New York: Penguin.

Nietzsche, F. 1990. *Beyond Good and Evil.* Translated by R. Hollingdale. New York: Penguin.

Nietzsche, F. 1991. *Ecce Homo.* Translated by R. Hollingdale. New York: Penguin.

Nisbet, R. 1974. *The Sociology of E. Durkheim.* New York: Oxford University Press.

Noel, P. 1992. "When The Word Is Given." In Hazen, D. (ed.), *Inside the L.A. Riots.* Los Angeles: Institute for Alternative Journalism.

North, C.C. 1926. "The City as a Community: An Introduction to a Research Project." In E. Burgess (ed.), *Urban Community.* Chicago: University of Chicago.

Nteta, C. 1987. "Revolutionary Self Consciousness as an Objective Force within the Process of Liberation: Biko and Gramsci." *Radical America* 21 (Sept.-Oct.) 5: 55-61.

Nye, F.I. 1958. *Family Relationships and Delinquent Behaviour.* New York: John Wiley.

O

Oakes, J. 1985. *Keeping Track.* New Haven: Yale University Press.

Oakley, A. 1981. *Subject Women.* New York: Pantheon.

Oakley, A. 1981. "Interviewing Women: An Contradiction in Terms." In H. Roberts (ed.), *Doing Feminist Research.* London: Routledge and Kegan Paul.

O'Bireck, G. 1996. *Not A Kid Anymore.* Toronto: Nelson.

O'Brien, M. 1981. *The Politics of Reproduction.* London: Routledge and Kegan Paul.

O'Connor, J. 1973. *The Fiscal Crisis of the State.* New York: St. Martin's.

Okihiro, N. and I. Waller. 1974. *Ecological Analysis of Crime.* Centre of Criminology, University of Toronto.

Ollman, B. 1976. *Alienation.* Cambridge: Cambridge University Press.

Olson, E.L. 1988. *No Place To Hide.* New York: Esther and Co.

Olson, J. and R. Wilson. 1984. *Native Americans in the Twentieth Century.* Provo, Utah: Brigham Young.

Omi, M. and H. Winant. 1989. *Racial Formation in the United States.* New York: Routledge.

O'Neill, J. 1972. *Sociology as a Skin Trade.* London: Heinemann.

O'Neill, J. 1985. *Five Bodies.* Ithaca: Cornell University Press.

O'Reilly, K. 1989. *"Racial Matters": The FBI's Secret File on Black America, 1960-1972.* New York: Free Press.

O'Reilly-Fleming, T. 1993. *Down and Out in Canada.* Toronto: Canadian Scholars' Press.

O'Sullivan, C. 1990. *Television.* San Diego: Greenhaven Press.

P

Page, C. 1988. *The Right of Lifers.* New York: Connie Page.

Pahl, R.E. 1970. *Patterns of Urban Life.* London: Longmans.

Pahl, R.E. 1970b. *Whose City? And Other Essays on Sociology and Planning.* London: Longmans.

Panitch, L. (ed.). 1977. "The Role and Nature of the Canadian State." In *The Canadian State: Political Economy and Political Power.* Toronto: University of Toronto Press.

Parisi, N. 1982. "Are Females Treated Differently? A Review of the Theories and Evidence on Sentencing and Parole Decisions." In N. Hahn Rafter and E. Stanko (eds.), *Judge, Lawyer, Victim, Thief: Women, Gender Roles and Criminal Justice.* Boston: Northeastern University Press.

Park, R. (ed.). 1952. *Human Communities.* New York: Free Press.

Park, R. and E. Burgess (eds.). 1925. *The City*. Chicago: University of Chicago Press.

Park, R.E. [1925], 1967. "The Urban Community as a Spatial Pattern and a Moral Order." In R.H. Turner (ed.), *Robert E. Park on Social Control and Collective Behavior*. Chicago: University of Chicago Press.

Park, R.E. 1936. "Human Ecology." *American Journal of Sociology* 42 (July): 1-15.

Parker, D.B. 1976. *Crime by Computer*. New York: Charles Scribner and Sons.

Parker, D.B. 1983 *Fighting Computer Crime*. New York.

Parker, R. 1994. "The Myth of Global News." *New Perspectives Quarterly* 2 (Winter)1.

Parsons, T. 1952. *The Social System*. New York: Free Press.

Parsons, T. 1952b. "The Superego and the Theory of Social Systems." *Psychiatry* 15 (1).

Parsons, T. 1954. "Sociology and Psychology." In J. Gillin (ed.), *For a Science of Social Man*. New York: Macmillan.

Parsons, T. 1958. "Social Structure and the Development of Personality: Freud's Contribution to the Integration of Psychology and Sociology." *Psychiatry* 21 (4).

Parsons, T. 1964. *Social Structure and Personality*. London: Collier Macmillan.

Parsons, T. 1966. *Societies: Evolutionary and Comparative Perspectives*. Englewood Cliffs: Prentice-Hall.

Parsons, T. [1937] 1968. *The Structure of Social Action*. New York: Free Press.

Parsons, T. 1977. *Social Systems and the Evolution of Action Theory*. New York: Free Press.

Parsons, T. 1978. "Comment on R. Stephen Warner's Toward a Redefinition of Action Theory: Paying the Cognitive Element its Due." *American Journal of Sociology* 83 (May) 6: 1350-1358.

Parsons, T., Shils, E., Naegale, K. and J.P. Pitts. 1965. *Theories of Society*. New York: Free Press.

Pashukanis, R. 1978. *Law and Marxism*. London: Ink Links.

Pasquino, P. 1978. "Theatrum Politicum: The Genealogy of Capital." *Police and the State of Prosperity Ideology and Consciousness* 4 (Autumn): 41-54.

Paternoster, R. 1984. "Prosecutorial Discretion in Requesting the Death Penalty: A Case of Victim-Based Racial Discrimination." *Law and Society Review* 18: 437-478.

Pearce, F. [1976] 1978. *Crimes of the Powerful*. London: Pluto.

Pearson, G. 1979. *The Deviant Imagination*. London: Macmillan.

Perlman, R. 1975. *Consumers and Social Services*. New York: J. Wiley and Sons.

Petersilia, J. 1980. "Criminal Career Research: A Review of Recent Evidence." In N. Morris and M. Tonry (eds.), *An Annual Review of Research*. Chicago: University of Chicago Press.

Pfohl, S. [1985] 1994. *Images of Deviance and Social Control: A Sociological History*. Boston: McGraw-Hill.

Philips, L. and H. Votey. 1987. "Rational Choice Models of Crimes by Youth." *The Review of Black Political Economy* 16 (1-2): 129-187.

Phillips, C. and S. Dinitz 1982. "Labelling and Juvenile Court Dispositions: Official Responses to a Cohort of Violent Juveniles." *The Sociological Quarterly* 23 (Spring): 267-278.

Phillipson, M. 1972. "Theory, Methodology and Conceptualization. In M. Phillipson et al. (eds.), *New Directions in Sociological Theory*. London: Macmillan.

Pickvance, R. (ed.). 1976. *Urban Sociology: Critical Essays*. London: Tavistock.

Pitch, T. 1985. "Critical Criminology, The Construction of Social Problems and the Question of Rape." *International Journal of the Sociology of Law* 13: 35-46.

Piven, F. 1981. "Deviant Behaviour and the Remaking of the World." *Social Problems* (June 28).

Piven, F. and R. Cloward 1971. *Regulating the Poor*. New York: Random House.

Platt, A. 1974. "Prospects for Radical Criminology in U.S.A." In I. Taylor et al. (eds.), *Critical Criminology*. London: Routledge and Kegan Paul; also in 1974, *Crime and Social Justice* 1: pp. 2-10.

Platt, A. 1977. *Child Savers: The Invention of Delinquency*. Chicago: University of Chicago Press.

Pleck, E. 1987. *Domestic Tyranny*. Toronto: Oxford University Press.

Plummer, K. 1983. *Documents of Life: An Introduction to the Problems of a Humanistic Method*. London: George Allen and Unwin.

Polan, D. 1982. "Toward a Theory of Law and Patriarchy." In D. Kairys (ed.), *The Politics of Law*. New York: Pantheon.

Polk, K. 1967. "Urban Social Areas and Delinquency." *Social Problems* 14: 320-325.

Polk, K. 1969. "On the Ecology of Delinquency." *Social Problems* 16 (Spring): 529-532.

Pollack, O. 1961. *The Criminality of Women*. New York: A.S. Barnes.

Pollack, O. 1979. "The Masked Character of Female Crime." In F. Adler and R. Simon (eds.), *The Criminology of Deviant Women*. Boston: Houghton-Mifflin.

Polsky, N. 1969. *Hustlers, Beats and Others*. Garden City: Anchor.

Ponting, J.R. and R. Gibbins. 1980. *Out of Irrelevance*. Toronto: Butterworth.

Pontusson, J. 1980. "Gramsci and Euro-communism: A Comparative Analyses of Class Rule and Socialist Transition." *Berkeley Journal of Sociology* 24-25: 185-248.

Pope, C. and W. Feyerherm. 1990. "Minorities and the Juvenile Justice System." Draft Report for the Office of Juvenile Justice and Delinquency. US Department of Justice.

Porter, J. 1965. *The Vertical Mosaic*. Toronto: University of Toronto Press.

Posner, J. 1990. "The Objectified Male: The New Male Image in Advertising." In G. Hofmann and Nemiroff (ed.), *Women and Men*. Montreal: Fitzhenry and Whiteside.

Poulantzas, N. 1973. *Political Power and Social Classes*. London: Verso.

Poulantzas, N. 1974. *Classes in Contemporary Capitalism*. London: New Left Review.

Poulantzas, N. 1978. *Classes in Contemporary Capitalism*. London: Verso.

Pozzolini, A. 1968. *Antonio Gramsci: An Introduction to His Thoughts*. London: Pluto.

Price, J.A. 1973. "The Stereotyping of North American Indians in Motion Pictures." *Ethnohistory* 5: 153-171.

Price, J.A. 1978. *Native Studies*. Toronto: McGraw-Hill.

Priest, L. 1989. *Conspiracy of Silence*. Toronto: McClelland & Stewart.

Prieur, D. and M. Rowles. 1992. "Putting a Stop to Violence and Inequality: A Union Woman's Guide." *Our Times* (June): 17-18.

Procacci, G. 1978. "Social Economy and the Government of Poverty." *Ideology and Consciousness* 4 (Autumn).

Prus, R. and S. Irini. 1980. *Hookers, Rounders and Desk Clerks*. Toronto: Gage.

Purich, D. 1986. *Peace River Past: A Canadian Adventure*. Toronto: Venture Press.

Pupo, N. 1988. "Preserving Patriarchy: Women, the Family and the State." In N. Mandell and A. Duffy (eds.), *Reconstructing The Canadian Family: Feminist Perspectives*. Toronto: Butterworth.

Q

Quinney, R. 1970. *The Social Reality of Crime*. Boston: Brown Little and Co.

Quinney, R. 1972. "The Ideology of Law: Notes for a Radical Alternative to Legal Oppression." *Issues in Criminology* 7 (Winter): 1.

Quinney, R. 1974. *Critique of Legal Order: Crime Control in Capitalist Society*. Boston: Little, Brown.

Quinney, R. 1975. *Criminology*. Boston: Little, Brown.

Quinney, R. 1977. *Class, State and Crime*. New York: Longman.

R

Radelet, M. 1994. "Executions of Whites for Crimes Against Blacks: Exceptions to the Rule?" In D. Baker (ed.), *Reading Racism and the Criminal Justice System*. Toronto: Canadian Scholars' Press.

Radelet, M. and G. Pierce. 1985. "Race and Prosecutorial Discretion in Homicide Cases: *Law and Society Review* 19: 918-927.

Rafky, D.M. 1978. "Racial Discrimination in Urban Police Departments." *Crime and Delinquency* (July): 233-242.

Rafter, N. 1985. *Partial Justice: Women in State Prisons 1800-1935*. Boston: Northeastern Press.

Raines, P. 1975. "Imputations of Deviance: A Retrospective Essay on the Labelling Perspective." *Social Problems* 23: 1-12.

Rank, M. and C. Lecroy. 1983. "Toward a Multiple Perspective in Family Theory and Practice: The Case of Social Exchange Theory, Symbolic Interactionism and Conflict Theory." *Journal of Applied Family and Child Studies* 32 (3): 441-448.

Ratner, R. 1985. "Inside the Liberal Boot: The Criminological Enterprise in Canada." In T. Fleming (ed.), *The New Criminologies in Canada*. Toronto: Oxford University Press.

Ratner, R. and J. McMullan (eds.). 1987. *State Control*. Vancouver: University of British Columbia.

Reasons, C. 1974. "The Politics of Drugs: An Inquiry in the Sociology of Social Problems." *Sociological Quarterly* 15, 381.

Reasons, C. 1975. "Social Thought and Social Structure: Competing Paradigms in Criminology." *Criminology* (November): 332-365.

Reasons, C. 1985. "Ideology, Law, Public Opinion and Workers' Health." In D. Gibson and J. Baldwin (eds.), *Law in a Clinical Society? Opinion and the Law in the 1990's*. Vancouver: Carswell Legal Publ.

Reasons, C. 1986. "Occupational Health and Safety in Two Jurisdictions: Canada and Australia." In R. Tomacs and K. Lucas (eds.), *Power, Regulation and Resistance: Studies in the Sociology of Law*. Canberra: School of Administrative Studies.

Reasons, C. and C. Goff. 1980. "Corporate Crime: A Cross-National Analysis." In G.Geis and E. Stotland (eds.), *White Collar Crime: Theory and Research*. Beverley Hills: Sage.

Reasons, C., Ross, L. and C. Paterson. 1981. *Assault on the Worker: Occupational Health and Safety in Canada.* Toronto: Butterworth.

Reckless, W. 1967. *The Crime Problem.* New York: Appleton Century-Crafts.

Reckless, W., Dinitz, S. and B. Kay. 1957. "The Self-Component in Political Delinquency and Potential Non-Delinquency." *American Sociological Review* 22: 566-570.

Reckless, W., Dinitz, S. and E. Murray. 1956. "Self-Concept as an Insulator Against Delinquency." *American Sociological Review* 21: 744-746.

Regan, T. 1986. "Bargaining and Governmental Directives: The Question of Limits to Negotiated Orders." *Canadian Review of Sociology and Anthropology* 23 (3): 383-398.

Regoli, P. and E. Poole. 1978. "The Commitment of Delinquents to Their Misdeeds: A Re-Examination." *Journal of Criminal Justice* 6: 261-269.

Reiman, J.H. [1979] 1990. *The Rich Get Richer and the Poor Get Prison-Ideology, Class, and Criminal Justice.* New York: Macmillan.

Reiss, A. and H. Rhodes. 1961. "The Distribution of Delinquency in the Social Class Structure." *American Sociological Review* 26: 720-732.

Report. 1988. *Task Force on Aboriginal Peoples in Federal Corrections Solicitor General: Final Report.* Ottawa: Supply and Services.

Report. 1991. *Aboriginal Justice Inquiry.* Winnipeg: Government Services.

Report of the Standing Committee on Justice and the Solicitor General. 1993. *Crime Prevention in Canada: Toward a National Strategy.* (February) Ottawa: Supply and Services.

Resch R.P. 1992. *Althusser and the Renewal of Marxist Social Theory.* Los Angeles: University of California Press.

Reuter, P., Rubinstein, J. and S. Wynn. 1983. *Racketeering in Legitimate Industries: Two Case Studies.* Washington, D.C.: National Institute of Justice.

Rex, J. and D. Manson. 1986. *Theories of Race and Ethnic Relations.* Cambridge: Cambridge Press.

Rice, M. 1990. "Challenging Orthodoxies in Feminist Theory: A Black Feminist Critique." In L. Gelsthrope and A. Morris (eds.), *Feminist Perspectives in Criminology.* Buckingham: Open University Press.

Rice, R. 1956. *Business of Crime.* Westport, Conn.: Greenwood Press.

Rich, A. 1980. "Compulsory Heterosexual and Lesbian Existence." *Signs* 5: 631-660.

Richards, P. and R. Berk. 1979. *Crime as Play: Delinquency in a Middle Class Suburb.* Boston: Ballinger.

Richardson. B. 1991. *Strangers Devour the Land.* Vancouver: Douglas and McIntyre.

Richmond, A. 1989. *Caribbean Immigrant in Canada: A Demo-Economic Analysis.* Ottawa: Statistics Canada.

Rivera, E. 1992. "The Marketing of the Late Malcolm X." *Toronto Star* (October 31): D5.

Roach, C. 1981. "Canadian Apartheid?" *Rikka* 8 (Winter): 4.

Roberts, D. and G. York. 1991. "Judges Urge Separate Native Justice System." *Globe and Mail* (August 30).

Roberts, J. 1994. "Crime and Race Statistics: Toward a Canadian Solution." *Canadian Journal of Criminology* 36, 2, (April): 175-185.

Roberts, J. and T. Gabor. 1990. "Lombrosian Wine in a New Bottle: Research on Crime and Race." *Canadian Journal of Criminology* 2: 291-313.

Robinson, C. 1992. "Black Intellectuals at the British Core: 1920's-1940's." In J. Gundara and I. Duffield (eds.), *Essays On The History of Blacks in Britain*. Aldershot, Hants: Avebury, Ashgate Publishing.

Robinson, S. 1950. "Ecological Correlations and the Behavior of Individuals." *American Sociological Review* XV: 351-357.

Roby, P. 1969. "Politics and Criminal Law: Revision of the New York State Penal Law on Prostitution." *Social Problems* 17 (Summer): 83-109.

Rock, P. 1973. "Phenomenalism and Essentialism in the Sociology of Deviance." *Sociology* 7: 17-29.

Rock, P. 1979. *The Making of Symbolic Interactionism*. London: Macmillan.

Rodney, W. [1972] 1982. *How Europe and Underdeveloped Africa*. Washington, D.C.: Howard University Press.

Roediger, D. 1991. *Wages of Whiteness*. London: Verso.

Romero, F.J. Gonzales. 1989. "Hispanic Underrepresentation in U. S. Job Training." *Currents* 5 (March): 4.

Rosen, L. and S. Turner. 1967. "An Evaluation of Lander Approach to Ecology of Delinquency." *Social Problems* XV.

Ross, J. 1992. "Campus Anti-Semitism: A Double Challenge." *Emunah* (Spring/Summer).

Rossi, S.R. and Rossi, J.S. 1985. "Gender Differences in the Perceptions of Women in Magazine Advertising." *Sex Roles* 12, 1033-1039.

Roth, J. 1970. "Comments on Secret Observation." In W. Filstead (ed.), *Qualitative Methodology*. Chicago: Rand McNally.

Roth, J. 1994. "Firearms and Violence." Report, National Institute of Justice (Feb) US Department of Justice, Washington, D.C.

Rothman, D. 1980. *Conscience and Convenience*. Boston: Little, Brown and Company.

Rowbotham, S. 1989. "Women's Consciousness, Men's World." In R. Gottlieb (ed.), *An Anthology of Western Marxism*. New York: Oxford University Press.

Royal Commission on Donald Marshall Jr. 1989. *Prosecution*. Halifax: Nova Scotia Government.

Rubington, E. 1982. "Deviant Subcultures." In M. Rosenberg, R. A. Stebbins and A. Turowetz (eds.), *The Sociology of Deviance*. New York: St. Martin's.

Rubington, E., and M.S. Weinberg. 1987. *Deviance: The Interactionist Perspective*. New York: MacMillan.

Ruby, C. 1992. "Gun Owners Should be on Shorter Leash than Dog Catchers, Argues Clayton Ruby." *Toronto Star*.

Rush, S. 1984. "Collective Rights and Collective Process: Missing Ingredients in the Canadian Constitution." *Socialist Studies* 2.

Russell, K. 1992. "Development of a Black Criminology and the Role of the Black Criminologist." *Justice Quarterly* 9 (December) 4: 667-684.

Ryazanoff, D. 1963. *The Communist Manifesto of K. Marx and F. Engels*. New York: Russell and Russell.

S

Sacco, V. and L. Kennedy. 1998. *The Criminal Event.* Toronto: ITP Nelson.

Safillos-Rothschild, C. 1972. *Toward A Sociology of Women.* Toronto: Xerox.

Sagarin, E. 1975. *Deviants and Deviance.* New York: Praeger.

Said, E. 1979. *Orientalism.* New York: Vintage.

Said, E. 1983. *The World, the Text and the Critic.* Cambridge: Harvard University Press.

Salamini, L. 1974. "Gramsci and the Marxist Sociology of Knowledge: An Analysis of Hegemony-Ideology-Knowledge." *Sociological Quarterly* 15: 338-359.

Salutin, R. 1987. "Keep Canadian Culture off the Table—Who's Kidding Who." In L. LaPierre (ed.), *If You Love This Country.* Toronto: McClelland and Stewart.

Sanders, A. 1990. "Battling Crimes Against Nature." *Time* (March, 12): 68-69.

Sarri, R. 1986. "Gender and Race Differences in Criminal Justice Processing." *Women's Studies International Forum* 9: 89-99.

Saxton, S. 1987. "The Greying of Symbolic Interactionism." *S.S.S.I. Notes* 13 (Winter) 3.

Scanlon, M. 1993 "Women In Prison." *Psychology Today* November / December.

Schecter, S. 1982. *Women and Male Violence.* Boston: South End Press.

Schelling, T. 1967. *Economic Analysis of Organized Crime.* President's Commission on Law Enforcement and Administration of Justice, Task Force Report on Organized Crime, Washington: U. S. Printing Office.

Schermerhorn, R. 1961. *Society and Power.* New York: Random.

Schietz, S. and J.N. Sprafkin. 1978. "Spot Messages within Saturday Morning Television Programs." In G. Tuchman. Ak. Daniels and J. Benet (eds.), *Hearth and Home: Images of Women in the Mass Media.* New York: Oxford U. Press.

Schmeiser, D. 1974. *The Native Offender and the Law.* Ottawa: Law Reform Commission of Canada.

Schrag, C. 1971. *Crime and Justice: American Style.* Washington, D.C.: Government Printing Office.

Schur, E. 1972. *Labelling Deviant Behavior.* New York: Harper and Row.

Schur, E. 1980. *The Politics of Deviance.* Englewood Cliffs: Prentice-Hall.

Schur, E. 1984. *Labelling Women Deviant: Gender, Stigma and Social Control.* Philadelphia: Temple University Press.

Schutz, Alfred. 1964. *Collected Papers II: Studies in Social Theory.* The Hague: Martinus Nijhoff.

Schwartz, M. and S. Tangri. 1967. "Delinquency Research and the Self Concept Variable." *Journal of Criminal Law, Criminology and Police Science* 58 (June): 182-190.

Schwartz, R. and J. Skolnick. 1962. "Two Studies of Legal Stigma." *Social Problems* 10: 133-142.

Schwendinger, H. and J. Schwendinger. 1977. "Social Class and the Definition of Crime." *Crime and Social Justice* 7 (Summer): 4-13.

Scott G.S. 1992. "The Hidden Hurdle." *Time,* (March 16): 42-45.

Scott, M.B. and S.M. Douglas. 1970. "Accounts, Deviance and Social Order." In J. Douglas (ed.), *Deviance and Respectability.* New York: Basic.

Scott, R. and J. Douglas (eds.). 1972. *Theoretical Perspectives on Deviance.* New York: Basic.

Scull, A. 1977. *Decarceration.* Englewood Cliffs, N.J.: Prentice-Hall.

Sellin, T. 1938. *Culture, Conflict and Crime.* New York: Social Science Research Council.

Senate Committee on Poverty. 1971. *Poverty in Canada.* Ottawa.

Sennett, R. 1970. *Classic Essays on the Culture of Cities.* New York: Appleton-Century-Crofts.

Shapiro, M. 1978. *Getting Doctored.* Kitchener: Between the Lines.

Sharrock, W. and B. Anderson. 1986. *The Ethnomethodologists.* Sussex: Ellis Horwood.

Shaw, C. 1930. *The Jack Roller.* Chicago: University of Chicago.

Shaw, C. and H. Mckay. 1931. *Social Factors in Juvenile Delinquency.* Washington: U. S. Government Printing Office.

Shaw, C. and H.D. McKay. [1942] (1969). *Juvenile Delinquency and Urban Areas.* Chicago: University of Chicago.

Shearing, C.D. 1973. "Towards a Phenomenological Sociology or Towards a Solution to the Parsonian Puzzle." *Catalyst* 7: 9-14.

Shearing, C. and R. Ericson. 1990. "Culture as Figurative Action." *British Journal of Criminology* 42, 4.

Sheley, J. 1991. *Criminology.* Belmont, California: Wadsworth.

Sherman, L. 1975. "An Evaluation of Police Women on Patrol in a Suburban Police Department." *Journal of Police Science and Administration* 3: 434-438.

Short, J. 1957. "Differential Association and Delinquency." *Social Problems* 4: 233-239.

Short, J. 1975. "The National History of an Applied Theory: Differential Opportunity and Mobilization for Youth." In N. J. Demerath (ed.), *Social Policy and Sociology.* New York: Academic Press.

Short, J., Rivera, R. and R. Tennyson. 1965. "Perceived Opportunities, Gang Membership and Delinquency." *American Sociological Review* 30: 56-67.

Short, J. and F. Strodbeck. 1965. *Group Process and Gang Delinquency.* Chicago: University of Chicago.

Shover, N. 1983. "The Later Stages of Ordinary Property Offender Careers." *Social Problems* 31 (1983) 2.

Shulman, N. 1972. *Urban Social Networks.* Ph.D. Dissertation, University of Toronto.

Shull, S. 1993. *A Kinder Gentler Racism? The Reagan-Bush Civil Rights Legacy.* London: ME Sharpe.

Siegal, H. 1977. "Gettin' it Together: Some Theoretical Considerations of Urban Ethnography Among Underclass Peoples." In R. Weppner (ed.), *Street Ethnography.* Beverly Hill: Sage.

Siegel, L. 1998. *Criminolgy.* New York: West/Wadsworth.

Signorielli, N. 1989. "Television and Conceptions about Sex Roles: Maintaining Conventionality and the Status Quo." *Sex Roles* 21: 341-360.

Silvera, M. 1983. *Silenced.* Toronto: Williams and Walker.

Silvera, M. 1990. "Man Royals and Sodomites: Some Thoughts on the Invisibility of Afro-Caribbean Lesbians." In S. Stone (ed.), *Lesbians in Canada.* Toronto: Between the Lines.

Silverman, R. and L. Kennedy. 1993. *Deadly Sins: Murder in Canada.* Scarborough: Nelson.

Simmel, G. [1950] 1969. "Types of Social Relationships by Degrees of Reciprocal Knowledge of Their Participants." In K. Wolff (ed.), *The Sociology of George Simmel.* New York: Free Press.

Simmel, G. [1950] 1969a. "The Isolated Individual and the Dyad." In K. Wolff (ed.), *The Sociology of George Simmel*. New York: Free Press.

Simmel, G. [1950] 1969b. *The Sociology of George Simmel*. Edited By K. Wolff. New York: Free Press.

Simmons, A. and K. Keohane. 1992. "Canadian Immigration Policy: Strategies and the Quest for Legitimacy." *Candian Review of Sociology and Anthropology* 29 (4): 421-452.

Simmons, J.L. 1965. "Public Stereotypes of Deviants." *Social Problems* 13: 222-232.

Simon, D. 1988. "Liberalism and White Collar Crime: Toward Resolving a Crisis." *Quarterly Journal of Ideology* 12 (January) 1: 19-30.

Simon, D. and D.S. Eitzen. 1986. *Elite Deviance*. Boston: Allyn and Bacon.

Simon, R. 1975. *Women and Crime*. Lexington, Mass.: D. C. Heath.

Simpson, S. 1989. "Feminist Theory, Crime and Justice." *Criminology* 27 (4): 605-631.

Simpson, S. 1991. "Caste, Class and Violent Crime Explaining Difference in Female Offending." *Criminology* 29 (1): 115-135.

Singer, P. 1980. *Marx*. Oxford: Oxford University Press.

Singer, P. and D. Wells. 1984. *The Reproduction Revolution: New Ways of Making Babies*. Oxford: Oxford University Press.

Skogan, W.G. and M. Maxfield. 1981. *Coping with Crime*. Beverly Hills: Sage.

Smandych, R. 1985. "Marxism and the Creation of Law." In T. Fleming (ed.), *The New Criminologies in Canada*. Toronto: Oxford University Press.

Smart, C. 1976. *Women, Crime and Criminology: A Feminist Critique*. London: Routledge and Kegan Paul.

Smart, C. 1981. "Law and the Control of Women's Sexuality: The Case of the 1950's." In B. Hutter and G. Williams (eds.), *Controlling Women: The Normal and the Deviant*. London: Croom Helm.

Smart, C. 1986 "Feminism and the Law: Some Problems of Analysers and Strategy." *Int J. of Soc of Law*. 14: 109-123.

Smart, C. 1989. *Feminism and the Power of Law*. London: Routledge.

Smith, D. 1978. "Organized Crime and Entrepreneurship." *International Journal of Criminology and Penology* 6: 161-172.

Smith, D. 1980. "Paragons, Pariahs and Pirates: A Spectrum Theory of Enterprise." *Crime and Delinquency* 26 (July): 358-386.

Smith, D.E. 1973. "Women's Perspective as a Radical Critique of Sociology." *Sociological Inquiry* 44 (1): 7-13.

Smith, D.E. 1974. "The Ideological Practice of Sociology." *Catalyst* 8: 39-54.

Smith, D.E. 1985. "Women, Class and Family." In V. Burnstyn and D. E. Smith (eds.), *Women, Class, Family and the State*. Toronto: Garamond.

Smith, D.E. 1987. *The Everyday World as Problematic: A Feminist Sociology*. Boston: North Eastern University Press.

Smith, M. 1979. *The City and Social Theory*. New York: St. Martin's Press.

Smith, V. 1992. "For the Future: Fighting Free Trade Fatalism." *Our Times* (December): 35-38.

Snider, L. 1978. "Corporate Crime in Canada: A Preliminary Report." *Canadian Journal of Criminology* 20 (April) 2: 142-168.

Snider, L. 1991a. "The Regulatory Dance: Understanding Reform Processes in Corporate Crime." *International Journal of the Sociology of Law* 19 (May) 2: 209-236.

Snider, L. 1991b. "The Potential of the Criminal Justice System to Promote Feminist Concerns." In E. Comack and S. Brickey (eds.), *The Social Basis of Law*. Halifax: Garamond.

Snider, L. 1991c. "Critical Criminology in Canada: Past, Present and Future." In R. Silverman, J. Teevan and V. Sacco (eds.), *Crime in Canadian Society*. Toronto: Butterworth.

Snider, L. 1993. *Bad Business: Corporate Crime In Canada*. Scarborough: Nelson Canada.

Solicitor General, Canada. 1993. *National Symposium on Community Safety and Crime Prevention*. Ottawa: Police and Security Branch.

Solicitor General. 1994. *Weapons Use in Canadian Schools*. (Walker, S.G.) User Report: Responding to Violence and Abuse No. 1994-05 Supply and Services.

Solivetti, L.M. 1987. "La Criminalita di Impresa: Alcuni Commenti Sul Problema delle Cause." *Sociologia del Diritto* 14 (1): 41-77.

Solomon, R.P. *Black Resistance in High School*. Albany: State University of New York Press.

Solomos, J. 1988. *Black Youth, Racism and the State—The Politics of Ideology and Polity*. Cambridge: Cambridge University Press.

Southern Poverty Law Center. 1991. *The Ku Klux Klan: A History of Racism and Violence*. 4th ed. S. Bullard (ed.). Alabama, Klanwatch In the USA.

Sowell, T. 1981. *Ethnic America*. New York: Basic.

Sowell, T. 1993. "Political Pricing." *Forbes* (July 5): 50.

Spann, G. 1993. *Race Against the Court: The Supreme Court and Minorities in Contemporary America*. New York: New York University Press.

Spears, G. and K. Seydegart. 1991. "Racial Minorities on TV Ontario." *Currents* (April): 19-20.

Spitzer, S. 1975. "Towards a Marxian Theory of Deviance." *Social Problems* 22 (June) 5: 638-651.

Spivak, G. C. 1985. "The Rani of Sirmur." F. Barker et, al. (ed.), *Europe and Its Others*, I. Colchester: University of Essex.

Spradley, J. 1979. *The Ethnographic Interview*. New York: Holt, Rinehart and Winston.

Stacey, J. 1988. "Can There be a Feminist Ethnography?" *Women's Studies International Quarterly* 11: 21-27.

Stanko, E. 1985. "Would You Believe this Woman?" In N. Hahn Raffer and E. Stanko (eds.), *Judge, Lawyer, Victim, Thief*. Boston: Northeastern University Press.

Stanley, L. and S. Wise 1983. *Breaking Out: Feminist Consciousness and Feminist Research*. London: Routledge and Kegan Paul.

Stanley, M. 1985. *The Experience of the Rape Victim with the Criminal Justice System Prior to Bill C-127*. Ottawa: Department of Justice.

Staples, R. 1975. "White Racism, Black Crime, and American Justice: An Application of the Colonial Model to Explain Crime and Race." *Phylon* 36 (1) March: 14-23.

Starr, G. 1984. "Popular Right in (and out of) the Constitution." *Socialist Studies* 2.

Statistics Canada. 1987. *Culture Statistics: Television Viewing in Canada*. Ottawa # 87-208.

Statistics Canada. 1990. *Women and Crime.* Juristat, Ottawa: Statistics Canada.

Statistics Canada. 1990b. *Canadian Social Trends* (Summer). Ottawa:. Supply and Services.

Statistics Canada. 1992. *Canadian Social Trends* (Autumn). Ottawa: Supply and Services.

Stebbins, R. 1970. "On Misunderstanding the Concept of Commitment." *Social Forces* 48: 526-529.

Stebbins, R. 1987. "Interactionist Theories." In R. Linden (ed.), *Criminology.* Toronto: Holt, Rinehart and Winston.

Steel, B.S. 1987. "Equality and Efficiency Trade Offs in Affirmative Action-Real or Imagined?: The Case of Women in Policing." *The Social Science Journal* 24: 53-70.

Steiberg N. 1994. "The Law of Unintended Consequences." *Rolling Stone* (May 5): 33.

Stein, N. 1960. *The Eclipse of Community.* Princeton: Princeton University Press.

Steinem, G. 1986. *Outrageous Acts and Everyday Rebellions.* New York: Penguin.

Steinem, G. 1993. *Revolution From Within.* Boston: Little, Brown and Co.

Sterling, T. 1978. "Does Smoking Kill Workers or Working Kill Smokers." *International Journal of Health Sciences* 8: 437-452.

Stewart, M. (ed.). 1977. *The City: Problems of Planning.* Harmondsworth: Penguin.

Stone, C. 1975. *Where the Law Ends.* New York: Harper/Torchbooks.

Stone, S. 1990. *Lesbians in Canada.* Toronto: Between the Lines.

Stone, G. and H. Faberman 1970. *Social Psychology Through Symbolic Interaction.* Waltham: Xerox.

Stonechild, S. 1984. "Nehiyawak." *Almighty Voice* 2.

Strasser, H. 1976. *The Normative Structure for Sociology.* London: Routledge and Kegan Paul.

Strauss, A. 1967. "Language and Identity." In J. Manis and B. Meltzer (eds.), *Symbolic Interactionism.* New York: Allyn and Bacon.

Strauss, A. 1978. *Negotiations: Varieties, Contexts, Processes and Social Order.* New York: Jossey-Bass.

Straus, M., Gelles, R. and S. Steinmetz. 1980. *Behind Closed Doors: Violence in the American Family.* New York: Anchor.

Straus, M.A. and R.J. Gelles 1986. "Societal Change and Change in Family Violence From 1975 to 1985 as Revealed by Two National Surveys." *Journal of Marriage and the Family* 48 (August): 465-479.

Sturino, F. 1978. *Post World War Canadian Immigrant Policy Towards Italians.* Toronto: Multicultural History Society of Ontario.

Stryker, S. and E. Craft 1982. "Deviance, Selves and Others Revisited." *Youth and Society* 14 (2): 159-183.

Sugar F. and L. Fox. 1989/90. "Nistum Peyako Seht'wawin Iskwewak: Breaking Chains." *Canaian Journal of Women and the Law* 3 (2)1989/1990: 465-482.

Sugarmann, J. 1993. "The NRA is Right: But We Still Need to Ban Handguns." In R. Monk (ed.), *Taking Sides.* Guilford, Conn.: Dushkin.

Sugarmann, J. and K. Rand. 1994. "Cease Fire." *Rolling Stone* (March 10): 30-42.

Sullivan, D. and R. Weitz. 1988. *Labour Pains.* London: Yale University Press.

Sullivan, G.L. and P.J. O'Connor. 1988. "Wome's Role Portrayals in Magazine Advertising." *Sex Roles* 18: 181-188.

Sullivan, R. 1994. "Tonya Harding: The Hard Fall." *Rolling Stone* (July 14-28): 80-118.

Surette, R. 1984. *Justice and the Media*. Springfield: Charles C. Thomas.

Surette, R. 1989. "Media Trials." *Journal of Criminal Justice* 17: 293-308.

Sutherland, E. 1924. *Criminology*. Philadelphia: J. B. Lippincott.

Sutherland, E. 1939. *Principles of Criminology*. Philadelphia: Lippincott.

Sutherland, E. 1941. "Crime in Business." *Annals* 217: 112-118.

Sutherland, E. 1945. "Is 'White Collar Crime' Crime?" *American Sociological Review* 10: 132-139.

Sutherland, E. 1949. *White Collar Crime*. New York: Holt, Rinehart and Winston (also in 1961, New York: Dryden).

Sutherland, E. and D. Cressey. 1978. *Principles of Criminology*, 10th ed. Philadelphia: Lippincott.

Suttles, G. 1968. *The Social Order of the Slum*. Chicago: University of Chicago Press.

Suttles, G. 1972. *The Social Construction of Communities*. Chicago: University of Chicago Press.

Swainson, D. 1988. "Riel and the Structure of Canadian History." In H. Bowsfield (ed.), *Louis Riel: Selected Readings*. Toronto: Copp Clark Pitman.

Sweet, L. 1986. "Corporate Criminals Must Pay." *Toronto Star* (April 14): C1.

Sydie, R.A. 1987. *Natural Women, Cultured Men: A Feminist Perspective on Sociological Theory*. Toronto: Methuen.

Sykes, G. and P. Matza. 1957. "Techniques of Neutralization: A Theory of Delinquency." *American Sociological Review* 22 (5): 664-670.

Syzmansky, A. 1978. *The Capitalist State and the Politics of Class*. Cambridge: Cambridge University Press.

Szasz, A. 1986. "Corporations, Organized Crime and the Disposal of Hazardous Waste: An Examination of a Crimogenic Regulatory Structure." *Criminology* 24 (February) 1: 1-27.

T

Talbot, C. 1984. *Growing up Black in Canada*. Toronto: Williams-Wallace.

Tangri, S. and M. Schwartz. 1967. "Delinquency Research and the Self Concept Variable." *Journal of Criminal Law, Criminology and Political Science* 58: 182-190.

Tannenbaum, F. 1938. *Crime and Community*. Boston: Ginn.

Tanner, J. and H. Krahn. 1991. "Part-time Work and Deviance Among High-School Seniors." *Canadian Journal of Sociology* 16, 3: 281-302.

Taras, D. and H. Holmes. 1993. "Introduction." In H. Holmes and D. Taras (eds.), *Seeing Ourselves, Media Power and Policy in Canada*. Toronto: Harcourt, Brace, Jovanovich.

Tarde, G. [1903] 1962. *The Laws of Emitation*. Gloucester, Mass.: Peter Smith.

Task Force, Report 1991. *Survey of Federally Sentenced Women, Task Force on Federally Sentenced Women on the Prison Survey*. Corrections Branch, Ministry of the Solicitor General of Canada #1991-4.

Tatartyn, L. 1979. *Dying for a Living*. New York: Deneau and Greenberg Publishers.

Tator, C. 1987. "Anti-Racist Education." *Currents* 4 (Winter) 4: 8-11.

Taylor, I. 1981. "Crime Waves in Post-War Britain." *Contemporary Crises* 5, 1: 43-62.

Taylor, I. 1983. *Crime, Capitalism and Crime*. Toronto: Butterworth.

Taylor, I., Walton, P. and J. Young. 1973. *The New Criminology*. London: Routledge and Kegan Paul.

Taylor, I., Walton, P. and J. Young (eds.). 1974. *Critical Criminology*. London: Routledge and Kegan Paul.

Terkel, S. 1992. *Race: How Blacks and Whites Think and Feel About the American Obsession*. New York: New Press.

Thio, A. 1972. "Class Bias in the Sociology of Deviance." *American Sociologist* 8 (February): 1-12.

Thio, A. 1975. "A Critical Look at Merton's Anomie Theory." *Pacific Sociological Review* 18 (April): 139-158.

Thio, A.1983. *Deviant Behavior*. Boston: Houghton Mifflin.

Thomas, P. 1996. "U.S. Crime Rate Falls to 10 Year Low." *The Toronto Star* Oct 3: A3.

Thomas, W. and F. Znaniecki. [1920] 1958. *The Polish Peasant in Europe and America*. Boston: R. C. Badger.

Thompson, E.P. 1963. *The Making of the English Working Class*. Harmondsworth: Penguin:.

Thompson, K. 1988. *Under Seige: Racial Violence in Britain Today*. London: Penguin.

Thompson, M., R. Ellis and A. Wildavsky. 1990. *Cultural Theory*. Boulder: Westview.

Thrasher, F. [1927] 1963. *The Gang*. Chicago: University of Chicago Press.

Thorne, B. and M. Detlefsen. 1986. "Advisory Citizen Participation in the Correctional Systems of Canada, the United Kingdom and Ireland." Unpublished monograph. Toronto.

Tilly, C. 1970. "An Anthology on the Town." In W. Mann (ed.), *The Underside of Toronto*. Toronto: McClelland and Stewart.

Tilly, C. 1974. *An Urban World*. Boston: Little, Brown and Company.

Tilly, C. 1978. *From Mobilization to Revolution*. Reading: Addison-Wesley.

Tittle, C. 1975. "Labelling and Crime: An Empirical Evaluation." In W. Gove (ed.), *The Labelling of Deviance*. New York: Halstead.

Toby, J. 1957. "Social Disorganization and Stake in Conformity: Complementary Factors in Predatory Behaviour of Hoodlums." *Journal of Criminal Law, Criminology and Police Science* 48 (May-June): 12-17.

Toby, J. 1957. "The Differential Impact of Family Disorganization." *American Sociological Review* 22 (October): 505-512.

Toby, J. 1979. "The New Criminology is the Old Sentimentality." *Criminology* 16: 516-526.

Toby, J. 1980. "The New Criminology is the Old Balony." In J. Inciardi (ed.), *Radical Criminology*. Beverly Hills: Sage.

Toennies, F. [1887] 1957. *Community and Association*. London: Routledge and Kegan Paul.

Toffler, A. and H. Toffler. 1994. "Apocalypse Right Now?" *Psychology Today* (January/February).

Tomlinson, G. 1985. "Producing Truth: The Social Construction of Encyclopedia Editing." *Proceedings of the Ethnographic and Qualitative Conference* Vol. 3.

Toner, B. 1977. *Facts About Rape*. London: Hutchenson.

Tong, R. 1989. *Feminist Thought: A Comprehensive Introduction*. San Francisco: Boulder/Westview.

Toronto Disarmament Network. 1992 (Summer).

Trice, H. 1970. "The Outsider's Role in Field Study." In W. Filstead (ed.), *Qualitative Methodology.* Chicago: Rand McNally.

Trigerr, B. 1985. *Natives and Newcomers.* Kingston: McGill-Queen's University Press.

Troper, H. and M. Weinfeld. 1988. *Old Wounds.* Markham: Penguin.

Trotman, A. 1993 *African-Caribbean Perspectives of Worldview: C.L.R. James Explores the Authentic Voice.* Doctoral Dissertation, York University, Sociology.

Trueman, P. 1980. *Smoke and Mirrors.* Toronto: McClelland and Stewart.

Tuchman, G. 1978. "The Symbolic Annihalation of Women by the Mass Media." In G. Tuchman, A. Kaplan Daniels and J. Benet (eds.), *Hearth and Home: Images of Women in the Mass Media.* New York: Oxford University Press.

Tucker, R. (ed.). 1978. *The Marx-Engels Reader,* Second Edition. New York: W.W. Norton and Company.

Tully, S. 1992. "What C.E.O.'s Really Make." *Fortune* (June 15): 94-99.

Tumin, M. 1965. "Functional Approach to Social Problems." *Social Problems* 12.

Turk, A. 1964. "Conflict and Criminality." *Journal of Criminal Law, Criminality and Police Science* 55.

Turk, A. 1966. "Conflict and Criminality." *American Sociological Review* 31 (June): 338-352.

Turk, A. 1967. "On Parsonian Approach to Theory Construction." *Sociological Quarterly* 8: 37-50.

Turk, A. 1969. *Criminality and Legal Order.* Chicago: Rand McNally and Company.

Turk, A. 1976. "Law as a Weapon in Social Conflict." *Social Problems* 23 (February) 3: 276-291.

Turk, A. 1976b. "Law, Conflict and Order: From Theorizing Towards Theories." *Canadian Review of Sociology and Anthropology* 13 (August) 3: 282-294.

Turk, A. 1977. "Class, Conflict and Criminalization." *Sociological Focus* 10: 209-220.

Turk, A. 1977. *Political Criminality.* Beverly Hills: Sage.

Turk, A. 1979. "Analysing Official Deviance: For Non-Partisan Conflict Analyses in Criminology." *Criminology* 16: 459-476.

Turk, A. 1986. "Law and Society." In L. Teperman and R. Richardson (eds.), *The Social: An Introduction to Sociology.* Toronto: Mcgraw-Hill.

Turner, R. 1967. *Robert Park: Selected Papers.* Chicago: University of Chicago Press.

Turner, R. (ed.). 1974. *Ethnomethodology.* New York: Penguin.

Turner, R. 1978. "The Public Perception of Protest." In J. Manis and B. Meltzer (eds.), *Symbolic Interaction.* Boston: Allyn and Bacon.

Tyler, T. 1994. "The Colour of Justice." *Toronto Star* (January 8): C1, C4.

U

Udry, J.R. 1977. "The Importance of Being Beautiful: A Rexamination of Racial Comparison." *American Journal of Sociology* 83, 154-160.

Unnever, J. and L. Hembroff. 1988. "The Prediction of Racial and Ethnic Sentencing Disparities: An Expectation States Approach." *Journal of Crime and Delinquency* 25: 53-82.

United Nations. 1992. *Human Development Report.* New York.

US Department of Health and Human Services. 1992. Centers for Disease Control and Prevention, Morbidity and Mortality. Weekly Report (December 18).

US Department of Justice. 1991. Bureau of Justice Statistics L. Jankowski Bulletin. Washington, D.C.

US Department of Justice. 1993. Bureau of Justice Statistics Bulletin. Washington, D.C.

United States Department of Justice, Bureau of Statistics. 1980. *Computer Crime*. Washington, D.C.: Government Printing House.

United States, Federal Bureau of Investigation. 1992. *Crime in the United States*.

V

Valverde, M. 1985. *Sex, Power and Pleasure*. Toronto: Women's Press.

Valverde, M. 1990. "The Rhetoric of Reform: Tropes and the Moral Subject." *International Journal of the Sociology of Law* 18.

Valverde, M. 1991. "Feminist Perspectives on Criminology." In Gladstone, R. Ericson and C. Shearing (eds.), *Criminology*. Toronto: Centre of Criminology.

Valverde, M. 1991b. "As if Subjects Existed: Analyzing Social Discourses." *Canadian Review of Sociology and Anthropology* 28 (2).

Vaughan, T. and L. Reynolds. 1968. "The Sociology of Symbolic Interactionism." *American Sociologist* 3 (August): 208-214.

Vaz, E. 1966. "Self-Reported Delinquency and Socio-Economic Status." *Canadian Journal of Criminology and Corrections* 8: 20-27.

Vaz, E. 1967. *Middle Class Juvenile*. New York: Harper Row.

Verdun-Jones, S. and G. Muirhead. 1979. "Natives in the Canadian Justice System." *Crime and Justice* 7/8 (1).

Verdun-Jones, S. and G. Muirhead. 1982. "The Native in the Criminal Justice System: Canadian Research." In C. Boydell and I. Connidis (eds.), *Canadian Criminal Justice*. Toronto: Holt, Rinehart and Winston.

Visano, L. 1982. "Public Urban Order: Police Knowledge and the State." Educational Deviance Ethnography Project and Critical Pedagogy Workgroup, OISE University of Toronto (March 11).

Visano, L.A. 1983. "Tramps, Tricks and Trouble: Street Transients and Their Controls." In T. Fleming and L.A. Visano (eds.), *Deviant Designations*. Toronto: Butterworth.

Visano, L.A. 1985. "Crime, Law and the State." In T. Fleming (ed.), *The New Criminologies in Canada*. Toronto: Oxford University Press.

Visano, L.A. 1987. *This Idle Trade*. Concord: Vita Sana.

Visano, L.A. 1988a. "Generic and Generative Dimensions of Interactionism." *International Journal of Comparative Sociology* XXIX (September) 3-4: 230-244.

Visano, L.A. 1988b. "V. Hans and N. Vidmar, Judging the Jury." *Criminal Justice Review* 13 (Spring) 1: 67-68.

Visano, L.A. 1990. "Crime as a Negotiable Commodity." *Journal of Human Justice* 2 (Autumn) 1: 105-116.

Visano, L.A. 1991. "The Impact of Age on Paid Sexual Encounters." In J.A. Lee (ed.), *Gay Midlife and Maturity*. New York: Harrington Press.

Visano, L. 1993. "Counting Crime." Unpublished paper, York University.

Visano, L. 1994. "The Culture of Capital as Carceral: Conditions and Contradictions." In K. McCormick (ed.), *Carceral Contexts*. Toronto: Canadian Scholars' Press.

Visano, L. 1996. "What Do They Know? Delinquency as Mediated Texts." In G. O'Bireck, *Not A Kid Anymore*. Toronto: Nelson.

Visano, L. 1996. "War on Drugs: From The Politics of Punishment to the Prospects of Peacekeeping." *Addictions: An International Research Journal* 1 (Fall): 81-95.

Visano, L. 1997a. "Bram's Stoker's *Dracula* as a Critical Ethnography: Mediated Moralities and Mysterious Mythologies." In Carol Davison (ed.), *Stoker's Dracula*. London/ Toronto: Dundurn Press.

Visano, L. 1997b. "From Localized Texts to Hegemonic Narratives: Contextualizing the "Games Pimps Play." In J. Hodgson, *Games Pimps Play*. Toronto: Canadian Scholars' Press.

Visher, C. 1983. "Gender, Police Arrest Decisions and Notions of Chivalry." *Criminology* 21: 5-28.

Vold, G.B. 1958. *Theoretical Criminology*. New York: Oxford University Press.

Vorst, J. et al. 1991. *Race, Class, Gender: Bonds and Barriers*. Toronto: Garamond.

W

Waitrowski, M., D. Griswald and M. Roberts. 1981. "Social Control Theory and Delinquency." *American Sociological Review* 46: 525-541.

Walby, S. 1986. *Patriarchy at Work*. Cambridge, UK: Polity.

Walcott, R. 1994. "The Need for a Politics of Difference." *Orbit* 25, 2.

Walker, J. 1980. *Racial Discrimination in Canada: The Black Experience*. Ottawa: Canadian Historical Association, #41.

Walker, J. 1982. *A History of Blacks in Canada*. Quebec: Government Printing House.

Walker, J. 1990. "Race and the Historian: Some Lessons From Canadian Public Policy." Toronto: Osgoode Hall.

Walker, L. 1979. *The Battered Woman*. New York: Harper and Row.

Walker, L. 1984. *The Battered Woman Syndrome*. New York: Springer Publishing.

Walker, S. 1985. "Racial Minority and Female Employment in Policing: The Implications of Glacial Change." *Crime and Delinquency* 31 (4): 555-572.

Wallace, M. 1991. *Black Macho and the Myth of the Superwoman*. New York: Verso.

Wallace, W. 1969. *Sociological Theory*. Chicago: Aldine.

Walsh, W. 1986. "Patrol Officer Arrest Rates: A Study of Social Organization of Police Work." *Justice Quarterly* 2: 271-290.

Ward, J. 1989. *Organizing for the Homeless*. Ottawa: Canadian Council on Social Development.

Warren, C. 1983. "The Politics of Trouble In An Adolescent Psychiatric Hospital." *Urban Life* 12: 327-348.

Warren, R. 1977. *Social Change and Human Purpose: Toward Understanding and Action*. Chicago: Rand McNally.

Watson, R. et al. 1993. "Death on the Spot: The End of Drug King." *Newsweek* (December 13): 18-21.

Waubageshig. 1970. *The Only Good Indian*. Toronto: New Press.

Waters, H. 1992. "Editorial." *Race and Class* 34 (July-September)1: v-vi.

Wax, M. 1980. "Paradoxes of Consent to the Practice of Fieldwork." *Social Problems* 27 (February) 3.

Waxler, J.G. 1985. "Roles Styles of Women Police Officers." *Sex Roles* 12: 749-755.

Wayne, J. 1971. *Networks of Informal Participation in a Suburban Context*. Ph. D. Dissertation, Sociology, University of Toronto.

Webber, D. 1987. "Community-Based Corrections and Community Consultation—A How to Manual." Ottawa: Solicitor-General, Ontario Region.

Webber, M. 1992. *Hungry for Change*. Toronto: Coach House.

Weber, M. [1930] 1958. *The Protestant Ethic and the Spirit of Capitalism*. Translated by T. Parsons. New York: Charles Scribner and Sons.

Weber, M. 1946. "Class, Status and Party." In H. Gerth and C.W. Mills (eds.), *From Max Weber: Essays in Sociology*. New York: Oxford Press.

Weber, M. 1958. *The City*.Translated and edited by D. Martindale and G. Neuwirth. New York: Free Press.

Weber, M. [1947] 1969. *The Theory of Social and Economic Organization*. Translated and edited by A. M. Henderson and T. Parsons. New York: Free Press.

Weber, M. 1969. *Max Weber on Law in Economy and Society*. Cambridge, Ma.: Harvard University Press.

Weigart, A. 1983. "Identity: Its Emergence Within Sociological Psychology." *Symbolic Interactionism* 6 (2): 183-206.

Weiler, K. 1988. *Women Teaching For Change*. New York: Bergin and Garvey.

Weinstein, C and E. Cummins. 1993. "The Crime of Punishment at Pelican Bay Maximum Security Prison." *Covert Action* Summer, (45): 38-45.

Weisheit, R. 1987. "Women in the State Police: Concerns of Male and Female Officers." *Journal of Police Science and Administration* 15: 137-144.

Welling, B. 1984. *Corporate Law in Canada*. Toronto: Butterworth.

Wellman, B. 1979. "The Community Question: The Intimate Network of East Yorkers." *American Journal of Sociology* 84 (5): 1201-1231.

Wellman, B. and B. Leighton. 1978. "Networks, Neighbourhoods and Communities." Research Paper #97. Centre for Urban and Community Studies, University of Toronto.

Wellman, B. and S. Berkowitz (eds.). 1988. *Social Structure: A Network Approach*. Cambridge: Cambridge University Press.

Wells, E. and J. Rankin. 1983. "Self Concept as a Mediating Factor in Delinquency." *Social Psychology Quarterly* 46 (March): 11-22.

Weppner, R. 1977. *Street Ethnography*. Beverly Hills: Sage.

West, C. 1993. "Black Intellectuals, Jewish Tensions: How to End the Impasse." *New York Times* April 14: A15.

West, W.G. 1978. "The Short-Term Careers of Serious Thieves." *Canadian Journal of Criminology* 20 (2): 169-190.

West, W.G. 1981. "Notes on the Possibility of a Neo-Marxist Ethnography." Unpublished paper O.I.S.E., University of Toronto.

West, W.G. 1984. *Young Offenders and the State*. Toronto: Butterworth.

White, P. 1986. *Native Women: A Statistical Overview*. Ottawa: Supply and Services.

White, R.D. 1986. *Law, Capitalism and the Right to Work*. Toronto: Garamond.

Whitehouse, P. 1983. "Race Bias and Social Enquiry Reports." *Probation Journal* 30 (2), 43-49.

Whyte, W.F. 1955. *Street Corner Society*. Chicago: University of Chicago Press.

Wiggins, D. 1993. "Critical Events Affecting Racism in Athletes." In D. Brooks and R. Althouse (eds.), *Racism in College Athletes*. Morgantown: Fitness Information Technology.

Wilks, J. 1967. *Ecological Correlates of Crime and Delinquency in the U. S.* Washington, D.C.: U. S. Government.

Williams, P. 1991. *The Alchemy of Race and Rights: Diary of A Law Professor.* Cambridge: Harvard Univesity.

Williams, P. 1994. "Spirit-Murdering the Messenger: The Discourse of Fingerpointing as the Law's Response to Racism." In Baker, D. (ed.), *Reading Racism and the Criminal Justice System.* Toronto: Canadian Scholars' Press.

Williams, R. 1990. *The American Indian in Western Legal Thought.* Oxford: Oxford University Press.

Williamson, J. 1978. *Decoding Advertisements.* London: Marion Boyars.

Willie, C. 1967. "Relative Contribution of Family Status and Economic Status to Delinquency." *Social Problems* XIV.

Willis, P. 1980. *Learning to Labour.* Farnborough: Gower.

Wilson, P. and D. Chappell. 1986. "Physician Fraud and Abuse in Canada: A Preliminary Examination." *Canadian Journal of Criminology* 28 (April): 129-146.

Wilson, T.P. 1970. "Normative and Interpretive Paradigms in Sociology." In J. Douglas (ed.), *Understanding Everyday Life.* Chicago: Aldine.

Wilson, W. J. 1987. *The Truly Disadvantaged.* Chicago: University of Chicago.

Winks, R.W. 1971. *The Negro in Canada: An Historical Sketch.* New Haven: Yale Press.

Winks, R. 1971. *The Blacks in Canada.* Montreal: McGill-Queen's University Press.

Winter, J. 1992. "Taking Care of Business: Corporate Connections in Mainstream Media." *Our Times* (June): 33-35.

Wirth, L. 1964. "Urbanism As a Way of Life." In A. J. Reiss (ed.), *Louis Wirth: On Cities and Social Life.* Chicago: University of Chicago.

Wiseman, J. 1979. *Stations of the Lost.* Chicago: University of Chicago Press.

Wiseman, J. 1979b. "Towards a Theory of Policing Intervention in Social Problems." *Social Problems* 27: 3-18.

Wiseman, J. 1985. "The Adaptation and Clustering of Generic Concept Through Application to Diverse Research Topics." Conference on Qualitative Research: An Ethnographic and Interactionist Perspective. University of Waterloo.

Wiseman, M.B. 1989. *The Ecstasies of Roland Barthes.* London: Routledge.

Wittgenstein, L. 1980 *Culture and Value.* Edited by G.H. Von Wright with Heikki Nyman, translated by Peter Winch. Chicago: The University of Chicago Press, 1980.

Wolf, N. 1991. *The Beauty Myth.* New York: Random House.

Wolf, N. 1993. *Fire with Fire.* Toronto: Random House.

Wolfe, C. 1986. "Legitimation of Oppression: Response and Reflexivity." *Symbolic Interaction* 9 (2): 217-234.

Wolff, R. 1989. "Gramsci, Marxism and Philosophy." *Rethinking Marxism* 2 (Summer)2: 41-54.

Wolff, K. (ed.). 1950. *The Sociology of George Simmel.* New York: Free Press.

Wolfgang, M., A. Kelly and H. Nolde. 1962. "Comparisons of the Executed and the Commuted Among Admissions to Death Row." *Journal of Criminal Law and Criminology* 53: 301-310.

Wood, A. 1981. *Karl Marx.* Boston: Routledge and Kegan Paul.

Wood, N. 1993. "A Reluctant Welcome." *Maclean's* (January 4): 26-27.

Woods, L. 1979. "Litigation on Behalf of Battered Women." *Women's Rights Law Reporter* 5 (1): 7-33.

Woodsworth, J.S. [1909] 1978. *Strangers Within Our Gates*. Toronto: University of Toronto Press.

Worrall, A. 1990. *Offending Women: Female Lawbreakers and the Criminal Justice System*. New York: Routledge.

Wright, B. 1990. *Black Robes, White Justice*. New York: Carol Publishing.

Wright, J. 1986. "The Armed Criminal in America." *Research in Brief.* U.S. Department of Justice, National Institute of Justice (November): 1-5.

Wright, J. 1993. "Second Thoughts About Gun Control." In R. Monk (ed.), *Taking Sides*. Guilford, Conn.: Dushkin.

Wright, J.W. 1993b. *The Universal Almanac 1994*. Kansas City: Universal Press.

Wright, J. and L. Marston. 1975 "The Ownership of the Means of Destruction: Weapons in The United States." *Social Problems* 23: 93.

Y

Yakabuski, K. 1994. "Nipping Crime in the Bud." *Toronto Star,* (April 17): C1 and C4.

Yablonsky, L. 1962. *The Violent Gang*. New York: Macmillan.

Yalnizyan, A. 1990. "Reflections on Full Employment." Unpublished paper, Conference on Canadian Political Economy in the Era of Free Trade, April 6-9, Carleton University.

Yinger, J. 1960. "Contra-culture and Subculture." *American Sociological Review* 25: 625-635.

Yollo, K. and M. Bograd (eds.). 1988. *Feminist Perspectives on Wife Abuse*. Newbury Park: Sage.

York, G. 1989. *The Dispossessed*. Toronto: Lester and Orpen Dennys.

York, G. 1991. "Justice Report Generates Caution." *Globe and Mail* (August 31): A5.

York, G. and L. Pindera 1991. *People of the Pines: The Warriors and Legacy of Oka*. Toronto: Little, Brown.

Z

Zapf, M. 1991. "Litigation Must Become Big Part of Environmental Fight." *The Lawyers Weekly: Special Supplement on Environmental Law*. (November 29): 1.

Zedner, L. 1991. *Women, Crime, and Custody in Victorian England*. New York: Oxford University Press.

Ziegel, J., Daniels, R.J., Johnston, D. and J.MacIntosh. 1989. *Partnerships and Business Corporations*. Toronto: Carswell.

Zatz, M. 1987. "The Changing Forms of Racial and Ethnic Biases in Sentencing." *Journal of Research in Crime and Delinquency* 24 (1): 69-92.

Zedner, L. 1991. *Women, Crime and Custody in Victorian England*. New York: Oxford University Press.

Zinn, H. 1971. "The Conspiracy of Law." In R. Wolff (ed.), *The Rule of Law*. New York: Simon and Shuster.

Zinn, H. 1994. "The Federal Bureau of Intimidation." *Covert Action* (Winter): 27-31.

Zorbaugh, H. 1929. *The Gold Coast and the Slum.* Chicago: University of Chicago Press.

Zwarun, S. 1984. "Dark Secret." *Chatelaine* (June).

Zwarun, S. 1991. "Arab Canadians: Victims of a Gulf War Backlash." *Chatelaine* (July).